Published by

The Naval & Military Press Ltd
Unit 5 Riverside, Brambleside
Bellbrook Industrial Estate
Uckfield, East Sussex
TN22 1QQ England

Tel: +44 (0)1825 749494

www.naval-military-press.com
www.nmarchive.com

TWENTY-FIVE YEARS

IN

THE RIFLE BRIGADE.

BY THE LATE

WILLIAM SURTEES,

QUARTERMASTER.

The Naval & Military Press Ltd

TO

MAJOR-GEN. SIR ANDREW F. BARNARD,

K.C.B. AND K.C.H.

AND THE OFFICERS OF THE RIFLE BRIGADE,

THESE REMAINS OF MY DECEASED BROTHER

ARE MOST RESPECTFULLY DEDICATED,

BY THEIR OBLIGED AND MOST

OBEDIENT SERVANT,

JOHN SURTEES.

PREFATORY NOTICE.

THE Author of the following Narrative entered the Army in early life. He commenced his military career in 1795, as a private soldier in the Northumberland Militia; and in the following year he volunteered into the Pompadours. In this regiment he first faced the enemy, during the expedition to Holland under the Duke of York. On getting his discharge from the Pompadours, in 1802, he again entered the service as a private in the Rifle Brigade, to which he was attached for a period of twenty-five years. From his steady conduct, and ardent love for his profession, he was soon advanced from the ranks, and, after various intermediate steps, was appointed Quartermaster; a situation which he held as long as he continued in the corps, enjoying the respect and esteem of his brother officers of all ranks, as is amply testified by the letters which form the Appendix to this volume.

Though, as Quartermaster, the Author was not called by duty to join in battle, yet he lost no opportunity of entering the scene of action, or of placing himself in a favourable situation for observing what was passing. It is unnecessary to enumerate the arduous services of the Rifle Brigade from 1802 to 1815.

During the whole of that period the Author was actively engaged with his corps.

The Narrative is faithfully—indeed literally—printed from the Author's MS. as he left it at his death.. The critical reader may therefore detect various inaccuracies which, had life been spared to the Author, would probably have been corrected; but he will find much to approve, and, hackneyed as Narratives of the Peninsular War have become, he will also find much that is new.   There is no embellishment in the style of the Author's composition, but there is a quiet Defoe-like sincerity and simplicity characteristic of his pages, and a strain of unaffected piety, that is very pleasing; and the scenes and descriptions which he gives, though sometimes singularly chosen, and reported quite with a manner of his own, are on the whole portrayed with strong graphic effect.   One word, however, before closing,—our Author is never vulgar.

A severe pulmonary affection compelled him to quit his corps in 1826. He retired to Corbridge, his native village, where he arrived on the 24th of October in that year, and continued there, respected and beloved, and constantly engaged in acts of benevolence, till the period of his death, 28th May, 1830.

November 23, 1832.

CONTENTS.

CHAPTER I.

CHAPTER II.

CHAPTER III.

CHAPTER IV.

CHAPTER VII.

CHAPTER VIII.

CHAPTER IX. ·

CHAPTER X.

CHAPTER XI.

CHAPTER XII.

CHAPTER XIII.

CHAPTER XIV.

CHAPTER XV.

CHAPTER XX.

TWENTY-FIVE YEARS

IN

THE RIFLE BRIGADE.

CHAPTER I.

Birth and Parentage—Enters the Militia—Volunteers into the Line—
Joins the Army destined for Holland—The Troops embark at Deal—
Land at the Helder—Laxity of discipline—March for Schagen—De-
tachment under Sir Ralph Abercromby sent to surprise Hoorne—
Hoorne surrenders.

I WAS born on the 4th of August, 1781, in the village
of Corbridge, in the county of Northumberland; of parents
who may be said to have been among the middle classes,
my father being a tradesman. They gave me such an edu-
cation as was customary with people of their station in life;
viz. reading, writing, and arithmetic. My mother having
sprung from a pious race, was the first to implant in my
mind any sense of religion; indeed, it is to the spiritual
seed sown in my heart by her during my youth, that I am
indebted, under God, for having been brought, many years
afterwards, to consider my ways, and to turn to Him.
Nevertheless, being naturally of a sensual and wicked disposition, I, as might be expected, spent a dissolute youth,
which often caused great pain and uneasiness to my good
and pious mother. But I did not continue long under the
paternal roof; for, having from my infancy a great predi-
lection for a military life, I embraced almost the first oppor-

A

tunity that offered, after I became sufficiently grown, to
enter into the militia of my native county. I enlisted on
the 15th of November, 1798, being then little more than
seventeen years of age. I entered this service with the determination that, should I not like a soldier's life, I would
then, after remaining a few years in it, return home; but,
if I did like it, to volunteer into the line, and make that my
occupation for life. It will readily be believed that this
undutiful step affected deeply my excellent parents; for
though my father was not *then* a religious man, he had a
heart susceptible of the tenderest feelings; and I really believe that no parents ever felt more deeply the combined
emotions of tender regret at my leaving them so young,
and for such a purpose, and at the disgrace which my way-
ward conduct had, as they imagined, brought upon myself.
But though evil in itself, God overruled it for good to me,
and, I trust, to them also. I would here remark that the
life of a soldier was by no means considered in my native
village, at that time, as at all creditable; and when I sometimes in my boyhood used to exhibit symptoms of a military inclination, I was often taunted with the then oppro-
brious expression, " Ay, thou likes the smell of poother,"
intimating thereby that I was likely to disgrace myself by
going for a soldier.

I left my family in much grief in the beginning of 1799,
and marched with several other recruits to join my regiment at Chelmsford in Essex, where we arrived in about
a month, and where I began my military career. I always
liked a soldier's life, consequently I did not suffer from
many of those parts of it which are so unpleasant to those
of a contrary disposition; and, as I took pleasure in it, I
of course made more progress in acquiring a knowledge
of my duty than some others who set out with me. I was

early placed in the first squad, an honour which I considered no trifling one in those days,—but none of us finished our drill; for, in July of the same year, an order was issued, permitting such men as chose to extend their services, to volunteer into the line, in order to recruit the army then destined for Holland. We had previously marched from Chelmsford to Colchester, a distance of twenty-one miles, which march was to me, I think, the severest I ever underwent; for being young, and totally unaccustomed to any thing like it, the weight of the musket, bayonet, accoutrements, and knapsack, appeared, towards the latter end of the march, to be almost intolerable; but I kept up, although excessively tired. This will show how necessary it is at all times to accustom troops, destined for service, to move in such order as they will be expected to do when they take the field—for, if unaccustomed to the carriage of the knapsack, and to frequent marches with it for exercise, they will be utterly unable to perform any movement against, or in the face of an enemy, with that celerity necessary to ensure success. I volunteered, with several of my comrades, into the 56th regiment, or Pompadours, so called from their facings being Madame Pompadour's favourite colour, and we set off (carried in waggons to accelerate our movements) for Canterbury, which we reached in two days and one night, having travelled without making a halt; and there we joined the skeleton of our regiment, just then returned from the West Indies, where twice, during the war, it had been nearly exterminated by disease.

In a few days after our arrival, a selection was made throughout the volunteers for fit subjects for the light company, when, fortunately, both myself and William Sutherland (who had been in the same company with me in the militia, and who, from our names and size being so nearly similar, had always stood next me in the ranks) were chosen for this, in my mind, honourable service.   I felt not a little proud at my advancement, as I considered it, (and as I believe the generality of soldiers consider it,) to be made a light-bob.

The regiment had not at this time either arms, appointments, or clothing; but, being in a few days sent off to Barham Downs, where the army for Holland was assembled and encamped, we soon after were supplied with the necessary equipment, and commenced without delay to drill and get the men in readiness for embarkation.   At this time the flank companies of all those regiments destined for Holland were separated from their battalions, and formed into what are termed flank battalions.   That in which my company was placed consisted of eleven light companies, the command of which was given to Lieut.-Col. Sharpe, of the 9th regiment, an experienced and gallant veteran, who had commanded a similar battalion in the eastern district, under the Earl of Chatham.   The grenadier battalion was composed of an equal number of grenadier companies, and belonged to the same regiments to which ours belonged. Before our arrival on Barham Downs, the first division of the expedition, under Sir Ralph Abercromby, had sailed; and we soon after were called out to fire a *feu de joie* for their capture of the Dutch fleet, and their having effected a landing and gained a victory near the Helder.   Nothing could be more brilliant than our display upon this occasion appeared to me—we were nearly 20,000 strong, I imagine, and, being formed in one extensive line, the firing of the *feu de joie* produced a fine effect.   To my non-military readers, perhaps, it will be necessary to explain what is termed a *feu de joie*.   The usual mode is, when formed in line, for the fire to commence by signal with the right file of the whole, and each of those on their left take it up rapidly in succession, so that, to a looker-on, it has the appearance of a wild-fire running along the line; but on this occasion we heightened the effect, by beginning with the right of the front rank only, and when it had passed along by the front, the left-hand man of the rear rank took it up, and so it passed along by the rear to the right again. It appeared to me, at that time, certainly the finest sight I had ever witnessed. Every heart present was elated with joy, and beat high to be led on to share in those glorious achievements which we were then celebrating; but, alas! we were then ignorant that we were as unfit at that time to suffer the toils and privations of a campaign, as if we had never seen a soldier; we were all young, and inexperienced in the highest degree, and our discipline, as might be naturally expected, was far from good; for, being an army hastily collected from every regiment of militia in the kingdom, the officers of course neither had that knowledge of the characters of their men, which is so essential, nor had the latter that confidence in their officers, which only a service together for some length of time can engender, and which is absolutely necessary to secure an unreserved and active obedience to their commands. But the period of our embarkation fast approached; previously to which, we were reviewed by his Royal Highness the Duke of York, (who was destined to command us,) accompanied by several others of the Royal Family, and by General Sir Charles Grey, my countryman. I believe they all expressed themselves highly satisfied with our appearance and movements, and hoped that we would shortly add fresh laurels to those already gained by our forerunners.

As it was expected to be a service of only a short duration, it was determined that the men should embark in what is called " light marching" or " service order," that is,

with only about half the usual complement of necessaries,
consequently every soldier had to leave a considerable portion of his things behind him ; and, in order to deposit them
safely, empty casks were procured for each company, into
which every man was ordered to stow his extra things, after
being properly packed and labelled with his name, &c. This
rather grieved me, for I had brought with me from home as
good a kit (as the soldiers term it) as any in the army. My
dear mother had prepared me shirts fine enough for any officer, and abundance of them, but of those thus left I never
saw one afterwards. During our stay in this camp, I never
enjoyed better health or greater lightness of spirits, forgetful or heedless of the deep and lasting anguish which my
late rash step must naturally inflict upon the hearts of my
tender and affectionate parents ; but I was no doubt stimu-
lated to this thoughtless forgetfulness of them, by witnessing the animating scenes around me, where all was bustle
and high anticipation of more glorious doings.

We marched from this camp to Deal, where we embarked
in transports already prepared to receive us. As soon as we
arrived we were instantly put on board, but never shall I
forget the effect which the sight of the sea, and such a number of ships of various sizes and descriptions, had upon me ;
for before this I had never been near the sea, although I
had marched from the north to the south of England. But,
to add to all the strange things which then met my view,
we were instantly on marching down put into a large boat
that lay high upon the beach ; which, when filled with
troops, they run down into the sea with astonishing rapidity, turning my stomach, as we entered the water, completely topsy-turvy. The effect of all this can better be
conceived than described ; we were immediately rowed off to,
and put on board our transport, which happened to be a

brig called the Zephyr of Shields. Here also every thing was quite new to me; but all was met and performed with the highest spirits, so far as sea-sickness permitted. We remained on board two or three days before the fleet was ready for sea; but at length we sailed with a favourable breeze, and in two or three days more we made the coast of Holland, and soon afterwards came to anchor within the Texel. Every thing being ready for landing, and the Helder being in our possession, we disembarked there on the 15th of September, 1799, having been just one week on board. We were formed on landing near the town, and waited till some others had disembarked, before we moved off. Among those regiments which landed, I remember the 35th was one. This regiment, after coming on shore, was drawn up close to us; they had not been long landed before the men began with their knives to cut off each other's hair, which then was worn in the shape of a club; this was done without any orders from their officers, and appeared to me, I confess, such a breach of discipline, as I could not have anticipated; for though on the whole it was an improvement, as later usage has shown, yet I apprehend for a body of soldiers, without any permission from higher authority, to take upon them to break through the long-established custom of the service, was such an utter renunciation of all obedience to authority, as directly to threaten with destruction the best interests of the army to which they belonged; however, at such a time it would perhaps have been attended with still worse consequences to have made an example of the offenders, although, had stricter discipline been enforced from the outset, I feel assured the army in general would have benefited by it.

Towards evening, we moved forward through the town of Helder, and proceeded on our route towards Schagen, and

halted for the night on the road, and where such as could find
houses, of which there were a few straggling ones in the
neighbourhood, got into them. I awoke in the night, and still
fancied myself on board ship; for the wind and rain were beating violently against the little hovel into which a few of us
had crept, and I imagined it was the dashing of the sea against
the bow of the vessel. Indeed so strong was this imagination,
that when I got up, I literally could not stand steady, not
having been long enough on board to acquire what is
termed my " sea legs;" that is, I had not learned the art
of standing steady when the vessel heeled; and, strange as
it may appear to a person who has never been at sea, I
believe most landsmen have the same feeling for some short
time after being put on shore. We had each man been supplied with a blanket while in camp on Barham Downs, but
had no proper or uniform mode of carrying them; we had
no great-coats, but made use of the blanket sometimes as a
substitute in the morning, when we turned out to proceed
on our march. We certainly made a strange appearance.
Some had their blankets thrown around them, others had
them twisted up like a horse collar, and tied over their
shoulders in the manner of a plaid; while some had them
stuffed into, and others tied on to the top of their knapsack; in short, we appeared like any thing but *regular*
troops. We moved forward as soon as we were formed, and
early in the day reached Schagen-bruck, where his Royal
Highness stood to inspect us as we marched past. Near
this place we fell in with some of the Russian regiments,
they having landed nearly at the same time, and of which
nation there were, I believe, about 20,000 troops expected
to join our army. But if we appeared irregular and gro-
tesque, I know not well how to describe them; their riflemen were shod with boots very much resembling those of

our fishermen, coming up considerably higher than the
knee ; thus rendering them, I should imagine, incapable of
celerity of movement, one of the chief requisites in a rifle
corps ; they also wore large cocked hats and long green
coats. Their grenadiers were dressed more apropos, having
high sugar-loaf shaped caps, mounted with a great deal of
brass, and projecting forward at the top, with long coats,
and gaiters reaching above the knee. Their regular infantry
were nearly similar to the grenadiers, only they wore cocked
hats instead of caps. The regiment which we saw on this
occasion had with it, I should think, full half as many followers as soldiers, some of whom carried immensely large
copper kettles; others the provisions, and others the officers'
baggage; in short, these were the scullions, the cooks, and,
as it were, the beasts of burden of the regiment ; but this
was a bad system, for it increased by one half the number of
mouths to fill, and must have been attended with the worst
consequences when provisions were scarce. The officers,
I remember, carried what was formerly used in our service,
a long sort of pole, with a head like a halberd, and called, I
believe, a "spontoon." This, on passing a general at a review, the officer twists and twirls around his head, precisely
as a drum-major in our service does his cane. When we
had passed his Royal Highness at the bridge, we moved forward to the town of Schagen, and took up our quarters in
the church. I thought this extremely odd, as I had been
accustomed to view so sacred an edifice with more reverence
than to suppose they would quarter soldiers in it ; but we
were stowed in it as thick as we could well be, and made the
best of our quarters ; some taking the chancel, others the
vestry, and some the body of the church ; nay, some even
took up their lodging in the reading-desk and pulpit. We
could contrive to make out the Lord's prayer in Dutch,

but could not well proceed further, although there is much
similarity between that language and the English of my
native county.   Here, for the first time, we learnt that
our brigade was what was called the *reserve*, and commanded
by Colonel M'Donald of the 55th regiment; but on this
occasion and in Egypt, the reserve was not what is generally understood by that term, for in both places it was
composed of some of the best troops in the expedition, and
was generally first called into action. On this occasion, the
reserve consisted of the 23d Welsh fusileers, the 55th regiment, the grenadier battalion before mentioned, and our
light battalion.

We remained here till the 18th, when towards evening
we were ordered under arms, having been previously supplied with provisions; and, after every preliminary was
adjusted, we set forward on our march towards the city
of Hoorne, situated on the Zuyder Zee.   Of our destination,
the men, of course, were totally ignorant, but no doubt
the officers knew. It turned out that about 8000 troops
had been appointed for this service, the execution of which
was intrusted to that gallant old veteran, and hitherto successful general, Sir Ralph Abercromby. The intention
was to make a rapid and extensive flank movement during
the night, and surprise and capture the said city, while his
Royal Highness was to attack the enemy in front. We
moved off as it became dark, but such was the state of
the roads that it became the most trying and distressing
march that I believe ever troops undertook; the roads were
literally knee deep in mud in most places, while every now
and then they were rendered nearly impassable, both by the
enemy having broken down the bridges over the innumerable canals and dikes which intersect this country, and
these canals in many places having overflowed their banks.

None but those who have experienced this or something similar, can form an idea of the fatigue attending a night march in such a country, where the column is large. We marched, I think, in sections of about eight file, that is, with eight men abreast in the front rank, and the like number in the rear rank covering them. Conceive, then, your arriving at an obstacle which the darkness of the night multiplies a hundred-fold. Not more than one man will attempt to pass this obstacle at the same time, and he has to grope his way; consequently all the other fifteen men must stand still, or nearly so, till he is over, before they each move on in turn. Multiply this by the 300 sections behind, and you will have a halt for the rear of probably an hour or more; standing all this while nearly up to the knees in mire; or, what is worse, as each regiment has accomplished the task of getting over, this of course causes the others in the rear to be drawing up towards it by degrees, so that probably you are compelled to stand (or, if you choose, you may lie down in the mud) for a quarter of an hour, or more perhaps; and then move on again for the space of a few hundred yards, and then another halt; so that could you lie down to enjoy a little rest, the constant cry of " forward" resounding in your ears, just as you begin to close your eyes, renders it the most tiresome and trying situation that I know of. It is true, the head of the column does not suffer in an equal proportion with those in the rear, or a night march in an enemy's country would be a dangerous operation.

During this march, I remember, when the road was extremely deep, some one on the right of my section called out that there was an excellent path a little beyond him; when one poor fellow moved in that direction, but had not made many steps, till souse he went into a deep canal. Whether the man who called out had been actually deceived by the smooth surface of the water, which appeared in the

dark like a nice level road; or whether he did it through mischief, I know not, but the poor simpleton who followed his
advice paid dearly for his curiosity, being with some difficulty extricated from his uncomfortable situation.   I may
observe that these canals or dikes skirt both sides of every
road in this part of Holland, and are even made use of as
fences for the fields, there not being any hedges or walls
that I remember to have seen.

About break of day we reached the city, which at once
surrendered; but just before daylight, I became so excessively weary that I could not continue in the ranks any
longer; indeed men had been dropping out for some hours
before, so that, I suppose, when the head of the column
reached Hoorne, one half the number had fallen out; for
it was beyond the powers of human nature to sustain such
excessive fatigue.   I, with two or three others, got behind
a house that stood by the roadside, and laid ourselves down
on a paved footpath which led from the back-door.   Never
in my life did I experience a greater luxury than this appeared to be, where something hard, and that would keep
me out of the deep and filthy mire, could be found to rest
upon.

I laid me down and slept as soundly as ever I did in my
life for about an hour, which quite refreshed me.   We then
got up and set off with all despatch to overtake the column,
which we came up with and joined just as they halted after
reaching the city.   None of the troops entered the place, I
believe; but my battalion being towards the rear of the column, was at a considerable distance from it.   All now lay
down to rest, and such as had houses near them occupied
them; but those who had not, chose the driest parts of the
canal bank or road, and all were soon buried in profound
sleep, excepting those who were placed on guard.

CHAPTER II.

The Russian Allies carry Bergen—Allow themselves to be surprised, and the whole Army forced to retire to their former position—Skirmishing in the vicinity of Old Patten—The Russians endeavour to force their way back to Bergen—The Russian and British Forces joined—The Enemy forced to abandon Egmont-op-Zee—Alkmaar surrenders—The Troops advance to Egmont Binnen—Skirmishing—General Engagement—The Enemy repulsed—The Forces retire to Zaand Wyck—Armistice concluded—Return to England.

FROM daylight we had heard a heavy and constant cannonade towards our right and rear. His Royal Highness, with the remainder of the army, as was before intimated, had moved forward and attacked the main body of the enemy; but as I did not witness this action, I forbear to relate what I heard concerning it, further than this, that the Russians who attacked the enemy posted in the neighbourhood of Bergen, having by some mismanagement allowed themselves to be surprised after having carried that village, the whole army had been obliged to retire to their former position. In consequence of this failure, I believe, we were ordered towards evening to fall in, and (what appeared annoying in the extreme) to retrace our weary footsteps by the same dirty road by which we had advanced. Nearly the same fatigue and misery were endured as in our advance; but the column did not keep so much together as before, the men falling out by hundreds, so that the stoppages were not quite so great.

We did not return to Schagen after our retreat, but were cantoned in some villages in front of that town ; and a few days afterwards we were moved to the right of Schagen, through Schagen-bruck, to a farm hamlet called Zaand Wyck.

Here we remained till the 1st of October ; but I should not omit to mention, that we had, during the intervening period, several marches, all of which were made by night, and in which similar sufferings and fatigue were endured as in the march to Hoorne. This, it may probably be remembered, was one of the wettest autumns almost upon record ; and in these marches we generally had the full benefit of the torrents which fell in this naturally wet country. I have actually seen the water running out at the bottom of the men's trowsers like that from the gutter which carries the rain from the roof of a house. When we had not a night march, we invariably had to be at our alarm post an hour before daybreak,—and that being about four miles distant from our quarter at this time, we never had what may be called a full night's rest.

Military men will know that the custom of being at the alarm post before daybreak is almost universal ; for, that being the usual time of attack, it behoves those who are apprehensive of a visit from the enemy to be on the look-out, and to be prepared to receive them when they come— here they remain, till, as the vulgar phrase goes, " You can see a white horse a mile off," that is, till it is clear daylight, and they have ascertained that no enemy is in the neighbourhood ; after which, if all be quiet, they retire to their quarters. Our accommodations at Zaand Wyck may be said to have been good, for our officers had a farmhouse to live in, and we had a good dry barn and other outhouses to lie down in ; and in which I enjoyed some comfortable nights' lodgings. But on the 1st of October, in the afternoon, we were ordered to fall in, it having been previously intimated to us that we might probably have a brush with the enemy.

We were, of course, all life and glee on receiving the information, and the usual quantity of provisions having been issued, and every other preparation made in the night, we moved off by the same road by which we had usually advanced to our alarm post. This we passed, and then entered a most unpleasant country to march through ; it being nearer the enemy, of course all bridges and other communications had been destroyed. As we moved on, a little after daylight we were overtaken by the 11th light dragoons, on which we were ordered to open to the right and left to let them pass us. They seemed in high spirits, and some of them cried out, as they passed us, " Go on, my lads, lather them well, and we'll come up and shave them."

Sir Walter Scott mentions this saying as made use of by some of the cavalry at Waterloo, as if it were at that time new ; but I can assure him it is as old as 1799, if not much older, for I certainly heard it used on this occasion, and I know not but it may have been said long before. The cavalry inclined, after passing us, to their left, while we kept down towards the sea ; and soon after, on ascending a small eminence, we got a view of the village of Old Patten, where we discovered about 10,000 or 12,000 of our army drawn up near the sea-beach. We passed them, and moved forward in the direction of a high range of sand-hills, which commenced about a mile beyond the village, and which overlooked all the plain below. Here the enemy was posted, and I was told that they began as soon as we were within reach to cannonade us ; but from the heads of the men in front, I could not perceive any appearance of such cannonade, nor do I believe that any of their shot reached us. A little farther on, however, we met a Russian yager, or rifleman, coming back and holding out his hand, which had been

wounded, and from which the blood was flowing pretty co-
piously.

This was the first blood that I had ever seen as drawn
in hostile conflict, and it certainly produced a somewhat
strange effect upon me ; it showed plainly that we were in
the immediate vicinity of that enemy we had so often talked
about, and whom we hoped to conquer ; that now the time
had arrived which would infallibly prove what every man,
boaster or not, was made of ; and that it might happen that
it was my lot to fall. Having reflected (rather confusedly I
own) on the passing scene before me, and offered up an occasional prayer to Him who alone can cover the head in the
day of battle, we now approached the bottom of this sandy
eminence, when my company was ordered to unfix bayonets, (for we had previously primed and loaded,) and dash
on at double quick time till we came in contact with the
enemy. No time was left for reflection now, the immediate
duty we had to perform occupied all our attention fully ; we
soon got into a smart fire from the enemy's riflemen, which
we found was the only description of troops, except a few
artillery, that we had to contend with, their main bodies of
heavy infantry being on the right and left of this sandy
range, which in some places was about a mile in breadth, in
others more or less.

After the fight had fairly commenced, we kept but little
order, owing partly to the want of discipline and experience
in our people, and partly to the nature of the ground, which
was rugged and uneven in the extreme, being one continued
range of sand-hills, with hollows more or less deep between
them ; and partly it may be attributed to the ardour of our
young men, who pressed on perhaps too rapidly. We continued to advance, and never once made a retrograde movement, the enemy regularly retiring from height to height

on our approach ; but they had greatly the advantage over us in point of shooting, their balls doing much more execution than ours ; indeed it cannot be wondered at, for they were all riflemen, trained to fire with precision, and armed with a weapon which seldom fails its object if truly pointed ; while we were (what shall I say) totally ignorant of that most essential part of a soldier's duty. They consequently suffered little from our fire; but we could not believe this, and tried to persuade ourselves they had either buried their dead in the sand before we came up to them, or carried them off as they retreated ; but experience has since taught me to know that we then must have done them little harm.

About the middle of the day, as I and a young man of the name of Thomas Bambrough (a countryman of my own, and who had volunteered with me,) were moving on in company, in passing through one of the valleys to an opposite height, we were assailed by a little volley from a group of the enemy which we discovered on a hill in front of us ; one of which shots took effect in poor Bambrough's thigh just about the ham ; he instantly fell, and roared out most piteously ; I laid down my musket and endeavoured to hoist him on my back, in order to take him out of the fire, which they now poured in without intermission ; but in this I failed, for he was so completely disabled by the wound, as to be rendered totally helpless, and it was so extremely painful that he could not bear the least movement.

I felt constrained to leave him, although I did so with reluctance, telling him that I would push on to the height we had first in view, to which I then perceived some more of our men had advanced, and would drive the enemy from their position ; of course all this was not literally told him, but something to that effect was said ; and I found that the moment I left him they ceased to fire on him ; and, as I pro-

A 2

mised, we did drive off the enemy. Shortly after, some of our own people came up to where poor Bambrough lay, and carried him off to the rear; he was sent to an hospital, where he soon after died, they not being able, I understand, to extract the ball. Soon after this, there were some tremendous volleys of musketry heard on our left, apparently down in the plain below us.   I, with one or two others, now inclined a little towards the left, in order to have a peep at the troops there, so hotly opposed to each other, in doing which, we still kept our line in front of the enemy's skirmishers.

We found it was the Russian army endeavouring to force their way towards the village of Bergen, the scene of their former disaster; but they were most distressingly retarded by the innumerable canals or ditches, by which the country was so intersected, and which were generally impassable by fording. · On some occasions I could perceive, when they had found an entrance into an enclosure, and had fought their way to the farther side of it, they were obliged to retrace their steps, and get out by the same way by which they had entered, the enemy all this while pouring into them a close and destructive fire. This appeared to me to be most trying to their patience, and very disheartening; but they bore it with great steadiness.

Meantime, our own heavy troops were advancing on the right by the sea-beach, where was a plain of sand, of perhaps from 100 to 200 yards in breadth; the sand-hills between the two wings, as I said before, being swept by us, assisted by a small corps of Russian riflemen. We moved on till we got a little in advance of the Russian army, (which, from the obstacles they had to contend with, did not make very rapid progress,) and immediately over the village of Bergen, which stood on the plain, close under the sand-hills. Here, the enemy being in possession of considerable field-works, plied us pretty plenteously with shells from their howitzers, (their guns they could not elevate sufficiently to reach us,) but from which we suffered very little; for our people being much extended, and the sand being deep, the bursting of the shells was attended with very little mischief. Indeed, for a long time, I did not know what they were; for, having several times heard a loud explosion pretty near, I actually looked round to see the gun, which I imagined had fired, but could perceive nothing but a cloud of smoke rising from the spot, and the small bushes and herbs about it on fire. I thought it strange, and it was not till it was several times repeated, that we discovered what it really was, for my comrades were equally ignorant with myself.

At length, towards the close of the afternoon, a loud and heavy fire of musketry broke out on our right, which continued for a considerable time, and then ceased. This was our heavy infantry, who had advanced by the sea-shore, and who had now approached the village of Egmont-op-Zee, where the enemy made a most determined stand, but at last were driven back with great slaughter, and our people took possession of the town. From this place the battle derives its name. A little after dark, the enemy abandoned Bergen also, so that we ceased any longer to be annoyed by their shells, which they continued to throw while they held possession of the place. But a short while before they retired, one was thrown, which pitched just close over my company, (for we had then been collected, and were formed in close order immediately above the town,) and where Colonel Sharpe and another officer were walking; it lay for a second or two hissing and burning, and might be expected every moment to explode. Their road lay close past it; the veteran however took no notice of it, but continued his walk and conversation the same as if nothing had occurred,

and without going an inch out of his way.   It burst with
a tremendous report, but fortunately without doing either
of them the least injury.   I confess I thought it rather *too
brave;* for it appeared to me that he might have walked a
little farther from it, or stopped for a moment or two without any imputation on his courage; but people do not all
see things exactly alike.

Our loss in this action was but trifling, considering the
extent of the operations.   We had in my company only
about fourteen or fifteen men killed and wounded; among
the latter were my two countrymen, Bambrough, as before
noticed, and Sutherland.   One man of our company, I was
told, in charging a fieldpiece, was struck down by the wind
of the ball, and which, although it did not touch him,
brought blood from his mouth, nose, and ears; he never
after thoroughly recovered the effects of it.   I do not remember ever to have felt more fatigued than I did after this
day's work.   We had marched before commencing the
action, I should think, twelve miles or more. We had been
kept upon the run the greater part of the day, and had fought
over nearly as much more ground, through loose sand, sometimes nearly up to the middle of the leg, and over ground
so extremely uneven, that a few miles of leisurely walking
on such, would be more than I should be able to accomplish
now; and we had been nearly all the day deprived of every
sort of liquid, for our canteens were soon emptied of what
little they contained in the morning, and having myself
fired nearly 150 rounds of ammunition, the powder of which,
in biting off the ends of the cartridges, had nearly choked
me.   What would I not have given for a good drink?   I
felt completely exhausted, and laid me down with the others
with great good-will on the top of one of the sand-hills.
But the night proved extremely wet, so that every one of

us was very soon as completely soaked as if he had been dragged through a river; and, to crown my misfortunes, I was without a blanket. Here I must confess my folly, that others similarly situated may profit by my experience. Soon after the commencement of the action a rumour was spread along the line of skirmishers, that the Duke, seeing the very arduous duty we had to perform, had said, "Never mind, my lads, if your knapsacks are any encumbrance to you, and impede your running, throw them off, and I will take care you shall be furnished with others." No sooner did this silly report reach my ears, than I, with many others, equally simple, believed it, without taking time to consider that if even it were true, a knapsack and a blanket, (for they were together,) to be useful should be at hand when wanted. But, simpleton like, away went knapsack and blanket, and I felt greatly relieved in getting rid of such a burden, and now pushed on after the enemy with increased vigour, trying at the same time to persuade myself the report was true; although I own I occasionally had my doubts on the subject. But night came on, as I have said, and such a one as I have seldom seen for wet, and then I plainly perceived that I had played the young soldier.

An officer of ours of the name of Lacy, who had formerly been the captain of the Northumberland light company, and who volunteered with us, offered any man half a guinea for the use of a blanket for that night only, but without being able to obtain one: this will give some idea of the kind of night it was. I had nothing for it, but just to put the cock of my musket between my knees, to keep it as dry as possible, and lay myself down as I was. I endeavoured to get as close as I could to one who had a blanket, and lay down with my head at his feet, which he had covered up very comfortably with his blanket. The rain pelted so heavily and so incessantly on my face, that I ventured after a while to pull a little corner of this man's blanket just to cover my cheek from the pitiless storm, and in this situation snatched a comfortable nap; but he awakening in the night, and finding that I had made free with the corner of his blanket, rudely pulled it from off my face, and rolled it round his feet again.

I was fain to lie still and let it pelt away, and even in this exposed situation I got some sleep, so completely were the powers of nature exhausted by fatigue. At length morning arose and showed us to ourselves, and such a group of sweeps we had seldom seen. Our clothing was literally all filth and dirt; our arms the colour of our coats with rust; and our faces as black as if we had come out of a coal-pit. In biting off the ends of the cartridges, there are generally a few grains of powder left sticking on the lips and about the mouth; these, accumulated as they must have been by the great quantity of ammunition each of us had fired, and with the profuse perspiration we were in during the heat of the day, added to the wet which fell upon us during the night, had caused the powder to run all over our faces; so that in the morning we cut the most ludicrous figure imaginable. However we immediately set about getting our arms again in trim, for though the enemy had left us masters of the field of action, they were not far distant from us. We soon got our firelocks again in fighting order; that is, they would go off, though the brightness, on which a clean soldier piques himself, was gone past recovery at this time. I now felt rather sore from firing my piece so often; the recoil against my shoulder and breast had blackened them, and rendered them rather painful, and the middle finger of my right hand was completely blackened and swoln from the same cause.

At this time it was reported that a sad accident had occurred in our battalion; a soldier of one of our companies, in cleaning his musket, had by some awkwardness allowed it to go off, and an officer being immediately in front of where he was standing, the ball had taken effect upon him, and killed him on the spot.

After getting ourselves brushed up a little, the whole battalion was brought together, and moved to the right into the town of Egmont-op-Zee, where the guards and some other regiments had been since the evening before, after beating the enemy out of it, as I before mentioned. We remained here for that day, during which Alkmaar surrendered, and then advanced to the village of Egmont Binnen, or Egmont-op-Hoof, I am not certain which it is called, a few miles in front, and close by the sea.

I omitted to mention, that our fight of the 2d took place over the ground from which Lord Duncan's victory derived its name, *i. e.* Camperdown. This headland, I fancy, we must have passed during that day's operations—But to return. We remained in Egmont Binnen till the morning of the 6th, when my battalion was ordered to fall in and march towards the outposts, a few miles in front, in order, as we understood, to relieve our grenadier battalion, which had been out since the day before. We advanced by the seashore, but had not gone far before we saw and heard unequivocal signs that we should have something more than outpost duty to perform; the fact is, the enemy was rapidly advancing, their force in front having been greatly augmented by reinforcements; but when about two miles from the village, we met a soldier of the 11th light dragoons bringing in a French officer, whom he had taken prisoner. He belonged to the chasseurs-à-cheval, a sort of mounted light troops, who can act either as infantry or cavalry, as occasion may require.   When we met them, and while they stood talking for a moment, I could not help thinking it would have made a fine subject for a painting; for the officer was most superbly dressed in dark green, with a richly embroidered pouch-belt over his shoulder, and with a deep cut across his cheek, from which the blood was streaming over an extremely handsome face; indeed he was altogether a most interesting figure, and, contrasted with the rough features and haughty bearing of the proud trooper who had taken him, produced a fine effect.   The fellow gave his horse a slap over the flank with the flat of his sword, and set off with his prisoner, crying out, that there were plenty more of them to take, and that he would soon return and bring in another.

As we advanced, we could plainly perceive the enemy in front, skirmishing with our grenadiers, and we also saw that they possessed a pretty strong body of cavalry—a species of troops we had not encountered on the 2d.   We could distinctly perceive the cavalry wading into the sea as far as their horses could go, in order, as we imagined, to see past the point of a projecting sand-hill, which obstructed their view of the beach beyond it; but when they perceived that the force which was advancing against them was not great, they attacked our grenadiers with increased vivacity, and we soon after came in contact with them, for they were advancing with as great rapidity as if no force was in front to oppose them.

We soon perceived that they were nearly four times our numbers, and were obliged to adopt such a *ruse de guerre* as is frequently practised by the weaker party, but which had no effect, I am sorry to say, on this occasion,—that is, while one part of our force was skirmishing, the remainder got behind sand-hills a little in rear, and letting the men's heads just show over their tops, as if standing in columns of battalions, tried to induce the enemy to believe that each separate body which apppeared was of that force ; but no, Johnny (as the soldiers sometimes call the French) was not so easily gulled, for they had previously ascertained pretty accurately the strength of our force in front of them, by the operation of the cavalry before mentioned. · They therefore pressed on us with the most desperate fury, and in over-whelming numbers.

We maintained the action as well as our limited means permitted, and for a while kept tolerable order ; but as the fight became hotter, and the disparity of force more apparent, I regret to say, our young troops fell into considerable disorder and confusion. This giving the enemy greater confidence, of course he availed himself of it, and attacked us with redoubled impetuosity ; and, I lament to say, our dismayed and disheartened young soldiers fell from one degree of confusion to another, till at length all order seemed entirely lost amongst us ; and what was at first a rather regular retreat, became at last a disorderly flight ; for wherever an attempt was made to check the ardour of the enemy, the immense inequality of force they possessed soon completely overthrew the few that stood ; and many were the brave fellows, both officers and men, who fell in this unequal contest, without their having the slightest chance of successfully opposing our impetuous foe.

The flight now became more like a race than any thing else, and I imagine they drove us not less than three or four miles without giving us time to breathe ; but when we had reached within about a mile of the village we had left in the morning, we perceived some regiments advancing to our succour ; among them was the 23d, which advanced in line, and showed so good and steady a front as quite delighted us. We could also perceive to our left, that the Russians had become engaged with the force in front of them, and were holding it at bay; indeed by this time the action had extended considerably into the country, and some others of the British troops, I understand, were soon engaged.

On the coming up of the reinforcement, the 23d in particular, our straggling and broken troops, which had been so wofully beaten, now united, and again advanced upon the enemy; and when the 23d had given them a volley or two, the French gave way and retreated with as great precipitation as they had advanced. In short the tables were turned upon them, and the pursuit of them now was equally rapid with our retreat before them a short while previously; and before the action ceased, we had driven them considerably beyond where we encountered them in the morning. Night scarcely put an end to the action, for the firing continued long after dark, each party being directed by the fire from the arms of their opponents; the unwillingness to desist on our part, I attribute to a desire of revenge for the disgrace they had inflicted on us in the morning. Towards the evening it came on exceedingly wet.

Nothing could surpass the steadiness and fine appearance of the 23d, on entering into action; but they were all old soldiers, while our two battalions were composed altogether, I may say, of volunteers from the militia, who had as little idea of service in the field, as if newly taken from the plough. I would just remark here, that from what I have witnessed upon different occasions, I should never be inclined to put very much confidence in raw troops of whatever nation, or of what stuff soever they may be composed, for it is certain, that without being at all deficient in point of courage, they have not that confidence in their own powers which soldiers who are inured to service possess; and if hastily or hotly set upon, while without the aid and example of others more experienced than themselves, it is many chances to one I think that they will give way. So it was on this occasion. Nothing could exceed the materials of which these two battalions were composed, had they had the advantage of a little more experience; and no troops could fight better than they did, after gaining the support and countenance of the old regiments which were sent to reinforce them.

But I confess with shame, we showed a great want of nerve in the early part of the day, although to any troops the occasion must have been one of severe trial. When the retreat had degenerated into a flight, and every one seemed intent only on making the best of his way to the rear, I, with some others who were among the hills, imagined we could get on faster if we took to the sea-beach, which, although it also was composed of deep sand, yet was level, and could not be so very fatiguing as climbing the innumerable hills over which we had to retreat. Away we accordingly set for the beach; but we had forgotten to calculate that if the beach would facilitate our retreat, it also would the enemy's advance. This we soon discovered, for we had scarcely descended from the hills when we found ourselves almost surrounded by the enemy; and it was not without the utmost exertion in our power that we were enabled to effect our escape, the balls flying thicker about us during our short stay here than they had done all the day before. My haversack was a great encumbrance to me on this occasion, for, having lost my knapsack as before related, I was obliged to stuff every thing I possessed into this inconvenient bag; which, hanging so low as to knock against my thighs, greatly impeded my progress to the rear, and had nigh got me lodged in a French prison.

A girl, who had followed a grenadier belonging to my regiment when he volunteered out of the militia, accompanied her protector during the whole of this day's operations, and shared equally with him every danger and fatigue to which he was exposed, and no argument could prevail upon her to leave him till the whole business was over, and till the battalion to which her sweetheart belonged was sent to the rear at night. I am not certain whether it was his Royal Highness's intention to have fought this day, or whether the action was brought on fortuitously; but certainly, although we began the fight under very unfavourable circumstances, and things looked rather awkward at one part of the day, no army ever got a more complete drubbing than the French did before the business terminated. I have since learnt that the action became general along the whole line towards the close of the day. Thus ended the last affair between the British and French troops during that unfortunate expedition.

The next day we fell back upon Egmont Binnen, leaving sufficiently strong outposts to occupy the ground we had taken, and this day I was fortunate enough to pick up the shell of an artilleryman's knapsack who had been killed in one of the late fights; but for necessaries I was totally destitute, and began soon after to feel the effects of my folly in throwing away my own. A little before midnight of the evening of the 7th, we were again ordered under arms with all dispatch and without noise, and had no doubt it was for the purpose of advancing as before, so as to reach the enemy's line by daylight next morning. How great then was our surprise and disappointment, when we turned our faces towards the rear, and filed out of the village by the road leading towards our old quarters ! We moved on in silence till we reached Egmont-op-Zee, where the flashes from a large coal fire erected by way of lighthouse, shed a melancholy gleam over our columns as we passed beneath the hill on which it was erected. Here also by the sea lay innumerable dead bodies, both of men and horses, together with broken tumbrils and other sad emblems of the devastation which a few days previously had been made on this very ground; for here it was that the heat and principal part of the action of the 2d took place, when the heavy columns of the opposing armies came in contact with each other. It would not be easy to describe our feelings as we moved sadly and silently along, knowing, as we now did, that we were for ever abandoning all the advantages that we had hitherto gained, after so much toil, privations, and loss as we had suffered; but it was useless to repine. Our leaders must know better than we could possibly do, what state the army was in, and what likelihood remained of effecting the object for which we came into the country; our duty therefore was to obey, without questioning the propriety of our present movement, however unpleasant it might be to our feelings.

We passed by Old Patten, near to which the action of the 2d commenced, and finally returned to our old quarters at Zaand Wyck, which we reached some time next day, and where I found my comrade Sutherland, who had been here for some days; his wound, which was through the shoulder, not having disabled him from making his way thus far. He had some mutton already cooked, of which I partook with great relish, for I needed refreshment much; and after taking a swig out of his canteen, I laid me down and slept most soundly, rejoiced and thankful that I had so comfortable a home to return to.

We remained in this quarter only a day or two, and then our brigade was removed towards the left of the line, which, as well as I remember, rested upon Kolhorn. My battalion occupied the village of Basingohorn, to which we had retired on a former occasion ; I mean on our retreat from Hoorne. This was one of the villages farthest in advance, consequently it became an outpost. A night or two passed quietly, but on the second or third night, a firing commenced from the advanced sentries all along the line. Whether the enemy had merely been making a reconnoissance, or whether they had intended to advance in force, and our discovering them altered their plan, I know not, but think the former the more probable ; but be as it may, it had the effect of turning out our whole line of outposts, which, as might be expected, prepared to give them the best reception we were able. I remember on this occasion putting in two balls when we were ordered to load, as I was determined not to spare them, for I (with all my comrades I believe) felt sore at having been obliged to yield up all the advantages we had gained, to an enemy which we certainly did not consider as having fairly won them from us in action, but who were more indebted to the severity of the weather, producing such disastrous consequences on our young army, than to their prowess in the field. They retired, however, without giving us an opportunity of welcoming them in the manner we intended. A few days after this, on the 19th October, it came to my turn to be one of the advanced sentries. About break of day, while musing of many things, of home with all its comforts, and contrasting it with my then rather uncomfortable situation, I was suddenly aroused from my reverie by the beating of drums and sounding of trumpets and music, &c., all along the French line. I could not conjecture the cause of all this, for although it is customary to sound and beat the réveille at this hour, yet never having heard the French do so before, I concluded something more than ordinary had occurred to cause them to do so on this occasion, and I need hardly inform my reader that I kept a good look-out, in order that they should not catch us napping. In a short while, however, the mystery was cleared up; for an officer of ours came round all the advanced sentries to tell us, that, as an armistice had been concluded, we were not any longer to prevent the country-people from passing and repassing, as we had formerly had orders to do. I imagine the festive noises which I heard arose from this circumstance having taken place, for I believe the French were tired enough of the business, although they had now become in some measure the assailants; or else the cessation of hostilities allowed them to resume their wonted custom of beating the réveille in the morning.

Seeing we had failed in our attempt to wrest the country from the French, and that no hope now remained of our ever being in a condition to effect it, the prospect of returning home once more became a pleasing consideration, and I fully gave way to it. My comrades also now began to turn their thoughts homeward, and cheerfulness once more beamed on countenances which for some days past had been rather gloomy. But by this time the dysentery had made sad ravages among our young and inexperienced soldiery, for on a day soon after this, we could in my company muster on parade only eighteen men out of one hundred, of which it was composed at the outset. This inefficiency was caused principally by disease, although we had certainly lost a fair proportion in the field. It was therefore well that our removal to a more favourable soil was about speedily to take place; and wisely had his Royal Highness acted in agreeing to evacuate a country, the climate of which had been so extremely prejudicial to his army. About this time also, I

began to have my personal trials and sufferings; for now I
began to feel the full effect of my folly on the 2d inst., in
throwing away my knapsack, for I had not a change of any
description, and the consequence may be easily conjectured.
Filth and vermin now began to add poignancy to my other
sufferings, but I bore up against them all as well as I was
able; and I have reason to thank God, that the strength of
a good constitution enabled me to continue my duty without yielding for one day to the accumulated effects of these
disagreeables.   Soon after this also, the good people of
England, commiserating our uncomfortable situation, sent
out presents of flannel shirts and shoes, which arrived most
opportunely.   I was not fortunate enough to obtain one of
the former necessary articles, but my sergeant kindly put
me down for a pair of shoes, of which I stood in great need,
and now beg to return my best thanks to the kind friends
who sent them, although at the time we expected we should
have to pay for them.   In a short while after this, the grenadiers and light battalions were broken up, and each company returned and joined its own proper regiment.   We
joined ours (the 56th) at a weeshaus (or poorhouse),
situated on the great canal which connects this part of
Holland with Alkmaer, and not far from Schagen-bruck.
Here we were occupied for a few days in putting things in
the best order we could, previous to our embarkation.

About the 3d November we marched for the Helder,
from whence we went on board.   On our way down, one
of my comrades, who was not over scrupulous in expressing
his sentiments, was railing bitterly against the mismanagement (as he imagined) of the expedition, and saying, "he
hoped the next time we came to that country, should we
ever come again, that we would leave it under more favourable circumstances."   General Manners (to whose brigade

we now belonged) was riding close behind, unknown to this complainer, and overheard every word he said. When the soldier had finished, the General most good-naturedly rode up to him, and began to argue the matter with him. "Why," says he, "although we are leaving the country, it is not from the enemy having compelled us to do so from his superior bravery or success in the field, for we have fought only five actions since landing, and in four of these we have been the conquerors; it is owing solely to the great sickness and consequent inefficiency of the army that we have been compelled to this measure." I could not but admire the affability and kindness of the General, and was fully satisfied myself, and so were all who heard him, of, I believe, the justness of the remarks he made. We reached the Helder the same day, where we remained doing duty till the 10th November, on which we embarked on board his Majesty's ship Romney, of fifty guns, commanded by Captain Lawford, (afterwards by Sir Home Popham.) She was only a small vessel of her class, and yet our whole regiment was put on board her; we indeed were not very strong, but she was crowded beyond measure, for many, nay, most of the troops had not literally lying room, each company having barely the space between two guns, which, I should think, is not more than twelve feet at the utmost, and even here the sailors, whether with or without orders I know not, slung their hammocks over us. I particularly remember this being the case, for I had the second night, by way of securing room to stretch myself, lain down between decks early in the evening, and had had some little repose, when a sailor, whose hammock was slung right over me, and while standing and making it, put his foot right on my cheek, and stood there till he had finished. I know not whether he knew that it was a human head he was treading on, but I judged it best to be as quiet as possible; preferring the pain of bearing his weight on my head, rather than, by moving or crying out, to incur the risk of his foot slipping, and peeling the skin off my face. The voyage was fortunately short, for in seven days we landed at Yarmouth, glad and rejoiced that this unpleasant and ill-fated expedition was terminated. I know not whether my reader is old enough to remember the autumn of which I have been speaking, but to me it appeared one of the wettest and most uncomfortable that I ever remember; and it was here, while exposed to its effects, that were laid, most probably, the seeds of that severe pulmonic affection from which I have since suffered so much.

CHAPTER III.

WE landed at Yarmouth on the 17th November, and the next day marched to Norwich, where we remained a few days, and where we found the people remarkably kind and attentive to our comforts ; and, indeed, we now cut a most sorry figure, being literally nothing but rags and dirt ; it was certainly a sad tax on the good landlords on whom we were billeted, to be compelled to find us lodgings, for we never left the beds unoccupied by some of the uncomfortable companions of our travels when we arose in the morning. I· here began to find myself very unwell, for though I had borne up against sickness in the field, I could not now receive my food without feeling the most afflicting nausea, my stomach being completely out of order ; and it was no wonder, for we had been compelled for several weeks past to drink the brackish water of the ditches of Holland, no springs (that ever I saw) being there to be found, and the little water in their wells, when we arrived in the country, being speedily exhausted. We had also been depri-

ved of salt nearly all the time of our sojourn in that country, one of the greatest privations that I know of. Through
the nursing of my kind landlady, however, I gradually regained my appetite, and with it my health, for which I have
reason to be truly thankful to Him who has ever dealt so
mercifully with me.

In a few days we left Norwich on our route to Chelmsford, and on our way passed through Bury St Edmunds,
where my late regiment, the Northumberland militia, was
quartered; they vied with each other in showing us kind
attentions, but our miserable appearance put the soldiers of
this regiment sadly out of love with the regular service.

We did not remain at Chelmsford long, but marched
again for Horsham in Sussex, on which occasion I for the
first time had a view of the metropolis, as we passed through
it, by way of Whitechapel and London Bridge, &c. At
Horsham we were quartered during the remainder of this
winter. About the 10th or 12th of February 1800, we
marched for Portsmouth, where we embarked for Ireland
on the 14th. On this occasion the regiment was put on
board two first-rate frigates; the Endymion was that on
which the left wing went on board, but I do not recollect
the name of the other. An agreement was entered into between the two captains, I understood, to sail for fifty
guineas, they both being considered fast vessels; our destination was Cork; they were to start together, and the
first there of course to be the winner.

We sailed with a favourable breeze, and got on most
delightfully, having, soon after sailing, parted from our
antagonist, and passing, if I recollect right, inside the
Isles of Scilly, we in a few days drew near our destined port.
But on the 19th, as we were pushing on with all our might,
having every stitch of sail set, a squall came on so suddenly,

that, before she could be stripped of her superfluous clothing, she was actually running bows under water, the sea
entering the bow-ports, and making its way along between
decks, like to wash every thing away before it. At this time
the log was hove, and we were going at the (I believe)
unparalleled rate of fifteen knots an hour. But unfortunately
for our captain, the vessel was completely driven out of her
course, and towards evening we entered the harbour of
Kinsale, thus losing the fifty guineas, although we were no
doubt the better sailer.

This was the first gale I had experienced, and I did not
relish it; but when we entered the harbour, where the
water was quite smooth, the sensation I felt was most
delightful, after having been buffeted most violently by
the sea without. The next day we landed, and were billeted
in Kinsale, and here I had the first view of Irishmen and
Irish manners. I need not attempt to describe them; for
could I, so many have done it before me, that the subject
is almost exhausted. In a day or two after landing, we
marched to Cork, where the right wing had been landed,
and with which we of course formed a junction.

We remained in Ireland from this time till the peace of
1802 was concluded, and were quartered successively in the
towns of Cork, Kilkenny, Clonmel, Fermoy, and Kinsale;
but as there was nothing which could interest a reader that
occurred to me during this period, I shall pass it over in
silence, save mentioning the following :—In the year 1800,
it is well known the utmost distress was experienced by the
poor of both countries, a scarcity, the effects of the wet
harvest of 1799, having grievously afflicted all the British
dominions. But in Ireland, the sufferings of the poor were
great, beyond the conception of an Englishman who has not

witnessed them, and many hundreds of them, I believe, actually perished of want.

But my tale relates more immediately to my own sufferings and those of my comrades; for we had then but what was termed a " black shilling a day," that is twelve pence Irish, an English or white shilling, or Hog, going in that country for thirteen pence; we had not then any beer money either, but had solely this black shilling to subsist on. Meat at this time was no less than 10d. per lb., of which each man received half a pound; bread was 5d. per lb., of which we also got half a pound. This half pound of bread, and half pound of meat, and that not of the best, was all we had to live on, and do our duty, which was not always of the easiest description. The remainder of our shilling was taken to furnish necessaries, washing, pipeclay, &c., for I do not remember that we ever laid in any sort of vegetables for the pot. Potatoes were out of the question, for they were no less than three shillings a stone of fourteen pounds.

Although we did not absolutely suffer want, the reader will perceive that we were but sparely dieted; the consequence was, innumerable robberies of potato fields, and gardens, &c., in the neighbourhood of our quarters; and many were the men that got punished for this crime, but it could not be put a stop to, for hunger is not easily borne. Indeed, on one occasion, I myself was seduced, by the persuasion of my comrades and by the cravings of hunger, into the commission of this crime. I remember well I was on what was termed the Commissariat guard, a short distance from the town of Fermoy, when my companions, thinking it a favourable opportunity for procuring something to eat, prevailed upon me to accompany them to a garden near the bridge, into which we entered, and each of us returned loaded with a fine cabbage, and which afforded us an excellent meal after our relief from guard. It is impossible to justify such an act, but the reader will be convinced, I trust, that sheer hunger alone urged me to the perpetration of this crime. Others, I have no doubt, were equally ill off, who did not resort to such disgraceful means of satisfying their hunger, but bore it with patient resignation. I believe that such was the case, and take shame to myself for yielding either to the calls of nature or the solicitations of my companions, some others of whom were not so scrupulous. During this distressing season I sold a watch which had formerly been my father's, and with which I felt extremely loath to part. I also received a little money from home, all, or nearly all, of which was expended in procuring food.

The hedges and fields, &c. in the vicinity, were ransacked in all directions, for the purpose of procuring bramble-berries, nettles, &c. &c.; in short, for any thing that was eatable. Such was our situation during several months, while under the command of Lieut.-Col. Skinner, who, although an excellent officer, had little idea of disposing of a soldier's pay to the best advantage; but latterly we were commanded by Major Keating, who, making the comfort of the soldiers under his command his continual study and delight, soon adopted a system which secured to us plenty in comparison of our former state. He left off the meat and bread save occasionally, and procured for us plenty of oatmeal and milk, by which means our wasted bodies began shortly after to resume quite another appearance.

We were quartered at Lap's Island, in Cork, when the news arrived of peace having been concluded; and as the bulk of the regiment had volunteered from the militia for five years, or during the war, measures were taken for discharging all those who did not re-enlist either into their own or other regiments. My mind was fully made up to return home; for although, as I said before, I never repented of having entered the regular service, yet I knew that the anxiety of my dear parents for my return was so great, that I had settled it fully in my own mind to leave the army.

Another reason operated with me partly in forming this resolution—I had persuaded myself that I ought to have been promoted—for I judged myself fully capable of conducting the duties of a non-commissioned officer, and I flattered myself my conduct had been generally unexceptionable; but I was disappointed, for the great numbers in my company, who were judged both more deserving and better qualified, and withal better-looking soldiers, put it out of the question for me to look forward to promotion.

I was in this state when an officer and a party of the Rifle corps arrived at Cork, to receive such of the men of the different regiments then about to be discharged, as chose to volunteer, for this novel, and, as some thought, dangerous service. I cannot account for the impulse with which I was urged on, from the moment I had seen one of the men, to enter this corps. Something strange seemed to push me on, contrary to the full determination to return home, which had possessed me an hour before. I will not attempt to account for it, but such was the fact. I immediately, with some others of my regiment, gave in my name as a volunteer for the Rifle corps, and was in consequence in a day or two sworn into that corps, in which I have ever considered it an honour to serve, and which I have reason to thank a kind and overruling Providence I ever entered.

No news of course could be so afflictive to my dear parents, as to hear of the last rash and irretrievable step which I had taken. It had wellnigh broken their hearts, for they fully calculated on my returning home, as I had written to that effect. Judge then of their surprise and sorrow, when they learnt that I had entered, what was deemed by some, a condemned corps, and that for life—and that the West Indies would no doubt soon be my grave.

On my leaving the 56th, the officers of my company expressed their regret that I should quit the regiment, and told me, that although the mode hitherto pursued of keeping all the best-looking men in the light company had kept many from obtaining promotion, who otherwise would have been made non-commissioned officers, yet that mode was no longer to be adhered to, and that I might shortly expect to be promoted into another company, if I would consent to remain. I thanked them, and told them I had made up my mind, on which they each gave me a certificate as to character, &c., recommending me to the officers of my new corps, and which were of service to me afterwards.

The sergeant who had been sent to receive us, at once became my stanch friend, and employed me, as the party was now become pretty strong, to act as a non-commissioned officer. Every thing went on quite smoothly, and I felt happy in my new corps, and in my new employment.

We marched soon after to Waterford, and thence to Passage, and there embarked for the Isle of Wight, and without encountering any remarkable event arrived at Cowes on the 27th June, 1802 ; here we remained a day or two, and then marched for the regiment in Sussex. We found them at East Bourne, although Blatchington was their quarter, but they had been sent out of it on account of the assizes or election, I do not remember which.

. We immediately commenced our light drill, in which I took great delight ; but most of all I liked the shooting at the target. As recruits, we were first drilled at what is termed the horse, *i. e.* a machine to assist young riflemen in taking aim. At this I pleased my commanding-officer so much the first time I tried, that he ordered me to the front, and told me to load, and fire at the target. I did, and made a pretty good shot, hitting pretty near the bull's eye ; on which he made me load again and fire, and hitting that also, he made me go on till I had fired ten rounds, all of which hit the target, and two of which had struck the bull's eye. The distance indeed was only fifty yards, but for a recruit, that is, a person unaccustomed to rifle-shooting, he called it a wonderful exhibition, and in consequence he gave me sixpence out of his pocket, and ordered me home. I thought the reward quite inadequate, so natural is it for us to overrate our own deservings.

This officer (Major Wade) was one of the best shots himself that I have almost ever seen. I have known him, and a soldier of the name of Smeaton, hold the target for each other at the distance of 150 yards, while the other fired at it, so steady and so accurate was both their shooting.

I continued to maintain my character as a good shot, which in a rifle corps is a great recommendation, and proceeded in acquiring a knowledge of my other duties with such steadiness as obtained the approbation of my officers. We soon after marched to Chatham—and while there, several non-commissioned officers being employed on the recruiting service, I was employed in doing the duty of one, having been appointed what is termed a " chosen man."

I must record the manner of my appointment. An acting-sergeant was doing the duty of pay-sergeant of our company, but he took it into his head to go all wrong, spending the money intrusted to him for the payment of the men. He of course was deprived of the situation ; and on this occasion it was, that the officer commanding the company came to me one day, and said to me, " Surtees, I shall be *forced* to make you a chosen man." I thanked him, but could not help reflecting on the strange mode of expressing himself which he had adopted. The fact is, I believe, without thinking about the opinion I must form of the compliment he was paying me, he had been indeed forced to it, for he had no one to pay the company besides ; and as I was not yet dismissed from the drill, it was an unprecedented measure. But he need not have told the *whole* truth on this occasion, for I should have been no worse a non-commissioned officer, had he been more complimentary ; but he was a *plain* man, and not much given to compliment.

On our march hither, some of the men broke into the plate chest of the officers' mess, while the baggage stopped in Maidstone ; one man was discovered, and tried for it, and sentenced to receive 800 lashes, all of which he took at one standing, and that without evincing much suffering ; this was the most I ever saw inflicted at one time.

We marched again from Chatham in September, and on the 2d of October arrived at Thorncliffe. While here, my parents interested Mr Beaumont, M.P. for my native county, to solicit my discharge from the Honourable Colonel Stewart, my then commanding-officer, they paying the regulated sum to the government. The colonel sent for me, and talked with me on the subject, and argued most forcibly in favour of my remaining in the regiment, saying he had intended to promote me the first vacancy ; and that he had no doubt whatever of seeing me one day an officer. I own my views were not so sanguine ; but his reasoning prevailed, and I consented to remain. Soon after, an opportunity offering, I was appointed corporal on the 24th of the same month.

Here again I had disappointed my beloved and tender parents, for it was not without considerable trouble and difficulty they obtained the interference of Mr Beaumont, and now I had again thrown cold water on all their endeavours to obtain my discharge. I fear I have much to answer for, as respects my conduct towards them. May God forgive me!

CHAPTER IV.

HAVING given satisfaction as a corporal, I was shortly after appointed acting-sergeant; and in that capacity also, having pleased my officers, I was, on a vacancy occurring on the 19th of February following, appointed sergeant, and given the payment of a company. My head was almost turned by such rapid promotion, and I began in earnest to contemplate the possibility of my colonel's predictions being one day verified. Kind Providence watched over me, however, and kept me from being too much elated, and of committing myself as I otherwise might have done. Indeed I many times did commit things which, if strictly searched into, would have brought censure upon me, and lowered the high opinion that both myself and others entertained of me; but nothing that openly violated the law by which I was then governed (although many of God's laws I daily transgressed) was done by me.

I was at this time, although careful to secure the good opinion of my officers, little solicitous to please Him who had alone lavished all this bounty upon me. Indeed I be-

lieve I was as ungodly at this time as I ever remember to
have been, and yet He caused me to prosper. Oh! how
I ought to feel shame and confusion of face at the recollection of such abused goodness and mercy! May He pardon
me for Christ's sake!

A short while before my appointment as sergeant, a most
melancholy occurrence took place in the neighbourhood of
our cantonment. A large Dutch East Indiaman, outward
bound to Batavia, and full of troops, in passing down channel, mistook, I understand, the light at Dungeness for one
on the French coast, and in consequence stood in towards
Dymchurch wall instead of keeping out to sea. As might
be expected, she was not long in striking on the wall, running with her bow quite close under the road, and in an
instant, almost, went to pieces; and although numbers of
people were early at the spot, and some, I believe, at the
very moment she struck, they could render the unfortunate
sufferers no effectual aid, although only a few yards distant
from them. Out of about 800 persons on board, only seven
men were saved. Many poor fellows, I understand, attempted
to swim on shore, some on planks, and others without any
aid; but such was the tremendous swell, and the general
destruction of the ship so rapid, that only those seven before mentioned succeeded; and they not without being all
more or less injured by pieces of the wreck. An admiral, I
understood, was on board, and perished; several beautiful
females were afterwards cast ashore among the dead, the
wives or daughters, no doubt, of some on board; they were
for the most part nearly naked, so that it is conjectured
they had been in bed.

As might be expected, the allurement to plunder so valuable a wreck was not resisted by the natives of this part
of the coast, but Colonel Stewart humanely placed strong

bodies of the regiment at different points where the wreck
had drifted, to secure as much of the property as he could
for the Dutch government, and also to collect and bring in
the numerous dead bodies which floated along the shore;
all of which he had decently interred in the churchyard at
Thorncliffe, and had the poor wounded survivors taken into
hospital, where every care was taken of them. Indeed nothing could exceed the unremitting attention which he paid
both to the dead and living on this most melancholy occasion, and for which he received, as he well merited, the
thanks of the Dutch government.

About this period we had several individuals serving in
the corps as soldiers, who had been officers in the army
during the late war, but who, from different causes, had
been reduced to the necessity of enlisting as private soldiers.
The first that I remember was a person of the name of
Conway Welch, who, I understood, had been an officer, and
I think the Adjutant of the Surrey Rangers. He got on to
the rank of Corporal, but, being excessively wild, I believe
he never attained a higher rank. I do not remember what
became of him.

The second was called Hughes; he was, I believe, when
he enlisted, actually in the receipt of half-pay as a lieutenant
of the line. He was a person of good conduct, and was
soon promoted to the rank of corporal, and the colonel took
him for his own private clerk, or secretary, as he was denominated; but he did not remain long in this situation, for
he was shortly after called upon full pay of his rank in the
army. I believe his case was a singular one.

The third unfortunate individual was of the name of Tait.
He had been a captain in the Caithness Legion, but reduced when the regiment was broken up at the peace. He
conducted himself extremely well for some time after he

came into the regiment, and got on so far as to become
pay-sergeant of a company.   But in this situation, having
considerable sums at his command, he became involved
through his dissipation, and being unable to extricate himself from his difficulties, he adopted the fatal resolution of
committing suicide, and accordingly, when quartered at
Woodbridge, he one day retired to his room, loaded his
rifle, and blew out his brains.

The story of the fourth individual is a scarcely less melancholy one.   His name was M'Laughlan.   I had known
him while serving in my late regiment, as he had been an
officer in the light company of the 35th regiment, and
stood next in the light battalion to the company to which
I belonged.   He, shortly before our embarkation for Holland, got involved, through a gambling transaction I heard,
and was in consequence obliged to dispose of his commission, which, it would appear from this, he had originally purchased.   But interest was made in his behalf, and he was
permitted to accompany his regiment to Holland in the
capacity of a volunteer, and he accordingly assumed the fire-
lock and bayonet in place of his former weapon, the sword.
He was fortunate enough to obtain another commission
before the return of the troops to England, but how he became deprived of that I have been unable to learn.   But
about the latter end of 1803, he enlisted as a private in my
corps.   His conduct here was far from good, and he consequently never rose higher, for he was continually in scrapes
from his dissipated habits; and becoming tired of the re-
straint laid upon him by the strict discipline which our excellent commanding-officer enforced, he one day made an
attempt to desert and join the French at Boulogne, and was
picked up by one of our cruisers in endeavouring to cross
the channel in an open boat.   He was brought back hand-

5

cuffed, and lodged in the guard-house one day when I happened to be sergeant commanding the guard.

As I looked on him, I could not help reflecting on the
strange vicissitudes which attend some men in their passage
through life.   Here was a person whom I had known only
a few years before while encamped on Barham Downs, a gay
and handsome young officer, moving in the circle of men of
gallantry and honour; and now behold him a wretched cul-
prit, stretched on the wooden guard-bed, manacled like a
felon.   In contrasting his miserable situation with my own
so much happier lot, what ample cause had I for gratitude
to that kind and indulgent Providence, which had preserved
me from those excesses, which entailed so much misery on
others.   He was shortly after tried by a general court-martial, and transported as a felon for life.   I understand a sister
of his was at Thorncliffe at the time of his trial, &c., the
wife of a brevet lieutenant-colonel in the 4th regiment.
What must she have felt !

It will be recollected that, in 1803, war again broke out
between this country and France, as my preceding story had
intimated.   The army was consequently augmented again,
and my corps, till now called the " Rifle Corps," was made
the 95th.   This year a camp was formed on Thorncliffe,
under the command of that able general and excellent man
Sir John Moore.   This was termed by some the " Vanguard of England," for here it was that the then threatened
invasion of this country by Bonaparte must most likely have
taken place, it being immediately opposite to the grand
camp then forming at Boulogne.   Daily rencontres took place
between our cruisers and his far-famed flotilla; and on one
occasion, the belief that he was sending forth his invincible
host was so great, that our camp was struck, the troops
turned out, and received each man his sixty rounds of am-

munition; the waggons and carts were all put in immediate requisition, and the inhabitants were flying in all directions. But to our disappointment, I will not say whether disagreeable or otherwise, it all ended in smoke; it happened to have been some of his flotilla making a movement along the coast, which had been set on by our cruisers and pretty roughly handled.

We remained in this camp till the 24th of November, I think, having occasionally before this period had our tents blown from over our heads by the autumnal gales. The next year a more formidable camp was formed on the same ground, the force having been augmented by a second line, composed of regiments of militia. This year also, like the last, passed over without witnessing the long-threatened invasion of Old England, although Bonaparte, in the pride of his heart and the vanity of his mind, had begun to erect a monument near Boulogne, to commemorate that glorious achievement. My regiment, on the breaking up of the camp, marched into Hythe Barracks, where we remained till the month of April, 1805.

In the spring of this year another volunteering from the militia into regiments of the line was ordered, on which occasion I was selected by my commanding-officer, Lieut.-Colonel Beckwith, to accompany Lieutenant Evans, of the regiment, down to my native county, to receive such men of the militia regiments there as chose to enter the 95th. On this occasion we were very successful, having obtained between seventy and eighty men from the different regiments in the north. It was on this occasion that I had the first opportunity, since I became a soldier, of visiting my native village, and my greatly-distressed parents and family. I need not describe the meeting that took place between us, on my first seeing them—it will be better conceived than told ;—suffice it to say, joy and sorrow were strangely mingled together—joy to see me once more safe and sound —but sorrow that the line of life I had adopted should so soon, so very soon, call upon me to part from them again. In fact, I could only remain with them three days, at the end of which, I had orders to join my party at Morpeth.

With this respectable batch of volunteers we marched, and joined the regiment at Canterbury, whither it had been removed during our absence, and, on our arrival, received the thanks of our commanding-officer for our exertions. Here, and at this time, a second battalion to the 95th was formed, the sergeant-majorship of which I was in hopes of obtaining ; but in this I was disappointed, for a sergeant, who was both much older than me, and had much stronger claims than I could pretend to, was selected for the situation ; and although he did not turn out so well afterwards as was expected, yet these circumstances ought to have satisfied me at the time that no injustice was done me by bestowing it upon him. But such was my folly, and the over-high opinion I entertained of my own merits, that I could not quietly acquiesce in this most just arrangement ; and foolishly imagining myself ill-used, the chagrin of which drove me to the adoption of one of the worst expedients possible, I immediately took to drinking and to the neglect of my proper duties, thinking, like an ass as I was, that I should thus revenge myself for my supposed ill-usage, forgetting that it was only on myself that this revenge could ultimately fall. However, the same good Providence which has mercifully and so continually watched over me, stepped in to my aid in this my most dangerous situation ; for one day my captain, who had always been my friend, sent for me, and urged upon me the folly and the baseness of my present conduct, and the unhappy consequences to myself that were likely to result from persisting in a course so absurd and blame-worthy. This, with my own reasoning on the subject, brought me at length to a better disposition of mind, and induced me once more to resume my duties with cheerfulness and alacrity.

I have mentioned this circumstance, because I believe I was nearer at this time to falling into my original nothingness, than I ever have been, either before or since; and I have no doubt that many an excellent non-commissioned officer and soldier have been involved in the like error, who have not been so fortunate as I was in escaping its consequences.

From Canterbury we marched to Brabourn Lees Barracks, in the same county, where we remained till some time in October, when we were called upon to embark for Lower Germany. During our stay at Brabourn Lees, a circumstance occurred which called forth an exhibition of as great magnanimity, on the part of Colonel Beckwith, as I almost ever remember to have witnessed: We had received about 200 Irish volunteers, who were wild and ungovernable in the extreme; a party of these, in strolling about one day, had fallen in with Mrs Beckwith, with her maid and child, taking a walk along the Ashford road. Not knowing, I imagine, who the lady and her maid were, they set on and assaulted them in the most violent and outrageous manner, proceeding to such lengths as perhaps delicacy forbids to mention. It was, I believe, discovered who they were. Accordingly, the next day, the Colonel formed the battalion into a square, and proceeded to relate the circumstance to the regiment; " But," says he, " although I know who the ruffians are, I will not proceed any farther in the business, because it was *my own wife* that they attacked; but, had it been the wife of the meanest soldier in the regiment, I solemnly declare I would have given you every lash which a court-martial might have sentenced you." Such a trait of generous forbearance is not often met with ; but by this, and similar instances of liberal feeling, he completely gained the heart of every soldier in the battalion, a thing not always attainable by very excellent commanding-officers.

About the latter end of October, 1805, we marched to Ramsgate, and there embarked, as before noticed, for Germany. It was my lot, on this occasion, to be put on board a small and ill-shaped collier brig, called the Jane of Shields, but the master I have forgot. She was a most miserable sailer, making on a wind almost as much lee as head-way, and in every respect ill adapted for the transport service. We had not been many days at sea before we lost the fleet, and in our endeavours to find it again were at one time on the coast of Jutland. All this time we had been beating against a contrary wind ; but while here, the wind became favourable, and we appeared to have nothing to do but to bear away for the mouth of the Elbe, which river it was our destination to enter ; but unfortunately, by some mismanagement, we fell quite away to leeward of it, and got entangled between the mainland and the Island of Wangeroog, not far from the mouth of Jade River, instead of the Elbe.

While in this uncomfortable situation, it came on to blow a tremendous gale, which rendered our position not only most unpleasant, but extremely perilous, for we were embayed, and the wind blowing on a lee shore, and the vessel became almost unmanageable, her bad sailing becoming distressingly more apparent the more she was put on her mettle. In the midst of the confusion attendant on such circumstances, the master (with what intention I know not,

whether to drown dull care, or to fortify him against his
exposure to the watery element) went down below, and
swallowed the best part of a bottle of brandy. In doing
which, his corner cupboard, with all its contents, came
rattling down about his ears. He would fain have had me
to pledge him, but I begged to be excused. The consequence was, he became quite drunk at the time when all
his abilities as a seaman were likely to be called into operation ; but he probably saw things clearest after having his
eye wet.

My commanding-officer now became quite alarmed for
the safety of the troops, seeing the master had incapacitated
himself, as he conceived, for the management of the vessel;
and, after a consultation among our officers, an attempt was
made to deprive him of the command, and intrust it to the
mate, who had in this case, in order to save as many of the
troops as possible, determined on running the vessel high
and dry, as he termed it, on the sandy beach, near the Jade
River.

At this proposal, however, the master stormed and blas-
phemed like a madman, swearing there was neither soldier
nor sailor on board the ship but himself. He went so far,
and became so outrageous, that our commanding-officer
talked of hanging him up at the yard-arm ; but it being a
ticklish thing to take the command of a ship from the person legally authorized to exercise it, the major did not en-
force the wishes of the officers. The poor mate sat down
on the companion and cried like a child, partly owing to the
abuse the captain gave him, and partly, I imagine, from the
hopelessness of our situation. The captain, in his refusal
to yield up the command, told the major he had been several times wrecked, and had been, I know not how many
times, exposed for a considerable length of time in the

water; and that he was not afraid to encounter it again. This, however, was but poor consolation to landsmen, who had not been accustomed to such duckings.

A desperate case requires a desperate remedy—so our captain thought—for he instantly clapped on the vessel the square mainsail, which every moment threatened to carry away the mast, and in which case, nothing could have prevented our destruction; however, Providence so ordered it, that she bore it through the gale, and he, after putting her on the outward tack, continued to stand from the land till he imagined he had completely weathered Wangeroog; but at midnight, when he ordered to put about the ship, had it not been for the cabin-boy providentially seeing close to leeward of us the light of Wangeroog, we should instantly have been upon the rocks. This will show either what a bad sailer the vessel was, or how far the master had miscalculated the distance; for he imagined himself by this time to be quite clear of all the land, and considerably out to sea. He continued, after this providential escape, to stand on on the same tack, and just cleared the island; and in the morning, the wind having somewhat abated, and shifted a little in our favour, we were enabled, soon after, to lay our course.

We arrived in the Elbe, and landed at Cuxhaven on the 18th of November, 1805, the day on which our fleet there was celebrating the victory of Trafalgar—clouded indeed it was by the death of the hero who fell while achieving it—yet glorious to the nation to which that fleet belonged. We, immediately after landing, marched for Dorum, a village twelve or fourteen miles distant, and from thence by Osterholtz and Bremer Lhe to the city of Bremen. On our arrival there, (my battalion forming the advanced guard,) we found the gates were shut against us; a Prussian garrison was in the town, the commandant of which seemingly did not know how to act, whether to admit us as allies, or not, the policy of his government at that time being so extremely ambiguous. Colonel Beckwith, who commanded the advance, was not however easily to be deterred from executing his orders, and he hesitated not to tell them, that if they did not choose to admit us peaceably, force should be resorted to to gain an entrance. This had the desired effect, for the gate was soon after thrown open, and we were received by the authorities of the town, and by the inhabitants in general, with the warmest expressions of friendship and cordial attachment ; the Prussian officers, all the while looking on, apparently not over-well pleased with the conduct of their hosts; they were soon afterwards, however, withdrawn from the territory, and we then remained sole occupiers of this part of the country.

Our army assembled in this city in considerable force, when it becoming necessary to establish outposts in advance, my battalion was sent out first to the town of Delmenhorst, and subsequently a part of it to the city of Oldenburg, and the remainder to the town of Wildishausen ; to this latter place two companies were detached, under the command of Major Travers, and to which he appointed me to act as sergeant-major. We did not remain long in this situation, but were again recalled from Wildishausen to Delmenhorst, and afterwards sent to join the other companies at Oldenburg.

Here we staid some time, during which we experienced the most unbounded hospitality and kindness from the whole of the inhabitants, but more particularly from the Duke. He actually did not know how sufficiently to express his friendly disposition towards our officers in general, —his kindness also extended to the soldiers,—for when we

afterwards received an order to retrograde again to Delmenhorst, he sent forward to the half-way house refresh-
ments of every description, for both officers and men; and
the night before we left this hospitable city, he gave a
splendid ball in honour of the officers of our corps, to which,
of course, every inhabitant of a suitable rank was invited.
Nay, I heard, and have no reason to doubt the correctness
of the report, that he wrote to the burgomaster of Bremen, to which city we again retired, to endeavour, if possible, to have us quartered in his immediate neighbourhood,
in the best part of the town, for that not only the officers,
but the soldiers of the corps, were perfect gentlemen; indeed, the conduct of the battalion at this time, under its
kind and excellent commanding-officer, was such as to entitle it to the highest praise. Our retreat on this occasion,
I understood, was rendered necessary, in consequence of the
defeat of the allied forces at Austerlitz, and of the fatal termination by that sanguinary action of the campaign in that
part of Germany.

Although I am no prophet, I predicted at this period
what the result would be to the King of Prussia, whose
hesitating and equivocal conduct kept him aloof from taking
an active part, when his co-operation might have been of
the utmost advantage to the general cause. It required no
second sight to perceive, that when Bonaparte could clear
his hands of his present antagonists, he would not hesitate
for a moment to turn his arms against a monarch on whom
he could not cordially rely, and whose dominions offered
such a strong temptation to an ambitious and aspiring mind
like his.

We continued to occupy Bremen till towards the beginning of February 1806, when the whole army gradually
drew down towards our place of embarkation, for the pur-

pose of evacuating the country, our stay now having been rendered useless by the unsuccessful and unfortunate turn which the allied affairs had taken.   My battalion covered the retreat of the army ; but as great numbers of the German Legion, which formed part of the British force in this country, were deserting and returning to their homes, we were sent away into the interior to endeavour to intercept such of them as might pass by the villages we occupied, and restore them to the army.   We took some, but not many ; and soon after we also retired, and went on board at Cuxhaven, and again returned to England, landing at Yarmouth on the 19th of the same month.

During the whole of my military career, I never witnessed so cordial an attachment to the British name and character, as was manifested during this service, by the good people among whom we had been residing.   Nothing was too good for us—and nothing was left undone by them to render us comfortable and happy.   It is true they have their vices like other people ; but barring one or two peculiar to continental nations, I believe them to be, generally speaking, as moral as any people among whom it has been my lot to sojourn.   But, oh ! with what shame and sorrow do I look back on the part I acted at this period—how profligate and abandoned was my conduct at the very time that a kind and gracious Providence was showering its choicest blessings upon me ! but, alas, I paid no regard to the remonstrances of conscience, which I endeavoured and succeeded in drowning in debauchery and intemperance.

CHAPTER IV.

Our Author made Quartermaster-Sergeant of the 2d battalion, which
he joins at Feversham, Kent—Expedition to Denmark—Embark at
Deal—Land at Vedbeck, Zealand—Partial Engagements—Siege of
Copenhagen—A Division under Sir Arthur Wellesley advance to
Kioge—Copenhagen capitulates—Amnesty between the Danish
Forces in the Island of Zealand, and the British—The British evacu-
ate Denmark—Embark at Copenhagen—Arrive in the Downs—Land
at Deal.

WE landed, as I before stated, at Yarmouth, and proceeded by way of Lowestoft to Woodbridge, in Suffolk, in
the barracks of which my battalion was quartered. Here
also was the 23d regiment, that which I had seen act so
nobly in Holland: and as it was determined by its commanding-officer to give the regiment some idea of light
movements, I was selected for the purpose of instructing
their non-commissioned officers. But I did not long continue to instruct them, for in the May following, an offer
was made me by Colonel Beckwith of the situation of sergeant-major in the Cornwall Miners, a regiment of militia,
with the prospect, he told me, of shortly becoming adjutant.
This, however, after due consideration, I declined accepting
—preferring to remain in a regiment and service which I
liked so well, and in which I hoped one day to rise to something higher than my present situation.   I believe my
conduct on this occasion was approved, for not long after,
it was intimated to me, that the offer I had refused, had
been made to the quartermaster-sergeant of our second

battalion, and that he had, after some hesitation, accepted it, thus leaving his situation open for me. Accordingly, I departed for the purpose of joining that battalion, and entering on my new duties.

I joined it at Feversham, in Kent. My means increasing, the sinfulness of my course of life was increased in proportion. It is true, I generally performed my various military duties to the satisfaction of my superiors; but could not at all times please my present commanding-officer, against whose wish and inclination I had been appointed to my present situation; he naturally wishing to have a person of his own selection. Soon after this, an expedition being ordered for South America, of which three companies of my present battalion were to form a part, I waited on him, and requested him to permit me to accompany them in the capacity of acting quarter-master. He said no; but if I chose to resign my present situation, and go as a sergeant, he would permit me. This I of course declined, as it would have been paying a bad compliment indeed to my benefactor, Colonel Beckwith, thus to give up for nothing what he had been at pains to procure for me.

This, and some other little things which occurred about the same time, proved to me that I was no favourite with my new lieutenant-colonel, and that it behoved me to be very guarded in my conduct. We were, after this, removed to Brabourn Lees again, and remained there, without any occurrence arising, till we were summoned to take part in the expedition fitting out for Denmark.

We accordingly repaired to Deal, where we embarked on the 26th of July, 1807, and shortly after sailed for our destination. We arrived in the Sound about the 10th of August, where the whole fleet was assembled; one of the largest I had yet seen. On the 16th, every thing having been previously got ready, we landed at the village of Ved-beck, in the island of Zealand, about ten or twelve miles below Copenhagen. It was a most beautiful and glorious sight to witness the debarkation of the first division, or advanced guard, to which my battalion belonged. The most perfect arrangements had been made by Sir Home Popham, who superintended the landing of the troops ; and nothing could exceed the beauty and regularity in which the different divisions of boats approached the shore, covered by some small brigs and bombs, which had orders to clear the beach by grape shot, of any enemy that might appear. Some light artillery also landed with us, prepared for immediate action, for it was not known but the Danes might attempt to oppose our landing, they having rejected every overture on the part of our commanders for the delivery of their fleet.

After landing, mine and the first battalion of my regiment were sent forward in the direction of Copenhagen ; and on this occasion, I for the first time saw the illustrious General, who has since made the world resound with his exploits. He commanded us, who formed the advance, and directed our two battalions during the operations of the day. But we met with no force of the enemy, save a small patrol of cavalry, which passed in front of us, and then retired towards the city ; this showed that they were observing our movements. We halted for the night at a village called, I think, Lingbye, on the great road from Copenhagen towards Elsineur. We rested on our arms all night, and early in the morning moved forward on the Copenhagen road, and about midday took up cantonments within a long gun-shot of the city, and began to invest the place. All was quiet till about three o'clock in the afternoon, when a general cry of turn out, set the whole of our people in motion. A considerable body of the enemy were advancing from the town, and by this time had attacked the advanced picquets on our left, towards the sea-shore; but instant succour being sent, they maintained their ground.

The force opposed to the enemy was but small, consisting of two companies of the 4th regiment, four of the 23d, and four of my battalion, with two light fieldpieces; in all not more than 1000 men, while the Danes were near 3000. Nevertheless, the moment the armies came in contact, they instantly gave way, leaving a considerable number of killed and wounded behind them, and retreated into the town.

On this occasion, I attached myself to my commanding-officer, who, with the surgeon, and some others of the staff, advanced with one of the guns on the great road, having some of our companies on each flank. He gave me his glass to take care of, with which I soon after busied myself in watching the motions of the enemy. I discovered at a short distance to our left and front, a considerable body of troops, dressed in long red coats, which I knew could not be British, for that description of dress had long been laid aside by us; I accordingly began, pointing them out as an excellent mark for the artillery, which was then with us; but I had scarcely spoken, when an officer present, cried out, after looking, did I wish the artillery to fire on our own people? The colonel also made some severe and reproachful remarks, telling me, if I would fight, to go and take a rifle. I said nothing; but he had scarcely finished his harangue, when a round shot came directly from this body of supposed British troops, which nigh carried away one of the legs of the first officer who spoke.

The enemy were soon repulsed, and the troops retired again to their former cantonments. After their troops retreated, a body of their gun-boats advanced against some of our small craft which happened to be rather close in shore, but their attack occasioned little injury, the distance being considerable.

The next morning the enemy opened a heavy and rather destructive fire of artillery upon our outposts, by which we lost an officer of artillery and several men ; their fire was chiefly directed against what was called the wind-mill battery, which was our farthest advance at this time.

On the 19th, my battalion was moved farther to the right, and nearer the town ; there was constant firing between the advanced posts of the two armies, and this continued for several days, during which the investment of the city was proceeding with, and batteries, &c. marked out for the purpose of bombarding it. All kinds of ordnance stores were at the same time disembarked, and sent off to the army with the utmost dispatch. In short, nothing could exceed the vigour with which the siege was now prosecuted, after the final rejection of pacific overtures by the Danish general.

On the 24th, we were ordered under arms at two o'clock in the morning, and immediately advanced, driving in the enemy's outposts, with the view of carrying our works nearer the town. In this movement we experienced considerable opposition and suffered some loss, from their guns on the town walls, and from musketry from the windows.

We this day established two strong and well advanced batteries, and at night set fire to a wind-mill in their possession, which obstructed our view of some of their works. During the whole of the 25th, there was a constant fire both of artillery and fire-arms, by which one of the light battalions of the German Legion suffered rather severely. My battalion relieved them at the outposts a little before dark, and was fortunate enough not to lose a man, where they had lost considerable numbers.

On the 26th, a corps or division of the army was assembled, and placed under the immediate orders of Sir Arthur Wellesley. It consisted of the following regiments, viz. 43d, 52d, 92d, 95th, and 6th Battalion King's German Legion, with six squadrons of German cavalry, and some artillery, and was destined to advance against a body of the enemy composed principally of militia, which had been for some time past collecting in the neighbourhood of Kioge.

At three o'clock P. M., we started from the neighbourhood of Copenhagen, the troops making their way through the country to the left of the great road to Roskild. I had charge of the baggage, which was carried on light German waggons, the bodies of which are formed chiefly of wicker-work, and are so light and easy of draught that the natives travel in them in the same manner nearly of our coaches— they going sometimes at a considerable rate.

I found it impracticable to continue in the same direction the troops had gone, for they presently left all traces of a road, and struck right across the country—and as I knew I should be expected to have the baggage with them that night if possible, I determined to run all hazards, and proceed along the great high-road in hopes of afterwards being enabled to find them out—accordingly I moved forward, and presently passed the outposts of the German cavalry stationed in the direction of Roskild; the men, I doubt not, wondering at my temerity in pushing on with a few baggage waggons, where they were all on the alert with swords drawn, and with carbines and pistols loaded. I own it was a hazardous undertaking, for a very small party of the enemy would easily have captured both me and my baggage; but I knew my commanding-officer to be such a person as to pay little attention to excuses of any kind when he wished a thing to be done, and withal he loved his comforts, and would not have been easily pacified had he been deprived of them. Fortunately, after advancing for some miles beyond the outposts of our army before mentioned, I fell in with a road branching off towards the left, apparently in the very direction the troops had taken.

Till I reached this point, I had advanced with considerable caution, and slowly ; determined, if any enemy should appear in front, to endeavour to effect a retreat. But now, having left the great road, and taken that which I judged would bring me to the neighbourhood of those I was seeking, I accordingly ordered all my guards to mount, and set off at a brisk trot, keeping a good look-out to my right flank, for fear of surprise, and fortunately fell in with the division at the very moment it was entering the road by which I had come. I received great credit for my generalship, and was complimented by the officers of my corps, they being the only people in the division, I believe, who had the comfort of their baggage that night. The name of the village where we halted is Caughstrup.

The next day we continued to advance in the direction of Kioge, and in the afternoon we reached a village which I forget the name of, and where evident traces appeared of the enemy having shortly left it ; indeed, we found two or three stragglers in the village, who were of course made prisoners. We halted outside the village for the night.

A short- while before we reached this village, I saw a body of troops dressed in red, marching on our right flank, at right angles to the road by which we were advancing, and which I instantly concluded must be a part of the enemy's force, as we had no troops in that direction. But remembering the rebuke I received on the 17th for inter-

fering with concerns that did not belong to me, I shut my
mouth in silence, and did not, I believe, mention the
matter. It is evident it was a part of the enemy's force, for
the General's information led him to take that very same
direction the next day ; and that being towards Roskild,
we set out and reached that city in the afternoon, but found
the enemy had again given us the slip, and doubled back to
nearly the same place from whence we had started.

The next morning about three o'clock we left Roskild,
and took the road for Kioge, near which it was now ascertained the enemy had come to a resolution to make a
stand. I forgot to mention that previous to this our force
had been divided and formed into two brigades ; the 52d,
92d, our 1st battalion, and some cavalry and artillery,
remaining under the command of Sir Arthur ; while the
43d, the 6th German Legion, and our five companies, with
the remainder of the cavalry, were put under the command
of Baron Linsengen, one of the generals of the German
Legion. Sir Arthur's people had not been with us for a
day or two back, but where I do not exactly know. But
this morning it was arranged that his brigade was to
march directly upon Kioge and attack it in front, while we
fetched a circuit behind, and came upon a part of their
force stationed in a forest or wood behind the town—and
thus cut off their retreat. But the poor creatures were
unable to stand above a round or two, and almost immediately broke and fled in all directions.

As we approached the wood we were destined to attack,
the appearance was certainly rather formidable ; for from
the immense cloud of dust they raised in performing their
movements, we calculated on meeting with a considerable body of troops ; and indeed, just as we approached
the wood, our cavalry laid hold of an officer of their horse,

dressed partly in uniform and partly as a civilian. From him we obtained information that they had in the field 12,000 men ; 5000 of which were armed with pikes, 1000 cavalry, and the remainder consisted of artillery and infantry. He must, I think, have overrated their numbers, or surely they might have made some sort of a stand against 5500 men, the strength of our division.

On Sir Arthur attacking them in the town of Kioge, they stood, as before said, only for a round or two, and fled, many of them coming in contact afterwards with our brigade ; but from the extent of (and intricate roads through) the wood, very few of them were made prisoners ; till towards evening, when a company of my battalion, with some of the German cavalry, overtook a considerable body in the village of Herfolge, apparently the rearguard of the enemy. In this village they made a stand, getting into the churchyard, which afforded an excellent position, it being considerably higher than any other part of the village. Here also they soon began to waver, and after a few shots from our people, they all laid down their arms and became prisoners of war. Their numbers were 1550 men, with 56 officers, and Major-General Oxholm, the second in command of this part of the Danish army. A considerable quantity of artillery, small arms, baggage, and provisions, &c., with two stands of colours, fell into the hands of the captors on this occasion. These poor creatures were instantly sent off as prisoners, and put on board our ships at Copenhagen ; many of them apparently quite glad that they had done with fighting. Great numbers of them had nothing better by way of shoeing than wooden clogs—a very inconvenient kind I should imagine for a rapid retreat.

The loss of the British during this day's operations was, as might be expected, quite trifling. I had this day followed the ill-natured advice of my commanding-officer on a former occasion, and had taken a rifle, but had little opportunity of using it, not having fired more than eight or ten shots. My battalion halted in the village of Herfolge for the night, and the next morning moved forward towards the town of Kingsted, that being the direction in which the broken fragments of the Danish army had retired.

Our two battalions had been employed all the day of the 29th, after the first onset, in scouring the woods from Kioge to Herfolge. We continued this service on the 30th also, and took numbers of poor creatures who had been engaged in yesterday's operations, but who had not yet been able totally to divest themselves of their military habiliments, although apparently anxious to do so. We reached Kingsted on the 31st, and finding that the only regular part of the late army had retired into one of the islands in the Great Belt, and that the militia portion had totally disbanded itself, we halted here till the fall of Copenhagen, which took place on the 7th of September. But to prevent surprise from any lurking parties of the enemy, which might still have kept together, and to deprive them of the means of injuring us, strong detachments were sent out to scour the country, and to bring in all the military arms they could discover. A party of this description, consisting of 100 cavalry, and 100 of my battalion mounted on light waggons, traversed the country for a considerable distance, and returned after having discovered and taken possession of ten pieces of ordnance of small calibre, and forty rifles belonging to the Kallundburg rifle company, with several muskets. They also gained correct information respecting the regular troops that had been lately opposed to us, and found they had retired into the islands of Falstar and Meon.

On the capitulation of Copenhagen, terms of amity and

peace were entered into between the Danish forces in the island of Zealand and the British; but these did not extend to the islands before mentioned, nor to the other parts of his Danish Majesty's dominions; consequently, we still remained at war with such of his forces as were not included in the capitulation; and he might at any time have collected an army, had he been able, and attacked us without any infringement of those terms. It behoved our generals, therefore, to watch against any attempt of this nature; and accordingly strong outposts were established all along the Belt, composed principally of the men of our two battalions. The 1st battalion occupied Kallundburg, Slagelse, Korsoer, and Skielskiore; whilst the following towns and ports were occupied by my battalion, viz. Mestyed, Lundbye, Wordingburg and Prestoe; thus forming a complete chain of posts around the west and south coasts of the island. We remained so posted till the 15th of October, by which time the greater part of the naval stores taken in the dockyard having been taken on board, and the period fast approaching for our evacuation of the country, we began to retire towards Copenhagen, which we reached on the 17th, and immediately embarked on board the Princess Caroline, a Danish seventy-four which had been surrendered with the others of that fleet, and which are mentioned below.*

* List of Ships and Vessels captured at Copenhagen, 7th September, 1807.

	Guns.		Guns.
Christian the Seventh,	98	Three Crowns, . . .	74
Neptune, ...	84	Shield, ...	74
Waldemer, ...	84	Crown Princess Maria, . .	74
Princess Sophia Fredrica .	84	Denmark, ...	74
Justice, ...	74	Norway, ...	74
Heir Apparent Frederick, .	74	Princess Caroline, . . .	74
Crown Prince Frederick, .	74	Conqueror, ...	64
Frien, ...	74	Norge, ...	74
Oden, ...	74	Dalmakin, ...	64

We remained in the roads till the 20th, when the fleet dropped down towards the Sound; and on the 21st the whole passed the Castle of Elsineur, with a favourable and pleasant breeze, the British ensign waving proudly from the lofty masts of their late gallant fleet; it must have been an extremely galling sight for them (the Danes) to witness, and I dare say they did not pray for many benedictions on our heads; I pitied them from the bottom of my heart. On taking leave of this country, I could not help remarking on the great similarity between its inhabitants and the Germans about Bremen—kind-hearted, hospitable, and inoffensive in the highest degree; and although suffering at that time so severely from the policy of our country, they were high in our praises as individuals and as a nation. I have great cause to speak well of those innocent and worthy people, for I have seldom experienced more kindness and attention than was shown me by them whenever circumstances rendered such kindness and attention suitable, particularly at Nestyde, where I met a young man who had formerly been in the West Indies, where he had learnt to speak a little English, (for of Danish I could not under-

	Guns.		Guns.
Pirle, ...	44	Elbe, ...	20
Wory Wife, ...	44	Eydeman, ...	20
Liberty, ...	44	Gluckstadt, ...	20
Iris, ...	44	Sarp, ...	18
Rotar, ...	44	Glowman, ...	18
Denry, ...	44	Nid Elvin, ...	18
Mayed, ...	36	Dolphin, ...	18
Triton, ...	28	Marcur, ...	18
Fredrington, ...	28	Cousier, ...	14
Kline Belt, ...	28	Flying Fish, ...	14
St Thomas, ...	22		—
Tylto, ...	24		Total, 40

Together with eleven gun boats, with two guns each in the bow, and fourteen do. with one gun in the bow and one astern.

stand a word.) He introduced me to one worthy man, who had been an officer, and fought in the famous action of Kioge above narrated. Poor fellow, he felt heartily ashamed of the sorry attempt they had made to act the part of an army, and I daresay would gladly have blotted from his memory for ever the recollection of the ridiculous part they had acted. I was not aware of this circumstance at first, and when it was brought upon the tapis in the course of conversation, (my young friend being interpreter,) I unluckily said, that " any man armed with a bludgeon only, could easily beat three such soldiers."

I felt quite ashamed of myself afterwards, when I discovered that he, poor man, had made one in that memorable action; but he took it all in good part, apparently conscious of the justness of my remark. Indeed, I was partly led on to use such expressions by the young fellow condemning so bitterly their conduct, and which I afterwards would have given something to have unsaid. He, however, bore no resentment, and kindly took me home and introduced me to his wife, and requested me to salute her with a kiss. I hesitated, thinking that I could not have understood him right, and feeling awkward in such a situation ; but my young friend assured me it was the custom there to do so, on which I of course complied. They are, in my opinion, an extremely moral race of people, no vices that I know of being practised by them, save occasionally a little drunkenness by some few individuals. I heartily wish them well.

We sailed, as I said before, on the 21st of October, and had fine weather till we arrived in Yarmouth Roads. We passed one Sunday on our voyage home, at a certain hour of which our pious naval commander (Lord Gambier) made signal for the whole fleet to lay to, and have divine service, that is, in such ships as there were chaplains on board of. This caused the irreligious and profligate part of our people on board the Princess Caroline to blaspheme and storm at a terrible rate, for being so long detained when the wind was so fair.

It happened, when we arrived in the Roads at Yarmouth, or near there, I think it was on the Galloper Sand, that a tremendous gale began to blow, which baffled all exertions to withstand it. We cast out the anchors, but without effect, for we ran away with them both, and in the endeavour to vere out cable, or rather by the rapidity with which it was dragged out of the ship by the force of the wind, our bits caught fire, which with considerable difficulty were got extinguished after great exertions. During the gale, I understand a sailor was blown off the foreyard; and nearly at the same moment a woman, one of our corporals' wives, fell down the hatches into the hold, and broke her back, of which, indeed, she afterwards recovered, but never after regained her upright posture.

Those scoffing gentlemen before mentioned, attributed the whole of our misfortunes to the delay occasioned by the divine service before adverted to, and were not sparing of invective against the individual who caused its performance, forgetful, it would seem, that *He*, whom that commander invoked on that day, holds the winds in His hand, and can at pleasure let them loose upon an ungodly fleet, whether for correction or judgment, at what time, and in what manner, best pleases him. I doubt not the excellent commander alluded to has been a blessing to many. May he long continue to ornament the exalted station he fills ! We weighed again after the storm abated, and proceeded round to the Downs, and the next day, the 16th of November, landed at Deal, and from thence marched to our old quarters at Hythe Barracks.

CHAPTER V.

Our Author marries—The Battalion to which he belongs ordered to join the Expedition fitting out for Corunna— Movements of the Army in Spain—Return to England.

SOME little time after our return from the Baltic, I obtained a short leave of absence, for the purpose of visiting my parents, and the other members of my family; and, during my stay in my native village, contracted a marriage with a young woman whom I had known from my boyhood, she having been one of my earliest schoolfellows. I cannot say that I enjoyed in the marriage state that happiness which I expected from it, partly owing to the frequent and long separations which my calling rendered unavoidable, and partly from other causes which have no connexion with my narrative. I believe, during the eight years which my wife lived after our union, I spent more than six of these in absence from her.

At the expiration of my leave, we set off to join the regiment, which still remained at Hythe, where we remained till the beginning of September following, when my battalion having again been ordered for foreign service in the expedition fitting out for Corunna, it became indispensable that my poor wife should return to Northumberland, and

D

remain under the protection of her parents, till my return, should it please God to spare me. This, no doubt, was a severe trial to us both, but particularly to her, who had such a journey to undertake, alone and unprotected, and she at the time far advanced in pregnancy ; but, however distressing, it must be undertaken, and I unfortunately could not be spared from the regiment, for our orders were to proceed immediately to Ramsgate, for embarkation.

We parted, after I had accompanied her as far as I was able, and seeing her safely stowed in the coach. It may be supposed that a new-married pair, under such circumstances, would part with heavy and afflicted hearts. -

My battalion embarked at Ramsgate on the 10th of September. On this occasion, I was very fortunate in getting on board an excellent transport, called the Nautilus, of Shields, commanded by Captain Watson (my wife's maiden name), and the steward, a native of the Hermitage, a place within four miles of my home. Of course, we were mutually glad to meet each other, and often talked over old Northumbrian stories, which recalled delightful recollections of our younger years. The fleet in which we sailed rendezvoused at Falmouth, whence we took our departure, and arrived at Corunna on the 26th of October.

On our passage, when we made Cape Ortegal, a pilot-boat came off, in which were the first Spaniards I remember to have seen; certainly, they did not prepossess me greatly in favour of their countrymen, but they are now so well known in England, that a description of those I here saw, would be only to repeat what has been so often and so much better told by others. We landed at Corunna, as before said, on the 26th, and a day or two after, proceeded up the country, halting for the first night at Betanzos. Our force consisted of cavalry, infantry, and artillery, in all, about 10,000 men, and was commanded by General Sir David Baird, and intended to co-operate, or form a junction, with that under Sir John Moore, then in Portugal, and who was then advancing into Spain.

My battalion, and some companies of the first battalion of my regiment, formed the advanced guard, a situation which I consider the most enviable of any in the army—for here all is untried, and, as it were, unbroken ground; every thing is fresh, and although attended sometimes with a little more danger of being cut off while separated from the main body, yet possessing so many countervailing advantages, that I hesitate not to say it is the most desirable post of any in an army.

At Betanzos, we began to experience the great defectiveness of our commissariat department, at this period of our history; for the gentleman sent forward to provide our two battalions with food, was so utterly unacquainted with his business, that he was actually afraid to make an attempt to issue provisions. Although bread had been baked by order of the Spanish authorities, he not understanding, as he said, the Spanish weights and measures, durst not issue any thing without his own, which were behind; but it was evident the troops could not remain without provisions. We were here, as in most of the towns we afterwards passed through, lodged in convents, the officers generally either being quartered on the inhabitants of the town, or lodged by the monks in their cells. On these occasions the men occupied only the corridors, into which straw was generally put by the authorities of the place, the men lying as close as pigs in a sty, which indeed was necessary to keep each other warm; but these lodgings were not to be complained of, as clean straw, and shelter overhead in that country, are no contemptible quarters.

We moved forward by fair and easy stages, by way of
Lugo, Villa Franca, Cacabelos, and Astorga; this latter
place we reached on the 19th November, but during the
march, we had experienced considerable difficulty in obtaining supplies both of provisions and the means of transport. This is a considerable town, containing probably
about 5000 inhabitants. Both it and Lugo are surrounded
by old Moorish walls, which may formerly have been considered strong, but which, according to the present mode
of warfare, would offer but a feeble resistance to a besieging
army. It contains a number of convents, both in the town
and suburbs, and, of course, a proportionate number of idle
monks, &c. Here, as in many towns in Spain, they have a
curious mode of keeping out of their houses unwelcome
visiters; for the doors being all made remarkably strong,
and kept constantly shut, you cannot enter till the inmates
have first reconnoitred you through an aperture above the
door, made for the purpose; and it is not till they are satisfied who you are, and with your business, that they will
open the door, which they generally do by a cord communicating with the latch from their peep-hole above.

Here we were pretty plentifully supplied with provisions,
and rested for some days, my battalion having been pushed
forward to a village called Zalada, about a league in front of
the town. After having been refreshed by a few days'
rest, my battalion was again pushed forward, and occupied
the town of Labeneza, about four leagues in front of Astorga, while the main body of the army assembled in and
around that town; but we had not remained more than a
few days in Labeneza, before a report arrived of the enemy
being in our front, and advancing in force; and we were
consequently recalled to Zalada, in order to form a junction
with our main body. Not long after this, about the latter

end of November, orders were received from Sir John Moore, for our division to retreat and fall back upon Corunna. This measure, I understand, was rendered necessary, in consequence of the Spanish armies having been completely beaten and dispersed, so that nothing remained to oppose an overwhelming French force, which it was ascertained had entered Spain, but the few British troops comprising the armies under Sir John Moore, and ours.

We accordingly set to the right-about, and fell back as far as Cacabelos, the main body occupying Villa Franca and its neighbourhood. This movement was not by any means liked by any of us; for, independent of its being so uncongenial to the spirit of Britons to turn their backs upon an enemy, we felt disappointed at what we saw and heard of the celebrated Spanish patriots. We had been given to understand that the whole nation was up in arms against the French, and that we should have been received, on entering their country, as liberators, and treated as brethren, but in both these points we were miserably disappointed; for, instead of a hearty welcome on our arrival, we could with great difficulty obtain leave to land, and still more to obtain the necessary supplies of carriages and provisions to enable us to come forward; and with regard to the patriotism of the people, whatever might have been their good-will to act in defence of their beloved country and Ferdinand, they appeared as little likely as any people I had ever seen, to effect any thing against such an enemy as the French. In fact, those of them who formed their armies, at least of those straggling parties we so often met, could be called nothing better than mere rabble—no organization, no subordination, but every one evidently pursued that plan which seemed right in his own eyes.

While we remained at Cacabelos, (a place famous for

good wine,) many were the schemes adopted by some of
our bibbers, to obtain a sufficient quantum of this excellent
beverage.   I understand they occasionally borrowed each
other's clothes; that is, a 43d man would borrow a rifleman's green jacket, and *vice versa*, and go and steal, or in
some other illegal mode obtain, a camp-kettle full or two ;
and when the owner came to point out the person who had
robbed him, of course he could not be found.

We had not remained above a day or two in our new
quarters, before an express arrived from Sir John Moore,
with orders for us to advance again immediately ; and
which, notwithstanding we had little or no prospect of assistance and co-operation from the Patriots, was cheerfully
complied with.   We retraced our former steps, passing
through Astorga and Labeneza, and reached Benevente on
the 15th December.

Our cavalry, consisting of the 7th, 10th, and 15th hussars,
under Lord Paget, had by this time come up from Corunna,
and had been pushed forward to join Sir John Moore's
force ; they fell in with a party of the French cavalry at the
town of Rueda, not far from Tordesillas, and of which they
either killed, or took prisoners, nearly the whole ; in fact,
through the whole of this service, nothing could exceed
the gallantry and intrepid conduct of our cavalry under
his lordship.   At this town, as well as at Astorga and
Villa Franca, depots of provisions began to be formed soon
after our arrival.

On the 17th December, we again advanced from Benevente, in order to form a junction with Sir John Moore's
army, and passing through Valderas, Majorga, and Sahagun, we reached the convent of Trianon, about a league in
front of the latter place.   On the 20th, here the two forces
were united, and a fresh distribution into brigades took

place. Ours, under Brigadier-general Crawford, was termed the Light Brigade, and consisted of the 1st battalion 43d, 2d battalion 52d, and the 3d battalion of my regiment.

The whole army was assembled in this neighbourhood, and consisted of about 26,000 men, the whole *now* under the command of Sir John Moore. Previous to our arrival at Sahagun, Lord Paget, with a part of the 10th and 15th hussars, discovered that a considerable body of the enemy's cavalry occupied that town. He therefore detached the 10th by a circuitous road, while he with the 15th approached it by the more direct one. They were, however, discovered by the French before reaching the town, which gave the enemy time to turn out and form to receive the attack. His lordship, when a favourable opportunity offered, charged the French, who were greatly superior in numbers, and completely overthrew them, taking two colonels, eleven other officers, and about 150 men.

On the evening of the 23d, the whole army was put in motion, with an intention, it was said, of attacking Marshal Soult, who, with a corps of about 16 or 18,000 men, was posted behind the River Carrion, his head-quarters being at Saldanha. The Spanish General Romana, was to take a part in this movement ; his small and sadly inefficient force had approached the left of our army, or rather we had drawn towards his position, and he was, I believe, perfectly willing to lend all the assistance in his power, in the contemplated attack ; but our General, I fancy, did not calculate upon any material help, from a force so greatly out of order as his was said to be. Soon after dark, the troops fell in ; and as it was understood an attack was going to be made on the enemy; every pulse beat high, in expectation of soon congratulating each other on a victory. All was life and animation ; and the necessary preparations, by the light of our blazing fires, for such an event as a battle, after the many long and harassing marches we had had, gave an interesting appearance to the scene.

When all was ready, the troops moved forward. It was a cold and bitter night, and there were some small brooks on the road. An officer of my battalion, who was not very well, when he came to one of those, instead of marching straight through, as it appears had been ordered, went a little way round by the bridge, although not off the road. A certain general officer, who happened to be there at the time, observed it, and getting into a great rage at the officer leaving his section, made him turn back, and march through and through repeatedly, by way of punishment. Such a mode of treating an officer, certainly appeared rather harsh; but this general piqued himself on his being able to make his brigade better marchers than any other troops in the army; and in this he certainly succeeded, although it was not without frequent exhibitions, such as the above. Our people had not gone far, however, till they were countermanded, and returned back to our convent. I rather think the main body of the army had not moved out of their cantonments; but ours being the advanced brigade, it was necessary we should move before the others.

It appears Sir John Moore, just before he intended to set out, had received information, not only of Soult having been greatly reinforced, but that several strong corps of the French army were marching directly upon us, by which, should he delay only a few days, we should be completely surrounded, and cut off from a retreat. This was most distressing information, for never was an army more eager to come in contact with the enemy than ours was at this moment, and never was there a fairer prospect of success, had things remained as they were; but now, instead of honour and glory being acquired, by showing the French what British troops could do in the field, it was evident nothing remained but to commence a retrograde movement, the worst and most unpleasant, in a British soldier's view, of any other.

Winter had now completely set in ; the face of the country being covered with deep snow, the weather was unusually severe. Our prospect, therefore, was by no means a pleasant one. To commence a retreat in front of a greatly superior force, and with the probability that other French armies might be before us, and intercept our retreat upon the sea, which was distant from us nearly 250 miles, with the country in our rear being already exhausted of every thing that could contribute to our support, and with such excessively bad weather to perform the retreat in, rendered it, I may say, as unpleasant a situation as troops could well be placed in. Added to which, our commissariat was by no means so efficient in those days as they have latterly become ; and our troops in general being young, and unaccustomed to privation, it was but too obvious, that should the retreat continue long, many would be the disasters attending it. On Christmas day, our brigade, as the rear of the infantry, commenced its uncomfortable retreat, and continued marching till late at night. when we reached a convent near Majorga. The next day, although we started early, we only reached the village of St Miguel about midnight.

Here I had considerable difficulty with the baggage. I had had charge of it all day, my guard being composed of officers' servants, &c., who, the moment they got into the village, set off to their masters, and left me alone with the mules, the troops having, by the time I got in, all lain down to sleep. Several of the muleteers had been pressed into the

service against their wills, and of course would have made
their escape whenever an opportunity offered. I was therefore compelled to drive them all into the churchyard, and
watch them myself, till luckily, after waiting in this situation a considerable time, without daring to go to sleep after
the fatigues of such a day, some men happened to wander
in that direction in search of meat, by whom I sent to our
quartermaster to request he would send a guard, which he
did soon after, and I had the happiness to be allowed to
throw myself down and take some rest.

This day Lord Paget had another brush with the French
cavalry, who, being apprized of our retreat, had advanced to
Majorga. He attacked them with that gallantry which
shone so conspicuously in the cavalry during the whole of
this service, and completely overthrew them, killing and
wounding many, and taking a number prisoners; in this
affair the 18th hussars were engaged, and behaved nobly.
The next day we reached Castro Gonzales, and Castro
Pipa. At the latter village, my battalion halted for the
night and the next day. These two villages command the
passage over the river Eslar, they being about equidistant
from the bridge, and something more than a mile apart on
high ground over the river, which runs about a league in
front of Benevente. Here we were obliged to remain during the time mentioned, in order that the heavy divisions
of the army might get sufficiently forward before we moved.

I had still the charge of the baggage, and not knowing
where my battalion was to be quartered for the night, I
had crossed the Eslar to the Benevente side, till I learnt long
after dark that Castro Pipa was its quarters. I consequently
turned back and recrossed the river, and just as I reached the
end of the bridge, I heard a shot immediately in my front.
The 43d regiment guarded the bridge. It turned out to be
a patrol of the enemy's cavalry who had come close to the

top of the slope leading down to the bridge, and where a double sentry of the 43d was posted. By some accident these two men were not loaded; the French dragoons were consequently permitted to come close up to them without their being able to give any alarm. One of them, however, run his bayonet into one of the Frenchmen's horses, and retreated, but the other was not only cut down with the sabre, but had a pistol fired at him, which was the report I had just heard. I saw the wounded man, who was severely hurt, but whether he survived or not I know not.

When I reached Castro Pipa, my commanding-officer would scarcely credit the report I gave him, conceiving it impossible the French could be such near neighbours. I was a good deal chagrined at his suspecting my veracity, but he had never been what I may call a friendly commanding-officer to me, as the story of the rifle at Copenhagen will prove; indeed, as I had been put into the situation I held contrary to his wish, it was hardly to be expected that he would show himself very friendly. During the night, however, our quarters were beat up, not indeed by the enemy, but by our brigadier, who was not sparing of his censure for our want of alertness in turning out. Indeed, we neither had so good a look-out as we ought to have kept, nor did we get under arms with that promptitude which was desirable, and from the cause before assigned; that is, that our commandant did not believe the enemy was so near.

I own I was not sorry that the General paid us such a visit, as it not only put us more upon our guard, a thing so indispensably necessary in the presence of an enemy, but it gave me some satisfaction for the dishonour put upon me by disbelieving my information.

The enemy did not disturb us during the remainder of

the night, and next morning the brigade was assembled on
the height above, and in front of the bridge ; considerable
bodies of the enemy's cavalry appearing in the plain before
us. Some skirmishing between our people and the enemy
took place, but nothing of any importance occurred. Our
brigade was left in this position to cover the working party
who were preparing to blow up the bridge, at which they
worked all day ; during the night our people were withdrawn from the farther side, and the explosion soon after
took place, but the destruction of the bridge was by no
means so effectual as was wished and expected. When we
turned out in the morning to move towards the bridge, I
(still having charge of my battalion's baggage) discovered
that a vast quantity of excellent biscuit was stored up in an
empty house in the village, which, no doubt, had been baked
for the purpose of supplying the magazine at Benevente;
and as our people had been but very indifferently supplied
with bread since we commenced the retreat, I determined
to load a bullock-cart with it, and try to get it to a place of
safety, where I hoped to be able to issue it to them.

I accordingly took a cart and two bullocks, there being
plenty in the village, and apparently without owners, for
the inhabitants had mostly either abandoned the place on the
appearance of the French, or had hid themselves. I loaded
the cart, but still I wanted a person to drive it ; and although
I used both promises and threats, I could not prevail upon
any person to go with me. I therefore mounted the cart
myself, and using my sword by way of a goad, I entered
the river at a place which looked like a ford, and had the
good fortune to reach the other side in safety. I mention
this to show that so much importance need not have been
attached to the destruction of the bridge, as both here, and
near Castro Gonzales, the river was perfectly fordable, for

near the latter place the French cavalry forded it on the following morning.

I now made my way to Benevente, where I remained during the day of the 28th; and at night, as before hinted, the troops which had been guarding the bridge arrived, leaving cavalry piquets on the plain between the town and the river. The next morning our people left Benevente, and as I was a little behind them with the baggage, on my reaching a height in rear of the town, I observed in the plain in front a considerable body of the enemy's cavalry, who had, as before stated, crossed the river near Castro Gonzales, and were advancing towards the town, opposed, though feebly at first, by the few of our cavalry left there on piquet; but the cavalry regiments which were in town quickly turning out to their support, they were at length completely able to oppose, and finally overthrow them.

During the time I remained here, I saw our brave dragoons make three most gallant and successful charges against superior numbers of the enemy, completely breaking and dispersing the different bodies against which the charges were made. The enemy appeared to be drawn up in different lines, the front one of which was that always charged; and I observed, that as our people advanced upon them, they were always received with a fire either from the carbines or pistols of the enemy, but this never appeared in the least to check the ardour of the charge, for in a minute or two after I observed the French troops retired in confusion, and formed behind the other lines. At length they were completely driven back to the ford by which they had crossed; and in a charge now made upon them, General le Febvre, with about seventy men, fell into our people's hands. These troops were a part of Bonaparte's Imperial Guard, and the flower of his army, being fine-looking men, dressed in dark-green long coats, with high bear-skin caps, and mustaches, which gave them a formidable appearance. It was said that Bonaparte was looking on at this affair, and witnessed the defeat of his hitherto invincible Old Guard ; it is certain that he slept the night before at Villalpando, a place only four leagues distant from the field. I now set off and overtook the baggage and the bullock cart, not having had an opportunity of issuing the biscuit ; but before I had proceeded above a few miles, the bullocks knocked up, and notwithstanding every exertion I found it impossible to get them any farther. Thus was I reluctantly compelled to abandon a cart-load of excellent biscuit, after having had so much trouble with it, at the time when I knew it was greatly needed by my hungry fellow soldiers, and to whom it would have been a most welcome offering. On this day's march, a most lamentable number of stragglers were overtaken by us, we being in rear of all the infantry ; they had either fallen out from excessive fatigue, or from having (as in too many instances) drunk too much ; indeed, the destruction of the magazine of provisions at the place we had left, enabled too many of them to obtain by one means or other considerable quantities of spirits, and which, of course, rendered them incapable of marching. This was a long and wearisome day's journey of nearly thirty miles ; we did not reach Labeneza till late at night, where a considerable quantity of ammunition was obliged to be destroyed, the animals failing which drew it.

The next day we reached our old quarters at Zalada, a league in front of Astorga, where we halted for the night, the remainder of the brigade going into the town. It was to this village, it may be remembered, that we were sent on our first advance, and subsequently after our first retreat from Labeneza; but besides these movements from the village and back again, during the time we remained in it, we almost every morning had orders to pack up and move a short distance out of the place. This was done no doubt to accustom us to a ready turning out, as till this period our baggage had been transported on bullock-carts; but now we had mules, and it was necessary to accustom those whose duty it was, to load the mules with dispatch. But on every occasion of this kind, the inhabitants always imagined we were actually going to leave them, and the moment we were clean gone, as they thought, they set to work and rung the church bell with all their might. This was either to testify their regret at losing our company, or to evince their gratitude to Heaven for having got rid of such a band of heretics, by which their most pure and holy dwellings had been defiled; it was laughable to see the long faces they put on when we, so contrary to their hopes and expectations, always returned to our wretched and uncomfortable quarters.

During the whole of the time we remained in this village, I, as a staff-sergeant, could find no better lodgings than a dirty open shed; the reader will therefore judge how ill the privates must have been off. Our fellows began about this time to pick up little bits of Spanish, and would often exercise their ability to converse in the native tongue, by telling the inhabitants that we were certainly going to "*marcha manana,*" that is, to march to-morrow, so that it became quite a by-word, which annoyed our hosts not a little. If I mistake not, the Padre of this village was a great knave, and did not scruple to help himself to such things as he had a mind for, belonging to our officers, whenever a fit opportunity presented itself. The next day, the 31st, we moved into Astorga, where we halted for an hour or two, till the destruction of the magazine there was completed, although nothing but rum remained; and here I witnessed such a brutal and swinish eagerness for drink as was quite disgusting. The rum casks were ordered to be staved, and to let the contents run out on the street, that they might not fall into the hands of the enemy : thus the rum which had cost so much trouble in bringing up all the way from Corunna was about to be lost for ever; a thing most heart-rending to the numerous soldiers looking on, who loved it so dearly. However, they were determined not to lose all, for when the heads of the casks were knocked in, and their contents permitted to run in streams down the gutters, some of those brutes deliberately took off their greasy caps, and laving up the rum and the mud together, drank, or rather ate, the swinish mixture. What noble soldiers would our country produce, were not that detestable vice of drunkenness so common among us; but to it how many have I seen deliberately sacrifice their own and country's honour, nay their very life itself, rather than forego the beastly gratification !

All this morning we had been told to keep a sharp lookout on the Leon side of Astorga, for the enemy was every moment expected to make his appearance from that quarter; however, we were not disturbed during the short time we remained. We here fell in with a considerable body of Romana's army, apparently all confusion, and destitute of every thing. We understood that they were not to be marched in the same line we were taking, but that it had been concerted between the two generals that our route should be kept free; however, here, and for several days afterwards, we suffered greatly from their contiguity.

We continued our march from Astorga the same day, and reached at night the village of Foncevadon, about

2

twenty miles distant. Here we pigged in as well as we were able, there being only five or six houses; but as we had a few tents with us, we managed not amiss. Till now our brigade had formed the rear of the infantry, there being some cavalry in rear of us; but it was now determined that ours and the Light German Brigade under Brigadier-general Charles Alten, should strike off from the great road, and take the route for Orense and Vigo. This was done, I understand, with a view to secure a passage across the Minho at the former place, should Sir John, with the main army, be compelled to retreat in that direction, and probably with the view also of drawing off a part of the enemy's overwhelming force from the pursuit of that body, and to induce them to follow us into the mountains. Notwithstanding this, they continued to pursue Sir John on the great road, whilst they left us free altogether.

I beg to notice here, that both Mr Gifford and Mr Moore (Sir John's brother), have fallen into a trifling error respecting the period of our separation from the main body, they both making us be detached before our arrival at Astorga, whereas it was not till we had passed a day's march beyond it that we were sent off. The thing is of no consequence, only it is as well to be correct.

The next day, the 1st of January 1809, we marched by a most difficult road through the mountains, to Ponferrada, situated about a league to the left of the great road to Corunna, on which the main army was retreating. When we got in, our commissary immediately made a requisition to the Alcalde of the town, to provide bread for the two brigades, as we began to be in most fearful want. He promised to set the bakers to work immediately, and in a few hours, he said, the bread would be ready. We called on him repeatedly, without obtaining any, he still alleging it was not yet quite ready, and putting us off from time to time, till midnight, when the patience of our commissary being fairly worn out, he yielded to the anger so naturally inspired by such shuffling conduct, and used some strong language to the Alcalde. Whereupon, we discovered at once that he had been only amusing us with promises he did not intend to fulfil; and told the commissary that he did not fear any of his threats, for that, as Romana's army had now also entered the town, he had no doubt they would protect him, and revenge any insult offered to him. The commissary had indeed talked about hanging him for his double-dealing, and leaving the troops utterly starving; but if he could have got any bread ready, it is most natural to suppose he would prefer letting his own countrymen have it; this, however, as might be expected, had a most pernicious effect upon our suffering soldiers, for when provisions could not be procured in the regular and ordinary mode, it is evident they would take them wherever they were to be found —for hunger is not easily borne, accompanied by incessant fatigue. In the morning, when we turned out to continue our march towards Orense, we heard a heavy firing towards our right and front, and this proved to be an attack made by the enemy's light troops upon our first battalion, who, with some cavalry, had been left in Cacabelos as a rear-guard. Our first battalion gained great credit for their conduct on this occasion. The force of the enemy greatly exceeded ours, yet our people drove them back with great loss, killing General Colbert, who commanded the advance. This was done by a noted pickle of the name of Tom Plunkett, who, fearless of all danger to himself, got sufficiently nigh to make sure of his mark, and shot him, which, with the fire of the others, caused great havoc in the enemy's ranks, and set them flying to the rear much faster than they advanced. Our situation was thus, in a manner, in rear of the enemy's advance guard, yet they did not turn in our direction. Cacabelos was distant from us only about a league.

Our road this day lay over high and almost inaccessible mountains, deeply covered with snow. On the top of one of these, as our General was passing the column, a cry was passed from the rear to open out to allow him to pass, the road being very narrow. One of our men, as the General came near, happened to say, loud enough for him to hear, that " he had more need to give us some bread," or words to that effect, which so exasperated the General, that he instantly halted the whole brigade, ordered the man to be tried by a drum-head court-martial, and flogged him on the spot. It was a severe, but perhaps necessary discipline, in order to check in the bud the seeds of murmuring and in-subordination, although I own it appeared harsh.

Our march was a long and toilsome one indeed, and did not terminate till about ten at night, when we reached St Domingo-Flores, where nothing could be procured but a very small quantity of black bread, the village being quite small. Tired with the journey, we felt rather inclined to sleep than eat ; and, wet and dirty as we were, we laid our-selves down till dawn, when we commenced another such day's march, and reached at night the village of La Rua. During these two days, want and fatigue had compelled many to fall out, some of whom, no doubt, perished in the snow on the bleak mountains, over which our road, or rather path, had lain ; others fell into the hands of the enemy, and some few rejoined us after having obtained some little re-freshment from the natives.

It would but be a repetition of the privations and fatigues we underwent, to notice all that befell us on our way thence to Orense, which place we reached on the 7th of January, having previously pushed on, by double forced marches, a few hundred men, to take possession of the bridge over the Minho at this place. Here we remained a day, and obtained provisions, then much needed by us all, for the men had been literally starving for several days past. We had time and opportunity here also to strip and change our linen, that is, those who had a change; the others washed the shirt they took off, sitting without one till it was dry. Indeed, by this time we were in a most miserable plight; our shoes, of course, were nearly all worn out, and many travelling barefoot; and our clothes, as might be expected, were ragged and filthy in the extreme; indeed they could not be otherwise, for I suppose none of us had put any thing off since we commenced the retreat. This day's rest, however, refreshed us greatly, and enabled us to perform the remainder of our toilsome journey with more comfort; indeed, since we had secured the passage of the Minho, and thus prevented the enemy from getting in before us, our minds were more at ease, for strong apprehensions were entertained that the French would have detached a corps from their main body to seize this pass, and thus cut off our retreat to Vigo. A part of Romana's army entered Orense before we left it, worse, if possible, in point of appearance than ourselves; but they, in their best days, are more like an armed mob than regularly organized soldiers.

It is a pity that Romana did not adopt the plan pointed out to him by Sir John Moore, either to retire into the Asturias with his army unbroken, or hang upon the flanks of the enemy as he passed through the mountains; and which he could have done with ease and safety, for these fellows could live where regular troops would starve, and there was no doubt but the peasantry would have assisted their countrymen with all their means. This would have in some measure retarded the too rapid progress of the French, and probably been the means of saving to our country one of its bravest and most skilful generals.

Some of our men who had been compelled to stop behind from fatigue and starvation, rejoined us here, having generally been assisted by the peasantry, who gave them food, and helped them forward.

On the 9th, in the morning, we left Orense, crossing the Minho to the north side of that river, and continued our march to the town of Ribadavia, situated at the junction of the rivers Avia and Minho, both of which, from the melting of the snow, and the immense quantities of rain that had fallen, were greatly swollen. So much so, that when I approached the town with the baggage, (the troops having gone on before,) and which I did not reach till near midnight, I found the road completely overflowed with water ; and being without a guide, I could not of course in the night be certain where the road lay, the whole bank of the river being completely under water. We were in consequence obliged to climb the mountains to our left, and proceed in the best manner we were able with the loaded mules ; but so precipitous were they in one place, that a load of ammunition slid off the mule's back, and the casks rolled rapidly down the hill towards the river. I durst not venture to leave them, although my chance of finding them in such a situation appeared small indeed ; however, we halted the remainder of the mules, while a few of us set off down the steep in the direction we had seen them go, and after a long and anxious groping in every hollow of the rocky mountain, succeeded in recovering them ; but the powder in them, and indeed nearly all the ammunition we had, was rendered completely useless, from the constant heavy rain that had fallen. I am almost astonished that no accident happened to either man or beast in this perilous journey, for our feet literally " stumbled upon the dark mountains," without either guide or path, and where the ground was most uneven and dangerous. We however at length reached our destination, wet and weary enough, and, just as we entered the town, were informed that the corridor of one of the convents where two of our companies were sleeping, had just fallen to the ground with a tremendous crash, and that several men had had their limbs broken by the fall; I do not remember that any were killed. It being so late, I could not procure any kind of quarter, so I was fain to sit down by the side of a fire kindled in the yard of this convent for the remainder of the night.

We next morning resumed our journey, and in three days more from this place we reached Vigo. On this last day's march we had a pretty high eminence to ascend at some distance from the town, from which the view of the town, the shipping, and the sea, broke all at once upon us. It was a most delightful prospect, and it was highly amusing to observe the joy which seemed to animate the woe-worn countenances of our ragged and dirty soldiers. Fellows without a shoe or a stocking, and who before were shuffling along with sore and lacerated feet like so many lame ducks, now made an attempt to dance for joy; laughter and mirth, and the joke, now succeeded to the gloomy silence with which they had in general prosecuted their wearisome journey for several days past, as the friendly element before them promised shortly to put a period to long and toilsome wanderings. Indeed, although I am a bad sailor, and suffer always severely when at sea, I do not remember ever to have witnessed a sight which inspired me with greater pleasure than the shipping and the sea did on this occasion.

The fleet of transports for the army under Sir John Moore, was just clearing the bay as we came in sight, but we observed that a sufficient number remained at Vigo to transport us to our native land, a place we sorely longed for, as we had often contrasted the happiness and security and comfort of our friends at home, with the poverty and misery we had lately witnessed in the country we were leaving; and this no doubt increased our anxiety for the change. We marched into Vigo, and were soon after put on board the vessels destined to receive us. It was my fortune to be sent on board the Alfred, 74, with two of our companies; a great number of men were still behind, for even the few last days' marches had deprived us of many who till then had braved the toils and privations of the journey, but who now had fairly sunk under exhaustion. The Commodore, therefore, remained as long in the bay as it was safe, sending the stragglers as they arrived on board the different ships; but within a few days after our arrival, the enemy entered the town, which of course precluded all hope of more escaping. We consequently weighed and stood out towards the outer bay, where we again came to anchor.

A Russian ship-of-war was in a small harbour in this bay, which it was intended to board and cut out. As we were then, I believe, on rather bad terms with that nation, never did I witness such alacrity and delight as our tars on board the Alfred manifested when buckling on their cutlasses for the occasion, and I feel certain that if confidence in themselves would tend to insure the victory, no men had a better chance of succeeding; but from some cause or other with which I am unacquainted, the enterprise was abandoned.

On the 21st January we weighed and stood out to sea; but a gale coming on we were obliged to come to anchor

again under the shelter of the Isle of Bagona. We did not
get to sea till the 24th, but on the 25th we spoke a frigate
going out to Lisbon with General Dyatt on board, who informed us of the fatal business at Corunna. Indeed the people on board this ship had, from vague reports, greatly magnified our loss on that occasion, telling us that the whole
army had been nearly cut to pieces, and that very few indeed had been able to effect their escape. We each, of course,
mourned for his particular friends, not doubting but they
had fallen among the rest. I think it was the same night
on which we saw this ship, a fatal accident had very 'nigh
taken place. Our captain was the Commodore, and the
captain of the Hindostan store-ship had charge of the rear
of the fleet ; his place was consequently always behind all
the other vessels. Some time after dark, however, our look-
out people gave notice of a large vessel on our starboard
quarter. We shortened sail and let her come up pretty
close to us, and made the private signal, but no answer was
returned. At length, when near enough, we hailed her, but
still no answer. An order was now given to stand to quarters and prepare for action, not doubting she was an enemy
which had got among the fleet. The guns were accordingly run out, the matches lit, and every thing prepared for
action. She appeared a large ship, but of what force they
could not guess. Again she was hailed, and again she dis-
regarded it. Our first lieutenant was now fully convinced
she was an enemy, and pleaded hard with the captain to give
the word fire, but the captain said he would hail her once
more, and if she did not answer he would fire. Providentially they heard us this time, and answered it was the
Hindostan. What they had been about I know not, for we
were quite near each other; and had she received our broadside, as was the intention had she not then answered, it is

most probable she would have gone down ; at all events the consequences must have been awful, for she had the whole of the 43d regiment on board, besides her own crew. Our captain certainly censured him in no very mild terms for leaving his station in the rear, and getting to the very head of the fleet. She was a very lofty ship, and carried forty-four guns I believe, and had not less than 1000 men on board, many of whom must have suffered had we fired upon her.

A few days after this we encountered a most tremendous gale, and came in sight of the English coast, somewhere near the Lizard or the Start ; but our master not knowing exactly where he was, we stood off again towards the French coast.

The next day the gale was if possible more severe, and the ship rolled so much that they were afraid her guns would break loose from their lashings, in consequence of which large spikes were driven in behind the wheels of each gun-carriage to prevent such an accident. In this situation, I know not whether I did not almost wish myself on the snowy mountains of Galicia again, rather than where I was, so miserable a sailor am I, and so much do I suffer from sea-sickness.

The fleet was by this time completely scattered, every one making the best shift he could for himself ; some got into Plymouth, some reached Portsmouth, and some, I believe, foundered in the gale, among which, if I mistake not, was a brig, on board of which my two companies had been first embarked, but were subsequently removed to the Alfred, and some of the German Legion, I think, put on board her.

At length we made the Isle of Wight, and subsequently Spithead, which we reached on the 31st, and the next day landed once more on the happy shore of our native Britain.

E

Thankful indeed I ought to have been for the ever watchful
care of an indulgent and kind Providence, who had brought
me safely through the toils and sufferings under which so
many more robust and hardy than myself had sunk; but, alas !
I had then no sense of the gratitude due for such unmerit-
ed favours, and instead of rendering thanks to Him who had
thus preserved me, I entered, with all the eagerness of a person devoid of reason and religion, into every vice and sen-
suality that presented itself. I here learnt with sorrow the
great loss which my friends in the first battalion had sustained, but glad nevertheless that it was not to the extent
we apprehended, and that none of my particular friends had
fallen.

We left Portsmouth, and returned to our old quarters at
Hythe, in Kent, passing again on the road my native county
militia at Battle, in Sussex, as I did at Bury, on my return
from Holland ; and truly our appearance on this occasion
was, if possible, more deplorable than on the former. However, our tattered and worn-out habiliments had the effect
of inspiring some of my countrymen in that regiment with
a desire of sharing in the glory, as they termed it, of suffering so much in the defence of our beloved country ; and
they accordingly made up their minds to volunteer into
our corps the first opportunity that offered, and which they
put in execution that same year, as will be told hereafter.
We took up our abode in the comfortable barracks at Hythe,
and immediately set about putting every thing in order,
and truly much was wanting to fit us again for duty as
soldiers.

CHAPTER VI.

Volunteering—Farther Promotion—Embarks for Portugal, with two Companies of the Second Battalion—Debark at Cadiz—Advance to the Isla—The French occupy all the adjacent Towns, except Cadiz and the Isla—Cannonading—Spanish Army—Detachment of the Allied Army sent round by Gibraltar and Chiclana, to take the Enemy in the rear of his works, and compel him either to fight or abandon them—Come up with a portion of the Enemy in the vicinity of Veger —Bravery of the British—The Enemy repulsed with great Loss, but, from the apathy and misconduct of General La Pena, and the Spaniards under his command, the French are allowed to retain their Works in the vicinity of Cadiz.

In April of this year, an order was issued to allow the militia regiments to volunteer, for the purpose of filling up the regiments of the line ; and I was sent by Colonel Beckwith (our two battalions being then both at Hythe) to receive those who chose to volunteer from the Northumberland militia before-mentioned, which had now been removed to Ipswich. Lieutenant Beckwith had the charge of our party, but proceeded *incog.* to Ipswich, the general orders not permitting officers of the line to be seen in the quarters of the militia. On our arrival at Ipswich, I had the pleasure of obtaining the names of thirty fine young fellows, among whom the patriots formerly mentioned of course were included. Several other militia regiments in this district also gave volunteers to us, so that in three days, from the commencement of the volunteering, we obtained upwards of 1100 men ; and had we not, by an order from the Horse-Guards, been precluded from taking any more, I doubt not we should have obtained several hundreds besides, for our regiment alone had near eighty names down for us, who were not allowed to enter from the above cause. Indeed the Commander-in-Chief, Sir David Dundas, (afterwards our Colonel,) appeared quite astonished, and not well pleased, that we had run away with so many men when others wanted them so much. He was obliged, however, to grant us a 3d battalion, as we had so many more men than were required to fill up the 1st and 2d ; and our respected Colonel, Major-general Coote Manningham, dying about this time of the fatigue he had undergone in Spain, Sir David took us to himself, and became our Colonel-in-Chief, giving the command of the 3d battalion to my respected (and now lamented) friend and benefactor, Major-general the Honourable William Stewart. The Lieutenant-colonelcy was given to Major Norman M‘Leod, our senior Major, and only two or three other steps were given to the officers of the regiment, although it was alone owing to their exertions in obtaining men, and to the high character the regiment had acquired, that such numbers had volunteered into it.

It becomes not me to censure or criticise the measures of government, but I cannot help thinking that more favour was certainly due to the corps as a body. For myself, I ought and must speak with gratitude, not of them, but of that kind Providence which has favoured me so far, so very far, beyond my deserts, for, on the 8th of June following, I was appointed Quartermaster of the 3d battalion.

Our 1st battalion was again sent out to join the army in Portugal, while mine was sent to Brabournlees to equip and drill our new levies. Every exertion was made to this effect, and the battalion was soon completed and rendered fit for service. Here my wife joined me again, the child to which she gave birth in my absence having died when six weeks old. This was the only child she ever had, and it was perhaps a providential dispensation, for she was extremely delicate, and by no means a healthy person, and it is not unlikely her offspring might have inherited her disease, that is, an affection of the chest. We had only lived a few months together, till another call for service separated us again.

In June 1810, we received orders to send out to Cadiz two companies of my battalion, together with the commanding-officer and staff, three others having been already sent thither in the spring. The melancholy business of parting with my wife was again to be gone through; but on this occasion I was favoured by being permitted to accompany her to London, where, parting from her with a heavy heart, I took my place for Chichester, at which place my detachment would be quartered next day, on their way to Portsmouth. I omitted to mention, that Lieutenant-colonel Barnard of the 1st or Royals, had exchanged with Lieutenant-colonel M'Leod some time previous, and he consequently was now going out as my commanding-officer. We embarked at Portsmouth on the 11th July, on board the Mercury frigate, armed *en flute*, and commanded by Captain Tancock.

We had a favourable passage, and landed at Cadiz on the 29th of that month. This city, it may be remembered, was besieged at this time by a French army under Marshal Victor; consequently, when we arrived, we were amused by seeing immense shells flying from one party to the other, but without doing any serious injury to either, the distance being too great to produce any effect of moment.

As we came in sight of Cadiz, the view was most enchant-
ing, for the city appeared as if composed of lofty and elegant
snow-white buildings, apparently rising from the bosom of
the ocean, for the land on which it is built cannot be seen
at a distance; added to which, the numerous and beautiful
towns about the bay, and a little beyond it, rendered it a
most delightful scene.   On the right was Cadiz, with its
lofty lighthouse, and its strong sea-walls rising out of the
water; on the left was Rota, an apparently neat little town.
Farther up the bay, on the same side, was Port St Mary's,
and beyond that Porto-Real, both considerable towns.   In
the centre rises the Isla de Leon, now called St Ferdinand;
beyond that Chiclana, composed of the elegant country
residences of the more wealthy Cadiz merchants; and, in
the distance, towering on the mountains behind, the dazzling
white town of Medina Sidonia shining in the sun; indeed
altogether imagination can scarcely picture to itself a more
interesting *coup-d'œil*, the scene being closed by the lofty
snow-clad mountains of Ronda.   We landed at Cadiz, and
remained for the night in the barracks situated in the barrier, on the land-side of the town, and which is remarkably
strong, the fortifications being composed of solid masonry,
and the barracks all bomb-proof. I suffered dreadfully from
the myriads of fleas which preyed upon me during the night,
and was glad when morning appeared.

   We marched next day to the Isla, (be it observed the town
is called by that name as well as the island on which it and
Cadiz are situated,) distant from Cadiz about seven miles;
the island is of a most singular form, being about ten
miles broad at the end next the continent, from which it is
separated by the river Santi Petri; immediately below the
town of Isla it begins to narrow very rapidly, forming from
thence to Cadiz nothing more than a narrow sand-bank, in

some places not more than a hundred yards across, and on which a causeway has been built to connect the two places. We took up our abode in the Isla, where the Spanish government, such as it was, at this time resided; and here I witnessed the first opening of the Spanish Cortes in 1810, which was attended with all the pomp and show of a truly Roman Catholic people. *Te Deums* and other pompous and brilliant ceremonies marked the event; indeed, here we had an opportunity of seeing a great number of the grandees of the Spanish nation, for, as I said before, the government had retired to this place from Madrid, and most of the courtiers and others attached to the government had assembled here, together with the deputies from the different provinces; altogether the scenes we witnessed here were sometimes very imposing.

The French occupied all the towns before named save Cadiz and Isla, their advanced piquets being thrown forward to near the river Santi Petri, except near the Bridge of Luaza, which is the only communication across from the island to the mainland; here our pickets were advanced a considerable distance beyond the bridge upon a causeway on which is the road leading to Seville, through a broad salt marsh on the banks of the river; it is here about two miles wide, and utterly impassable, except to those who know the footpaths across it, being intersected at every few paces by deep salt-pits or pans. The enemy, as mentioned before, had their sentries at some parts pretty far into the centre of this marsh, and there were some fellows in the Spanish service called by the name of " creepers," they obtaining their livelihood by killing sea-fowl and other animals in this marsh; and so dexterous were they at this *creeping*, that they could steal upon the birds unperceived, which enabled them to get them with ease. Sometimes a fellow of this

calling would set off on a *creeping* excursion, and instead of
bagging a wild-duck, or some other such bird, would plunge
his stiletto into the heart of an unsuspecting French sentry,
and leave him weltering in his gore.   This was a noble ex-
ploit in their estimation, and marks strongly the character
of the Spaniard, who, inured to blood by the frequency of
their bull-fights and other similar exhibitions, hesitates not
a moment at assassination if urged on by what he deems his
own or country's wrongs ; this inhuman act, of course, was
perpetrated in the dark.

I may mention, in connexion with this, that on the Christmas of 1810, it was reported that sixteen people had been
assassinated in Isla alone, on the evening or night before ;
it is probable the number may have been exaggerated, but
the thing was such an almost everyday occurrence that it
appeared not to excite the least horror at its atrocity.   I
had occasion to go down the town during the Christmas day,
and I saw still lying at the corner of one of the most frequented streets, one of the unhappy beings who had thus
fallen.   No one seemed inclined to own him ; and his body,
foul with blood and dust, was thus permitted to remain in
the public streets without any enquiry being made with respect to the perpetrator of so foul a deed.   In truth they
are, as it were, trained up to this recklessness of human life
from their infancy, for in the town of Isla there was a sort
of naval academy, where a number of boys, from perhaps
eight to twelve years of age, were educated ; these urchins
were permitted to wear swords, and it is really astonishing
how desirous they appeared to make use of them, for they
could scarcely ever pass along the streets without trying the
sharpness of their points upon the backs of pigs or dogs, or
any other unfortunate animal that came in their way.

The French also occupied a long low tongue of land which

stretches out into the Bay of Cadiz, taking its rise from between Port St Mary's and Porto Real, and extending to within about two and a half miles of Cadiz, and about one from Puntalis, a fort erected on the island opposite the extremity of this low tongue; this is called the Trocadero, since become famous as the field on which the Duke D'Angouleme, and Prince Carignan of Naples, gained so many honours. On the point of this tongue the enemy's principal batteries were erected, and from thence they contrived occasionally, but not often, and never with any great effect, to throw shells into the town of Cadiz. The mortar now in St James' Park, called the " Prince Regent's bomb," was cast at Seville on purpose to enable them to reach the town, no ordnance of common dimensions being capable of throwing a shell so far; but it did not answer the end proposed, or at least the effect expected from it, for it was imagined by them, that if they could once succeed in throwing shells into the city, the inhabitants would become so alarmed that they would compel the military to surrender. This, however, was far from being realized, although they did throw a few in; but the distance being so great, they were necessarily thrown much at random, some of them falling short of the town, others flying completely over into the bay near the lighthouse on the other side, and some few, as I said, falling in the city, but from which very few casualties occurred.* I am told they were obliged to have the mortar

* The distance to which the French threw these shells is truly amazing. The longest range of heavy iron sea-mortars is only about 4200 yards, whereas the distance from the French batteries on the Trocadero to the nearest point of Cadiz was, I believe, 4500 or more; but they exceeded this considerably, for, as I said above, some of their shells fell in the sea beyond the town, near the lighthouse, a distance of at least 500 or 600 yards farther. The shells were always half filled with lead, to increase

slung in chains at the time of firing it, the concussion being
so great as to destroy the bed in which it was fixed. As
may be supposed, there was constant war between our fort
Puntalis, before mentioned, and the enemy's batteries on
this point ; in fact our people had orders to throw a thirteen-
inch shell every quarter of an hour, besides the occasional
firing from the guns and other mortars when any thing appeared on the opposite side; and you may be certain the French
were not behind us in the expenditure of ammunition ; they
were remarkably fond of firing what are termed salvos, that is,
volleys of artillery. On one occasion I happened to be looking out from a high tower near Isla, call the Tore Alto, and
while all was deep and profound silence, and I happened to be
looking towards the point of Trocadero, in a moment the
smoke rose from at least 100 pieces of artillery, fired by signal, and the noise they made was tremendous. Our poor little
fort of Puntalis appeared almost enveloped in the dust raised
by the striking of the shot, and the smoke from them which
fell about it, and seemed as if almost deprived of power by
so sudden and unexpected a salute ; but she began at length
to return the compliment, although feebly in comparison of.
the tremendous volley she had received. This and such like
were of frequent occurrence, scarcely a day passing without
something interesting taking place.

To enable us to cope in some measure with the French,
a large double fortified sea-mortar was brought from Gibraltar, which threw thirteen-inch shells. It was brought up
to the back of the town of Isla, near some powder magazines, and an attempt made there to throw some shells over

their flight, so that when they burst the mischief they occasioned was
never extensive ; I believe not more than about half-a-dozen individuals
suffered from them in all.

to the Trocadero. The first trial, an empty shell was put in, with not less than thirty-two pounds of powder in the chamber. On firing it, the shell flew all to atoms, from the violent shock occasioned by so great a quantity of powder; and the shell being too weak for that description of mortar, another was tried filled with sand, to give it more weight and solidity; this answered the purpose, for it fell on the land on the opposite coast, but still, from the great range, much uncertainty must naturally attend the practice, and it was eventually given up. The next day, however, we were saluted from the opposite side with both shot and shell, the French thus showing us that they were better able to play at long bowls than we were; neither, however, did their practice continue, for there was nothing at the point where their shot and shells fell to be injured by them, the magazines before noticed being now empty.

On another occasion an attack was made by our people on the Trocadero itself, where it was reported the French had got a considerable number of boats, &c., laid up on shore, about halfway between the point and Porto Real; our folks took gun-boats and boats with rockets, the intention being to set fire to the enemy's craft. They accordingly advanced in good style, keeping as far, however, as possible out of the range of the French batteries at the point, which, as they were directed towards Cadiz and Puntalis, could not easily bring their artillery to bear upon our boats. They reached the place where it was said the French craft was lying, and fired a considerable number of rockets, but without being able to effect any thing farther than burning one boat, I believe. As they were returning, however, they met the French commander, who had been down to the point in a light boat, and he, like a brave fellow, determined to run completely the gauntlet rather than return, keeping as close in shore, however, as possible. The whole of our gun-boats fired at him as he passed, and knocked the water up about him in all directions without ever once touching him, although, to look at him, one would have imagined it impossible he could escape; but here the old soldier's adage was verified, for there was still more room to miss than to hit him, and he accordingly escaped scot-free.

While here, I had a most ample opportunity of closely viewing the Spanish army, great numbers being stationed in and about the Isla, and great numbers constantly coming into and going out of the place, after receiving such equipment as the government was able to provide for them. Nothing could exceed the hardy and robust appearance of the men in general; and had they been clothed, appointed, and disciplined like either their enemies or their allies, there could not have been a finer soldiery. I cannot, however, say so much for their officers; most of them appeared to be utterly unfit and unable to command their men. Those who had the means, seemed to think of nothing else but dressing like apes or mountebanks, and intriguing with the women. It was really absurd and ludicrous to see the strange figures they generally made themselves. In one regiment alone you might have observed more different uniforms than both we and the French have in all our armies. One would have had on a blue coat turned up with red, with a chaco and a straight sword, the uniform prescribed for officers of the infantry, I believe; the next would have most likely had on a hussar dress, with an enormous sabre dangling by his side; another would have had a red coat, a fourth yellow, a fifth white, and so on. In short, all the colours of the rainbow were generally exhibited in the uniforms of one regiment's officers; and every one of them appeared to vie with the other who could make the greatest harlequin of himself, whilst those of them who were mounted would caper and prance about the streets like so many fools, riding with their legs at full stretch, and the toe of the boot (if they had one) just touching the stirrup, and drawing the reins continually through the fingers of their right hand; and if by any chance an ape of this kind came near the window of his dulcinea, and thought there was a likelihood of her seeing him, I pitied the poor foot-passengers who might happen to be near him, for he would make his unfortunate Rosinante prance and caper by the immense long bit in its mouth, and the pieces of iron in the shape of spurs on his (shoes perhaps), till the poor animal was like to fall under him. In short, they had all the pride, arrogance, and self-sufficiency of the best officers in the world, with the very least of all pretension to have an high opinion of themselves; it is true they were not all alike, but the majority of them were the most haughty, and at the same time the most contemptible creatures in the shape of officers, that I ever beheld. It was, therefore, not to be expected that the soldiers would or could look upon them with that degree of respect and reverence so essential to a due maintenance of subordination in an army.

About the month of February 1811, it was concerted between the Spanish government and General Graham, who commanded us, to undertake an expedition which should land in the vicinity of Gibraltar; and being there reinforced by some troops from that fortress, the whole should move forward in the direction of Chiclana, and, taking the enemy in the rear of his works, compel him either to abandon them or fight a battle. Accordingly, on the 18th of that month, we embarked on board some small vessels that had been fitted up for the occasion in the bay of Cadiz, and, sailing soon after, we reached Algeziras, ten miles on this side of Gibraltar, and landed there on the 24th. Our force con-

sisted of a brigade of artillery, with ten guns; two battalions
of Foot Guards; the 28th, 67th, and 87th regiments; a
battalion composed of flank companies from Gibraltar; two
companies of the 47th regiment, and two of the 20th Portuguese regiment, with six companies of our corps and one
squadron of cavalry,—in all about 4500 men. The Spanish
army, under the command of General La Pena, (who, being
senior officer, directed the whole,) consisted of two divisions,—in all from ten to eleven thousand. We were not
allowed to take any baggage with us, consequently we could
not expect much comfort during the service, which was
expected to be short. The day we landed we bivouacked
on a height near Algeziras, and the next morning moved
on towards Tarifa, where we remained for that day and the
next, to allow time to get the artillery and cavalry horses
on shore. Here I observed a strange custom among the
females of this place, the remains, I apprehend, of the
Moorish fashion, (which no doubt would continue longer in
this place than others, it being immediately opposite to and
in sight of Africa.) The Spanish women all wear what they
term a mantilla, that is, a kind of scarf made of cloth, generally black, which they throw over their heads lengthwise,
letting the two ends come over their shoulders, and meeting
and crossing on the breast, it forms a sort of head-dress which
shows only the face, and keeps them close and snug about
the head; but here, they bring it so far forward as to completely cover the face, leaving nothing but a very small hole
in front of their left eye (I think it is), at which they peep
out, without showing any part of the face. Colonel Brown
of the 28th, who was then a most wild and eccentric character, although now I understand completely altered, could
not relish this hiding of their beauty by the modest dames
of Tarifa. All, therefore, that he met in the streets he stop-

ped, and made them open the mantilla, that he might have a fair peep at them, to the great scandal of the good ladies of this still Moorish town, and which, had it been on any other occasion, might have been attended with unpleasant consequences to himself.

When every thing was ready we moved forward from Tarifa, and halted for the night on a height about twelve miles distant. The next day we reached Casas Vejas, or "Old Houses," where we bivouacked on a scrubby hill, the weather being very bitter, which we felt in all its force, having no covering whatever. Next day we had to cross a considerable lake of fresh water, by a sort of ford which crossed it about the middle. We had started before daylight, and, through some mismanagement, did not reach this lake till near mid-day, although it was only a few miles distant from our last night's quarters. One division of the Spaniards led the column, and another was behind us, we being thus in the centre, as being the least thought of probably by our Spanish Commander-in-Chief; for indeed we had often heard it said in and about Isla, " what fine-looking and well-disciplined soldiers the British are !—what a pity they cannot fight !" So thought La Pena, probably ; but by two o'clock the first division of Spaniards had not near got over the lake, at which the patience of our General was so completely exhausted, that he requested the Spanish General to allow him to bring forward the British troops, to show him the way how he and they would act. My battalion led the van, and were ordered to march straight through it without any picking of steps, and to go forward in regular sections, one man supporting another. They went in and marched right through it, as if it had been plain ground, the water taking them generally about mid-deep. The rest of the British army followed, and were all through in less than half an hour; a one-horse cart, indeed, stuck fast in the middle of it, from the wheels having got entangled between the large stones at the bottom. General Graham seeing this, instantly dismounted, and, plunging in, set his shoulder to the wheel, and fairly lifted it clear of the obstruction.

La Pena, and those about him, after witnessing the example set them by our General and his troops, seemed really ashamed of their former conduct, and, setting to in good earnest, they contrived to urge their soldiers and officers to take the water with more freedom, and before dark the whole army had got over. While we were so long detained by the first division of Spaniards getting across, I, with several other mounted people, rode forward to the ford, to ascertain the cause of our stoppage for so long a time. The Spaniards were going into the water one at a time,—here one, and there one,—while the creatures of officers were making the men carry them on their backs. Had the whole army acted thus, we should not have got over before daylight next morning.

When all were across, and the columns formed, we moved forward, and reached the neighbourhood of Veger, which stands on a high hill not far distant from the memorable Cape Trafalgar. We halted in an olive-grove below the town, and bivouacked for the night; it was bitter cold, and the troops could find but little wood for firing, which they much needed, from having got so completely wet in crossing the lake.

We remained at Veger all the next day, and a little after dark commenced our march. We being now in the neighbourhood of the enemy, it became necessary to conceal our movements as much as possible. During the night we passed the fishing town of Conil, and, keeping near the

1

coast, we arrived the next morning on the plain of Chiclana. I quote from our General's dispatch, as it states the thing in a much more clear and satisfactory manner than I could do. He says,—" After a night march of sixteen hours from the camp (bivouack) near Veger, we arrived on the morning of the 5th on the low ridge of Barossa, about four miles from the Santi Petri river. This height extends inland about a mile and a half, continuing on the north the extensive heathy plain of Chiclana. A great pine-forest skirts the plain, and circles round the height at some distance, terminating down towards Santi Petri, the intermediate space between the north side of the height and the forest being uneven and broken."

The two Spanish divisions had preceded us, who, after having rested a while on the plain, moved down towards the Santi Petri, where a bridge was to be thrown over by the troops in the Isla de Leon, and thus open a communication between the two armies, that is, between those inside the island and us.

The General goes on to say,—" A well-conducted and successful attack on the rear of the enemy's lines, near Santi Petri, by the vanguard of the Spanish army under Brigadier-general Ladrizabel, having opened the communication with the Isla de Leon, I received General La Pena's directions to move down from the position of Barossa to that of the Torre de Bermesa, about half-way to the Santi Petri river, over which a bridge had been lately established. This latter position occupies a narrow woody ridge, the right on the sea-cliff, and the left falling down to the Almanza creek, on the edge of the marsh ; a hard sandy beach gives an easy communication between the western points of these two positions.

" My division being halted on the eastern slope of the

Barossa height, was marched about twelve o'clock through the wood towards Bermesa, (cavalry patrols having previously been sent towards Chiclana, without meeting with the enemy.) On the march I received notice that the enemy had appeared in force on the plain, and was advancing towards the heights of Barossa. As I considered that position as the key of Santi Petri, I immediately countermarched, in order to support the troops left for its defence; and the alacrity with which this manœuvre was executed, served as a favourable omen. It was, however, impossible, in such intricate and difficult ground, to preserve order in the columns, and there never was time to restore it entirely. But before we could get ourselves quite disentangled from the wood, the troops on the Barossa hill were seen returning from it, while the enemy's left wing was rapidly ascending. At the same time his right wing stood on the plain, on the edge of the wood, within cannon-shot. A retreat in the face of such an enemy, already within reach of the easy communication by the sea-beach, must have involved the whole allied army in all the danger of being attacked during the unavoidable confusion of the different corps arriving on the narrow ridge of Bermesa nearly at the same time.

" Trusting to the known heroism of British troops, regardless of the numbers and position of the enemy, an immediate attack was determined on. Major Duncan soon opened a powerful battery of ten guns in the centre. Brigadier-general Dilkes, with the brigade of Guards, Lieutenant-colonel Brown's (of the 28th) flank battalion, Lieutenant-colonel Norcott's two companies of the 2d rifle corps, and Major Acheson, with a part of the 67th, (separated from the regiment in the wood,) formed on the right.

" Colonel Wheately's brigade, (consisting of the 28th, 67th, and 87th,) with three companies of the Coldstream

Guards, under Lieutenant-colonel Jackson (separated like-wise from his battalion in the wood), and Lieutenant-colonel Barnard's flank battalion (being two companies 47th, two ditto 20th Portuguese, and four of third battalion 95th) formed on the left. As soon as the infantry was thus hastily got together, the guns advanced to a more favourable position, and kept up a destructive fire. The right wing proceeded to the attack of General Ruffin's division on the hill, while Lieutenant-colonel Barnard's flank battalion, and Lieutenant-colonel Bush's detachment of the 20th Portuguese, were warmly engaged with the enemy's tirailleurs on our left.

" General Laval's division, notwithstanding the havoc made by Major Duncan's battery, continued to advance in very imposing masses, opening his fire of musketry, and was only checked by that of the left wing. The left wing now advanced firing. A most destructive charge, by the three companies of the Guards and the 87th regiment, supported by all the remainder of the wing, decided the defeat of General Laval's division.

" The eagle of the 8th regiment of light infantry, which suffered immensely, and a howitzer, rewarded this charge, and remained in possession of Major Gough of the 87th regiment. These attacks were zealously supported by Colonel Bilson with the 28th regiment, and Lieutenant-colonel Prevost with a part of the 67th. A reserve, formed beyond the narrow valley, across which the enemy was closely pursued, next shared the same fate, and was routed by the same means.

" Meanwhile, the right wing was not less successful. The enemy, confident of success, met General Dilkes on the ascent of the hill, and the contest was sanguinary; but the undaunted perseverance of the brigade of Guards, of

Lieutenant-colonel Brown's battalion, and of Lieutenant-colonel Norcott's and Major Acheson's detachments, overcame every obstacle, and General Ruffin's division was driven from the heights in confusion, leaving two pieces of cannon.

" No expressions of mine could do justice to the conduct of the troops throughout—nothing less than the almost unparalleled exertions of every officer, the invincible bravery of every soldier, and the most determined devotion of the honour of his Majesty's arms in all, could have achieved this brilliant success against such a formidable enemy, so posted. In less than an hour and a half from the commencement of the action, the enemy was in full retreat. The retiring divisions met, halted, and seemed inclined to form ; a new and more advanced position of our artillery quickly dispersed them. The exhausted state of the troops made pursuit impossible. A position was taken up on the eastern side of the hill ; and we were strengthened on our right by the return of two Spanish regiments, that had been attached before to my division, but which I had left on the hill, and which had been ordered to retire.

" An eagle, six pieces of cannon, the General of Division Ruffin, and the General of Brigade Rousseau, wounded and taken ; the Chief of the Staff, General Bellegarde, and aide-de-camp of Marshal Victor, and the colonel of the 8th regiment, with many other officers killed, and several wounded and taken prisoners, the field covered with the dead bodies of the enemy, attest that my confidence in this division was nobly repaid. The animated charges of the 87th regiment were most conspicuous. Lieutenant-colonel Barnard, (twice wounded,) and the officers of his flank-battalion, executed the duty of skirmishing in advance with the enemy in a masterly manner ; and were ably seconded by Lieutenant-Colonel Bush, of the 20th Portuguese, who (likewise twice wounded) fell into the enemy's hands, but was afterwards rescued."

The dispatch contains many more acknowledgments, which, as they have no connexion with my narrative, I have omitted.

I beg now to make such remarks and observations as may tend to throw light upon the different parts of the foregoing dispatch.

The two Spanish battalions attached to our division, together with Lieutenant-colonel Brown's flank-battalion, were left upon the height of Barossa, when we moved down into the wood, in order to secure that position till we had possessed ourselves of the height of Bermesa; but we had not left the plain more than half an hour, I think, and descended into the wood, till an officer came galloping after us, saying the French had debouched from the wood, and were moving on to the high ground in our rear, and had attacked the troops left there for its defence. Orders were instantly given us to countermarch, and to get on to the plain and into action as soon as possible. In coming about, one of the guns got entangled with a pine-tree; there was no time to disengage it, and setting to with the whip, they pushed the horses forward, and tore up the tree completely by the roots, although one of considerable size. I thought (as our General says) it appeared a good omen, and that a trifling obstacle would not be allowed to impede their career.

When we reached the plain, and perceived the enemy, never did a finer sight present itself. They were manœuvring on the high ground before us; and as Home says,

> " The hill they gained, and moving on its top,
> Of more than mortal size, towering, they seemed
> An host angelic, clad in burning arms."

Those immediately in front of my battalion were the famed
8th regiment, and consisted of two battalions of 700 men
each; one was composed of grenadiers, and the other of
voltigeurs, or light infantry. The grenadiers had long
waving red plumes in their caps, at least a foot in length;
while the light infantry had feathers of the same length
and make, but green, with yellow tops. The whole of the
French army had on their best or holyday suits of clothing,
with their arms as bright as silver, and glancing in the sun
as they moved in column, gave them really a noble and
martial appearance. We had no sooner cleared the wood
than we inclined to our left, and went immediately at them.
Major Duncan's guns commenced playing upon their column the moment he could get a clear piece of ground.
The two companies of the 47th, attached to my battalion,
were taken to cover and remain with the guns. Our people extended as we went up the hill, the Portuguese supporting us in the rear; and in a very short time we were
hotly engaged with the fellows with the beautiful green
feathers, many of which fell on the ground in a short time.
As we advanced, the battalions to our right and in rear of
us got formed in line, and moving forward in fine style,
took up stronger ground in advance; the guns in the centre
also moving onward, and causing dreadful havoc in the
enemy's ranks.

Early in the action my horse was killed, being shot in
the head, which ball, had his head not stopped it, would in
all probability have entered my body. He fell like a stone.
I then went on and joined the ranks, and finding a rifle of
a man that had just fallen, (poor little Croudace's servant,
who afterwards fell himself,) I took a few shots at them in
revenge for my horse. At this time the grenadier battalion
of the 8th, with their waving red plumes, began to advance

in close column, the drums beating all the time the *pas de charge*. They were supported by other columns in their rear, together with one, the French 54th, which they sent into the wood to try to turn our left. The 8th advanced, notwithstanding the galling fire kept up by our people and the Portuguese, every shot almost of which must have told, as they were in a solid body, not more than from 100 to 150 yards' distance. Our people were of course compelled to give way to this imposing column, when the regiments on our right and in our rear, opening out upon them a destructive fire, and the 87th and Guards immediately after attacking them with the bayonet, their rout and discomfiture was complete. The 8th, which suffered most, and from whom the eagle was taken, never yet got into line— nor did they intend, I believe—but advanced as a solid body, (occasionally firing from their front,) till, coming in contact with the regiments above mentioned, and in this state receiving the charge, their loss was excessive, for they could not get away. I understand, when the 87th charged, Ensign Keogh of that regiment made the first attempt to wrench the eagle from the officer who carried it ; but in so doing he was run through by several of those who supported it, and fell lifeless to the ground. Sergeant Masterson of that regiment then dashed at it, and was more fortunate, he succeeding in securing it. I understand there was some dispute between them and the Guards, who charged at the same time with the 87th, to whom it properly belonged ; but I imagine the 87th must have been the captors, for Sergeant Masterson soon after received a commission for his gallantry, and is now a captain in that regiment.

The 54th, the French regiment, which had been sent into the wood to turn our left flank, by some means got

entangled; for, except their light company, no part of the
regiment ever got into action again; and when their columns were routed, they found some difficulty in effecting
their retreat. There is something rather extraordinary and
very interesting in the story of the eagle and the 8th regiment, if it be true, and which I see no reason to doubt.
They were one of the regiments, it is said, which were
engaged at Talavera, and were particularly distinguished;
and it is further said, that the 87th was one of the regiments opposed to them, and over which they gained some
advantage; that is, the French troops caused the British
brigade, in which the 87th was serving, to retire with considerable loss; and that it was for their conduct in this
action that Bonaparte had placed a golden wreath of laurel
round the neck of the regimental eagle with his own hand.
If such was the case, it is most remarkable that the very
regiment by whom they should have obtained this honour,
should be the regiment that deprived them of their eagle,
which had been so highly honoured. But here, poor fellows, although they did not lose their honour, they lost
very nearly the whole regiment; for out of 1400 which
entered the field, not more than 200 of them entered Chiclana after the action. Indeed I never witnessed any field
so thickly strewed with dead as this plain was after the
action; and I feel confident, and all accounts agree in con-
firming the opinion, that the loss of the French on this
occasion was little short of 3000 men; ours was about
1250. Here then we have a loss of 4000 men in about an
hour and a half, out of about 12,000 which composed the
two armies.

In this action, Colonel Bush was almost absurdly brave
and conspicuous. As soon as he got his Portuguese fairly
into action, he rode slowly backward and forward among

them, with his spectacles on, crying out as the balls whistled past him, "Que bella musica!" what delightful music! Poor fellow, he did not ride there many minutes; for, being within a very short distance of the enemy's tirailleurs so conspicuous an object, it was not to be expected he could escape. He died a few days after the action.

Colonel Barnard, my commandant, (now Sir Andrew,) about the middle of the action, received a severe wound, and was borne away to the rear. Whilst the surgeon was dressing him, another shot struck him, and inflicted, I believe, a worse wound than the former. The horses of my battalion suffered greatly in proportion to their numbers. We had only four in the field, two of which, Major Ross's and my own, were killed, and Colonel Barnard's wounded; only the adjutant's escaped with a whole skin. Indeed there was scarcely an officer or soldier in the action that had not marks of shot about him. The caps of the tall guardsmen were riddled as it were; while the greater part of the enemy's shot passed over our little fellows, who were both too near them, and too low for their fire. I may remark on this subject that the French generally fire high, but here I think unusually so; for, after a considerable quantity of ammunition had been expended by my battalion, it became my duty to look out for a fresh supply. I accordingly posted off to the rear, where I expected to have found some mules which had been attached to us, with ammunition on their backs; but on my way thither, the ground was actually ploughing up on all sides by the enemy's large shot, and their musket-balls falling very thick; so much so, that some of our mules far to the rear had been wounded, and the others had dispersed. Hence also the second wound which my gallant commander received, where he ought to have been completely out of danger. Some ammunition for our rifles was, however, found in a one-horse cart belonging to the artillery, and out of it those whose ammunition was expended were replenished. But during my absence to the rear, the gallant and decisive charge had been made; and when I again reached the front, I perceived the enemy's columns in full retreat, covered by the remainder of their light troops, closely followed by some of my people. The retreat was accordingly sounded to recall them from the pursuit, and our brave and victorious little army cheered the enemy as his beaten and disheartened columns left the field.

Immediately after our army began to move off towards the Isla, our General being, as I understood, so much exasperated with the apathy evinced by the Spanish General, that he would no longer co-operate with him, and consequently drew off our troops into the Isle of Leon. My battalion, however, was destined to remain on the field all night to protect the numerous wounded from any marauders, or small parties and cavalry patrols of the enemy, which might happen to return. However, not a Frenchman made his appearance there again that night. When it was determined to withdraw the British army, Major Duncan, with great humanity, (approved of course by our excellent General,) cast off from the artillery-carriages all the spare ammunition, in order to make room for as many of our wounded officers and soldiers as those carriages could accommodate, and thus a considerable number of them were carried from the field immediately.

After they had left us, and my battalion was still standing in front of the position last occupied by our troops, all having retired but ourselves, and it now began to draw towards night, and we were preparing to move off, an unfortunate French sergeant attracted our notice. Poor fellow, he had been shot in the small of the back, and (on our surgeon examining him) pronounced to be mortally. He appeared to be a man above forty, and apparently a veteran, who had fought many a hard field; and was, I think, one of the most respectable-looking men of his class that I have seen. When he saw us preparing to leave him to his fate, the expression of his countenance became the most piteous and beseeching imaginable; imploring us in French not to leave him there to perish. My heart bled for him; but unhappily we had no means of removing him, had there even been a hope of his recovery. When he saw that his fate was inevitable, he crawled in the best manner he was able to a broken ammunition-box, and raising himself on his knees, supported by it, besought that Being who never casts out the cry of the unfortunate, and who, I sincerely hope, imparted to him that strength and comfort which his unhappy circumstances so greatly required. I doubt not he was a sincere Christian; never shall I forget the impression his unhappy fate made on my mind. To be left in solitude and darkness on this blood-stained heath, with the prospect of his own certain death before his eyes, and without any to comfort him in his last agony, must indeed have been a severe trial to his fortitude. Would to God I could have relieved him! His case was not singular, it is true; but none ever presented itself to my view under such truly affecting circumstances as this unhappy veteran's did.

After dark, my battalion retired over the field where the thickest of the dead and wounded were strewed, and many were the dying groans which struck upon our ears, as we traversed this bloody field; but, except these groans, no sound was heard, where lately the din of arms had been

loud and fierce, and where war had raged in all its fury ;
till coming to the house upon the sea-beach, where many
of the wounded had been collected, we were formed into
square on a sand-hill near it, and in this position rested on
our arms for the remainder of the night. On our way
from the front, we passed not far from where my horse had
fallen ; and as saddlery was scarce at Cadiz, I thought it
would be prudent to try to recover that on which I had
been riding. I found it ; but my horse having fallen with his
back inclined to the front, it was perforated by shot in five
places, and the tree was broken.   However, I disengaged
it, and giving it to one of the men, whose rifle I carried in
return, I got it safely into Isla.

About twelve at night, poor General Rousseau died, a
cannon-shot having carried away the greater part of the
flesh of one of his thighs ; and as no other troops were
near, the task of paying him the last sad duty devolved upon
me.   I went to the house aforesaid, and procured a shovel
or a spade, and digging a hole in the sand by the light of
the moon, his body was deposited, where it in all probability will remain till the last trumpet shall summon it to
rise. Poor drunken Gilles, one of the men I had employed
on the occasion, pronounced the only service as he was
committed to the dust, which was, " God rest his soul!" I
indeed sincerely hope so. Poor Rousseau had been a noble
soldier ; in his pocket was found a leave which he had obtained to return to France on account of ill health; but in
the prospect of the approaching action he had delayed his
departure, and thus fell a victim as it were to his patriotism
and his sense of honour. He was military governor of Xeres
de la Frontera, from whence we have our wine called Sherry,
a corruption of Xeres. He was a small slender person, and

apparently had suffered greatly from ill health. During the night some Spaniards were sent into the field to look for and bring off the guns we had taken, which they did.

As it approached towards morning, Major Ross, seeing all was quiet, moved us off by the beach towards our former quarters; and passing over the position of Bermesa, which the Spaniards still occupied, and crossing the Santi Petri by the lately erected bridge, we returned weary and hungry to La Isla, and where our friends received us once again with great cordiality. If my reader is not tired of the subject, I would just beg to draw his attention for a moment to the circumstances attending this action. The French troops were at least 7500 (some say 8000) strong, well clothed and appointed, and apparently well fed, and fresh from their cantonments, none of them probably having marched more than four miles. They were some of the best in the French service, and commanded by one of Bonaparte's ablest generals, a marshal of France, Victor, Duke of Belluno. They occupied a fine position, having the ground completely at their choice; while we did not muster more than 4500 at most. We had been marching for sixteen hours successively through the night over bad roads; and being taken in a manner by surprise, we came out of the wood *beneath* the enemy, broken and disjointed, and were instantly hurried into action.

The French fought desperately; for when their marauding columns came down upon us with an intrepidity seldom seen in the French army, and opening out their heavy and destructive fire, my heart quaked within me for the safety of our little army, and the honour of our country, for I thought it would be impossible to resist them. However, the steady valour of our troops repelled the assailants, and, taking advantage of their proximity, charged as before stated, and completely overthrew them. It is certain, as General Graham says, that *all* must have done their duty on this occasion; notwithstanding, we may sing with great propriety, " Non nobis, Domine"—" Not unto us, O Lord, but unto thy name be the praise ;" for it is certain we must have been specially favoured by a kind Providence, or it is impossible we could have gained *such* a victory under so many and so great disadvantages ; for never was victory more complete. In less than three hours from the first glimpse we had of them as we debouched from the wood, a Frenchman was not to be seen in all the field, save the numerous killed and wounded.

Although our General did not say any thing in his public dispatch of the abominable conduct of La Pena, no doubt he stated truly in his private information how ill that General had behaved ; for he and the 10,000 or 11,000 Spaniards he had with him remained within two miles of the field of action, quiet and passive spectators of the scene, without making one effort to support us had we been beaten, or to take advantage of the victory should we gain it ; and the consequence was, the French retained their ground and works by which they invested Cadiz and La Isla, whereas, had he made the slightest movement during or after the fight, they would have all gone off, and the siege would have been raised, for it is evident they contemplated and were prepared for this, the soldiers having each three or four days' bread in his possession.

A considerable number of other officers besides Generals Ruffin and Rousseau were taken. Ruffin was wounded in the neck by a rifle-shot, which touched the spinal marrow, depriving him of the use of his limbs. He was soon after embarked for England, but died as he came within sight of the Isle of Wight. He was an immense and a fine-looking man, about six feet two inches or six feet three inches high, and ate enormously. He every day received a mess from our General's table. The other officers also were treated with the greatest politeness and attention, dining first at one regimental mess, and then at another. They were fully sensible of the kindness shown them, and expressed themselves very grateful. They were afterwards sent to England.

I cannot omit here noticing the high estimation in which General Graham was held by every officer and soldier of this little army. I may truly say, he lived in their affections; they not only looked up to him with confidence as their commander, but they esteemed and respected him as their firm friend and protector, which indeed he always showed himself to be.

In all my fighting I never was in an action where the chances of death were so numerous as in this; and I may say, I never was in an action where I was less prepared to die. It is therefore of the Lord's mercies that he spared me —I hope, for good at last.

CHAPTER VII.

The 2d Battalion of the Pompadours ordered to proceed to Portugal—
Our Author visits England—Returns to Portugal, and joins his Re-
giment at Rodrigo—The Army move towards Badajos—Siege of
Badajos—Badajos surrenders—Insubordination among the Troops
—Quelled by the prompt measures of Lord Wellington.

WE remained at Isla till June, without any thing of importance occurring, but at this time I was brought nigh to
death's door by the bursting of a bloodvessel in the lungs.
I was so ill that it was deemed necessary to send me home
for change of air, it being exceedingly hot at this time at
Isla.   I was accordingly removed to Cadiz to wait for the
first ship returning to England, and while there I suffered
greatly, not being able to lie down in bed.   However, before a vessel could be had, an order was received for my
battalion to proceed to Portugal, and our esteemed commander was likewise ordered to proceed to that country. As
I felt myself somewhat better, I obtained permission to accompany my battalion to Portugal, and I accordingly embarked with it at Cadiz on the 30th of that month, on board
a transport, the name of which I forget.   General Graham

intended to have gone in a 50 gun ship that was leaving that port for England, he being to be left at Lisbon in passing. He sent an aide-de-camp on board to prepare for his reception; but he met with such treatment while on board, as induced the General to alter his plan and go in a frigate, on board which some of our people were embarked. It is said, that after the aide-de-camp had been shown the accommodation, the captain intimated to him, that it was expected the military officers would always keep on the leeward side of the quarter-deck. The windward side on board a man-of-war is considered the most honourable, therefore this was in fact putting the General beneath himself. He suffered, however, for his ill-timed assumption of supremacy, for there was a quantity of specie at Cadiz which was to be transported at the same time for the use of the army in Portugal, and which was intended to have gone in the ship with the General; but after this reception of his aide-de-camp, and the imperious condition attached to his going in this ship, he went on board the frigate with his suite, and took the money with him, thus depriving him of a considerable premium for its transport, to which he would have been entitled had the General gone with him. He, however, being the senior officer, we were all put under his charge, save the frigate before mentioned, and we were greatly annoyed by him during our passage, which our master said he prolonged in looking out for American merchantmen, there being then an appearance of war between the two countries. They said he actually detained one or two which left Cadiz when we did, and that he fired small arms into them to bring them to, although war had not been declared. One day during the passage he made a signal to the transports which we did not immediately perceive. We were astonished at the report of a gun, and at the same time a cannon-shot whizzed past our rigging. This is not, I believe, customary, a blank gun being generally fired first, and when nothing else will do, a shot a-head of the vessel, but he appeared not to stand on any ceremony.

We were glad when the voyage was over, it continuing from the 30th June to the 19th July, although three or four days only is the usual time.

We landed at Lisbon, and immediately set about preparing for our journey up the country to join the army ; but Colonel Barnard having received letters respecting the settlement of our late Colonel (General Manningham's) affairs, which could not be easily arranged without my presence, determined to send me home for the purpose, with a promise, however, that I should immediately come out again. I accordingly embarked on board the same transport with a ship full of all kinds and descriptions of people, sick and wounded, and lame and lazy ; such a motley group I have seldom seen. Our paymaster also returned home with me, and besides him I did not know a person on board.

We had a long and tedious passage, not reaching Portsmouth till the 27th August, although we embarked on the 1st of that month. When we entered the chops of the Channel, there was a considerable swell in the sea. Our master, for some purpose or other, had got up from the hold a small quantity of ballast (gravel), which was laid upon the quarter-deck. A fine stout young Irishman, an officer on board, came up the companion, and seeing the ballast lying there, asked where it came from.

" Why, don't you see," says the master, " how rough the sea is ? it has been washed up from the bottom and thrown upon the deck."

The Hibernian seemed quite astonished at the effect of the swell, but believed the story with all the simple-hearted credulity of a Johnny-raw, as the soldiers term a young and inexperienced soldier. Our paymaster was a little of a gourmand, and having for some time been deprived of luxuries, determined to indulge a little now we had come to the land of plenty. On our road, therefore, to London, (he and another officer and myself posting it,) we stopped at Godalming for dinner; he would needs have a carp, which he happened to see in a pond in the garden, made ready for our dinner. It was prepared according to his request, and with it and other good things we contrived to fare pretty well; although, according to my taste, a fresh herring would have been preferable. But lo, and behold! when the bill was called for, the awful sum of *half a guinea* for the carp was added to the other items of the dinner, which amounted to quite enough without it. To remonstrate would have been useless; we therefore paid the bill and set off, determined to be more economical in future.

I passed through London, and reached the depôt of my battalion, then stationed at Ashford in Kent, where, after having arranged the business for which I had been sent home, I obtained a three months' leave of absence to visit my native place, where I arrived, thank God, in a much improved state of health, and where I found all my friends and connexions as well as could be expected, and no doubt happy to see me.

About the middle of November of the same year, I started once more for foreign service, and embarked at Portsmouth for Lisbon on the 22d of that month, on board a small brig heavily laden with corn for the army in Portugal. We remained some time wind-bound, but at length got to sea and proceeded on our voyage, but shortly after the wind headed us and began to blow very fresh. We were therefore compelled to run for the Race of Portland, where we came to anchor. But the wind coming more favourable in a day or two, we weighed again, and got as far on our voyage as opposite Torbay ; but here again the wind coming foul, we were obliged to enter the bay and drop anchor again. We were detained here a good many days, during which I went ashore with another officer, who was on board with me, and indulged in some Devonshire clotted cream at Brixham.

In about a week we again started, and got about half way across the Bay of Biscay, when a heavy gale overtook us, and in which we lost a considerable portion of our quarter-bulwarks (I think they are called). Indeed, from the brig being so heavily laden, the water being within a very little of her gunwale, she did not weather the heavy seas which struck her very well, for during the night one came clean over her, partly filling the cabin where we lay with water; and I own I had considerable apprehension for our safety, which I believe was pretty universal on board. It pleased Him, however, who ruleth over all things, to bring us through the gale without further injury, although we appeared next morning in a very shattered condition, and after a few more days' sailing, we reached the Tagus, and landed at Lisbon about the middle of January 1812, and immediately commenced equipping for a campaign with the army which was at this time besieging Ciudad Rodrigo. I had to purchase a riding-horse and a mule to carry my baggage, and a great deal more of essential requisites to enable me to do my duty in the field ; and to say truth, I had not, by any means, sufficient funds to meet these considerable expenses, and was consequently forced to borrow, and glad enough to find a friend who could and would lend me enough for the occasion. And here I cannot but remark, that it seemed peculiarly hard on junior officers, on their taking the field, to be compelled to furnish all this equipment at their own expense. I have known several who did not recover from the debt they thus incurred (could they find a friend, as I did, to lend them what they wanted) for a considerable time after they had joined the army; nay, I believe some never recovered it, and the persons who were kind enough to oblige them lost several large sums in this manner. In my own case, I know, I was most wofully put to it to raise a sufficiency for this purpose; and many, I know, have been compelled to take the field without the necessary equipment to render them efficient. They were thus of little service to the army for a considerable time after joining, and many of them were obliged to leave it again, after striving to do their duty, inadequately provided with the conveniences and comforts requisite to enable a man to bear up against the fatigues he had to encounter. It struck me as but just, and in this opinion I am not singular, that all officers who have not sufficient pay and allowances to enable them to provide themselves with the means of transport, ought to be furnished in the first instance at the public expense, and then be afterwards obliged to keep them in a fit state for service at their own.

I set out from Lisbon soon after, and joined my regiment, which was one of those that formed the light division, and found them cantoned in the neighbourhood of Rodrigo, that fortress having fallen some days previous to my arrival. I had not been many days with the regiment till the division was assembled at a village called Ituera, on the banks of the Azava, to carry into execution the sentence of a general court-martial, before which seven men of the division had been arraigned for desertion to the enemy, they having been taken in Rodrigo at the capture of that place. They were of course all found guilty, as they were taken as it were out

of the enemy's ranks, and never attempted to plead not
guilty ; but they had said in palliation of their heinous crime,
that they were forced to desert from want of food and clothing ; indeed the army had not been so well supplied for a
short while previously, as they had been accustomed to, but
there never was any thing like want.   I understood the
clothing also was getting bad, but the men could not be got
up the country for want of transport, and they were no
worse off than their comrades. Indeed, from all I could learn,
they had acted in a most diabolical manner ; for at the attack of the breaches in assaulting the place, they were distinctly heard crying out to one another, " Now here comes
the light division ; let us give it them, the rascals," or something to that effect, and had, it is said, done more injury to
the assailing party than twice their number of Frenchmen.
Death of course was their sentence, and now the wretched
victims of delusion were to atone with their lives for one of
the greatest crimes known in the criminal code of the army.

   The division was formed into three sides square, on a
plain in front of the village, the graves of the hapless beings
occupying a part of the fourth face of the square. When all
was ready, and a firing party from each regiment had been
formed in the centre, the provost-marshal went to the
guard-tent, where the prisoners were in waiting, to conduct
them to the place of execution. They soon after appeared,
poor wretches, moving towards the square, with faces pale
and wan, and with all the dejection such a situation is calculated to produce.   Their arms had been pinioned one by
one as they came out from the guard-tent, and all being
ready, the melancholy procession advanced towards the centre of the square. The proceedings of the court which tried
them, together with the sentence, and the approval of the
Commander of the Forces, was read by the Assistant Adju-

tant-general, in the hearing of the whole division; which concluded, the prisoners were marched round in front of every regiment, that all might see and avoid their unhappy fate. They were then moved towards their graves. I ought to observe that the chaplain of the division had been with them in the guard-tent some little time previously to their leaving it, and when they quitted as above described, he followed them at a considerable distance, apparently ashamed of his peculiar calling, and the duty incumbent on him in such a conjuncture. They were led, as I said before, towards their graves; and when they reached the bank of earth in front of each, they were made to kneel down with their faces fronting the square, and then being one after another blindfolded, and left for a few moments to their own reflections or their prayers, the provost-marshal proceeded to the firing party, who had been previously loaded, and directing the men of each regiment to fire at their own prisoner, he advanced them to within about ten or twelve paces of the wretched men, and giving the signals by motion for their making ready and firing, the whole fired at once, and plunged the unhappy criminals into eternity. There was, indeed, one melancholy exception to this. One of the prisoners belonged to the troop of horse artillery attached to the division, and it seems the provost, in giving his orders for the soldiers of each regiment to fire at their own man, had not recollected that the artillery had no men there to fire. He was thus left sitting on his knees, when the others had fallen all around him. What his feelings must have been it is in vain to guess; but, poor fellow, he was not suffered long to remain in suspense, for a reserve party immediately approaching, they fired and stretched him also along with his companions in crime and misery; and in such of the others as they perceived life still remaining, they also immediately put an end to their sufferings, by placing their muskets close to their body, and firing into them.   One poor man, when he received his death wound, sprung to a considerable height, and giving a loud shriek, he fell, and instantly expired.

When all was finished, the division was formed into column, and marched round in front of the bodies, where each soldier might distinctly perceive the sad and melancholy effects of such a fatal dereliction of duty.   They were then, without more ado, thrown into their graves, which were filled up without delay, and the division separating, each regiment marched to its quarters.

I cannot describe the uncomfortable feelings this spectacle produced in my mind—nay, not only there, but in my body also—for I felt sick at heart; a sort of loathing ensued; and from the recollection of what I then suffered, I could not easily be persuaded to witness such another scene, if I had the option of staying away.   Death in the hundred shapes it assumes on the field of battle seems honourable, and not near so revolting to the feelings, and withal comes suddenly; but to witness the slow and melancholy preparations for an execution such as this, is productive, in any heart that can feel, of the most unpleasant sensations, I think, imaginable.

One of the poor wretches was the little shoemaker of our Highland company, by name M'Guiniss, whom I had known for many years, and who formerly bore an excellent character; but he had most likely been seduced by some of his companions to commit this heinous crime.

Not many days after this, the whole army began to move towards Badajos.   On the 26th of February we left our cantonments, and passing by way of Castello Branca and Villa Velha, we reached a village not far from Niza, called

Povo das Meadas, where my battalion took up its quarters for a time. From hence I was dispatched to Lisbon for the regimental clothing, which had then arrived at that port; but being unable to procure the means of transport, I was obliged to return without it. I rejoined them in the camp before Badajos about the 25th of March, and witnessed the siege of that fortress from this period to its fall on the 6th of April. The breaches having been reported practicable by the engineers on the 5th, in the evening the army was assembled for the assault, and was disposed as follows: the 3d division under General Picton was ordered to attack the citadel, and to endeavour to establish himself there by escalade; the 4th and light divisions, the former under General Colville, and the latter commanded by Colonel Barnard, were destined for the breaches; the 5th division, which had not co-operated hitherto in the siege, but brought this evening into the neighbourhood, was ordered to occupy the ground in front of the town by way of reserve. One brigade of that division was ordered to make a false attack on a work called the Pardeleras, which was connected with the town, although not actually belonging to it. Another brigade of the same division was ordered to make another false attack round towards the gate near the river Guadiana, which latter was to be turned into a real attack, if circumstances permitted General Walker, who commanded it, to do so. There was also a brigade of Portuguese, which was ordered to attack St Cristoval, a fort on the other side of the river. Every thing was arranged in the clearest and most satisfactory manner; all knew what they had to do, the point they were to occupy in the attack having been pointed out to most of them the day before. Soon after dark, the different divisions began to move towards their destined posts, all elated with the certainty of success.

I was then in the mess of the senior captain of my battalion, who commanded it on this occasion; and my other messmates were poor little Croudace and Cary, both lieutenants, the latter acting adjutant, and another. We had taken a farewell glass before we got up from dinner, not knowing which of them would survive the bloody fray that was likely soon to commence. Poor Croudace, a native of the county of Durham, and consequently a near countryman, put into my hand a small leather purse, containing half a doubloon, and requested me to take care of it for him, as he did not know whose fate it might be to fall or to survive. I took it according to his wish, and put it into my pocket, and, after a little more conversation, and another glass, for the poor little fellow liked his wine, we parted, and they moved off. Although I had thus, as it were, settled it in my mind that I would not go with them on this occasion, for my services could have been of but very little utility, yet, when they went away, I felt as if I was left desolate as it were, and was quite uneasy at parting from my beloved comrades, whom I had always accompanied hitherto. I therefore slung over my back my haversack, containing my pistol and a few other things, and moved forward, to try if I could find them; but falling in with some of my friends, staff-officers of the 43d, who were in the same brigade, they strongly dissuaded me from it, representing to me the folly of uselessly exposing myself, and the little service I could render there; and one of them requested me to accompany him to a hill immediately in front of the breaches, where we could see the business as it proceeded.

We waited till about ten o'clock, when the fire first commenced from the castle upon the 3d division, as they approached it; but the fire from thence did not appear

very heavy.   Not long after it opened out at the breaches,
and was most awfully severe; indeed it was so heavy
and so incessant, that it appeared like one continued
sheet of fire along the ramparts near the breaches, and
we could distinctly see the faces of the French troops,
although the distance was near a mile.   All sorts of arms,
&c. were playing at once, guns, mortars, musketry, gre-
nades, and shells thrown from the walls, while every few
minutes explosions from mines were taking place.   The
firing too appeared to have such a strange death-like sound,
quite different from all I had ever heard before.   This was
occasioned by the muzzles being pointed downwards into
the ditch, which gave the report an unusual and appalling
effect.   This continued without a moment's cessation, or
without any apparent advantage being gained by our
struggling but awfully circumstanced comrades.   Lord
Wellington had also taken his stand upon this hill, and appeared quite uneasy at the troops seeming to make no progress, and often asked, or rather repeated to himself, " What
can be the matter ?"

· The enemy had adopted an excellent plan to ascertain
where our columns were posted ; they threw an immense
number of light balls on all sides of the town, and when
they found out where there was a large body, a rocket was
fired in the direction of where it stood, and instantly every
gun, mortar, and howitzer, not previously engaged, was
turned in that direction, and grievous was the destruction
their shot made in the ranks of these columns.   Still our
people at the breaches did not get forward, although we
distinctly heard, with emotion, the bugles of our division
sounding the advance.   His lordship seemed now to lose
all patience, and aides-de-camp were sent to ascertain the
cause of the delay.   They flew like lightning, while the

whole rampart round the town seemed enveloped in one
flame of fire. Our brave but unsuccessful comrades were
heard cheering every now and then ; but still the fire at the
breaches did not slacken.   At length a dispatch arrived
from General Picton, stating, that he had established himself in the castle.   This was cheering news to his lordship, who expressed very strongly the gratitude he felt for
that gallant General.

During the reading of the dispatch, which was done by
torchlight, the enemy, perceiving the light, and that a number of people had assembled on the hill, directed a shell in
that direction ; but it fell short, and did us no injury.   His
lordship now rode off, and ordered our people at the
breaches to retire, as the town was now perfectly secure. I
also set off to inform my people of the happy circumstance.
I found them drawn off from the glacis a few hundred yards ;
but, oh ! what a difference in their appearance now from
what they were previous to the attack ! The whole division
scarcely mustered at this time 2000 men, so many had
been killed and wounded, and many had been sent to the
rear with the latter. I informed them that General Picton
had got possession of the castle, but my story appeared to
them an incredible tale ; for it was actually impossible, they
thought ; and although they made me repeat it over and over
again, they could scarcely bring their minds to credit such
unexpected news.

It was now dawn of day, and the firing had ceased at
every point.   Here I learnt the fate of my two beloved
friends and messmates : Croudace had been shot through
the body, and carried to the rear ; Cary had fallen, but they
could not tell what had become of him.   I now went forward towards the breaches, where I found that several men
of both the 4th and light divisions had remained ; and when

General Picton moved from the castle towards that point, which I believe he stated in his dispatch to be his intention, the enemy, finding themselves attacked in rear, began to abandon the defence of the breaches, and our people were then enabled to enter. Never did I witness any thing like the artificial impediments which the enemy had here thrown up, which, added to the natural ones, that is, to the breaches not having been so perfectly practicable as was desirable, rendered it next to impossible to enter, even after all opposition on their part had ceased. In one breach (the large one) this was literally the case ; for at the top of it was fixed a chevaux-de-frize extending the whole width of the breach, and composed of a strong beam of wood, with sharp-pointed sword-blades fixed in every direction, they being generally about three quarters of a yard long, and so closely set together, that it was impossible either to leap over them or penetrate between them, and the whole so firmly fixed to the works at the top, that it could not be moved. In addition, they had fitted a number of long and thick planks, with spikes about an inch or more in length, and laid them all down the breach, but fixed at the top, so that it was impossible for any one to get up without falling on these. Beyond the chevaux-de-frize several ditches had been cut, into which those must have fallen who surmounted the obstacles on the breach ; but I believe none did, although I saw one Portuguese lying dead upon the ramparts ; but I imagine he must either have been thrown up there by some explosion, or been one of those of the 3d division who came from the castle. In addition to all the above, from the covered way down into the ditch was, I should imagine, at least thirty feet ; our people had descended by ladders, and, I doubt not, in the dark, and, in the hurry and confusion of the moment, many were thrown down

and killed. In the middle of the large ditch a smaller one
had been cut, which was filled with water, and in which,
added to the inundation close to the right of the breaches,
(which had been caused by bringing the river partly into
the ditch,) numbers were drowned. Small mines had been
constructed all along in the ditch, which were exploded
when it was filled with people, and which produced infinite
mischief.

On the top of the ramparts the enemy had a considerable
number of shells of the largest size, ready filled and fused ;
and when our people had filled the ditch below, these were
lighted, and thrown over on their heads, each shell being
capable of destroying from twelve to twenty men or more.
They had beams of wood also laid on the ramparts, with
old carriage-wheels, and every sort of missile imaginable,
which were poured upon the unfortunate people below.

When these things are taken into consideration, added to
the incessant and destructive fire of from 3000 to 4000 men,
all emulous to do their duty, at the short distance of perhaps twenty yards,.with the ditch as full as it could possibly stow, the reader will be able to form some idea of the
destruction that must naturally ensue : and awful indeed it
was, for, within the space of less than an acre of ground, I
should imagine not less than from 1200 to 1500 men were
lying: it was a heart-rending sight. I learnt afterwards
that many were the desperate efforts that had been made to
ascend the breaches, but all in vain ; that many had nearly
reached the top, but they being either shot or blown up,
the others were forced down again. Another and another
trial still was made, but each succeeding party shared the
fate of their predecessors. At last the bottoms of the
breaches were nearly blocked up with the bodies of those
who fell.

By this time, General Philippon, the French governor, had surrendered. When he found the 3d division had got possession of the castle, and were preparing to move down to second the attack of the breaches by taking the enemy in rear, and that General Walker, with a part of the 5th division, had escaladed, and established themselves at the other end of the town, he deemed further resistance useless, and retired, with the garrison, to St Cristoval, on the opposite side of the river; and shortly after the whole surrendered prisoners of war, the troops, after being stripped of their arms and accoutrements, being marched along in the ditch to one of the gates, from whence they were escorted on their way to Elvas. They passed near the breaches while I was there, and I had a full view of them as they moved along. I thought they seemed under great apprehension for their safety, as they appeared quite downcast and dejected, which is not generally the case with French prisoners, who will shrug their shoulders, and tell you it is the fortune of war; but these poor fellows, who certainly had made a noble defence, seemed low-spirited and timid to a degree. Certainly by the rules of war, I believe, they might have been put to death, for having stood an assault of the place; but a British general does not resort to the same measures which their Marshal Suchet did at Tarragona, when he put all, both soldiers and inhabitants, to the sword.

Soon after daylight, the remaining men of attacking divisions began to rush into the town, in hopes of sharing, with those who had already entered, the plunder they imagined it would afford; and though every thing was done by Colonel Barnard, aided by the other officers, to keep out those of the light division, it was useless, although he even risked his life to prevent their entering. He had bravely, during the attack, repeatedly ascended the breach, in hopes·

of overcoming the obstacles which presented themselves, but he had always been driven back, although he escaped unhurt where all was death around him; and now his life nearly fell a sacrifice, in endeavouring to restore that discipline in his division which this unfortunate and unsuccessful assault had considerably impaired. He opposed his personal and bodily strength to the entrance of the plunderers, but in vain. They rushed in, in spite of all opposition; and in wrenching a musket from one of the soldiers of the 52d, who was forcing past him, he fell, and was nigh precipitated into the ditch. He, however, finding resistance here in vain, set off, accompanied by several other officers, into the town, to endeavour to restrain, as much as lay in his power, the licentiousness of those inside, whose bad passions, it was but too evident, would be let loose upon the defenceless inhabitants.

I had been in company with Captain Percival, my commanding-officer before alluded to, from the time of my first coming down to the division before daylight; and now he and I, hearing the heart-piercing and afflicting groans which arose from the numbers of wounded still lying in the ditch, set to work to get as many of these poor fellows removed as was in our power. This we found a most arduous and difficult undertaking, as we could not do it without the aid of a considerable number of men; and it was a work of danger to attempt to force the now lawless soldiers to obey, and stop with us till this work of necessity and humanity was accomplished.

All thought of what they owed their wounded comrades, and of the probability that ere long a similar fate might be their own, was swallowed up in their abominable rage for drink and plunder; however, by perseverance, and by occasionally using his stick, my commandant at length compelled a few fellows to lend their assistance in removing what we could into the town, where it was intended that hospitals should be established. But this was a most heart-rending duty, for, from the innumerable cries of,—" Oh ! for God's sake, come and remove me !" it was difficult to select the most proper objects for such care. Those who appeared likely to die, of course it would have been but cruelty to put them to the pain of a removal; and many who, from the nature of their wounds, required great care and attention in carrying them, the half-drunken brutes whom we were forced to employ exceedingly tortured and injured; nay, in carrying one man out of the ditch they very frequently kicked or trode upon several others, whom to touch was like death to them, and which produced the most agonizing cries imaginable.

I remember at this time Colonel (the late Sir Niel) Campbell passed out at the breach, and, as he had formerly been a Captain in our regiment, many of the poor fellows who lay there knew him, and beseeched him in the most piteous manner to have them removed. He came to me, and urged upon me in the strongest manner to use every exertion to get the poor fellows away. This evinced he had a feeling heart; but he was not probably aware, that for that very purpose both my commanding-officer and myself had been labouring for hours; but it soon began to grow excessively hot, and what with the toil and the heat of the sun, and the very unpleasant effluvia which now arose from the numerous dead and wounded, we were both compelled, about mid-day, to desist from our distressing though gratifying labours.

It was now between twelve and one o'clock, and though we had had a great many removed, a much greater number lay groaning in the ditch; but our strength was exhausted, for he was lame and unable to move much, and I had been obliged to assist in carrying many myself, the drunken scoundrels whom we had pressed into the service seldom making more than one or two trips till they deserted us. But my lamented friend and messmate, poor Cary, was still to search for, and, after a considerable time, he was found beneath one of the ladders by which they had descended into the ditch. He was shot through the head, and I doubt not received his death-wound on the ladder, from which in all probability he fell. He was stripped completely naked, save a flannel waistcoat which he wore next his skin. I had him taken up and placed upon a shutter, (he still breathed a little, though quite insensible,) and carried him to the camp. A sergeant and some men, whom we had pressed to carry him, were so drunk that they let him fall from off their shoulders, and his body fell with great force to the ground. I shuddered, but poor Cary, I believe, was past all feeling, or the fall would have greatly injured him. We laid him in bed in his tent, but it was not long ere my kind, esteemed, and lamented friend breathed his last. Poor Croudace had also died immediately after reaching the hospital, whither he had been carried when he was shot.

Thus I lost two of my most particular and intimate acquaintances, from both of whom I had received many acts of kindness and friendship. They will long live in my memory. Cary was buried next day behind our tents, one of the officers (my other messmate) reading the funeral service.

I cannot help adverting to some of the scenes which I witnessed in the ditch, while employed there as above noticed. One of the first strange sights that attracted our notice, was soon after our arrival. An officer with yellow facings came out of the town with a frail fair one leaning on his arm, and carrying in her other hand a cage with a bird in it ; and she tripped it over the bodies of the dead and dying with all the ease and indifference of a person moving in a ball-room,—no more concern being evinced by either of them, than if nothing extraordinary had occurred. It was really lamentable to see such an utter absence of all right feeling.

Soon after this the men began to come out with their plunder. Some of them had dressed themselves in priests' or friars' garments—some appeared in female dresses, as nuns, &c. ; and, in short, all the whimsical and fantastical figures imaginable almost were to be seen coming reeling out of the town, for by this time they were nearly all drunk. I penetrated no farther into the town that day than to a house a little beyond the breach, where I had deposited the wounded ; but I saw enough in this short trip to disgust me with the doings in Badajos at this time. I learnt that no house, church, or convent, was held sacred by the infuriated and now ungovernable soldiery, but that priests or nuns, and common people, all shared alike, and that any who showed the least resistance were instantly sacrificed to their fury. They had a method of firing through the lock of any door that happened to be shut against them, which almost invariably had the effect of forcing it open ; and such scenes were witnessed in the streets as baffle description.

One man of our first battalion, I am told, had got a hogshead of brandy into the streets, and, getting his mess-tin, and filling it from the cask, and seating himself astride like Bacchus, swore that every person who came past should drink, be who he may. His commanding-officer happened to be one who came that way, and he was compelled to

take the tin and drink, for, had he refused, it is not improbable the wretch would have shot him, for his rifle was
loaded by his side, and the soldiers had by this time become
quite past all control.   Another, who had been fortunate
enough to obtain a considerable quantity of doubloons, put
them in his haversack, and was making his way out of the
town, but was induced, before he left it, to drink more
than he could carry. He laid him down somewhere to take
a nap, and awoke soon after without even his shoes, and not
only were the doubloons gone, but all his own necessaries
also.

In short, a thousand of the most tragi-comical spectacles
that can possibly be imagined, might be witnessed in this
devoted city.   The officers did all they could to repress
these outrages, but the soldiers were now so completely
dispersed that one quarter of them could not be found;
and indeed the only benefit almost that the officers could
render was, by each placing himself in a house, which generally secured it from being broken open and plundered.
The different camps of our army were for several days after
more like rag-fairs than military encampments, such quantities of wearing-apparel of all kinds were disposing of by
one set of plunderers to the other.   But they were not
content with what they had brought out of Badajos; they
had now got such relish for plunder, that they could not
leave it off when driven out of the town.

A night or two after the surrender of the place, they
stole no less than eight horses and mules belonging to my
battalion, and took them to some of the other divisions,
where they sold them as animals captured from the enemy.
I lost on this occasion an excellent little mule, worth at
least L.20, and for which I of course never obtained a

farthing. We used every exertion to discover both the perpetrators and the animals, but without success.

An English army is perhaps, generally speaking, under stricter discipline than any other in the world; but in proportion as they are held tight while they are in hand, if circumstances occur to give them liberty, I know of no army more difficult to restrain when once broke loose. A reason may perhaps be assigned for it in part. On such occasions as this siege, where they were long and much exposed to fatigue almost insupportable, to the most trying scenes of difficulty and danger, which were generally borne with cheerfulness and alacrity, they perhaps reasoned with themselves and one another in this manner,—that as they had borne so much and so patiently to get possession of the place, it was but fair that they should have some indulgence when their work and trials were crowned with success, especially as the armies of other powers make it a rule generally to give an assaulted fortress up to plunder. They had also become quite reckless of life from so long exposure to death; but an English army cannot plunder like the French. The latter keep themselves more sober, and look more to the solid and substantial benefit to be derived from it, while the former sacrifice every thing to drink; and when once in a state of intoxication, with all the bad passions set loose at the same time, I know not what they will hesitate to perpetrate.

The reader will judge of the state of our soldiers who had been engaged in the siege, when Lord Wellington found it absolutely necessary to order in a Portuguese brigade to force the stragglers out of the town at the point of the bayonet. At this time I think I was fairly tired of life, so disgusting and so sickening were the scenes the few last days had presented. I had also lost two of those for whom

I had a great regard, together with several others of my brother officers, all excellent young men, with still a greater number wounded,—in all, in our fifteen companies, to the amount of twenty-six,—and men in equal proportion. It was indeed a trying time.

Notwithstanding what has been said above of the bad conduct of the British troops on this occasion, I am fully persuaded there is more humanity and generosity to be found in the breast of an English soldier than in any other in the world, for, except when inflamed by drink, I am confident it would be most revolting to his feelings to be ordered to proceed with cool deliberation to the execution of such horrid butcheries as we read of in the armies of other nations.—No! When calm and sober, no man acts with more tenderness towards those in his power than an English soldier. Bonaparte would not have found in them the willing actors in his political tragedy in Egypt, when he coolly fusiladed several thousands of his unfortunate Turkish prisoners, as related by Sir R. Wilson.

If I may be permitted to make a few remarks on the taking of this strong fortress, and of the conduct of the besiegers, I would say that never in the annals of military warfare was greater devotion shown by those of all ranks, from the General to the common soldier. The arduous and dangerous service of the trenches was cheerfully performed by every individual whose duty called him there; but the most conspicuous gallantry was manifested in the assault. Conceive of the heroic Picton and his brave division escalading a wall probably forty feet high, built on the summit of an almost inaccessible rock, and with troops at the top of all to oppose them as they reached its summit. It is true the enemy were not numerous here, having only about

200 men in the castle, but still one man in this situation was able to destroy probably twenty of the assailants, by throwing down a ladder after it had been set up ; most of those ascending would be crushed to death by the fall over such a precipice. But he carried every thing before him, and after establishing his own division in this commanding situation, he either actually did, or prepared to move upon the body of the enemy, who were defending the breaches. General Walker also, who commanded a part of the 5th division, bravely forced an entrance into the town at the opposite side, overcoming every one of the numerous barriers and obstacles which presented themselves ; and where he himself, in the act, I believe, of mounting the rampart, received a most desperate wound. It was said, but I know not how truly, that when he fell, the French soldier who wounded him was about to repeat the blow, which in all probability would have deprived him of life, but that the General, whether intentionally or not it is not said, made the masonic sign, which was understood by one of the Frenchmen, and that he instantly interfered in his behalf and stopped the blow. They say the General some time after found out that his brave deliverer had been sent to Scotland with his fellow-prisoners, and that he had him searched for and handsomely rewarded, and, I believe, procured him his liberty.

It is well known, I believe, to be the rule in all services like the assault of fortresses, &c., that those, both officers and men, who form the forlorn hope and the storming party, are volunteers, these being services of extreme danger, and which generally procure for the officers who survive a step of promotion ; but it might as well have gone (in the light division at least) as a tour of duty, for on all occasions of this nature, with only one or two exceptions, the senior officers of each rank insisted upon being sent on that duty. Nay, in one instance this heroic feeling was carried to an almost censurable excess.   Lieutenant Harvest of the 43d having been some time the senior of his rank in that regiment, and there being a vacancy for a captain, he had been recommended for the company; and although he had not been gazetted, yet it had been intimated to him through his commanding-officer that his name should shortly appear as captain.   Thus his promotion was perfectly secure; notwithstanding, when volunteers were called for for the storming party, he insisted on his right of going as senior lieutenant; so over scrupulous was he that his permitting a junior officer to occupy this post might be construed to the detriment of his honour.   He went, and fell; and thus not only lost his company but his life, and by his too refined sense of honour deprived another officer, probably, of that promotion which would have been the consequence of going on this duty had he survived.

Among the men also the same noble enthusiasm prevailed, for he who was selected for this dangerous service out of the superabundant numbers who always volunteered, was envied by his comrades as truly fortunate.   In fact, it required a character for good conduct to entitle a man to this honourable employment.   Whatever, therefore, their other faults might be, a want of bravery was not one of them.

CHAPTER VIII.

The army leave Badajos on the 11th of April, and move into quarters
near the river Agueda, where they remain till the 11th of June—
Advance towards Salamanca, which, with the exception of three
forts, the enemy had evacuated—The forts invested—The main bodies
of both armies bivouack within a mile and a half of each other, in
the vicinity of Monte Rubio and Morisco—The forts of Salamanca
surrender—The main body of the enemy retire to Tordesillas—
Movements of the army.

On the 11th April we left Badajos to return again to
the neighbourhood of Rodrigo, the French having, during
the absence of our army from that frontier, made an irruption into Portugal, and penetrated as far down as below
Castello Branca, completely ravaging the country. Our
first march was to Campa Mayor, where we were quartered
in the town. We next day reached Arronches, where we
bivouacked in a wood near it. The following day we marched into Portalegre, and on the 14th, Niza; the 15th we
crossed the Tagus at Villa Velha, and moved on to Larna-
das. Here we began to perceive some of the effects of the
recent visit from the French; but at Castello Branca,
which we reached next day, the devastation they had caused
was truly deplorable. We halted here one day to refresh
the troops and get forward our supplies, and the next day
reached Escallas da Cima. Here we began to get very
close upon the rear of the enemy; it therefore became

us to move forward with circumspection, for our force on this side the Tagus was yet but small. We advanced, however, and occupied successively St Miguel d'Arch, Penamacor, and St Bartholomo, near Sabugal, which last town we passed through on the 23d, and bivouacked that night at Alfyates. The utter desolation of Sabugal was beyond conception ; filth and misery presented themselves in every direction. It had been made a depot for provisions by the French, I imagine, for on all sides the entrails and other offal of bullocks and sheep polluted the atmosphere by the abominable stench they caused, and had attracted multitudes of vultures and other birds of prey, who had by this time become horribly tame and familiar : one vulture sat so long upon a dead horse as I was riding along the road, that he allowed me to come near enough to make a cut at him with my sword, as he stretched his enormous wings to mount up from his prey.

On the 24th we reached Ituera, where we halted for two days. We had now entered Spain, and it not being intended as yet to commence another active campaign, we moved into quarters near the river Agueda, my battalion and the 43d occupying the village of La Encina, or " The Oak." Here it was necessary that every exertion should be used to re-equip and prepare the troops for service, as it was intimated that another campaign would speedily commence.

All the winter and spring hitherto had been spent in active service, consequently much required putting to rights before we again took the field ; all hands were therefore employed to patch up and repair our clothing and shoes, and to get every thing in good order when our services were again to be called for.

While we were here, I began to experience some of the

ill effects of a deep-rooted enmity which one of my brother
officers had conceived against me, though till now partly
concealed. I was unconscious of having given him any
cause for this; but he, without ever giving me any opportunity for explanation, used all his influence in endeavouring to injure me in the opinion of two of my superior officers, who had hitherto been friendly to me; and not only
with them, but, I have reason to believe, with our acting
brigadier, whose mind, with the others also, he completely
estranged from me for a time. But though he misled them
then, they did not retain the ill opinion of me which his
misrepresentations had produced, for there are testimonials
from all three at the end of this volume. I was not so
fully aware of his dislike of me, till one day I was dining
at the table of our acting brigadier, when he and one of
those before noticed were also guests. I overheard him
telling this officer, (with an intention, I almost imagine,
that I should hear,) that I must be a bad man, for that I
was sitting silent when all the rest were talking, in order
that I might listen to their conversation. But I was the
junior officer there, and it did not become me to be talka-
tive; besides, I never was loquacious. I said nothing,
(although some may blame me for it, but I loved peace,)
trusting that one day such forbearance would not be forgotten; but I felt it deeply, and mourned over it in secret
with great bitterness of spirit.

In this place also I began to receive very pressing letters
from the merchants in England, from whom I had purchased a quantity of goods when last at home, but which, for
want of transport, could not be got up to the army in order
to their being disposed of; and, in short, scarcely a post
arrived that did not bring some unwelcome and distressing
tidings. I had purchased a fine mule in place of that stolen

from me at Badajos, for which I had given about £30.
I sent him down to Lisbon with my batman, to bring up as
many of the goods as the mule could carry; but he had not
been long gone till I had the mortification to learn that
this mule also was lost. The man said he had been stolen,
but I had every reason afterwards to believe that he had
sold him. Be it observed, I could but very ill afford losses
of this extent out of my pay and scanty allowances; but I
endeavoured to bear up as well as I could against these misfortunes, although it is certain I was not able to bring religion to my aid at this time of trial, for I had lived hitherto
in total neglect of that most momentous of all concerns,
and, although I endeavoured to amuse myself occasionally
by fishing in the Agueda, my mind began to be greatly
depressed.

About this time an order was issued for each British
regiment in the Peninsula to endeavour to enlist fifty Spaniards to be incorporated in the regiment. I was sent in
company with another officer into the mountains of Gata,
not far from the city of Placentia. We were not successful, for although we obtained the names of some who promised they would follow us to La Encina, they never made
their appearance. However, the beauty and magnificence
of the mountain scenery amply repaid us for our trouble.
From this village also I had the pleasure of visiting, for the
first time, the lately captured fortress of Ciudad Rodrigo,
and some of my brother officers who had shared in the toils
and dangers of the siege, pointed out to me the most remarkable scenes about it. Like Badajos, it had been battered
till practicable breaches were made to admit the besiegers,
and then stormed in the same manner, but its defence was
feeble compared with Badajos; and yet, to look over the
ground in the neighbourhood of the trenches, one would

imagine it impossible for troops to have lived, so completely was it ploughed up with shot and shells, each of the latter generally making an excavation sufficiently large in which to bury a horse.

Whilst we remained in these cantonments, the officers of the division once or twice got up a sort of " pic-nic," every one contributing something towards the feast, which was held in a large wood in the neighbourhood of Ituera. On our way from La Encina to this assembly, we passed over the ground where the 5th and 77th regiments had so distinguished themselves in September 1811, against a very superior force of the enemy's cavalry. The bones of the combatants lay bleaching upon the plain, the flesh having been very soon devoured by the innumerable birds of prey, which appeared as if collected from every part of the Peninsula. Indeed so numerous were the battles and skirmishes which took place along this frontier, together with the offal from the animals killed for the use of the armies, that they were no doubt bettter fed than they had in general been accustomed to.

But the period of our stay in this vicinity drew to a close, and on the 11th June we broke up from our cantonments, and passing the Agueda, the division assembled in a wood about a mile or two in front of Rodrigo.   While we were here a rather remarkable phenomenon appeared about midday, or soon after; the sun, which shone most brightly, and the moon, with several stars, appeared all at the same time, the latter being distinctly visible.   This of course attracted great numbers, and many were the sage remarks that were made, some believing it ominous of disastrous events; and indeed very shortly afterwards a circumstance occurred which in some degree confirmed their prediction. A grenadier of the 88th regiment (I think it was) had come over from his own division, to endeavour to prevail upon his wife, who had deserted him and taken up with a sergeant of our first battalion, to return with him, she having, as I understand, left him with one or more children, the first of their marriage, which he was anxious she should come and take care of. They had often, I fancy, quarrelled, and he had probably used her ill, but he was now desirous of a reconciliation, and entreated her to return with him to his regiment. He prevailed upon her to accompany him to some distance from the bivouack, that they might the more freely discuss the subject, for she had hitherto refused to agree to his request, being probably better provided for by the sergeant than she had been with him. While walking in a field close to the wood in which the bivouack was situated, and arguing the point with some heat, and she still persisting in remaining where she was, he became so exasperated at her continued refusal, that he, in a rage of jealousy and anger, drew his bayonet and plunged it in her bosom. Her cries soon brought people to the spot, who at once secured him, and he was instantly committed to the provost prison tent, and her body of course brought in and buried. Poor creature! she was one of the gayest of the females which graced our rural balls near Ituera only a short while previous, and had often danced with old General Vandaleur on those occasions. I believe he was not brought to trial for it, as her ill conduct probably had been considered as in some measure palliating what he did, and that he might be supposed to have been irritated to a degree of madness when he perpetrated the fatal act. I subsequently learnt that he was a brave soldier, and that he afterwards fell in the hard-fought battle of the Pyreneés.

We moved forward the next day in the direction of Salamanca, halting on the 13th at Alba de Yeltes, on the

14th at Sancho Bueno, the 15th at Matillo, in a large plain in front of which we bivouacked, where were the most luxuriant meadows I think I ever saw, the horses on our arrival being literally up to their bellies in fine rich grass. What a pity the natives know nothing of hay-making ! This fine herbage is permitted to stand there till it perishes, and yet in the winter they are frequently very ill off for provender for their cattle ; indeed I do not exactly know how they contrive to feed them in that season, but I know we were always greatly put to our shifts to procure any sort of long forage for our animals, being generally compelled by necessity to resort to this grass, rotten and dead as it was. I believe they use a considerable quantity of straw, which they chop very short, and which in truth is no bad substitute for hay; but when it is so very plentiful and so good, common sense, one would imagine, would induce them to preserve it.

Lord Wellington in the following season caused a considerable quantity of hay to be made in Portugal, getting scythes, &c. out from England, but we never returned that way afterwards to reap the benefit of it.   All this immensely rich and extensive plain is in a complete state of nature— no enclosures to mark the different boundaries of the proprietors, should it have any, but where there are " landmarks," the mode of ancient days is resorted to.

On the 16th we moved forward to within about five miles of Salamanca, and bivouacked near a range of low hills extending from the Rio Valmuso (which we had just crossed) to the city.   In front of this place our cavalry fell in with that of the enemy, with whom they had a *petit affaire*, and had captured a few of them, who, in the afternoon, passed our bivouack, on their way to the rear. We observed as they passed that they wore long queues, which had an odd appearance in our eyes, the British army having for so many years left them off.

Next morning we advanced towards the city. We had gone, I think, about three miles, when ascending one of those heights over which the road passes, we had a most interesting view of this beautiful place. It seemed thickly studded with elegant and highly ornamented spires, springing from the numerous cathedrals and colleges, &c. which it contained; but what heightened the effect was an immense column of smoke rising from some magazines which the enemy (not having time to carry off) had set on fire. We feared it was but the prelude to the whole city sharing the same fate, for their barbarous conduct in Portugal during Massena's retreat, rendered it but too doubtful they were resorting to the same mode of warfare here. They still retained possession of a portion of the town, in which they had constructed three forts; one very strong, and capable of containing about 500 or 600 men; the other two were smaller, to cover and act as supports to the principal one. In constructing these works they had destroyed the greater part of the colleges, and a considerable number of other public buildings, besides several extensive streets which Salamanca had formerly contained; but even now it was still a beautiful and interesting city. One of these works commanded the bridge, which rendered our crossing the Tormes here impracticable. We were in consequence moved about a league higher up the river, where we crossed by a rather deep ford. However, all got safely over, and we halted for the night on a small plain, a short distance from the ford, the main body of the enemy having retired and left 800 men in the forts before mentioned. These occupied but about one-third of the town, of course the remainder was open and free, and, as might be expected, every one was anxious to have a peep at this famous university. Consequently away a number of us scampered, and soon entered the city, the inhabitants of which were overjoyed to see us. The nuns were seen waving white handkerchiefs out of their iron-grated windows, and the Padres and other respectable inhabitants welcomed us with a thousand vivas, embracing us, and using every means of testifying their joy at our arrival.

I need not attempt to describe the place, for I am not able, and it has so often been described that my reader will not be disappointed at my declining to do it here ; suffice it to say, the buildings in general, and the religious edifices in particular, were most superb ; but the Goths had destroyed the finest portion of the city.

The forts were immediately invested, and we went and had a look also at them. They seemed remarkably strong, having been constructed principally of hewn stones, taken from the buildings they had destroyed ; and on all sides of them a space of perhaps two hundred yards or more was cleared away to make room for the play of their artillery, and to prevent a lodgement being made by the besiegers.

We next day moved from our bivouack near the ford, and marched to the village of Aldea Secco, in front of which our cavalry and the enemy had a rencontre, after which the latter retired: this was about a league and a half in front of Salamanca. Next day we were suddenly assembled in consequence of the enemy, in great force, making his appearance at some distance in front of our bivouack. We were then removed from the plain, and took up a position on a height called Monte Rubio, or Red Hill, a little to the right. Soon after, also, the other divisions of our army began to assemble on the height, and our Chief arriving on the spot, every thing had the appearance of something serious being about to take place.

Here also, for the first time, I saw Don Carlos de Es-
pagna with his few followers.   These were better clothed
and equipped than almost any other Spanish troops that I
had seen.   The day passed over, however, without the French
making any attack, and without any movement being made
on our side, farther than putting the different divisions into
position as they arrived on the ground.   The French were
continually receiving reinforcements, or rather their different divisions were rapidly arriving in succession, when they
all bivouacked in the plain in front of us, at perhaps a mile
and a half distance, and near to the village of Morisco. This
they very soon gutted of every portable article, whether it
was food, clothes, furniture, or whatever they could carry
off; nay, they unroofed the greater part of the houses for
fuel for the troops, but this latter proceeding could not be
avoided, there being no wood near them.   Englishmen may
well feel thankful that their dwellings have not been exposed to such visitors, who, in half an hour, will convert a
comfortable and smiling village into a heap of ruins.

We remained in this position for some days, the two armies, like two experienced pugilists, each waiting for the
other to strike the first blow, by which he would in some
measure lay himself open.   It was not, however, Lord Wellington's game to commence operations, seeing a part of our
army was then employed in the siege of the forts in Salamanca; besides, it is said, when some one ventured to hint
that we should attack the enemy, that his lordship judged
it would make a difference of 3000 men less on the side of
the attacking army.   I know not if this story be true, but
certainly great prudence was displayed on both sides. However, the enemy had occasionally cannonaded us a little from
the first; but about three days after their arrival, they made
a very brisk and vigorous attack upon a conical hill imme-

diately in front of our position, and a little to the right of Morisco. It was defended by the seventh division, which repelled the attack with great gallantry, driving the enemy down the hill again with great precipitation. The 68th regiment distinguished itself greatly, but in their pursuit of the beaten enemy, they advanced too far into the plain, and which the French observing, a forward movement was made again by them, and before our people could recover the high ground, Captain M'Kay and Lieutenant M'Donald, with a considerable number of their men, were made prisoners. Poor M'Kay received I know not how many bayonet wounds on this occasion, I believe not less than ten or twelve, but none of them very serious of course, or he could not have survived. He, with the others, were taken into the French lines, but he was so ill when they retired a few days after, that they were obliged to leave him in Morisco. The enemy's artillery played upon our line during the greater part of this attack, and caused us some loss, but not of any consequence, the horses appearing to have suffered more than the troops.

The French seemed disappointed and annoyed at our sticking so pertinaciously to the hills on this occasion, and told M'Donald (from whom I afterwards had this information) that it was only when we had every advantage on our side that we durst give them battle. Our armies were, I think, pretty nearly equal, each having perhaps about 40,000, but they were, I believe, superior in cavalry, and of course the plain was the very ground for them. Marmont seeing himself thus foiled, withdrew from before us, and made a movement to his left, crossing the Tormes with a considerable part of his force, and advanced on the other side of the river towards Salamanca. Our heavy German cavalry, under General Baron Back, opposed them here, and greatly distinguished themselves, driving the enemy's cavalry from the field. Our army made corresponding movements with the enemy, changing in parts our position.

Meantime the siege of the forts had been proceeding with from the first day of our arrival, and as the distance from Monte Rubio to the town was not great, several of us rode in to see how the siege was progressing, as the Americans have it. An attempt had been made to carry them by escalade, but it had failed; General Bowes, who led the attacking party, with several officers and men, having fallen in the attempt. His lordship now deemed it necessary to batter them regularly previous to another assault being made upon them. Heavy ordnance was therefore got into battery, which not only effected a breach in the smaller fort nearest the principal one, but which also threw a considerable quantity of hot shot into a building in the centre of it, which served as a barrack to the troops, the roof of which was presently set on fire, and the only shelter they had was thus destroyed. They thus were compelled on the 27th to surrender prisoners of war.

It is not easy to describe the effect produced on those inhabitants who lived nearest to the forts while the siege was going forward. Just as I entered one of our batteries, which had been established close behind a street, still occupied by the people, one of our artillerymen was carried out shot by a musket ball in the breast, and dead; the poor people when he was brought out into the street assembled round his body, and set up the most piteous lamentations imaginable. This impressed me with the good feeling which must have existed in their minds towards the English, for they are not a people, as the reader will be aware, who are very susceptible of horror at the sight of blood. A few hours after these forts surrendered, I went to visit the principal one—the devastation caused by our hot shot on the house before mentioned was awful. They had been obliged to make this their hospital also as well as barrack, and it was really lamentable to see the poor wounded Frenchmen lying there in a house that was literally falling about their ears, the roof having been completely fired, while burning beams and rafters were continually dropping upon these poor helpless beings. A French surgeon was still in charge of these men, and he had the politeness to show us all over the fort. As it had appeared from the outside, it was in reality remarkably strong, and the place where our people had made an attempt to escalade it, was pointed out to us; he said it was heavily mined, and that if our people had carried it by escalade, the mines would most likely have been sprung. There was fixed immediately opposite the gate a beam of wood, with holes bored in it, and about twenty musket barrels fitted into them, so as to command the entrance. These, I imagine, it was intended to have fired by a train, as our people forced the gate, and it would have been like a little volley, which must have swept away the first of the assailants. The inhabitants seemed greatly rejoiced when this business was concluded, and peace once more established in their city, and they vied with each other in showing us every mark of attention and kindness, looking upon us as their deliverers.

If I am not mistaken, it was here where our illustrious Chief played off a sort of innocent *ruse* upon some of the Padres of the place. Soon after our arrival, and before the attempt upon the forts had failed, he went to visit some of the principal cathedrals, &c. which remained entire ; the priests of course were proud to show their churches on such an occasion. He admired them greatly, and praised them much ; but what seemed particularly to attract his attention was the extreme whiteness and cleanness of their walls and

ceilings, although they were so very lofty. He enquired how
they managed to get up to them to keep them so ; and the
unsuspecting Padre, without hesitation, led him to where
they kept the immensely long ladders by which they ascended. This was just the very thing he wanted in his meditated
attempt upon the forts, and of course they, with others of
a similar description, were procured for that service. I will
not vouch for the truth of the above, although I heard it,
and I think it was not unlikely to have taken place. Indeed
had he made a formal demand for such things, it is not improbable they might have denied they had them ; but his
having seen them himself precluded this.

The forts surrendered on the 27th, and on the 28th the
enemy's main body retired altogether ; for they soon learned
the fate of the besieged, as they had occasionally communicated in some measure by rockets thrown up, and answered.
On the same day, our division moved forward to Castilbanos ;
and the day following to Parada de Rubiallis. On the 30th,
we reached Castrillo de Aguerino ; and on the 1st of July,
the town of Ravel-del-Rey. The next day, we moved on
towards Rueda, a considerable town. Here we found the
French in some force, their main body having retired across
the Duero to Tordesillas. The force in and about Rueda
consisted of both cavalry and infantry, and seemed to act as
a rearguard till the enemy's columns had time to file over
the bridge at Tordesillas. I was at some distance in front
of our division, the cavalry having preceded it, with whom
I went forward. As we approached the place, a pretty large
column of the enemy's infantry left it, and moved in the
direction of the bridge. Some of our horse-artillery at this
time came up, and fired Shrapnel shells into it, which did
considerable execution ; one shell particularly having killed
and wounded great numbers, among whom was an officer,

I think one of the handsomest men I had almost ever seen. Our cavalry had a little brush with some squadrons of the enemy a little further on in the plain, and captured a few prisoners. One of these was the sergeant-major of one of their hussar regiments, and of all the men I ever saw taken, this man evinced the greatest trepidation and alarm. He was absolutely like to sink to the earth, either from fear of what awaited himself, or from the effects of the contest in which he had been engaged. He had lost his cap in the fray, and seemed like a person deprived of his senses. He must, notwithstanding, have been looked upon by the French as a good soldier, and a valuable non-commissioned officer; for I learned afterwards that they sent in a request that he might be exchanged for one of our sergeants whom they had captured, as it was intended immediately to promote him to the adjutancy of his regiment; of course this was immediately complied with. The enemy retired to Tordesillas, and we bivouacked near Rueda, a part of the officers being permitted to go into houses in the town during the day.

In this situation we remained for a day and a night; but the sun being so powerful, the troops began to feel the ill effects of the heat. They were accordingly brought into the town and quartered in the houses. Here I experienced more of that hostility before spoken of, on the following occasion. In the number of houses allotted to my battalion, there happened to be some of the best of them without stables; but as there was not time to examine farther than their outward appearance, this could not be known by me. I therefore marked off the houses according to custom, giving the best, in point of appearance, to the senior officers in succession, and so on till all were served. It so happened that the house allotted to this officer, who had nearly the best in the battalion given him, had no stable. This I was, from the fore-mentioned cause, totally ignorant of. Neither had I any stable in the house I occupied, but, after some trouble, I had found one in a house occupied by some of the men, where I had put up my horses and mules, and went about the other duties of my station. In the evening I was informed by my servant that my animals had been turned out by this officer, and his own put in, in their stead ; and that mine were running loose in a yard, he not caring what became of them. My saddlery, and all the mule-apparatus, (precious articles in this country,) had also been cast out. He was my *senior* officer, and I was consequently obliged to bear this ill-treatment.

I mention this little circumstance, because it will show with what determined and unrelenting hostility he pursued me. Indeed it might not have been so trifling an affair, for had I not heard of it in time, I might have lost every horse and mule I possessed, which would have been one of the most serious disasters that could have befallen me. I could obtain no redress, for the captain before mentioned, who commanded the battalion, and this officer, being on rather unfriendly terms, he felt delicate in interfering in my behalf. Indeed I have some reason to believe, that it was partly on account of his enmity to this captain (with whom I still messed) that he so persecuted me.

I own I was on this occasion strongly tempted to demand that satisfaction which the rules of honour (as they are termed) dictate, for I then had not a Christian feeling on this subject ; but after consideration and consultation with some friends, it was feared he might take advantage of his superior rank, not only to decline giving me that satisfaction, but to report me, and thus destroy my prospects for life, for he would have been compelled to the latter step had he not acceded to my demand; and from the feeling he displayed towards me, there is not the least doubt he would have rejoiced at such an opportunity of ruining me. At this time, also, I had very few *real* friends who would have stood by me; for his secret machinations, and his having the ear of our brigadier, tended greatly to estrange my former friends from me.

All this, as might be expected, tended powerfully to depress my spirits, and to cast a gloom over a mind but too susceptible of impressions of that nature; for there is not any thing almost I would not do or submit to, to live on good terms with those I associate with, and indeed with all men. My mind was also much harassed at this time by receiving very unpleasant letters from England on the subject of the goods I before mentioned, and which had not yet reached any farther than Abrantes; and as the men began to be ill off for want of clothing, I obtained leave to proceed forthwith to Abrantes, to endeavour to get both the clothing and goods brought up to the regiment. I therefore set off, accompanied by one servant on a mule, leaving the other animals with the battalion, and proceeded on the 16th on my journey, and passing through Ravel-del-Rey, I halted for the night in a village where the seventh division was quartered. As I knew some of the officers of the 51st, I took up my abode with them for the night, and they indeed received me very kindly. My friends spent the evening very merrily; but, about midnight, they were called out and put under arms, expecting shortly to turn in again, as they told me; but they were marched off, and left the place entirely, leaving only my servant and myself in occupation of the town.

It seems that Marmont, with his whole force, had moved from Tordesillas, and had threatened Lord Wellington's

communication with Salamanca. In order, then, to keep up
a corresponding movement, and be ready to take advantage
of any false step the enemy might make, his lordship withdrew his whole force, and began to retire as Marmont advanced. Thus, in the morning, to my surprise, all the army
had left the neighbourhood, and as I was not certain who
the next visitors might be, I quickly decamped from a village now left open to the enemy. I got on at a considerable pace, as both my servant and myself were riding, and
on the 19th I reached Salamanca.

During yesterday's march I heard a considerable cannonade to my right and rear, and I afterwards learnt that the
two armies had come nearly in contact with each other,
and some skirmishing and exchange of shots had taken
place. I did not stop in Salamanca longer than to draw
rations for ourselves and animals, being anxious to get on
as fast as possible, to try to get up the supplies while the
army remained near the frontiers, for it was still expected
they would advance into the heart of Spain, notwithstanding the present partial retreat. I accordingly moved on
that evening to Matilla, and continued thus making stages
of thirty or forty miles a-day, and on the 25th I reached
Abrantes; but on the preceding day I was overtaken by
Lord Clinton, going home with the dispatches relative·to
the glorious and decisive battle of Salamanca, which took
place on the 22d. His lordship was nearly worn out, being
actually asleep on his horse as he rode past me, for he had
never once stopped from the time he first set out. I learnt
the news from the person who accompanied him. It is
impossible to describe the joy this information created
among the Portuguese inhabitants of the village. I stopped
for the night at Gaviæ.

I found at Abrantes a detachment of our second battalion proceeding to join the army ; but, to my sorrow, learnt there was no chance of procuring transports for the clothing, &c., for months to come. This was distressing information to me, and of course added to the despondency already preying upon my spirits ; for the merchants' letters I was continually receiving began to be most importunate, and indeed attributing the non-remittal of their money to a want of principle, and talked of reporting my conduct to the Commander-in-Chief.

Want of a proper religious feeling, under such circumstances, as might be expected, laid me open to great temptations. I therefore, to drown sorrow, and because I had always been too much addicted to it, began to give way to intemperance, and, falling in with a number of officers of very dissipated habits, I was led on to indulge in the most vile and abominable of all vices, *drunkenness*, to an excess almost incredible. But the gloom still seemed to thicken, and a dark cloud seemed impending over me, of which I was fully aware, and wrote home to my friends to that effect. At length my birthday, the 4th of August, arrived, and which must, as my unhappy companions in sin urged on me, be kept with all due jollity. Accordingly, a dozen of strong port-wine was procured, and we boozed away most joyfully, the whole being drank by about four or five of us. This produced constipation in the bowels, and had nigh brought me to my end ; but my mind was more affected, if possible, than my body. About two days after this debauch, on my retiring to bed at night, I felt an unusual inclination to rise up and fall down on my knees, to offer up my evening prayer ; for, notwithstanding all my wickedness and forgetfulness of God, I had not altogether abandoned the *form* of *saying* my prayers at night, but it was always after I lay down. I resisted this impulse, however, to rise and pray, and, after mumbling over **my** *form* without the *spirit*, I endeavoured to compose myself to sleep. I did sleep for a while, during which I was troubled with some confused and incoherent dreams; but soon after awaking, gracious God! what were my feelings then? Despair, black despair, had seized upon me. I rushed out of bed, and rolled upon the floor like one distracted, as indeed I was.   Oh! what would I then have given that I had never been born, or that I could cease to exist! Had it been possible, by throwing my body into the flames, to annihilate for ever my consciousness of being, how gladly would I have done it!   But no—the terrors of the Lord were upon me, and drank up my spirits; and no one who has not been in a similar situation can form the most distant idea of the misery which preyed upon me.   The pains of hell got hold upon me, and hope seemed for ever to be shut out from my mind.   I believed I had sinned past all redemption; that the mercy of God could not possibly be extended to me; and of the efficacy of the Redeemer's blood I knew nothing. Oh! this was a time much to be remembered by me, for none but He who afflicted me, and my soul which bore the affliction, knows what I then suffered!

At length the morning came, but with it no comfort for me.   One of my sinful and dissolute companions came to see me, but he seemed greatly shocked at the recital of my woful tale, and I believe then formed for himself resolutions of amendment, which I fear, poor fellow, he never was able to fulfil.   He did not long survive, but was shortly after called to his awful account, whilst I am spared,—a monument of the long-suffering mercy of God.   Amongst all my companions in error and wickedness, I could not procure a Bible, and, as a proof of the ungodly state I was then in, I had not one myself.   This poor friend, however, had a

Prayer-book, which he lent me, and out of which I eagerly sought for comfort and hope, but in vain, for all was against me. Yes—and all who make God their enemy, will find in the hour of need, that every other creature and thing will fail to yield them comfort ; but I had sinned too deeply and too perseveringly to find peace speedily. Oh ! in what black array did the sins of my whole life pass before me, and how did I sigh for annihilation ; or, if I could in any way atone for my wickedness, if I could but go and bury myself in a cave or den of the earth, and forego for ever all intercourse with mankind, how easily and how cheaply did I then conceive I should purchase pardon and peace ! But, alas ! I knew nothing of the way of reconciliation with an offended God, although I had been duly instructed in my youth. I was in such agony of mind that I scarcely heeded my body, but was prevailed upon to have a surgeon, who administered what he considered necessary, but without effect. My bowels had ceased to perform their functions, and this no doubt would greatly affect my head ; still, although this, as a *second* cause of the distraction of my mind, was easily discoverable, yet the *great first cause*, not only of my disorder, but of all its effects, was the God against whom I had so grievously sinned, and from whom alone I could hope for the removal of my present sufferings. But hope was at this time banished from my breast, and I gave myself up to all the agonies of a soul that is lost for ever ; but still I could not *rest* in this sad situation. I therefore now determined to set off for Lisbon, in hopes that I might obtain from the chaplain, who was stationed there, some slight alleviation of my misery, for none but Roman Catholic priests were to be found where I then was. I accordingly set off, accompanied by my servant, but in such a hurry, and so utterly regardless of all worldly concerns, that I left my baggage in my quarters, which was taken care of by the friend before mentioned.

I started in the afternoon of the second day after my attack. The sun was scorching hot above my head, but I regarded it not, seeing there was a hotter fire within me; indeed I believed I could not mortify my flesh sufficiently, so blind was I at this time of the nature of atonement. My feeling was, that I had an Almighty enemy over me; that His eye was upon me for evil, let me go where I would; and that I could not possibly escape from the destruction which He would shortly inflict upon my soul. How gladly, as I rode along, would I have solicited the rocks and mountains to fall upon me, and hide me from His sight, did I believe they could have availed for this purpose! But no— I felt it was impossible, and that I must endure for a short while longer the lighter punishment he had then laid upon me; and by and by I must drink to the dregs the cup of His everlasting indignation. O, sinners! be persuaded to flee from the wrath to come, for indeed one of the slightest terrors of the Almighty is enough to drive to distraction the strongest mind, and to appal the stoutest heart!

I arrived at Galigao, the place of my intended rest for the night—and here I was attacked with ague and fever in addition to my other disorder—this was the effect of my exposure to the sun in so weak a state. But I cared not for my body. I knew that would return to the dust from whence it was taken. But oh! the never-dying soul—to think that it should endure eternal and omnipotent wrath, overwhelmed me with dread indescribable. My mind, it is true, was affected by my disorder; but it could not be termed insanity or madness, for I even now remember with great distinctness the feelings I then experienced, and those feelings remained with me for a considerable time afterwards.

Here I felt myself extremely ill, and believed I could not survive till morning. I consequently got my servant to make down my bed in a corner of the room I occupied, with his own near it, and told him to leave the candle burning, for that my time could not be long. I was compelled to submit, and quietly lay myself down, in dreadful expectation of the fatal hour, and when, as I imagined, the infernal fiend would be commissioned to seize and carry off my soul to its abode of everlasting misery. I could not pray, nor had I any the most distant hope that my sentence could be reversed, for I fully believed it had been finally pronounced by Him who changeth not.

During this woful night, I appeared to possess a sort of second self, a being which existed and thought and reasoned quite distinct from that *me* who was stretched upon the floor, and which appeared to upbraid me with the misery it was then suffering, and was still to suffer, for the sins of my past abandoned life. I know not whether any other person in despair ever experienced this feeling ; but to me it was quite obvious, for I remember distinctly the sin to which it more particularly drew my guilty attention. Was not this the soul which will exist when the body is dissolved, and may not such an upbraiding take place between the body and the soul when the former shall be raised to join the latter in the judgment ? But the fact is, my soul was that night as it were on the point of taking its departure from the tenement of clay, and seemed strong to endure the everlasting wrath of God.

I do not know whether I slept any during this dreadful night ; but morning came, and with it a certainty that I was still in this world, but without the hope that this might have

been expected to produce.   I felt as in a fire, yet I scarcely
durst put my burning hands into the water my servant
brought me.   I felt convinced that I had forfeited all claim
to any thing like blessings, and that curses, both in body
and soul, were alone my due.

Ill as I was, however, I proceeded on my melancholy
journey, not with any hope that a minister of religion could
give *me* any relief, but a drowning man will catch at a straw.
Oh! how strong, how awfully strong, did my soul appear
at this time, to endure the tremendous wrath of Omnipo-
tence, whilst my body seemed fast sinking into its original
element!

I reached Lisbon in two days from this time, having taken
a boat at Santarem.   I ate nothing, with a trifling exception. I had no inclination for food, nor did I think I ought,
for the reason before given; my only sustenance was a little
water which I kept in a bottle, and with which I now and
then moistened my parched lips.

I arrived at Lisbon about daybreak in the morning, and
proceeded as well as I was able to a friend's house, and
knocked at the door; but shocked indeed were he and his
wife, when they saw me standing below, more like a ghost
than an inhabitant of this world.   Indeed it is not easy to
describe my looks at this time; there must have been much
of that spiritual misery depicted in them which a confirmed
despair no doubt produces.   They took me in, and after
hearing my woful tale, prepared to do for me the best that
lay in their power; they gave me their own bed, taking a
pallet for themselves, and treated me as if I had been their
brother.   He, poor fellow, is no more, but his beloved and
kind partner still lives, and may she always enjoy that happiness she seemed so desirous of contributing to on this occasion, and everlasting happiness hereafter!   As soon as it

could be conveniently done, the clergyman was sent for, and also a medical officer, although from neither had I any hope. But, alas! from the former, although a kind and sympathizing man, I derived but little benefit. He did not direct me to the only source of a sin-sick being's hopes, the Lamb of God which taketh away the sins of the world. He made my hopes to centre too much in my own resolutions and after-doings. No doubt, as my sins had been enormous and flagrant, my repentance ought to be proportioned; but when he saw me bowed down under an indescribable sense of guilt, oh! had he, like Paul to the jailer, pointed me to the Saviour, how unutterably precious and acceptable would it have been to my soul! I do not remember that any one character in scripture is described as having felt more fully and more keenly the sinfulness of sin, and of its consequent danger to the soul, than I did at this time. How thankfully would I have accepted the mode of salvation pointed out in the gospel; for indeed I was but too much (as all natural men are) inclined to expect pardon and happiness from the things which, if God spared me, I intended to perform. But He only knows best. This kind gentleman wrote me out prayers, and seemed much interested in my welfare; notwithstanding, the gloom of despair still hung heavy on me, and at length; and when the kind medical friend was enabled, after repeated efforts, to procure me some relief, I felt as if it was only the prolonging of my existence, in order that I might fill up the measure of my iniquity. This, I am now fully persuaded, was a suggestion of the Father of Lies, in hopes probably of prevailing upon me to adopt the awful and miserable resolution of Judas to get rid of life.

I thank God this was the only temptation of that nature which he permitted me to be exercised with; for I felt no inclination even in my darkest hours to commit suicide, fully believing that the utmost of my sufferings here could bear no proportion to those of the damned in hell. I consequently had no inclination to hasten them by rushing into eternity; this, it is evident, was of the merciful goodness of the Lord, and for which I am bound to be truly thankful.

I continued in this state of mind for several months, and could not, with all my reading, praying, and doing, find peace. My reading and praying seemed to me more like an irksome task, than an exercise in which I took delight. I had formed a resolution from the first to retire from the service, where it appeared to me I was exposed to so many temptations; but here the experienced Christian will perceive how erroneous were my views, and I think feel pleased that I never fully effected my purpose, although I made preparations for it. Indeed I could not well feel *certain* that I should act right by retiring from the post to which God's providence had appointed me, although my firm determination was to live devoted to Him. But, alas! how wofully have I failed of maintaining that resolution!

My health now gradually improved, under the kind and fostering attentions of my warm-hearted host and hostess, and it became necessary that I should resume my station at Abrantes, which I did, in hopes of being able to obtain transport from thence, although the army was at this time in the neighbourhood of Madrid. But after returning to Abrantes I suffered a relapse, and was again brought to the borders of the grave, my mind still deeply impressed with my former ill forebodings, although not quite so distressing as before. I got my servant to read to me while I lay groaning on the floor, for I could not bear to sleep in a bed at this time, but felt little comfort from his endeavours, the Scriptures being at this time "a sealed book" to me; so true is it that till the grace of God dispels our darkness we have no light in us.

I think it is probable that some of my readers, on perusing this part of my narrative, will be inclined to say, " surely this man must have been an uncommon and atrocious sinner, above all others, or he never would have suffered thus." I acknowledge with shame that I have been a most abominable and vile sinner, deserving of all the Lord laid upon me, and much more, for I was, and am, fully deserving of hell fire; and should that be my portion (as, through the merits and sufferings of my Saviour, I have a humble hope it will not be), I must acknowledge the kindness and justice of God, although I perish for ever.   But I would say to such readers, as our Saviour said to the Jews, that " except *ye* repent, *ye* shall likewise perish."   Others may be inclined, on the contrary, to say, that all this was merely the effect of disease, and not at all to be resolved into God's hatred of sin and punishment of it in this instance. I acknowledge that it was the effect of disease. But when God laid that disease upon me, He knew what effect it would produce upon my mind ; consequently, both disease and mental agony came from Him ; and, because I knew it came from Him, " I held my tongue and said nothing." And I have now, and I hope shall have for ever, the greatest cause to bless His holy name for this, as one of the greatest mercies He ever showed me, for having thus taught me to know how evil and bitter a thing sin is, and to set a juster estimate upon his favour. He thus taught me also to value and love the Saviour, who alone can deliver me from the punishment, the power, the pollution, and the love of sin, and to make me happy for ever.   Blessed be His holy name, for He has done to me all things well, and I humbly hope to enjoy His favour for ever.

During my stay at Lisbon, my batman, whom I before mentioned as having lost, or rather sold, my mule, and who had here rejoined me to take care of the horse and mule I had with me, either from remorse, or some other cause, made an attempt to cut his throat, and succeeded so far as to sever the windpipe, I believe, but did not quite effect his purpose. He was found in a field near Lisbon bleeding nearly to death, and brought into the hospital, where, with great care, and after some time, he recovered. Indeed 1812 was a sickly year, and many were affected strongly in the mind, several having committed suicide, I believe.

While I lay here ill the second time, I received a letter from the regiment telling me that the paymastership had become vacant, the poor old gentleman with whom I returned to England last year, having come out again to the Peninsula, and got as far as Rodrigo on his way to the regiment, and there, being attacked with the same disease I had suffered so much from, died; and that as General Stewart, our colonel, had arrived at Lisbon, I was to go and wait upon him, and that letters would be written from the regiment requesting him to recommend me for the situation.

I with great difficulty again reached Lisbon, and waited upon the general, but to my great mortification I found the promised letters from the regiment had never been received, and that another person had, in consequence, been recommended, he being the son of the late paymaster, and had applied some time before. My disappointment did not prey upon my mind, for at this time I set very light indeed by the good things of this world, and felt conscious that I already possessed much more than I deserved. I was compelled through illness to remain again in Lisbon some time, but found great difficulty to obtain permission from the commandant for so doing. My general, however, procured

me leave to stay till I should be able to resume my post at
Abrantes. Here, not only myself, but all the officers who
were then in Lisbon, and also at the army, suffered much
from the want of subsistence. I had at this period seven
months' pay due me, and could not obtain a dollar from the
public chest, although I wrote a note to the commandant
showing him how I was suffering from want of money.

The army had in the meantime pursued the French, as
before noticed, on one side to Madrid, and on the other to
Burgos ; but the attempt to take the latter by storm having
failed, and the enemy having been able to assemble a more
numerous force than Lord Wellington had before it, he was
obliged to retire from both those places to the frontiers of
Portugal. The division from Cadiz, the siege of which having
been raised by our forward movement in summer, had joined
the army at Madrid. Much was suffered, I understand,
during this retreat, the troops having been exposed to great
privations, and the weather being exceedingly wet and unpleasant. My division, after the retreat, took up its
quarters again in the villages on the Portuguese side of
Rodrigo—my battalion being stationed at the village of
Espeja. The army, as might be expected from the late
severe and harassing service they had been engaged in,
began to be extremely ill off indeed for want of clothing,
many of the men being nearly quite naked ; in consequence,
the most pressing orders were sent from head-quarters to
use every means possible to have the supplies immediately
forwarded, for Abrantes at this time contained stores belonging to almost every regiment in the army. My health
having been considerably improved, I again returned to
that depot, and, after waiting a few weeks, the means of
transport were at last given me by the commissary there.
I need not say with what alacrity I prepared for and com-

menced my long wished for journey. I had got a sufficient
escort assigned me, from a detachment of our men being
about to join the regiment.

We started about the beginning of January 1813, and
proceeded on our route by way of Niza, &c. I had been
obliged to buy another horse from some cause which I do not
now recollect, but when we were leaving the town just
named, I found, on turning out to move off, that a large
nail had been driven right up into the centre of one of
his feet. Whether this was done accidentally, or by design, I never could learn, but the consequence was the
loss of the horse. I had great trouble also to keep the
convoy, which consisted of about a dozen bullock carts, with
as many soldiers as an escort, together; the drivers, if they
were not strictly guarded, very often made their escape,
taking their bullocks with them during the night, and
leaving the cart in our possession, glad, I dare say, that they
got off so cheaply, for they seemed to have a great antipathy
to go with us. I was therefore compelled to collect them
all together near Castello Branco, and making the soldiers
load their rifles before them, told them as well as I was able
that they had orders to shoot the first who attempted to
desert with his bullocks. This had a good effect, for I believe
we lost no more till we reached the regiment; but, as we
approached the frontiers of Spain, several of the drivers ran
away without their cattle, preferring the loss of both bullocks,
cart, and payment, rather than enter that country, of which
the peasantry in general seemed to have a great dread.
Those who stuck by us to the last, were rewarded with the
bullocks and carts of the deserters; but I think we did not
take more than two or three out of the twelve to the regiment, the rest had all made their escape. Nothing can be
conceived more tiresome than travelling with such a convoy.

The carts are all constructed upon the principle of the Irish car; that is, the axle rolls round with the wheels, they being firmly united; consequently the creaking noise created by the friction is loud and most unpleasant, and they have no idea of grease or tar to diminish this, but believe in many parts, if not in all, the noise to be a sort of holy noise, which keeps the devil from them. I found, in removing these stores, that great robberies had taken place upon them, several of the bales having been opened while on board ship, great quantities of goods taken out, and their place filled up with old transport bedding, &c. I found it necessary, however, to endeavour to bear up against all this, for my mind would not suffer me to dwell too much upon such misfortunes. At length I arrived at the regiment, where indeed I was a welcome guest, for they were greatly in need of all kinds of equipment.

The officer who had rendered my life so unhappy before, had left the regiment, and gone into another far distant from my present place of abode, for which I was truly thankful, and his absence I found produced a great change in my favour; for every one seemed glad to see me, and sympathized with me in my late alarming illness; in fact, the face of things was entirely changed for the better. I myself had benefited much by my late chastisement. I had learned to think meanly of myself, and to be kind and submissive to all to whom I owed submission; a virtue which, I fear, I was but too deficient in before.

All things now went well with me. The goods, which before had been such a source of uneasiness and trouble, were rapidly disposing of, and thus the prospect of my soon being able to pay my creditors became every day brighter. But, in the mean time, what I had hinted at before took place: one of the merchants had actually reported me to his Royal Highness the Duke of York. This might, indeed, have deprived me of my commission, had his Royal Highness been harsh with me; but he caused a letter to be written to my commanding-officer, (now Sir Andrew Barnard,) to call on me to explain why I had not remitted the merchant what I owed him, and to account for my not answering his letters, which he said I had failed to do for several months. My answer was very simple, as the reader is aware; but, with respect to the letters, I showed the colonel one, in which the merchant acknowledged having received one from me a short time previously. This also was satisfactory, and I had moreover remitted him a short while before L.300 of the money I owed him. The colonel was fully satisfied, and wrote off to his Royal Highness accordingly, and I heard no more of the business. Soon after the captain, who had been acting as paymaster, was obliged to return to England, on account of ill health. After some necessary steps I was appointed to this duty, it being an addition of 10s. per diem to my pay. According to the army regulations, a person in my situation could not be appointed acting paymaster; but a committee of three captains was formed, who took all the responsibility of my transactions upon themselves, giving me, as before said, the whole 10s. per diem. This showed, at least, that they were not afraid to trust themselves in my hands; for I might have involved them deeply. In short, whatever I did (almost) prospered, and a kind Providence seemed to smile upon me; and I believe that from this to the close of the Peninsular campaigns was the happiest part of my life. I have reason, therefore, to bless God for his unbounded goodness to me.

CHAPTER IX.

Preparations for the Field—Amusements in winter quarters—Grand Review—Advance of the Army in pursuit of the Enemy—Come up with their rearguard in the vicinity of Hornilla de Camino—Skirmishing—Encounter with the 1st brigade of the Enemy, who are beaten, and forced to retreat—Our Army advance in pursuit—An affair between the rearguard of the Enemy and our 4th Brigade—Vittoria—General Engagement—The Enemy defeated—Remarks.

I BEGIN this chapter, through the mercy and goodness of God, with brighter prospects than any I have written hitherto; for though I was still ignorant of the peculiar doctrines of Christianity, I believed God was at peace with me, and, from my late dreadful sufferings for sin, I certainly walked very circumspectly, and I believe I had also more of the genuine feelings of a Christian, though not the knowledge; for I was lowly in my own eyes, and loved all mankind. In me was fully verified at this time that sublime, but seemingly ill understood, saying of our Saviour's, " Blessed are the meek, for they shall inherit the earth." I now was meek and lowly, and I had friends in abundance, and may truly be said to have possessed or inherited the earth, for I had plenty of every necessary good, and, withal, peace and contentment. I could not enjoy more had I been in possession of more. Alas ! how lamentable is it that chastisement should produce a better effect upon me, than love and gratitude to God is capable of doing ; for, to my shame be it spoken, pride and selfishness now prevail much more in my heart than they were able to do then ; and I find it much more difficult now to bring my mind down to that lowly and contrite feeling which with God is so acceptable, and with the possession of which only He promises to dwell.

As the officer whom I have had occasion so often to mention owed me a trifle of money, I wrote to him, in as friendly a manner as I could, hoping, now we were separated, that his enmity would cease, and I was desirous of being at peace with all mankind ; for, as I said before, I never yet knew why he was my enemy. He wrote back, with an order for the money, telling me, he hoped never to hear from me again, for that. he was anxious to forget that such a person had ever existed in the world. This, as might be supposed, wounded my feelings deeply, but I remembered that I had myself sinned as deeply against God, and that He might raise up such instruments for my correction as seemed good to Him. My feelings, therefore, towards this person were more of regret and pity than of resentment, and I think I did not forget to pray to God for him. Poor fellow, he has a good while since been called to his account, and that in rather an awful manner ; he fell in a duel, but which (from all I could learn) he was engaged in from the best motives, that of endeavouring to prevent the seduction of a young female belonging to his regiment. I hope he is at peace.

During our stay in winter-quarters every exertion was made to put the troops in a proper state to take the field again, so soon as the season was sufficiently advanced. While we remained here also every sort of innocent amusement, at least generally innocent, was had recourse to, both by officers and men, not only to pass the time of inactivity with pleasure, but to keep up that readiness for action always so necessary in a state of warfare. We accordingly had races, balls, plays, and every other description of pastime our situation admitted of. We in Espija established what was termed a *trigger* club, each one in turn giving an entertainment at his house, and at which, as the name would imply, as much game was produced as our sportsmen could procure. The plays were generally held at Gallegos, the quarter of the 43d, and which were indeed got up in a surprising style, considering the means of doing so. A *walking* club was established in our 1st battalion, which was quartered at Alamada ; we were of course frequently favoured with the company of its members, for they thought nothing of setting out, each with a long pole in his hand, and walking twenty or more miles to dinner. Thus harmony and a brotherly feeling was promoted amongst the officers of the division, —a thing of great moment where regiments have to act together, as well as pleasant to all parties. Some of our people also occasionally had a wolf-hunt, for these animals were quite numerous in this part of the country ; nay, so bold were they when pressed with hunger, that they did not scruple sometimes to enter our villages, and devour whatever fell in their way that they could master. An officer of ours had an ass or a mule torn to pieces one night while standing in the yard behind his house. The mode of hunting them was, to have a certain number with arms stationed at the different passes in the wood, whilst a large party of drivers scoured the wood in line, driving every thing before them, when the animals, coming upon the armed people, were shot ; but I do not think they were at all successful : it requires people accustomed to the business to enable them to kill many. There is a premium given for every wolf's head, but I forget how much it is.

I sometimes took a trip to the Azava, or the Agueda, on a fishing excursion ; but I was ill off for fishing tackle : the hooks the Spaniards make are the clumsiest things imaginable, and would not, I am persuaded, be made with less dexterity by the natives of New Zealand. Those which we were forced to use for fly-hooks had a hole or eye at the top, like the crook which you will sometimes see in a butcher's shop, intended to be hung upon another, which was formed by turning the wire down again, and through this they run their line ; besides, they almost invariably broke, and I have been wofully tantalized sometimes by having the hook break off the only fly that the fish were taking ; notwithstanding, I caught some very fine trout in the Agueda, this river abounding with them. I sometimes also caught barbel in that river ; but it was literally swarming with a sort of roach, or what some of our people called rock-fish : they generally feed from some stuff they find on the large stones. But as the season approached which was to call us to the field, a review of the whole division was ordered to take place on the plain of Espija, and which, I think, was as brilliant a spectacle of that description as it was possible for 5000 men to make. Every regiment was in high and complete order, the whole having by this time been fully equipped for the campaign : the movements, too, were beautiful, and executed with great precision and promptitude, and, as might be anticipated, called forth the unqualified approbation of our illustrious Chief.

A new and different arrangement was made this campaign with respect to both officers and men in their field-equipment. Experience had proved that constant bivouacking injured the men's health, as the mode they had adopted last year, though very ingenious, was not calcu-

lated to protect them sufficiently from exposure to the
weather.   They had last campaign been ordered each man
to have loops sewed on at the corner of his blanket ; thus,
when in the field, two of these were united, and spread over
two stand of arms set up at the ends for poles, and being
fastened down at the other corners with bayonets, they formed a sort of tent, into which perhaps four men might creep ;
but then they had thus only two blankets to serve as a bed
for the whole four men ; consequently they would, in cold
weather, be much exposed.   This campaign each company
received four tents ; thus allowing about twenty men for
each, and the officers of each company had one among them,
and the field and staff officers in like proportion.   These
were carried on mules, which before had carried the camp-
kettles ; but these being exchanged for smaller ones, the
men carried them in turns upon their knapsacks.   Thus it
rarely happened that the tents were not on the ground
nearly as soon as the men ; but strict orders were given always to encamp out of sight of the enemy, if practicable,
that they might not be able to calculate our numbers.
How very different from the ancient mode of encamping !
each of which being more like a town laid out with regular
streets, &c. &c. But war was a very different thing in those
days, and could Marlborough have risen to see one of our
straggling and irregular mountain camps, I know not what
his feelings would have been : he would, I fear, have
thought we had sadly degenerated.

All being now ready for opening the campaign, a part of
the army, under Sir Thomas Graham, crossed the Douro
low down in Portugal, and proceeded up the right bank,
while we, with Sir Rowland Hill's corps, moved forward in
the direction of Salamanca and Toro. On the 21st of
May, our division broke up from its cantonments, and

assembled at the village of St Felices el Chico, a few miles
below Ciudad. Rodrigo, each regiment having had the
Agueda to ford in its march to this camp. Our division at
this time consisted of the following corps :—viz. the 1st
brigade, under General Kempt, was composed of the 43d
regiment, 17th Portuguese, and the 1st and 3d battalions of
my regiment ; the 2d brigade, under General Skerrit, contained the 52d regiment, 1st and 3d Portuguese caçadores,
and the 2d battalion of my regiment ; one troop of horse
artillery, under Colonel Ross, was attached to the division ;
the whole being under the command of General Charles
Alten. On the 22d, we moved on to Martin del Rey, near
the river Yeltes, by the side of which we encamped. On
the 23d, we marched to and·encamped near San Munoz,
where the division had, I understand, suffered considerably
during the retreat of last year, from the. French having
gained ground upon them, and severely cannonaded them
from a height near this village. On the 25th, we moved
on to Robliza, having halted the day before to enable the
other division to come up with us. We next morning
moved forward to the little river Valmuzo, a few miles on
the Portugal side of Salamanca, and alluded to in my former
advance. Here we halted for three hours during mid-day
and cooked, and in the afternoon advanced to the ford of
El Canto, on the river Tormes, and about two leagues below Salamanca. Here we encamped for the night, and remained next day also. Lord Wellington, with some cavalry
we understood, had entered Salamanca, where only a small
force of the enemy's cavalry had been found, and which retired immediately ; but I believe some little skirmishing
took place between the parties. On the morning of the
28th we forded the Tormes, and advanced towards Aldea

Nueva de Figuera, which we reached late in the day, the distance being about twenty-four miles.

While we lay at El Canto, a few of our officers visited Salamanca, in hopes of meeting some of their old friends of last year; but not a *viva* greeted their ears on entering the city; a sort of suspicious look of recognition was all they could obtain from those people, who had received us only last summer with such extravagant demonstrations of joy. No doubt they had been made to suffer for their former expressions of attachment to us, for the French had in almost every place their partisans, who doubtless would not fail to give them, on their return, an account of the manner in which the English had been received, and the contributions would be laid on accordingly.

We remained at Aldea from the 28th May to the 2d of June, waiting for information from the corps under Sir Thomas Graham, it being intended to form a junction at or about Toro, where it was expected the enemy had a considerable force; this was distant from us about thirty miles. While we continued here, I took a trip to Sir Rowland Hill's division, where I had a townsman, an officer in the 28th, but had not the satisfaction of seeing him. I had other friends in that division, however, with whom I and my companions spent the day in great harmony and satisfaction, and at evening returned to our camp, about four miles distant, highly gratified.

On the 2d of June, we set off early in the morning, and arrived at Villa Buena about mid-day, where we halted for three hours to cook and refresh, after which we continued our march towards Toro, which we reached in the evening, but the enemy having destroyed the bridge across the Douro at this place, we encamped for the night in some fields on the left bank of the river. We learnt here that the hussars

attached to Sir Thomas Graham's division had attacked a
corps of French cavalry soon after their having quitted Toro,
and with whom a very smart affair had taken place, the
enemy being completely routed, and about 150 prisoners
taken from them. Our cavalry, I believe, lost an officer on
this occasion, who fell into the hands of the enemy.   Nothing could exceed the miserable appearance of the horses
taken from the French on this occasion ; they appeared really
half starved, although at this season there was plenty of
green forage to be had; they must either have been sadly
neglected, or have been doing exceeding hard duty.

The bridge having been rendered passable for the men,
the division crossed on the following morning, the horses
and mules fording the river. We left Toro immediately, and
moved on in pursuit of the enemy, and encamped that night
at Terra Buena.   On the 4th, we reached the convent of
Espinar, and encamped on a height just over it.   It was a
most picturesque and beautiful piece of country around this
convent, but itself appeared to have been lately rendered
uninhabitable.   I believe the monks had been driven away
by the French, but not a soul remained to enquire of; all
about the building was desolation.   We next day advanced
to the village of Muderra, and on the 6th to Amperdia, and
on the 7th we marched through the city of Palentia, and
encamped outside the walls, on the banks of the river Carrion.

Here the inhabitants evinced the same degree of enthusiasm on our entrance as we had been accustomed to witness
in other large towns, till the French had taught them a little more circumspection, and which, the good people of Palentia would have been most probably fully taught, had these
good friends of theirs ever got possession of their city again.
Some time after we had pitched our camp, and were strolling

about the city, the lifeguards entered, and were of course saluted with repeated vivas. One of the men, a rather country-looking young fellow, cried out, " Ay, the folks be always glad to see we lifeguards," happily supposing, no doubt, that they were intended as a particular compliment to his corps alone. All the country through which we had marched for several days past, was one continued plain of waving corn, mostly wheat of the very finest description. There are no hedges or dikes, but, as before noticed, only landmarks to divide the different fields, so that its appearance is like an immense sea, stretching as far as the eye can reach, the long corn undulating with the wind as the waves in the ocean.

On the 8th we marched forward and encamped at the village of Tamara, the weather having, from being exceedingly fine, and indeed rather hot, set in extremely wet and cold, and thus rendered marching very unpleasant. We next day reached La Peña, (the name, it may be remembered, of the Barossa Spanish hero,) the weather continuing very coarse and stormy. On the 10th we continued to advance, and marching through the village of Framosa, and passing over a canal which crosses here, we halted for the night on the right bank of the river Pisuerga, near the village of Lantadilla. In all these late movements, we had experienced a great deficiency of fuel for cooking and drying our clothes when wet, neither forest nor bush-wood being to be seen for days together, and indeed scarcely one solitary tree to be met with—nothing but corn ; so that we were occasionally compelled to resort to the cruel and unchristianlike expedient of pulling down houses to obtain the timber with which they were built for the purpose of cooking, or we must have eaten our food raw. This, however, was done in a regular and systematic order, the Alcalde of the village

I

pointing out such of the houses as were to be doomed to
the fire, and the troops taking no more than was absolutely
necessary.　It is astonishing to me how the natives themselves exist for want of this article of first necessity.

From this village we moved forward on the 11th, and
crossing the Pisuerga, marched on the town of Pallacio,
which we passed, and reached the village of Landrino, near
which we encamped for the night.

From the time we left Toro, the enemy had been gradually retiring before us, having withdrawn his forces from
all the strong places on the Douro, and seemed concentra-
ting somewhere in the direction of Burgos or Vittoria. Excepting our cavalry, no part of our forces ever had the satisfaction of seeing a Frenchman hitherto during the whole
of this long and rapid march ; but on the morning of the
12th, as we now approached Burgos, it was fully expected
that we should be able to get a sight of the fugitives ; and
accordingly, after we had left our last night's quarters, and
marched a few miles in the direction of the city, a pretty
strong body of the enemy's cavalry was seen drawn out on
a high plain, a little above the village of Hornilla de Ca-
miño.　These were supported by a division of infantry
formed in square, and occupying the outer edge of the high
plain facing the way we advanced, and apparently observing
our motions.　On discovering this force, our division was
halted to give the cavalry attached to us time to ride forward to reconnoitre, and ascertain more exactly the force
before us, than could be done while we were on the low
ground.

I rode forward with our cavalry, which, passing by the
enemy's square of infantry, approached the main body of
their cavalry.　It not being, however, the intention of the
French to fight here, they slowly and orderly retired before

us across the plain; but as we had left the square of infantry nearly behind us, the guns attached to our cavalry turned, in that direction, for this body seemed indifferent about the movements of our cavalry, and it was not till our division began to ascend the hill that they evinced the slightest intention of stirring. On seeing them, however, they quickly decamped, and as they had to pass within 150 yards of the position our guns had taken up, I imagined considerable execution must have been done upon them before they got out of our reach. But, strange to say, I believe only one single man was knocked down by the great numbers of shot fired at them. It must have been owing to the relative situations of the two parties; they passed down a hollow way which led from the high plain in the direction of the Burgos road, and which covered them completely till they came immediately below our guns, when it became a difficult matter to depress them so as to bear upon the enemy's square as they passed us. However the whole turned round and gave us a regular volley, for, as we were so much above them, there was no danger from their firing in square; but this, although the shots flew pretty thick about us, was not productive of any mischief that I remember. They retired across the plain below us, pursued by another division of ours which had advanced on our right, and between whom and the French a pretty smart skirmish took place. So soon as their infantry were clear from us, their guns opened out from the opposite side of the river upon us on the height, but, the distance being considerable, their shot did little execution. It was evident this force was only left here as a rearguard, to ascertain our movements and force, &c. We encamped for the night near the road by which we had ascended the high plain; but were awoke early next morning by a tremendous explosion which shook the

earth beneath us, although at the distance of 6 or 7 miles
from Burgos, the castle of which the enemy had blown up,
and retired altogether. We soon after commenced our march,
and, leaving that city to our right, made a long march in the
direction of the Ebro, and halted for the night near the
village of Tovar. The next day we moved on to Quintanajar,
and on the 15th, after a long march, we reached the Ebro,
and halted at the village of Puente Arrenas, situated in the
delightful valley of Veras. This is one of the most
picturesque and beautiful valleys in Europe, I dare say.
When you arrive at the brow of the high ground over the
Ebro, a sight breaks upon you all at once which is indescri-
bably grand and beautiful ;—a large river rolling under you,
beyond which a rich and fertile valley, laden with the fruits
of a hundred orchards, with charming villas and farm-houses
dispersed through all the lawn ; a stupendous bridge, of
I know not how many arches, leading you across this
magnificent river ; and the whole closed by high and beetling
rocks jutting out of the high woody bank on the opposite
side. It really appeared like enchantment when we first
arrived within sight of it, from the long' dreary plains we
had been so long traversing. Here, for the first time since
we entered Spain, did we meet with " manteca de vaca," or
" cow butter," all the other we had been compelled to use
hitherto for want of better, was what they call " manteca
de puerco," or "hog's-lard." The women who brought it
wore a quite different dress from those we had seen in the
parts we had passed through ; the women had on generally
yellow stockings, with abundance of petticoats of red, yellow,
green, &c. &c., and were all very stout-made ; they were, I
believe, from Asturias. Poor creatures, many of them
followed us with loads of butter, wine, cheese, &c. &c., even
into France, so pleased were they with the excellent prices

their merchandise brought amongst us; indeed, we had been so long debarred the enjoyment of butter and cheese, that we would have given almost any price to get them sweet and good. They carried their loads (and tremendous ones they were) as the flesh-wives in Newcastle carry theirs, that is, by passing a broad leather belt across the forehead and over the shoulders, and so underneath the heavy load upon their back. They were a civil and obliging race of beings, and apparently much more industrious and cleanly than the rest of their country people.

We left this delightful spot on the morning of the 16th, following the course of the river upwards for about a league, then turning short to the right, passed through an enclosed country, and halted for the night at the town of Medina del Pomar. This is a considerable-sized place, in which was a nunnery, the inmates of which greeted us with hearty welcomes and vivas, with waving of handkerchiefs, &c., through their strongly iron-grated windows, where they more resembled criminals of the worst description shut up in a strong prison, poor things, than people who had devoted themselves to the service of their Maker. Next morning, we moved forward through a country almost without roads; we were, in fact, crossing the country in order to get nearer to the great road leading from Madrid to Vittoria, and on which the enemy's army was then retiring. We encamped for the night, after a fatiguing day's march, on a woody height near the little river Loza. We took the high ground on this occasion for our encampment, although extremely inconvenient and uncomfortable, being among stumps and brush-wood, where there was scarcely room to pitch our tents; this was in consequence of being in the neighbourhood of a considerable force of the enemy, which was retreating, as before noticed, along the great road.

The next morning, the 18th of June, we started pretty early, and calculating that we should this day come in contact with the above force, we marched in such a manner as to be ready, when that event took place, to take advantage of any favourable circumstances that might offer. We had in our front a squadron of Hussars belonging to the German Legion, and which were generally attached to our division. About mid-day the squadron in front of us reached the village of San Millan, where the road on which we were then marching, and the great road on which the enemy was retreating, unite; the latter descending from a high table-land just above the village, and passing a narrow defile between two high rocks. Our cavalry, on reaching this village, descried the advance of the French, composed also of cavalry; and what was not a little singular, they also were Germans in the French service. Our brave Hussars instantly charged those of the enemy, and immediately overthrew the body opposed to them, and in the charge captured several men and horses, which they brought in prisoners.

By this time the head of the division had reached the spot, (my 1st battalion leading,) which in a few minutes got warmly engaged with the enemy's voltigeurs, a considerable number of whom had advanced to oppose us, in order that the main body of their division might be enabled, under cover of their fire, to pass through the village on the way towards Vittoria. Our people, however, pressed them so hard, that the whole of their leading brigade was obliged to join in the action. At this moment our illustrious Chief came galloping up; for, whenever any thing was to be done, he was always present. He had also taken care to have our 4th division moved so as to arrive at the village of Espija, a town about a league in front of us on the great road, nearly about the same time, so that, should the French contrive to get away

from us, they might fall into their hands. He immediately
sent me off to the leading company of our people who were
engaged, for the guide they had had with them, in order
that he might conduct his lordship to Espija; but that
was no place for a Spanish peasant who had neither honour
nor glory to gain, and he had accordingly made his escape
the moment our folks got into action. His lordship instantly
dashed off without a guide, while our two battalions, that is,
the 1st and 3d of my regiment, kept advancing upon the
enemy, and fairly drove them through the village, being
supported by the other regiments of the brigade, but who
had not any occasion to come into action.

The first brigade of the enemy being thus beaten, retreated along the great road in the direction of Espija, leaving
their second brigade and all their baggage to their fate.
These latter being pressed by our second or rear brigade, and
seeing us in possession of the village, and the road they had
to pass, immediately broke in all directions, and dispersed
themselves in the mountains over the village, each man
making the best of his way. This their baggage could not
do, and it consequently fell into the hands of the captors,
an easy and valuable booty; but although my brigade, by
beating and dispersing the enemy at the village, had been
the principal cause of its capture, yet those whose hands it
fell into had not the generosity to offer the least share of it
to us, but divided it amongst themselves.

During the skirmish in the village, a French hussar
chased one of our officers several times round one of the
trees growing by the side of the road, and repeatedly cut at
him with his sabre, and it is likely would have cut him
down at last, had not the officer seen a rifle lying near, belonging to a man just killed; and luckily it was loaded when
he picked it up. He waited for the Frenchman, and coolly

shot him through the body, and instantly seized his horse as lawful prize; had the rifle missed fire he was gone. We had not rested long after this brush till we heard a firing in our front, where indeed it was expected. The troops which had just left us, I imagine, had been attacked by the 4th division, and we, the 1st brigade, were instantly ordered to their support should they need it; but before we reached Espija, the enemy was completely beaten, and had retired in the direction of Vittoria. We had to retrace our steps and join our other brigade, and encamped for the night in the neighbourhood of San Millan.

Our loss on this occasion was but trifling, considering the smartness of the affair. An officer of my regiment, of the name of Haggup, a countryman of my own, received a most dangerous wound in the abdomen, of which it was feared he would die, but he soon after completely recovered. An aide-de-camp of the French General was wounded, and taken prisoner, but he soon after died, poor fellow. Along with the captured baggage were a number of Spanish ladies, who had been attached to the French officers to whom it belonged, but they did not appear over faithful to their protectors, for most of them, I believe, preferred remaining in the hands of their captors, to being forwarded after their beaten and now ill-provided former companions; such is generally the fidelity to be expected from that sort of people.

On the 19th we advanced by the same road the French had retired, till we reached the town of Salinas, where there were very extensive salt-works, as the name of the place denotes. We encamped for the night near the village of Pobes, on a small rivulet named Bayas, I believe. Near the end of our march to-day we had a view of the enemy's rear-guard, as they rounded the end of a mountain, which lay immediately before us, and over which the road to Vittoria passes. After rounding the mountain, this part of the enemy's force fell in with our 4th division again, which had been moved forward from Espija by another road. A very smart skirmish was the consequence, which we distinctly heard, and in which a good number fell on both sides. The French retired from hence into their position in front of Vittoria. During the next day, while we halted here, it began to be whispered that the enemy had concentrated his forces in and around Vittoria, which was distant from us perhaps about ten or a dozen miles, and that the divisions of our own army had that day approached nearer together, which indicated a determination on the part of our Chief to try his hand with King Joseph, should he be bold enough to stay where he then was.

Many, of course, and various would be the reflections which occupied the minds of the different individuals composing the two armies; but I can speak from experience, that those are of a much more pleasing nature which a consciousness of superiority and a good prospect of success inspires, than those which a retreating army are compelled to entertain.

Pretty early in the morning of the 21st, we fell in and moved forward by the way the French rearguard beforementioned had taken, and after having passed the end of the mountain and descended into the valley on the other side, we saw evident proofs that the affair between our 4th division and the French, above alluded to, must have been pretty warm. We continued to advance on the road to Vittoria, till, on ascending a rising ground, the French army appeared in position immediately in front of us. It was a noble and animating sight, for they appeared as numerous almost as grashoppers, and were posted as nearly as I can recollect in the following order. Immediately before us ran the river Zadora, passing from our left and front to our right and rear: In the centre of an extensive plain rose a pretty lofty conical hill, from which extended to their left a sloping plain, through which the great road lay, and terminated by a long range of mountains, stretching from Puebla de Arlanzon, just above the river, to a considerable distance beyond Vittoria. The city was shut out of our view by the conical hill before mentioned, and was distant from it about four or five miles; to the right of this hill, along the bank of the river, it appeared broken, and not easily approachable. On the face of the conical hill, and to its very summit, it appeared as thickly set with troops as if they had been bees clustering together; it was also thickly studded with . batteries and other field-works. On the plain between that and the long range of mountains, the troops appeared to stand so thick that you might imagine you could walk on their heads. There did not appear any great force on the mountains to their left, and what they had to the right of the conical hill and towards Vittoria we could not discern, but it turned out they had a strong force there. There were several small villages in the plain and on the side of the mountains; the largest stood rather to the right of the plain, with a wood immediately behind it; this, I believe, is called Subijana de Alva. On the bank of the river also were three or four villages, most of them on our side, with a bridge at each village. The French army did not extend immediately to the river bank, but was placed at some little distance beyond it. The river was easily fordable.

Our army began to arrive by divisions, and was posted as follows—General Hill with the 2d division, consisting of about 12,000 men, was on our extreme right, except about 3000 or 4000 Spaniards under General Morillo, who were still more to the right, and facing the long range of mountains before mentioned. In the centre was his lordship with the 3d, 4th, 7th, and light divisions, perhaps 25,000 strong, with the main force of artillery and cavalry. Sir Thomas Graham had been early detached to our left with the 1st and 5th divisions and some Portuguese, about 12,000 in all, to turn the enemy's right flank, and to try to cut him off from the great road leading from Vittoria to France, which ran in that direction.

Whilst this movement was executing, and the different divisions were getting into their several stations, we, who had arrived first, were allowed to pile our arms and sit down. His lordship, with a numerous staff, went down a little nearer to the river to reconnoitre the enemy's position. I wandered down with them, and got as near as I could in order to ascertain the opinion of the big-wigs as to the business about to take place. One staff-officer, after carefully examining the position of the enemy through his glass, gave it as his opinion, that we should scarcely be able to make any impression upon so numerous an army, and so very strongly posted; but this opinion must have been dictated, I think, by his rather desponding temperament, for I believe it was entirely singular.

The enemy, however, did not fail to notice this movement of our General and his staff, and instantly detached a corps of voltigeurs, who, rushing down to the river, dashed across the bridge at the village of Villoses, and immediately took possession of a small woody height on our side of the river, from whence they opened a fire on his lordship and those that were with him. This of course could not be borne; and as my battalion was the leading battalion of the column and nearest at hand, we were ordered (with two companies of our 1st battalion, which stood next to us) to take our arms, and drive those fellows across the river again. Thus we had,

I believe, the high honour of commencing the action on that memorable day. We soon chased the voltigeurs from the woody height, down through the village, and over the bridge, where they took post and remained, we not having orders to pursue them any farther. We took possession of the village, and continued skirmishing with the enemy, a good many men falling on both sides, as the river was not more probably than thirty or forty yards wide, and a constant fire was kept up by both parties till the French were afterwards driven away by our divisions crossing lower down the river.

After we had chased the enemy along the bridge, and they were fairly clear of the village, a French battery, situated a little above the river towards the conical hill, opened its fire upon us, from which we suffered a good deal, one shot having taken our people, who were lining a garden wall, in flank, and swept away five or six at a stroke; after this we kept more under cover.

Almost the first person who fell on our side was a lieutenant of the name of Campbell. He had, I am sure, a strong presentiment of his death, for he had, I believe, made his will the evening before; and when we first came in sight of the French army, and the others were all animated with life and glee at the prospect of gaining laurels in abundance, he, poor fellow, sat down by himself quite pensive, and seemed lost in thought. He received a shot in the forehead which terminated his career in a moment as it were, and plunged him into an eternity of bliss or woe. I hope he was prepared, but scarcely dare say I believe he was. Our duty having been accomplished by taking possession of this village, and keeping the French from coming over, we had now leisure to look round us and see what was going forward and we had certainly a noble field for observation. My commanding-officer, with the rest of the staff-officers and myself, together with half a company of men, took up our station at the church, which, standing high, gave us a fine opportunity of witnessing the movements of both armies.

A short while after we had taken post here, we observed the smoke to arise in dense columns in the direction which Sir Thomas Graham had taken, which showed he had commenced the attack on that flank of the enemy, and this was the signal for commencing operations on our right and centre. Sir Rowland Hill's people, with the Spaniards, instantly forded the river, and advanced along the top and side of the mountains before mentioned; and as this was done in considerable force, it seemed to disconcert King Joseph a good deal, for instantly his aides-de-camp were seen galloping in every direction, and the troops which stood upon the plain began to move in that direction, while those upon the conical hill began to descend in great numbers into the plain. This was precisely what our Chief had calculated upon; and now, by a rapid movement, he threw the centre divisions across the river, by the bridges of Trespuentes and Nanclara, a little below our village, and attacking the remaining troops upon the conical hill, they were overthrown as fast as our divisions reached them. The 2d, Sir Thomas Picton's division, here particularly distinguished itself.

General Hill's people were by this time very warmly engaged, for the enemy having, as stated above, strongly reinforced that point, they made a rather obstinate defence, particularly at the village and wood of Subijana de Alva, which latter was filled with their light troops, and where our 28th regiment, which was opposed to them, suffered considerably, and were not able to make much impression. The action had now become general, and our people on every side advancing; at this moment old Douro, who never failed to

inspire confidence wherever he appeared, came dashing down
into our village, and seeing the light troops which had been
opposed to us had retired, instantly ordered us to advance,
and join our division on the other side of the river. We accordingly moved forward, and marched with all expedition
to reach our point ; but the French had now begun to retire,
and our people to follow them, so that we found it difficult
to overtake them, and did not do so till they had passed the
conical hill.   When we came near that eminence, I rode up
to have a peep at the field before us, and never did I witness
a more interesting and magnificent sight.   A beautiful and
extensive plain lay before me, covered with the cavalry,
infantry, and artillery of the contending armies; while the
noise and din, occasioned by repeated volleys and rolls of fire
from the infantry, with the rattle of upwards of 200 pieces
of artillery, almost stunned the ear. Near the end of this plain,
and to the left, arose the lofty spires of Vittoria; and beyond
that again, the smoke arising from the attack of Sir Thomas
Graham's people added animation to the scene.

I had not contemplated the scene before me above a
minute or two, till a howitzer-shell from the French fell
close at my feet. My horse's bridle was hooked on my arm,
and I was standing looking through my glass; but when this
unwelcome visiter descended so near me, I thought it high
time to be packing. My horse, however, not having the
same fear of the consequences that I had, would not move
but at a snail's pace. I was, therefore, constrained to leave
him to take his chance, and get myself out of the way. It
burst, but providentially without injuring either horse or
man, but in the scramble I lost the top of my glass, which
I could not afterwards find.

I got down the hill, and joined my people, who had by
this time passed it; and just at this juncture I observed a

body of troops a little to our right, moving in the same direction we were. They were dressed in blue, and had caps
covered with white canvass. I took them for Spaniards;
but upon consideration that no Spaniards ought to be there,
and a closer inspection, I found they were a battalion of
French, and most likely those who had been so warmly engaged with the 28th at the village of Subijana, and who
having stood perhaps too long, and afterwards having the
wood to traverse, they had been detained considerably behind the rest of the army; for by this time our advance,
and consequently the French rear, could not be less than
half a mile in front of us. I pointed them out to one of our
lieutenant-colonels; but as we had received orders to push
on with all haste, and he not liking to disobey his orders,
and withal a ravine being between them and us, which
would have prevented our closing with them, they were
allowed to move quietly off, which they did with a pretty
quick but steady pace. Before we reached our division, we
had to pass a village, over against which was a very strong
French battery, and where they peppered us considerably,
but without doing much harm, I believe. We here joined
our brigade. Immediately in front of this village the enemy made one of his longest stands. Our brigade now
formed lines of battalions, and lay down in some ploughed
fields, while their artillery kept playing upon us. On our
left the 3d division was warmly engaged. In about half an
hour we moved in that direction. The 45th we found posted
behind a thin thorn hedge, with its commanding-officer
poor Colonel Ridewood, whom I had known before, lying on
its right, gasping in the agonies of death. A great many men
of this regiment had fallen here. We passed them, and continued to advance along the plain by brigades and battalions;
but we found the ground much intersected with ditches, which

would have retarded us had we wished to advance rapidly;
but from some cause or other, which we could not then
comprehend, we never pressed upon the enemy closely, but
gave them time to get quietly away. We were still, however, in expectation of their making their final stand; for
at every short interval a beautiful little position presented
itself, which the French invariably occupied in the finest
style possible, forming their lines on these little eminences
with the greatest precision, and in beautiful order; but they
never stood to let us get at them, for the moment we began
to come within musket-shot, they instantly began to retire to
another, which they took and abandoned in like manner. All
this time, indeed, there was continual skirmishing going on
between the light troops of the two armies, and a constant
cannonade, and occasionally the heavy lines came in contact;
but their infantry appeared to us to leave the field in the main
unbroken.

We continued these movements till near dark, by which
time we had considerably passed Vittoria, and the enemy's
artillery had nearly ceased. Our cavalry now got at them;
and although, from the nature of the ground, their movements were greatly cramped, yet they continued to charge,
and nearly captured King Joseph. We halted when we had
got about four miles beyond Vittoria, which we passed on
the left hand. We thought we had indeed gained a victory, but it appeared to us to be a most barren and useless one;
and many were not over well pleased that the enemy had
been allowed to get off so easily. But our noble Chief
knew well what he was about, for he reaped all the fruits
from this that could have been possibly gained from the
most bloody battle. Indeed it was far from being a bloodless victory, but he certainly did not sacrifice one half the
men that some in the action would have done: they thought

we should have pressed the enemy far more, and brought him to closer action.

After we halted, I (being the only quartermaster present) was sent in search of the baggage belonging to the division, and which had followed us far as they could along the great road. I passed through Vittoria on my way to the rear in search of it, and saw as I entered it several of Morillo's men, who had descended from the mountains and come into the town. From the vivas and other marks of gratulation which some of the inhabitants were rendering these ragged ruffians, a stranger would have thought that Don Morilhl, with his 3000 or 4000 Spaniards, had achieved the whole victory themselves. It is certain they are a vainglorious people.

I passed through the town, and, taking the great road, I soon had ocular proofs of the value of our day's work; the road being literally blocked up with every description of carriage-guns, tumbrils, waggons, &c. &c. which filled the great high-road for nearly two miles to the rear of Vittoria. I found it difficult to make my way through them, but at last fell in with the baggage; I could not, however, get it through, and was obliged to leave it, after giving directions where to find the division in the morning. I again passed through Vittoria in returning to the division; but oh, what scenes had I now to witness ! The followers of an army are sometimes very numerous, and here they were abundantly so; muleteers, Portuguese and Spanish concubines, with every description of vagabond you can imagine. These were by this time all labouring hard in their avocation of breaking open and plundering the carriages and waggons, &c. that had been left by the enemy. Among these were hundreds of soldiers, who were now beginning to feel the effects of the wine, &c. which they had found in the enemy's baggage ; and such a Babel was here to be witnessed as is not easy to conceive.

I had some difficulty in forcing my way through the town, at the end of which I was accosted by five or six soldiers' wives, belonging to one of our light cavalry regiments, who wished to accompany me, in order that they might find their husbands, as that regiment was attached in some measure to our division. Of course it would have been cruel to refuse them ; and as they were all mounted, away we posted, but had great difficulty to make out where the division now was. Many were the waggons and other carriages we passed on the road, either broken down, upset, or with people plundering them ; and I did not reach the division till 10 o'clock at night. I was very glad when I found them, being then excessively fatigued and hungry ; and just as I reached my people, I found the mess to which I belonged cooking a piece of thin mutton, which they had cut off from a sheep that had been taken from the enemy. This was all the plunder I got that memorable day, although, had I done as many others did, I might have obtained a great deal both of money and other valuables ; for, as I said before, the numerous carriages I passed gave me an opportunity which many would have rejoiced at of possessing myself of immense wealth ; but plundering never was my forte. One officer whom I knew got, I believe, near L.1000 worth of money, and other valuable property ; and innumerable others got considerable sums, more or less. I am glad now that I refrained from what *might* have been accomplished with ease and safety, but what also *might* have entailed upon me disgrace and ruin. One officer I heard of, who, while in the rear, where he ought not to have been, found a box full of money, most likely silver, but very heavy. A German dragoon coming up at the same moment laid claim to half of it, and when this officer took hold of it to remove it, the German also laid hold to prevent him. A sort of scuffle ensued, when the German made use of most abusive and mutinous language, with threats, which the officer was obliged to submit to, knowing, as both of them did, how far he had descended from his station, thus putting it in the power of the soldier to treat him as a brother plunderer. Surely the mention of such an occurrence is enough to deter any man who possesses the least spark of honour from ever putting it in the power of a soldier to treat him so. Besides, if an officer plunders before his men, what may not soldiers be expected to do?

In looking back upon the events of this day, I cannot help being struck with the bad generalship of those who commanded the French army. Marshal Jourdan, I understand, was Joseph's adviser on this occasion. He had always borne the character of an able General, but here he showed but little ability. Why did he so much weaken his force on the conical hill to support his left? Had he maintained his ground there, which is strong by nature, and they had rendered it stronger by art, he might have completely checked us on the right; for if we had advanced too far on that side, our wings would have been separated, which would have been a dangerous experiment; and I think Lord Wellington would not have hazarded it. And after leaving his first position, why did he not fight at every one of the beautiful little positions which he afterwards took up but never defended? This conduct is most unaccountable, for had he made a longer stand, even although he should be beaten, which no doubt he would have ultimately been, yet, by making this stand, he might have got off the greater part of his materiél, instead of which he carried off with him one gun and one howitzer only, leaving upwards of 250

pieces of ordnance in our hands. Most of his infantry left
the field apparently unbroken ; for only here and there they
had stood to let our people get at them. It is true Sir
Thomas Graham early cut off their retreat by the great road
to France ; but what then ? This ought to have made them
fight the more desperately, to enable them to get off the better
by the Pamplona road. The infantry should have stood
till the last, and not retired till fairly beaten out of the field.
Nothing could be finer than the movements of our army.

Every thing our Chief attempted succeeded to a tittle.
The only thing I did not like was the delay we occasionally
made in following up the enemy ; but I could not, of course,
comprehend the general movements, from seeing only a
small part of them, and I believe the victory would not have
been more decisive by being more bloody. We lost in the
village, where we first began the fight, nearly thirty men, with
the officer before mentioned as killed, and a considerable
number wounded. There was something remarkable in the
fate of one of the men who were killed by the cannon-shot
I before noticed. This man was remarkably averse to fighting, and had shown, on all occasions, a disposition to leave
that kind of work as soon as practicable. Poor fellow ! his
failing was known to all ; and on this occasion those about
him had orders to watch him, and keep him to his duty.
They had not been in the village many minutes when this
fatal shot swept him and about five others into eternity in
a moment. It has often been remarked, that this description
of people are generally the first to fall.

It may not be generally known, perhaps, that a battle
was fought on the 3d April 1367, a little higher up this
river, near the village of Novarete, between our Edward the
Black Prince, and Henry the Bastard, who had usurped the
throne of Don Pedro, King of Castile. The history of it is

given by Froissart, who says, " a little before the two armies met, the Prince of Wales, with eyes and hands uplifted towards heaven, exclaimed, ' God of truth, the Father of Jesus Christ, who hast made and fashioned me, grant, through thy benign grace, that the success of this battle may be for me and my army ; for thou knowest that in truth I have been emboldened to undertake it in the support of justice and reason, to reinstate the king upon his throne, who has been disinherited and driven from it, as well as from his country.' " This zealous prayer was immediately followed by the onset, the Prince crying aloud, " Advance banners, in the name of God and St George !"

" At the commencement," says Froissart, " the French and Arragonese made a desperate resistance, and gave the good knights of England much trouble ; but at last, when all the divisions of the Prince were formed into one large body, the enemy could no longer keep their ground, but began to fly in great disorder ; and Henry, the usurper, perceiving his army defeated, without hope of recovery, called for his horse, mounted it, and galloped off among the crowd of runaways. The English pursued them through the town of Najara, where they gained considerable plunder ; for King Henry and his army had come thither with much splendour, and after the defeat they had not leisure to return to place in security what they had left behind them in the morning."

There is a striking coincidence in many parts of the two actions and their consequences, which the reader cannot fail to notice. The most material difference, I think, in the two stories is, the offering up of the prayer by the Prince, and the modern practice of not recognising, publicly at least, the hand of God at all in any of our victories. This is to be lamented.

CHAPTER X.

Advance in pursuit of the Enemy—Our Forces retreat, in order to counteract Soult's movements for the succour of Pamplona—Total defeat of Soult in the several Actions near Pamplona—Our Forces again advance—Come up with the retreating Enemy at the Bridge of Yanzi—The Enemy take up a position behind Vera—A considerable body of the Enemy attacked at the Pass of Eschallar, and forced to retreat.

WE remained in bivouack all night where the battle had terminated ; and did not begin to move till near mid-day on the 22d, when we set off in the track of the enemy, and at night reached Salvatiera, where King Joseph had slept the night after the action.

The poor beaten French must have had a long march after the fight, for this was probably sixteen or eighteen miles from Vittoria. We started early on the morning of the 23d, and very soon began to overtake the rear of the enemy. They now resorted to a system of retarding our march, at once both cruel and cowardly ; every village they passed through they set on fire. Of course this caused us some delay, as the road generally ran through the middle of the village, and the country on each side was enclosed, but still nothing could justify such barbarity to the unoffending natives, who were thus deprived of house and home, and probably all they possessed in the world. We overtook their rearguard near a village about two leagues from Salvatiera. They attempted to make a stand while the village was in flames, but a shrapnell shell from our horse artillery set them instantly in motion. We came upon a considerable body of them again near the village of La Cunca, where we again cannonaded them, and where our people had some slight skirmishing with their rear.

We encamped for the night near this village, and again started after them in the morning early. My battalion led the column to-day, the post of honour. We had marched, I think, about eight or ten miles without overtaking any of the flying foe before us, but at last we came to an open country, that which we had traversed being pretty thickly enclosed, with bad roads and wet weather, which rendered marching very uncomfortable. Here a halt was ordered, as the enemy was in front in some force ; here for the first time we got upon the great road leading from Pamplona towards Bayonne; and here, where it turned the corner of a mountain, forming a pretty acute angle, they had the only gun and howitzer they had saved from the fight in position, and ready to receive us. The men of my battalion, and a part of our 1st battalion, were ordered to put their knapsacks up behind the hussars of the German Legion, as it was not expected they would be wanted, and it thus rendered our people better able to run. The enemy appeared to have two battalions here, one of which remained on the great road near the two pieces of artillery, while the other moved off more to our right, down a valley which they imagined would, at the other end, let them out into the great road again.

We now began to move forward, and as I happened to be the first mounted person who left the enclosed road we had been in, I was honoured with the first shot from their gun, which, although a good shot, did me no injury. Our people

now pushed on at them pretty smartly, which caused them,
after firing a round or two more, to limber up and retire
with their artillery, though they of course retired as leisurely
as possible, to give time for their troops, whom they were covering, to get away. The skirmishing between them and our
people continued for about two miles, they gradually retiring
before us; but when they came to a sort of pass in the road,
formed by two rocks nearly meeting in the middle, their
bugles or trumpets sounded first the halt to their troops,
and afterwards the advance upon us. We could not comprehend the meaning of this, till in a few minutes the battalion
which we had observed go down towards the right, suddenly made its appearance out of a wood among our skirmishers. Of course a sharp contest now took place, and the firing
on both sides became more brisk; this battalion, it appears,
had miscalculated on getting out of the valley, down which
it had retired, and had been compelled, at whatever risk, to
make the great road again before they passed the rocks before mentioned; and in order to let it do so, the other skir.
mishers had advanced to cover its movement. This battalion suffered considerably before it reached the road, and we
did not get off scot-free, having lost out of our five companies about twenty-four men.

Our artillery being pretty near at hand, Colonel Ross
brought up two guns, and fired into their retreating column,
doing considerable execution. We now moved forward in
close pursuit of the enemy for about two miles farther, when
a shot from Colonel Ross's guns having struck one of the
leaders in their gun, and our people at this time pressing
them so closely as not to give time to disentangle the dead
horse, they unwillingly were compelled to throw their only
gun into the ditch, and there abandon it. We continued
the pursuit till we drove them under the walls of Pamplo-

na, which I understand, poor wretches, they were not allowed to enter, on account of the scarcity of provisions in that fortress, and which after events proved was the case. We retired to the village of Aldava and others in the neighbourhood, where we remained for the night.

On the morning of the 25th, we advanced on the road to Pamplona, the enemy having all retired towards France, till we came within about one mile and a half of it, when we branched off to the left, and moved along a range of hills at about a mile distant from the works of the place, till we reached the town of Villaba, on the mountain-road from Pamplona to France; thus cutting off all retreat from the garrison, and thus in fact investing the place. During our movements to-day, my people being in the rear of the 17th Portuguese regiment, I was riding in company with my commanding-officer at the head of the battalion, when the horse of the Portuguese major threw out with both his hind feet with all his might, and struck me with one foot on my thigh, and the other on the calf of the leg. The blow was so severe that I nearly fainted, and was obliged to dismount and throw myself on the ground; but as no bones were broken, I gathered myself up again, and mounted and set off after the troops.

We encamped on the Pamplona side of Villaba, distant from the former about one mile and a half. The captain in whose mess I was, with his company, was that night ordered on picquet with in about three quarters of a mile of the city. I went there to get my dinner, during which several poor people, who had made their escape from the place, came and welcomed us in the name of the people, telling us they were heartily tired of their present lodgers; of course there would be different opinions among them, but I believe the generality at that time hated the French most cordially.

K

There was a division of the French army under General Clausel, which had not partaken of the flight at Vittoria, being then stationed at Logrona, and he having learnt the fate of his companions in arms, and their retreat into France, was moving through the country to our right, in order to effect his retreat also. Next morning, therefore, the 3d and our divisions were despatched in pursuit of this French corps. We marched that day to near Taffala, and halted at the village of Muro, at the junction of the great road from Logrona with that we now occupied, but we learnt that Clausel had kept more to his right, and was directing his course towards the mountain-road, which passes near Caceda and Languessa, into France.

We accordingly passed through Taffala and Olite, and encamped for the night. Next day we started early, and moved on till mid-day, when we halted for an hour or two to cook and refresh near the village of Murillo del Fruto. We here came upon the river Arragon. This had been already a long day's march, and the greater part of the division were ready to lie down now, but a much longer portion still remained to be accomplished. Accordingly, we set off after a short rest, and traversed the right bank of this river for about ten hours longer. Night marches at all times are unpleasant, but much more so on such a road or path as this was, and every one so nearly tired before beginning it.

We crossed the Arragon at the village of Galla Pienzo, and lay down in a field not far from the village of Caseda. Very few of the division reached this place until daylight next morning. But when I got in I unfortunately lay down on a ridge immediately behind our column, and where, had I given it a thought, I was continually liable to be disturbed. And indeed I was most wofully disturbed, for every fresh batch that came in tumbled themselves down upon me, or in blundering about in the dark were sure to stumble over me. It must be observed that my leg by this time, instead of getting better, had begun to swell dreadfully and to suppurate, consequently I was in a high state of fever; and to the thumps and kicks which I received in the dark during this uncomfortable night, I cannot but attribute much of my subsequent suffering.   Next morning we discovered that all our labour had been in vain, for Clausel had got the start of us, and had got off by another road into France.

We next day moved into Languessa, from which we were not far distant, but I could no longer accompany or precede the troops, my leg was now so bad. I was therefore obliged to get a pillow laid on my holsters, and then ride with my leg resting upon it, (a most uncomfortable position, could I have found a better,) while one of my men led my horse, and thus follow them as well as I was able.   We rested in Languessa all the 30th and 1st July; and on the 2d reached Deriza, having passed through Monreal.   Here I was obliged to be lifted off my horse, and put to bed. I was almost stupid from the pain I suffered; for my leg was now swoln as large as my thigh.   We next day moved into Villaba, from whence we had started in pursuit of Clausel, and thence into some villages on the plain, close to Pamplona.   Here I believe some works were thrown up to shelter the troops, either against the shot from the fortress, or a sally from the garrison.   This continued all next day. I remained very ill in bed.

On the 5th, the division left this quarter, and set off on the road towards France; but I could not follow them.   I got with great difficulty from my present station, which was now occupied by other troops, and stopped at a village, the name of which I forget, just over the ridge where I received my hurt, and a few miles distant from Villaba.

Here I found out that Dr Jones of the 40th regiment was in the latter town; and, as he had formerly been in our regiment, I took the liberty of requesting he would come and see me. This I found out by my servant going in for provisions. He very kindly came, and gave me the best advice he could. By this time my leg had burst, and had discharged a prodigious quantity of matter.

I remained in this village till about the 10th, during which time a priest had shown himself remarkably kind and attentive; there were very few inhabitants remaining besides him. He told me in one of the conversations that I had with him, that, from the first entry of the French troops into this country, one million had passed out of France into Spain, for he had had good opportunities of making a just calculation; and that, out of that vast number, not more than 200,000 had returned, thus proving that the enemy had lost in that country 800,000 men. And this is not to be wondered at, for nearly the whole population during that time had been in arms against them; and, although not acting as soldiers in the field, they never failed to assassinate the French wherever they could accomplish it. He said, moreover, that Mina, with his little band, could produce documents to prove that he had destroyed 40,000 Frenchmen.

About the 10th, I set off from this village, as my leg had by this time become somewhat easier; and, passing through Lantz, Elizonda, and St Estevan, arrived at Sumbilla on the 13th, still obliged to ride sideways with my leg over the pillow and holster. Here I found my division; and, as this journey had again brought my leg to nearly as bad a state as before, I was obliged to have it opened in two places, but without reaching the matter, as nothing but blood was discharged.

On the 15th, my division moved forward to the town of

Vera, the last town on the Spanish frontier. Here the enemy had taken up a strong position, both in front and rear of the town; the front position was on Santa Barbara, an exceeding high and almost inaccessible mountain. They were dislodged from the position before the town by my brigade, and retired into the Puerta, or Pass of Vera. I was not present on this occasion, having been again compelled to stay behind on account of my leg. While I remained at Sumbilla, I had been obliged to have my horse shod by a Spanish blacksmith, who drove a nail right into the quick. This I did not discover till several days after, when I found my horse quite lame.

On the 18th, I again crept on after my people, whom I found encamped on the height of Santa Barbara, from which I before said they had driven the enemy. Here we remained till the 26th. During this time my horse's foot had also suppurated, and he was quite unable to move. My leg also was daily discharging a vast quantity of matter, so that I felt at this time very uncomfortable; particularly as very stormy weather came on while we were here, which killed a great number of our animals, horses and mules, I believe not fewer than seven or eight in one night.

It will be known to the reader, perhaps, that on the 25th, Soult (who had now been appointed to the command of the French army) made an attack upon our posts at Ronces-valles and Maya, and had driven the divisions stationed there from their posts. He moved on towards Pamplona, in hopes either of beating back our army to Vittoria, (as he vainly talked,) or of being able to supply Pamplona with provisions, which it greatly needed. In consequence of this movement of the enemy, we also were compelled to fall back, although the troops in front of us made no de-monstration of advancing.

Accordingly, on the 26th, we began our retrograde movement, being myself at that time in as pitiable a plight as can
well be conceived.   My horse was so utterly lame, that he
could scarcely hop on three legs, while I was totally unable
to walk a step.   My kind friend Captain Perceval, with
whom I had long messed, helped me out of my trouble, by
dividing the load of one of his baggage-ponies among the
other animals, and lending it me to ride upon. We retired
from the height, and crossed the river Bidassoa, near Lizacca,
through which we passed, and kept along the mountains on
the left bank of that river till we reached a height opposite
Sumbilla, where we pitched our tents, and remained for the
night.   We did not move all next day ; but just as night
set in, we were ordered under arms, and continued our
retreat.   This was a still more distressing night-march
than any I had previously witnessed.

We were now, it may be noticed, in the midst of the
mountains of the Pyrenees, where precipices abound ; consequently the precaution to avoid falling over them would be
doubled.   One little streamlet, I well remember, delayed
the division probably two hours.   It came down from the
sides of the mountain which overhung the road, and crossed
it at a very dark and ugly-looking place, making a considerable noise as it fell from rock to rock.   This of course
made every one extremely cautious ; and in consequence a
poor good-natured corporal, who was killed soon after, got
himself into the middle of the streamlet, and took hold of
every person's hand as he passed, conducting him safely to
the other side.   Poor fellow, he was extremely anxious to
help me and my miserable little pony safely over.   This
and a few other places, something similar, prevented us
reaching our destination till an hour after daylight next

morning, although the whole distance was not more than ten miles.

We arrived at Zubietta in the morning. This place is about a league to the right of St Estevan, more into the mountains. Here we remained that day, and the next day moved higher up the mountain, behind the town, where we encamped, and remained till evening, when we again commenced our retreat. We had not quite so bad a march of it this night, the road being much more even, although, just at the outset, our adjutant, in riding along, had his cap pulled off by the bough of a tree, and in endeavouring to save it from falling, he pulled his horse right over a small precipice, which the two rolled down together. Luckily it was not a deep ravine into which he fell, or he would not have escaped so well : neither man nor horse were much hurt. We reached the village of Saldias in the morning, where we remained for the day. Last night my servant told me he had been obliged to leave my little horse behind, as he could not get him to hop any farther. I felt grieved at this, for he had brought me all the way from Lisbon, and shared both my good and bad fortune ; however, it was no use to fret, for that would not improve my situation, which indeed was not an enviable one, my leg all this time being extremely painful.

On the 30th, we made an excessively long march, (by day,) and at night reached Lecumberg, where we encamped. During the latter part of this day's march, we had heard an incessant cannonade and firing of musketry in the direction of Pamplona, from which we were apprehensive that Soult had penetrated too far ; but as it did not appear to recede, we believed our people had been able to hold him in check at least. We were now on the great road from Bayonne to Pamplona, in order to keep up the communication between

our right, where the fighting was now going on, and Sir
Thomas Graham, who was besieging St Sebastian. We were
here also to intercept any of the enemy's columns that
might either advance or retreat by this road.   Towards
evening of the 31st, an aide-de-camp arrived from Lord
Wellington, more dead than alive from the excessive fatigue
which he had undergone for the last three or four days, with
news of the total defeat of Soult in the several actions near-
Pamplona, termed the Battle of the Pyrenees, and ordering
us to retrace our steps, and again advance.   We set off in
the evening, and reached Larissa, where we halted for the
night. It was whispered that it was expected we should
have gone much farther this night, but I am not certain
whether it is true ; but certainly we might have proceeded
to Saldias, if absolutely necessary.

On the morning of the 1st of August, we again started
pretty early.   It was again reported this morning that another dispatch had been received during the night, directing
us to proceed with all haste, as the enemy were retreating
by St Estevan, and that we were to attack them wherever
we met them.   We now of course stepped out very freely,
and presently gained Zubietta.   Here I had ridden forward
to get a shoe fastened on, my horse having cast one in
coming over the mountains ; during which time the quartermaster had been called for some purpose or other, as I was
not there.

My General was not well satisfied : he saw me in this
village, and asked me why I had not been present when I
was wanted.   I told him the cause, but he still did not appear satisfied, and, by way of punishment, directed me to remain in the village till the baggage came up, and show them
the way the division had gone.   I may here observe, that
it was a little unreasonable in my General to find any fault

with me on this occasion ; for, had I not got the shoe put on
my horse, I could not have been of any use at all as a quartermaster.   My punishment indeed was slight, and I rather
think he was glad to find any excuse to delay me for the purpose for which I was left.   I am confident the officers of
the infantry suffered more anxiety and even loss on account
of the great want of farriers or horse-shoers in their regiments, than from almost any other cause.   Without the
officer was pretty high in rank, he had not only to pay most
exorbitantly for any thing of this kind which he got done,
but to beg and pray, and to look upon it as a favour conferred on him.   Most of the good shoers were taken by the
staff or general officers, consequently only the inferior ones
were left for the regimental officers, and in several cases
none at all.   The consequence of all this was, the loss of
several valuable animals, both horses and mules ; besides, in
some cases, the officers being rendered incapable of performing their duty as they otherwise would have done.   To this
I attribute a considerable loss in animals during this service.
It might easily be remedied by each infantry regiment having
a proper establishment of farriers, (say two,) with tools, &c.
in proportion, and the means of carrying them ; and then
every officer, whose duty requires him to be mounted, might
be served.   I myself bought tools to the amount of L.4, and
never had but one horse shod with them.   I could not get
a man to do it.   As soon as I saw the baggage on the right
way, I pushed forward, and joined the division again.   We
were literally at this time climbing up a mountain, where I
could not ride, but was obliged to crawl up, and pull my
horse after me.   My leg by this time had much improved.
We followed the road by which we had retreated a few days
before, and at length came to the rivulet that had so alarmed us all on our night-march.   It was really surprising that

we should have been stopped so long by such a trifle; but
in such a situation, and at such a time, things of that kind
are magnified a thousandfold by the imagination. We
passed our old camp ground opposite to Sumbilla, and here
we came in view of the enemy's columns retreating along
the road on the opposite bank of the Bidassoa. This gave
our men new life; but here the 52d and other regiments of
the 2d brigade were obliged to halt: they could proceed no
farther.

'We had marched by this time to-day two and a half of
the stages we made in retreating; but the 2d brigade had
been in the rear of the column all day, and had consequently
suffered much from stoppages, &c. My battalion, our 1st
battalion, and the 43d regiment, continued to move on, and
as they approached, the enemy seemed to acquire fresh
vigour. At length we reached the point of attack,—the
bridge of Yanzi,—and here the 1st battalion turning down
towards the river, at once left the wood and ground above
the bridge to be occupied by us. The enemy sent a pretty
strong corps of light troops across, which got engaged with
our people; but we soon drove down through the wood
again towards the bridge. At length, we got two companies posted just over the bridge, in front of which all the
rear of the French column had to pass. Poor creatures! they
became so alarmed, that they instantly began to cut away,
and cast off, all the loads of baggage, and both cavalry and
infantry, &c. to make the best of their way. But the
mountain on their right was inaccessible; consequently they
had all, as it were, to run the gauntlet. Great was the execution done amongst the enemy at this bridge, and many
were the schemes they tried to avoid passing. At length
they got a battalion up behind a stone wall above the road, on
the opposite side, from whose fire we received some damage;

consequently those poor people who had afterwards to pass were not so much exposed. Just about the close of the business, my kind friend, Captain Perceval, received a shot through his right wrist. His left hand had been closed for a length of time before, in consequence of a wound through that wrist, which had contracted his fingers, besides being lame from a wound in the hip. Now he was rendered completely useless. Towards dusk I went with him a little to the rear, and got his tent pitched, and made as comfortable as circumstances would admit. I pitied the French on this occasion, they seemed so much alarmed. The whole of their baggage fell into the hands of our 4th division, who were closely following them up on their side of the Bidassoa.

In this affair, the French were reduced to a dreadful dilemma; great numbers of their wounded had been brought off from the battles of the 28th, 29th, and 30th, near Pamplona, which were carried on biers or stretches by men of this division. When they saw us in front of them, where they had to pass, as it were, immediately under the muzzles of our pieces, they were compelled to adopt the cruel alternative of either throwing their wounded men down to perish, or run the risk of being shot or taken themselves. I believe the former, shocking as it seems, was generally adopted; and I have reason to believe that the greater part of them were thrown into the river; for, from the point where we first came in view of them to near where this affair took place, the Bidassoa was literally filled with the dead bodies of Frenchmen, and they could have come into it in no other way. We lost only a very few men on this occasion, not more than six or eight, while that of the enemy must have been extremely severe. Here the effects of rifle-shooting were plainly visible.

In remarking on this affair, I beg to draw the reader's attention to the following circumstances; viz. probably never troops made such a march over such a country before. We travelled at least thirty-two miles over mountains such as I before described, where you were sometimes nearly obliged to scramble upon your hands and knees. The day was exceedingly hot, and occasionally there was a great want of water. I am told that one of the regiments in our 2d brigade, which, it may be remembered, were obliged to halt, as they could go no farther, had no less than 200 men fell out, unable to keep up, and that some of them actually died of fatigue. I heard of one poor fellow, who, when he came to water and had drunk, lost his senses, fell to the ground, and shortly after expired. I have reason to be proud of my battalion on this occasion, which, when the roll was called, just before the action commenced, had only nine men fallen out; but they had been in the front all day, a great advantage in marching, particularly over a mountainous country.

This day's work gave me a higher idea of the powers of human nature, when properly trained, than ever I possessed before; for when you consider that each of those soldiers carried a weight of not less probably than forty or fifty lbs. and some much more, it cannot but be surprising that men should be able to sustain such fatigue for such a length of time—at the end of which to fight, and gain a victory.

Next morning were clearly observable the effects of the evening's work. In the house, the yard, and on the road opposite the bridge, were a great number of dead Frenchmen; and to the rear, by the way they had advanced, the road was literally strewed with baggage, and equipments of every description. Some of our people picked up a number of visiting cards, with General Vandermason on them, very elegant; so that his baggage, no doubt, had been cast off, as well as that of inferior people.

Soon after daylight, we were ordered to fall in, and move forward towards Vera. Just as we cleared the bridge, old Douro, with his staff, came riding up, who, when he saw how we had handled the enemy the night before, gave his head a significant nod, and smiled, which conveyed most intelligibly his approbation. We soon reached the neighbourhood of Vera, behind which, in the pass of that name, as before stated, the enemy took up a strong position, from which their picquets had never yet been driven. We were ordered to encamp a little below the bridge leading to Lezacca, between that and Vera, while the other regiments were intended to occupy the heights of Santa Barbara, from which we had before retreated. But towards mid-day it was discovered that the enemy still had a considerable body of troops in and about the pass of Echallar, a few miles to our right. Our brigade was therefore ordered again under arms, with the intention of co-operating with the 7th division in an attack upon those people. It was a thick mist, so that we could scarcely see twenty yards before us; but when we reached the bottom of an immensely high hill, on which the enemy were posted, we presently discovered whereabouts we had them.

Our 1st battalion extended to the right, and my battalion moved straight forward up the hill. For a considerable time the enemy's fire did us no injury, being deceived, I imagine, by the denseness of the fog. They fired almost always over our heads, some of which shots struck the men of the 43d, a considerable way below us. At length we began to approach the summit of the mountain, where the enemy were of course much more condensed, the ground they had to occupy being much smaller. Our people were advancing regularly up the hill, when we run right up against a rock, on the top of which was collected an immense body of the French, and from whom our people received a most destructive fire, knocking down fourteen men in an instant.   This unlooked-for circumstance checked our people, and made some of them retire for an instant behind a broken part in the mountain, from which they kept up the best fire they could.   During this transaction, the French, who were not more than ten or twelve yards distant, were calling out to us in Spanish to advance, and abusing us most lustily.   A Spaniard (one of the recruits I formerly mentioned) was so much annoyed, that he began in his turn to abuse the French ; and, as if words were not enough, accompanying them with the best shot he could give them. Poor fellow, he was instantly shot through the body, and fell to rise no more.

They now began to get courage, and made a show of advancing upon us : they did do so on the right against our 1st battalion, but my commanding-officer calling out to cheer our people, set up a shout, which had the effect of intimidating them, and they did not dare to advance. I was now sent away by Colonel Barnard to request the 43d (who were behind us) to send a company to support our 1st battalion, which they instantly did ; and just as I returned, I found the French had evacuated the rock from which they had annoyed us, on the top of which we found a great number of caps and pouches, &c., belonging to men who had fallen there.   We followed them over the hill, but they now gave us leg-bail, posting down into the valley towards France with all expedition.

The 7th division had some pretty sharp work before they dislodged the people in front of them, and had suffered very severely in effecting their object.   When every thing was

settled, one of our men thought he saw a man hiding behind a tree just below us : he went to see what it was, and
dragged out by the neck a French soldier of the 2d light
infantry. Poor fellow, he came out shrugging his shoulders,
and, putting on a most beseeching look, begged we would
spare him, as he was only a " pauvre Italien." Of course
no injury was done him, only the soldier who took him
claiming and taking from him his knapsack, which appeared a fine full one, and which he appropriated to himself. I
thought it cruel, and would have prevented it, had my voice
been of any weight ; and yet, had it not been taken from
him now, it would very soon after, when he became a
prisoner.

One battalion was ordered to remain and occupy this
hill, which dreadfully alarmed me, lest it should be ours,
for it was bitter, bleak, and cold. Luckily a Portuguese
battalion was ordered up, and we returned to our snug
camp by the river side ; and here, as if to crown our good
fortune, one of our men, who had been left behind in
charge of the tents, had got some meat roasted for our
mess, of which we all partook with great delight and thankfulness.

A friend of mine of our 1st battalion, during the advance the French had made upon that battalion, was nigh
falling into their hands. They rushed at him, but he perceiving, and endeavouring to avoid them, fell into a bush,
which scratched him most wofully, and in the fray lost his
cap and sword. They grasped at the latter, (which was
not drawn,) but which luckily broke loose from the belt, or
they would have had him. This hill was always known
afterwards by the name of Barnard's Hill, in honour of
Colonel Barnard, who commanded on the occasion.

CHAPTER XI.

The Author, from a mistake, loses his Servants for a few days—A Feast of Death—A Feast of Life—Fighting near St Sebastian—Singular instance of Spanish Bravery—St Sebastian is captured, but no Details given, the Author not having been present—Attack of the Pass of Vera.

WE remained at rest here for some time, during which I, as acting paymaster, had several trips to Tolosa, a considerable town on the great road from Bayonne to Madrid, where the paymaster-general had taken up his residence with the military chest. In one of them I went and had a peep at St Sebastian, the siege of which was then going on. While here, I received directions from General Sir William Stewart to attend him at Villaba, where he lay wounded, he having received two balls in the late actions. I set off, directing my servants with my baggage to follow close after me: by some means they were delayed a few minutes, and, supposing I was going again to the paymaster-general at Tolosa, went off in that direction, without asking any questions. I imagined they knew very well where I was going, and still went on slowly, every now and then looking back to see if I could descry them coming ; but although there was no appearance of them, I simply enough continued my route till I reached St Estevan ; and here I put up for the night, thinking, of course, they would come by and by. In the morning, I was fully convinced they must have gone some other road, and as all my books, &c., from which I wanted information, were in my baggage, I thought it useless to proceed any farther. In retracing my steps, which I did leisurely, I had an opportunity of seeing the great number of bodies which the French had thrown into the river, the road running close by its brink nearly all the way. It was really shocking to behold such numerous wrecks of mortality, with the disgusting appearance which most of them had assumed ; many of them were half eaten by the fish, and of others the flesh was hanging in rags, and bleaching in the stream. Of course I returned home, but did not see my servants again for several days, as it took three or four to accomplish the journey to Tolosa and back, and they had waited there a day for me.

On the day that I was absent, all the officers of my corps had had a sumptuous and splendid entertainment, it being the 25th August, the anniversary of the regiment's first formation. They had dug a ditch in an oblong shape in the middle of a field, the centre of which served for a table, while they sat with their feet in the ditch. I am told the French, who were just above, and overlooked them from the heights behind the town, assembled and viewed them, as if in astonishment to see them regaling themselves with so much glee in the midst of the wild Pyrenean mountains. No doubt the wine went merrily round, and many were the toasts which were drunk with three-times-three.

During this interval, I often amused myself with fishing
in the Bidassoa, in which there were many excellent trout,
and I was pretty successful, for I had got some tackle from
one of our captains, which he had brought from England.
On one of these occasions, while I was wading in a pool, I
spied a fine salmon laying just below me; I threw in and
brought my flies right over him, at which he instantly rose,
but I missed him. I tried again, and hooked him, but in a
moment he plunged right across the river, carrying with
him all my flies and part of my line, for I had no reel. I
might have calculated upon this, if I had thought for a moment; but the opportunity was so tempting, that I could
not resist it.

At length the 31st of August arrived, the day on which
St Sebastian was to be stormed. We knew this, for we had
furnished a number of volunteers, both officers and men, to
take part in the assault; many of our higher officers had gone
to witness the glorious spectacle. But early in the morning,
we were all astonished at the bugle sounding through
the camp the alarm, or assembly, and instantly orders were
given for the tents to be struck, the baggage to be packed,
and to set off with it to the rear without a moment's delay,
for the French were advancing; of course all this was done
in as short a time as possible, and the troops were ordered
to move on to a hill just over the bridge of Vera. A
detachment of ours had joined the evening before, and it
cannot easily be conceived the strange effect this sudden
alarm had on some of them. One of them, a lieutenant,
was all in a bustle getting his pistols put in fighting order,
and came to me begging I would take some money to keep
for him. I told him that it was likely to be in as much
danger with me as with himself, and of course declined.
The old hands, on the contrary, were as cool and quiet about

it as if it was an everyday occurrence. We moved to the height before mentioned, and saw a cloud of fellows with white caps coming down to the left of the town, and of course prepared to give them the best reception we could. I was sent with orders to my commanding-officer from the General, ' that he was, when pressed, to retire till he got on the ridge just over his house, (which was on the road a little to the rear of where we then were,) and that he was to stand there as long as it was possible.' I thought something very warm was going to occur, seeing such a cloud of Frenchmen were then approaching us, but we were all disappointed; they went quickly to their right after descending from the heights, and forded the river below the town, setting their faces towards St Sebastian. All this was effected under a cannonade from the heights.

Our 1st brigade (except my battalion) was then ordered to cross the river by the Lezacca bridge a little behind us, and to move parallel to the enemy along the ridge above that town, which had all along been Lord Wellington's head-quarters. As soon as they got across, they sent a body of troops to the bridge of Vera, close to which some of our people were stationed, and from thence they kept firing on us all day from some small mountain guns, which they had brought down with them, and occasionally with musketry. We were now somewhat curiously situated. The French position was on the side we occupied, while the other side of the bridge had been fortified by the Spanish General Longa, to protect himself during the last excursion of the French towards Pamplona; but now they occupied the side on which the intrenchments had been thrown up, and turned them against us of course; they did little execution by their fire. Lord Wellington, seeing the intention of the enemy, assembled all the British troops he could easily collect, and brought them in rear of a corps of Spaniards, which met the French in this direction; and finding this a fair opportunity of seeing what the Don could do, withheld the British, and let the Spaniards attack them by themselves. They had now the best chance of showing their valour that ever had or might present itself; they had the high ground, and the enemy had to climb up on their hands and knees to get at them; besides, they had behind them backers that would not see them get foul play. So away they set at them, and indeed they did tumble the French down in good style, upsetting them in all directions; so that our English division had nothing to do but to look on. This was the only time I ever knew the Spaniards act in a body like good soldiers.

The enemy, being beaten, were obliged of course to retrograde; but it came on one of the bitterest nights I have almost ever witnessed; the rain fell in torrents, and the lightning was very vivid. The French endeavoured to retrace their steps during the night, fording the river where they had crossed it in the morning; but the heavy rain had so swoln the river by midnight, that they could not continue any longer to wade it. A considerable number of them still remained on the other side, and no way presented itself of extricating themselves, but by forcing their passage across the bridge, near which a company of our 2d battalion, under Captain Cadoux, was posted, with one of ours, a short distance in the rear, to support him. Captain Cadoux's people were stationed in houses about thirty yards from the bridge, and had a double sentry on the bridge. The enemy's column approached very quietly, and then made a rush; but the rain having wet the priming of the sentries' rifles, they could not get them to go off to give the necessary alarm, and were in a moment driven from their post. The French then, seeing they had effected a passage, set up a shout, and rushed towards the houses where Cadoux's people were, who turned out at once, and with the supporting company, opened a deadly fire upon the enemy's column ; but poor Cadoux fell instantly almost, as he had imprudently mounted his horse on the first alarm ; his lieutenant also was severely wounded. The firing of course soon brought the whole brigade to the spot, which kept up a constant and well-directed fire during the whole of their progress along the little plain towards Vera.

The enemy suffered dreadfully on this occasion, leaving the ground literally strewed with their dead, who, like the others before mentioned, were next morning thrown into the river ; so that the fish had ample feeding for some time after. Some people afterwards reflected upon General Skerrott, who commanded here, for not posting a stronger force at the bridge, and for not blocking it up with an abbatis ; the former he might and ought to have done ; but the latter was impracticable, from the enemy holding the breastwork at the other end of the bridge, which was not more than about thirty yards long. Had a battalion been posted there, it is probable the French, who were compelled to have recourse to this daring attempt, might have been induced to surrender ; but I believe the General never imagined they had need to make such an attempt. Our loss on this occasion was rather severe also. A great many of Captain Cadoux's men fell ; Lieutenant Travers, who commanded the company of my battalion, was wounded, and a considerable number of men were killed and wounded ; among the former, some of the poor fellows who had joined from England only the day before.

Thus was Soult's second attempt frustrated, and St Sebastian fell into our hands. As I was not present at that glorious exhibition of British valour and prowess, I cannot take upon me to give any account of its capture. The volunteers who went from our division to assist in the storm or assault, sustained their full share in the casualties attendant thereon. The field-officer, Colonel Hunt of the 52d, was severely wounded; a lieutenant of the 43d, brother to Mr O'Connell, the famous Roman Catholic advocate, was killed; two lieutenants of our first battalion, named Percival and Hamilton, were severely wounded. The latter, I believe, was a volunteer on the occasion, not being entitled, from his standing, to take it as a tour of duty. He was conspicuously brave, and received two severe wounds, from which it would scarcely be imagined possible any one could recover.

A few days after the surrender of St Sebastian, I had again occasion to go to Tolosa for money, and took the road by Passages, the port where we now received all our supplies from England; and also to see the ruins of that late formidable fortress. When I reached it, the houses were still on fire, and not I believe half-a-dozen in the whole town that remained habitable, or the inhabitants had quite deserted it. I went up to the citadel and examined it, and I believe this, with proper casemates or bomb-proofs, might be rendered one of the strongest places in Spain, next to Gibraltar; but the French had suffered dreadfully from our shells, which had literally ploughed the ground on the top of this naturally strong height, and from which cause they had been compelled to surrender.

St Sebastian was indeed a melancholy spectacle at this time. I returned from Tolosa by a part of the road which we had traversed in our late retreat and advance again, as I now began to hope I might perhaps recover my little horse, for I suspected from some cause that my servant, instead of having been obliged to abandon him, because of his lameness, as he told me, had sold him at that time ; and this I actually found had been the case. I compelled him to tell me where he had disposed of him, and, with my broken Spanish, traced him from thence for near twenty miles farther into the mountains, where I found him in a village, the name of which I do not recollect, but where a squadron of our German hussars were quartered. I of course claimed and took possession of the horse, giving the person the amount he had paid for him ; but he being still lame, the commanding-officer of the hussars kindly permitted me to leave him with his farrier till he got well. He afterwards sent him to me, and would not even allow the farrier to receive any remuneration for his trouble, so kindly and politely did he behave.

September passed away without any thing remarkable occurring. My friend Captain (now Major) Perceval had been obliged to return to England, and Captain Balvaird succeeded him as senior captain of my battalion. I still continued in that company's mess. At length it was determined to attack the Puerta, or Pass of Vera, which the enemy had rendered exceedingly strong. The left of our army, under Sir Thomas Graham, were ordered to attack in their front, and force the passage of the Bidassoa, and establish themselves in France. We were merely to drive them from the heights above the town of Vera, taking possession of all the strong ground between that and France. The fourth division was brought up to support our attack, and formed immediately in rear of the town. One of the captains who formed the Committee of Paymastership, and who, it may be remembered, were held responsible for my accounts, and the due appropriation of all public money which might come into my hands, took a fancy that I exposed myself too much, and requested the commanding-officer, Colonel Ross, to prohibit my again entering into action, except for the purpose of bringing ammunition, &c., when my duty required me; in consequence of which the adjutant was sent to me this morning, previous to the operations commencing, with an order for me not to accompany the battalion. It may seem to the reader perhaps like affectation when I tell him I felt hurt at this order, and determined not very strictly to comply with it, for I believed that my respected commanding-officer had no objection that I should accompany him, did not this untoward circumstance interfere with my so doing. Accordingly I remained a looker-on among the fourth division. My battalion was destined to commence this attack by driving the enemy from a high and rugged hill on the right of the Pass, which was a necessary operation before the Pass itself could be attacked. Accordingly he extended the battalion, and encircled its base on the side next to Vera; and I believe, without firing a shot almost, he marched right up to the top of the hill, notwithstanding the sturdy resistance made by the enemy, and in a very short space of time completely cleared this formidable height.

This operation was the admiration of the whole fourth division, (for it was clearly observable by every one,) and they were most lavish of their praises for such a workman-like movement. When my people approached the top of the hill, I felt alarmed for their safety and their honour, for the French commander closed all his force to one point, and, forming them into line, made them fix bayonets, apparently with a determination to charge them down the hill again; and I saw that my people, for they could not perceive what the French were doing, were likely to be taken by surprise. Whether the Frenchman's heart failed him I know not, but when Colonel Ross reached the top of the hill, the enemy went to the right about, and instantly retired.

I felt proud of belonging to that corps, and happy at such a termination of this dangerous operation, and feeling a desire I could no longer resist, I set off to join them. By the time I reached the height just mentioned, the attack of the Puerta was going on, and a most arduous undertaking it was. My brigade attacked the right or strongest pass, which they carried in fine style, without much loss, although the enemy had a breastwork at every available point of ground. Our 2d brigade did not attack the left Pass quite so soon as the other, and when they had got about half way up they encountered the most formidable opposition.

A redoubt which the enemy possessed was filled with men, who waited till our battalion came within a few yards of them, and then poured in the most destructive fire imaginable, making the battalion recoil, and leaving one-third of its numbers on the ensanguined ground. But the 52d regiment being close behind, promptly supported them when rushing on together to the charge, and the French, after some hard fighting, were finally driven from this stronghold. After this they never made any obstinate stand, although there was occasional fighting all the way from the Pass down into the plain below, where some of our people followed them ; but it not being intended to quit for the present this high and formidable barrier, they were afterwards recalled. The boundary lines passed along this ridge.

We lost a few men on ascending the first hill, and a few in skirmishing afterwards, but our loss was not severe. But that of the 2d battalion, before noticed, was awful ; several

L

of that battalion who fell in this action had only a few days before joined from England, and this was their first action. On looking at the ground on which this affair took place, one would imagine it almost impossible that any army could force a passage through such innumerable difficulties. The hill itself was nearly impassable, and with the numerous redoubts and breastworks, with which it was literally covered, no troops in the world, I think, but British, would have dared to attempt it.

We found that the French, who occupied this station, had rendered themselves extremely comfortable, considering the kind of country and ground where they were posted. They had been at great pains in building very convenient and substantial huts in lines and streets, the same as an encampment, and which were indeed remarkably clean and neat. They had even built arm-racks at the end of each line, where their arms were stowed away most securely, and where they were preserved from the effects of the bad weather. Indeed, from the pains they had taken to render themselves comfortable here, it would appear as if they had not expected to be driven from it so soon.

The left of our army, under Sir Thomas Graham, also established themselves within the French territory. A corps of Spaniards on our left, between us and Sir Thomas, had likewise made a forward movement corresponding with the British. Some Spaniards were on the right of our division also, and were destined to drive the French from Là Rhune, an exceeding high rock, which overlooks all the other mountains, as well as the plain below. This they failed to accomplish, the enemy keeping possession all that night, and the skirmishing between the two forces continuing till after dark.

My battalion was sent on the outpost duty in the even-

ing down into the French plain below, and relieved the
Spanish General Longa, whose corps, with our 2d brigade,
were ordered to assist in the morning in dislodging the
enemy from La Rhune. I will not say whether the sight of
the red-coats coming against them the next morning had
the effect of alarming them, but they certainly evacuated
that exceedingly strong post without much farther opposition, and established themselves on a similar rock, but lower,
on the French side, and called by them Petit or Little Rhune.
But the possession of this lofty peak gave us the power of
overlooking all their movements for miles around us, as
well as of surveying La Belle France as far as the eye could
see, and indeed, compared with the bleak and barren mountains in which we had so long been residing, it did appear
a beautiful country, although, in reality, it is far from being
such. But we gazed upon it with strange and mingled
emotions, hardly believing it possible that we had now
reached and entered the territory of that once formidable
nation whose victorious armies had penetrated to the farthest
confines of Europe, who had overrun and subdued some of
the most warlike nations of the continent, and who had so
often threatened, and as often alarmed, the inhabitants of
England with the invasion of that sacred soil, on which
never yet a Frenchman has dared, in hostile array, to set
his foot since the days of the Norman William, but who
met there either with a prison or a grave.

We now pitched our camps by battalions, each occupying
a post more or less important, and the enemy began again
to construct their huts, and make themselves as comfortable
as their circumstances would admit ; Soult, no doubt, being
mightily chagrined that we had now fairly beat them out of
Spain, when he (as we now learnt) had promised his followers that he would soon lead them again to the plains of

Vittoria, where they might again retrieve their lost honours, and at which city they would celebrate the Emperor's birth-day. He thus boasted, and no doubt would have effected his purpose, had he not been so promptly met near Pamplona by his never-to-be outmanœuvred antagonist.

We now began to suffer greatly from the severity of the weather. It became exceedingly wet and stormy; and not infrequently the tents were blown away from over our heads, or the pole was forced up through the top, letting the wet canvass fall comfortably down about our ears while we were perhaps in a sound sleep. I had two streams flow-ing past my head, one went round the trench outside my tent, while the other I was fain to let pass through it; their murmurs lulled me to sleep, and I do not remember that ever I slept sounder than I did here, having made my couch comfortable by gathering dry fern, and spreading my mat-tress upon it.

Whilst we remained here, a few officers were appointed to watch the motions of the enemy from an old work which we understood had been constructed by the Spaniards and emigrant French against their revolutionary neighbours, whom they endeavoured to keep from entering Spain; and, of course, this was the daily lounge of those who had no better employment, not only that they might themselves see, but hear also from others what of importance was pass-ing. On one of these occasions, a vessel was descried (for the sea was not more than five or six miles from us) ma-king for the harbour of Bayonne, or St Jean de Luz, with a small schooner following her in chase, and every now and then giving her a shot. The vessel, (which turned out to be a French brig going with provisions for the few French-men who still retained the castle of Santona,) seeing she could not get clear of her unwelcome neighbours, her crew set her on fire, and taking to their boats, abandoned her, and escaped on shore—she soon after blew up with a tremendous explosion.

On the 31st of this month Pamplona surrendered, the garrison, consisting of 4000 men, under Major-general Cassan, the governor, becoming prisoners of war. They had been compelled to adopt this measure from sheer starvation, of which they, I understand, had suffered dreadfully. I happened to be at Passages on the day they reached that port, where they embarked, on their way to England. The General was a stout, handsome, and intelligent-looking man, and such a one as I should imagine would make a noble officer. The soldiers seemed quite unconcerned about their fate ; whether from the change being actually an improvement of their condition, or from the lightness and gaiety of their natural temper, I know not, but they were jesting and making as merry as if nothing had happened.

During the time we lay on these mountains, I regret to state my gallant and respected commanding-officer, Colonel Ross, suffered so much from rheumatism, that he was compelled to leave the regiment, and take up his abode at Rentaria, a village near to Passages.

It was reported that Lord Wellington intended attacking the enemy along his whole line, early in November, but the weather having rendered the roads impassable, it was postponed. On the day previous to the intended attack, the commanding-officer had been taken up to La Rhune, and the post that each corps had to occupy, with the movements they were intended to make, were clearly pointed out to them ; an excellent plan, when practicable, as it leaves no one any excuse for mistakes or blunders during the action.

At length, on the 10th of that month, I believe, it was

settled to take place; but on the 9th I was ordered to set off with the mules of the battalion, to fetch corn from Passages, a distance of about thirty miles. I suspected this was a scheme of the captain I before mentioned, as one of the committee of paymastership, in order the more effectually to keep me out of danger, for certainly had any thing serious happened me, they would have had some difficulty in rendering their accounts. It was not quite certain the attack was to take place next day, although it had been so rumoured; however, I was determined to try and reach the division as early as possible on that day. I accordingly got my business done in Passages as early as I could get the commissary to work; and having got the corn, and come on to Rentaria, which I reached about mid-day, I took the liberty of leaving the animals in the charge of the non-commissioned officer who had accompanied me; and calling on Colonel Ross, obtained his permission to let the sergeant proceed in charge of them to the regiment, while I might, if I chose, push on at a quicker rate. I had heard by this time, that the action had commenced by daylight that morning. I accordingly set off at as quick a pace as my starved animal could carry me; and passing Irun, and crossing the Bidassoa, and keeping along the great road for a considerable distance, I then inclined to my right, and skirted the Pyrenees along the whole plain. I had thus an opportunity of witnessing the conflict carrying on by the left wing of our army, as I passed along towards La Rhune, but with every exertion of myself and my poor jaded horse, night closed in upon me before I had nearly reached the station of the light division. I was compelled to work my way through a country which I had not hitherto passed, and which having been the scene of a sanguinary combat,

presented no very pleasing aspect.   At last I heard some
strange and foreign voices before me, for it was now quite
dark, on which I turned into a field, and waited till they
passed, by which I learned they were Spaniards.   I was apprehensive I might have kept too far to the left, and had
got into the French lines, which would not have been so
comfortable ; but after finding them to be men of General
Frere's Spanish division, I then had hopes of shortly meeting with my own people.   Directed by those good Spaniards,
I at last reached Petit La Rhune, the late formidable position of the enemy, on which the blazes from a thousand of
their huts were rising to the clouds, and enlightening the
atmosphere around.   But it being now ten o'clock, I found
myself incapable of proceeding farther, more particularly as
the Portuguese, among whom I now found myself, could
not give me any certain directions which way my division
had gone.   I was fain therefore to take up my abode, and
gladly did so, in a cottage with Colonel St Clair and several
other officers of the sixth Caçadores.   Let it not be supposed that a fighting disposition induced me to use so much
exertion to reach my division on this occasion—no ; but as
I considered that a sort of trick had been played off upon
me, I did what I could to render it nugatory ; no man liking,
as I imagine, to be the dupe of any other party's manœuvres,
with whatever friendly intention these may have been put in
operation.   I arose next morning early, and hastened to
the point where I expected to meet my brave comrades,
anxious to learn the fate of all I loved amongst them.   I
saw them and the third division at a considerable distance,
each on a height in front, appearing like flocks of sheep
huddled together as close as possible.   I soon reached them,
and learned with sorrow, that the brave Colonel Barnard
was, as they supposed, mortally wounded, the ball having

passed through the chest, and that little Lieutenant Doyle
was killed.

This was a most stupendous action ; the scene of operations extending from right to left, embracing, I imagine, not
less than thirty miles of country. The centre had fallen to
the share of my division, which, in the eyes of the best
judges, was the strongest part of the enemy's line, for it had
been fortified with the most consummate skill, and no la-
hour had been spared to render it impregnable, as the enemy
had been busily employed in the construction of forts, redoubts, and other fieldworks of every denomination, from
the day we drove them from the Pass of Vera; one in particular, a stone built fort, in the shape of a star, was exceedingly strong, and which was attacked and carried in the finest
style possible, I understand, by the 43d regiment ; the 52d
also surrounded a fort in which the French 88th regiment
was posted, the brave commander of which not having received any orders to evacuate it, remained till the retreat of
the French left him no other alternative than to surrender
at discretion.   The part my battalion had to play, was to
cross the valley separating the two La Rhunes in double
quick time, and attack the French rock by a gorge, which
allowed a passage from that valley into their position. This
was to be in conjunction with the attack of the Star Fort
by the 43d, as it in some measure took that work in reverse.
In short, every corps in the division, and I believe in the
army, had a most arduous duty to perform, and most nobly
did they execute it.   The left of our army, under Sir
Thomas Graham, did not succeed in driving the enemy
from his innumerable works which covered St Jean de Luz,
and which he retained possession of till the next morning;
when the centre, that is the 3d and light divisions, together
with the Spaniards on our right and left centre, made a

movement in advance, and crossed the Nivelle river, from
which this action derives its name. Our movement, which
threatened to separate the wings of the French army, caused the enemy to abandon his strong position in front of
St Jean de Luz, as well as that town, on which occasion he
attempted, and partly succeeded in destroying the bridge
over the Nivelle at that place; but it being soon after repaired, Sir Thomas Graham's corps took up their quarters
in the town.

We encamped for the night in front of the village of
Serres, or Sarre, or Zarre. It had rained hard all the day
of the 11th, and it continued almost without intermission
till our camp was literally swimming. I remember perfectly
that the water in my tent was several inches deep; and
when I awoke in the morning, I found a Portuguese boy
(who had followed us, and had attached himself to our mess
as a sort of servant) was sitting holding by the tent-pole,
that being the only place where he could find rest for the
sole of his foot. In short, we were as wet, clothes and beds
and all, as if we had been dragged through a river. The
evening before, I well remember, we had been highly
amused by my Scotch quartermaster-sergeant and his
friends, who had taken up their abode close by, singing, till
they rather grew tiresome,

" We are nae fou', we're nae that fou',
But just a drappie in our e'e."

This of course was done to drive away dull care, and to
make the best of an uncomfortable situation.

The next day towards afternoon, a considerable firing
was heard on our right, which had continued but a short
while, till our gallant and unwearied Chief came galloping
up, with some few of his staff following, who could with

difficulty keep pace with him, and asking most anxiously whereabouts and what the firing was. We could only point out the direction in which we heard it, but could give him no account as to its cause. Away he galloped in the direction we pointed out, and no doubt soon reached the spot.

I forgot to mention, that a man of the Brunswick Oels corps had been hung the day before for plundering by the Provost Marshal, no doubt in compliance with superior orders. It was necessary thus to give the army an example of severity, in order to deter them from committing those acts to which all armies are but too prone. We found indeed very little to plunder, had we been so inclined ; for the greater part of the inhabitants had left their houses, taking every thing portable with them. This they had been induced to do from the false statements which Soult had set forth in some proclamations he issued about this time, in which he described the English as savages, nay, even as cannibals, who would not scruple to commit the most monstrous atrocities ; so ignorant were the generality of these poor peasants, that many of them implicitly believed his representations. This, no doubt, was done with the view of raising the whole population in arms against us, in order to defend their homes against such a set of wretches as he made it appear we were ; but, although many of the natives joined the French army at this time, with which they were incorporated and led to battle, the result of his famous proclamations was not equal to his expectations ; for a great part of them declined warlike proceedings, and retired into the interior of the country with their families, leaving only a very small proportion indeed who remained in their houses. As might be expected, the empty houses suffered dreadfully ; every piece of furniture almost being destroyed, either for fire-wood, or in seeking for valuables; while the houses of those who remained in general escaped.

General Harispe, being a Basque himself, had the organizing of the new levies now raised; indeed, many of these had taken a part in the irruption into Spain on the 25th July for the relief of Pamplona, and many of them fell on that occasion. We were not so fully aware of the extent of the misrepresentation to which Soult had gone in these proclamations, till some time after we had entered France, and had penetrated considerably into the interior, when some of our officers, either during or after a march, entered the cottage of a peasant who had not left his home, to get a little milk. The poor woman was remarkably civil, offering them any thing the house afforded. They got some milk, for which they offered her money, but which she declined. Her child was running about the house at this time, which, coming near one of the officers, he took it between his knees, and patted it on the head, with which the child seemed very well pleased; but the poor mother, standing at a little distance, and eyeing most intently every motion of the officer, was like to swoon with fear and agitation. But as the mother had declined receiving any thing for the milk, the officer who had the child gave it some small coin, and letting it go, it ran to its mother, who snatched it up into her arms with the utmost joy, and altering her look, began to say, she thought they had been deceived; for that they had been led to believe from the proclamations of Soult, that we were such barbarians that we would not scruple to kill and eat their children, and which was the cause of her late fear and anxiety, as she expected the officer had taken the child for that purpose; but now she found we were not such people as she had been led to believe. Of course the officer laughed most heartily at having been suspected of a man-eating propensity, and soon convinced the poor woman that the English were not quite such barbarians as that, whatever she might have heard to the contrary.

CHAPTER XII.

The British Army advance farther into France—Pass the Nive—
Soult's Plans baffled—Two or three battalions of the Nassau and
Frankfort regiments come over from the French—French Politesse
—Threatened Attack by the French—Battle of the Nive—Account of
the Basques.

WE left our wet camp on the 15th, and advanced to the
village of Arbonne, where, for the first time during the
campaign, we were quartered in houses, except once or twice.
During our stay in the camp at Serres, or Zarre, we sent
our baggage animals to Passages for corn, on which occasion I lost another horse, the batman pretending it had
been stolen, but which, no doubt, he sold, as that trick had
often been resorted to by this time, and there was no de-
tecting it.

On the 17th we left Arbonne, and advanced to Arcangues, sending forward picquets to the village of Bassozari,
about half a mile in front. My battalion took up into
quarters in some straggling houses in front of the church
of Arcangues, while our first battalion occupied the chateau
and outhouses of Arcangues, about a quarter of a mile to the
right and front of the church. The enemy's picquets were

close to Bassozari, so that in some places scarcely a quarter
of a mile intervened between our quarters and their outposts.   They allowed us to take up our outposts very
quietly, they being now established in their intrenched
camp in front of Bayonne, and which was not far distant from
our advance.   There were some houses in the line of posts
occupied by the French, which, if in our possession, would
add greatly both to our security and convenience, and which
it was determined to wrest from them if practicable.

Accordingly, on the 23d the division was put under arms,
and our brigade, being in front, had this task assigned to
them.   The 43d, not having had so much work during the
campaign as our two battalions had, was selected for the
purpose of driving in the enemy's picquets, whilst we supported them.   They accordingly attacked and carried the
houses without a moment's delay; but unfortunately, Captain Hobkirk of that regiment, advancing with his company
beyond the line at which it was intended to halt, got immediately in front of some of their intrenchments, from which
he could not extricate himself, in consequence of which our
first battalion was ordered to advance to cover his retreat;
but he had by this time fallen into the hands of the enemy,
with a considerable number of his men : his lieutenant was
killed, and altogether the company suffered great loss.   The
remainder retreated, our first battalion people holding the
houses it was intended to occupy.   This occurred on the
left of the ridge.

On the right, and adjoining a marsh which separated us
from some high ground near the river Nive, and which was
occupied by another division of our army, were two or three
houses also which it was intended to take, as their possession secured us a passage across this marsh by a causeway,
which connected two eminences, that on which we stood,

and that occupied by the other division, the principal object
upon the latter being a large château called Garratt's House.
One company of the 43d also took those houses, supported
by some more of that regiment and my battalion; but after
they were taken, from what cause I know not, an order
was sent to evacuate them, on which the 43d retired.
Soon after, they were again ordered to be re-occupied, when
a company of ours advanced, and took possession, but had
not been there many minutes till another order was sent
for them to be evacuated. This order, however, had scarcely
reached them, when a charge was made on them by a body
of French cavalry, supported by a strong column of infantry.
The officer who commanded the company, either from the
order he had received, or from want of presence of mind,
called to his men to run to the rear when the cavalry
charged him, by which he did not suffer much in point of
losing men, for only one was wounded by the cavalry; but
it had a bad appearance to run away from cavalry, a description of force which we had learnt by this time almost to
despise, especially as, from his post, he might have knocked
down great numbers of them, and finally have repulsed
them, had he allowed his men to fire. The houses were,
however, eventually taken possession of by another company of our battalion the next day, which retained them in
despite of the enemy. The man who was wounded by the
cavalry was shot in the head by a pistol ball: he came to
the surgeon, where the main body of the battalion was standing, to be dressed; while this was doing, and the orderly
man holding a tin-full of water near, from which the surgeon was sponging and cleaning the wound, a ball came,
and, striking the tin, carried it right out from between the
hands of the orderly. I was standing close by, and shall
not easily forget the blank look which, as might be expect-

ed, the poor orderly put on. There was a good deal of firing all day, which, except what the 43d suffered, as before noticed, did little damage to the brigade.

On the occasion of our company taking these houses the next day, a very young officer, who happened to command it, evinced great fortitude and presence of mind. He advanced on the enemy, who, being then rather inclined to quietness, retreated gradually before him ; but after reaching the hedge, just beyond the principal house, told him (for they were quite near enough to speak) that he must not advance any farther, or they would be compelled to fire on him. The young fellow, solicitous about nothing but obeying his orders, told them that he was determined to have the house, and immediately putting his men under the best cover he could, called out that they might begin to fire whenever they pleased, he was ready for them. This young officer (whose name was Cary, and brother to my friend who fell at Badajos) spoke excellent French, so that the enemy understood him perfectly. The enemy did not contend any longer for the post, but planted their sentries within about thirty yards of ours. These sentries, indeed, were still so posted as to prevent a passage across by the causeway, had they been so inclined ; but the next day I went with another officer across by this road, on which occasion we actually passed to the rear of the French sentries.

A disposition had for some time been gaining ground with both armies, to mitigate the miseries of warfare, as much as was consistent with each doing their duty to their country ; and it had by this time proceeded to such an extent, as to allow us to place that confidence in them that they would not molest us even if we passed their outposts for the purpose I have mentioned. And this mutual confidence in each other was productive of the most comfortable results to both parties. We could move about at any time, and almost in any place, shooting or otherwise amusing ourselves, without the dread of falling in with an enemy's patrol, or of getting among their sentries. They never molested us from this time, except when we either advanced upon them, or they upon us, in hostile array. Our division had two main picquets ; all this took place at the right picquet. A few days after I happened to be at the advanced post on the left, commanded by one of my battalion, when the French officers beckoned to us. We, to show we were peaceably inclined, pulled off our swords, and advanced to meet them.   A number of inhabitants, who had left their houses on our first entering the country, having heard that we were not what we had been represented, were desirous of returning to their homes, and the officers wished us to admit them, and see them safe through the advanced posts. This of course we gladly promised, and the poor people were quite overjoyed at being permitted to visit their dwelling-places once again ; but, poor creatures, I fear they would find little there except the bare walls, if indeed these remained entire, for, from the reasons before assigned, it could scarcely be expected that houses without inhabitants, in the midst of an invading army, would be much respected. Each individual among them, old and young, carried heavy bundles on their heads, no doubt they having removed every thing that was valuable, if portable.

The French officers were extremely polite, and asked us many questions of the news of the day, &c. ; but the commander-in-chief, hearing of the familiarity which subsisted between the two armies, issued an order, prohibiting British officers from holding conversations with the enemy ; for as all these conversations were necessarily conducted in French,

L 2

(very few indeed of their officers being able to speak English,) he was apprehensive they might gain such information from our people, from their imperfect knowledge of the French language, as might materially injure our future proceedings. Before this order was issued, the most unbounded confidence subsisted between us, and which it was a pity to put a stop to, except for such weighty reasons. They used to get us such things as we wanted from Bayonne, particularly brandy, which was cheap and plentiful, and we in return gave them occasionally a little tea, of which some of them had learnt to be fond. Some of them also, who had been prisoners of war in England, sent letters through our army-post to their sweethearts in England, our people receiving the letters and forwarding them. They told us also how Hobkirk was situated, and were astonished at the extent and splendour of his equipage, (for he was a great dandy,) and could scarcely be persuaded he was only a captain.

My present commanding-officer, who was the senior captain, and in whose mess I then was, had sent to England, and got out from thence two immense pies, weighing nearly a hundred-weight each, and packed in tin cases. They were composed of every kind of game, and the best description of fowls, such as turkeys, &c., with the bones taken out, and the meat baked till it became like brawn when cut in slices. They were most excellent. One of these he had made a present of to our Major-general, and the other we were eating in the mess. We had also at this time a considerable quantity of good wine, which, by some accident, we had got hold of. We also had bought a pig and killed it, both living quite sumptuously at present, and having a good stock for future use.

But while we ourselves fared so well, our poor horse

and mules were literally starving. There was no kind of
forage for them, except what they could pick up in the now
completely exhausted fields around us. We had nothing
else to give them.

In this way we were going on, when, on the 9th of December, Lord Wellington, determining on passing the Nive,
preparatory to future operations, ordered our division and
all the left, under Sir John Hope, who had now succeeded
Sir Thomas Graham, to make a movement in advance, in
order that the enemy's attention might be attracted to this
point, while he threw over some divisions to the right bank
of that river. My battalion had to advance along the ridge
by which I had formerly passed in peace, to meet the returning inhabitants, as may be recollected; but now the
face of affairs was completely altered;—a heavy fire was
kept up by the French picquets from the moment they saw
us advance in arms, but we soon drove them from their
advanced works, and they were obliged to take shelter in
their intrenched camp, which was remarkably strong, and
which it was not intended we should attack. We accordingly halted on the brow of the ridge, while they kept up
an incessant fire, both from their guns and infantry, but
which, considering its extent and duration, was not by any
means a destructive fire.

Sir John Hope had a more laborious task to perform, or
else his troops went beyond the point intended, for they
continued the fight nearly all day, and at one time were
considerably in advance, but afterwards recalled.

The passage of the Nive was completely effected, and in
the evening we returned to our comfortable houses, a short
distance in the rear, and went to bed as usual. Next
morning, however, very early, orders were given to turn
out immediately, and stand to our arms, for the enemy was

advancing ; and indeed, when I came to the door, I heard a good deal of firing. The troops turned out at once, but the mules were to get, and the baggage to pack, and send away to the rear, or it might be lost ; so I set myself about this with all dispatch ; but before any of it was put up, I saw posting by me, with all expedition, a civil officer, who had only a short while joined us, and who, in his hurry, had put up all he could scrape together on his horse, on which he himself was riding. His boots, tied together, were slung over the horse's neck, and in short he looked more like a bagman than an officer, from the number of things he had hanging about him. It was most laughable to see him. I called out and asked him why he was in such a hurry, but he did not stop to give me an answer.

I got up our baggage very well, but what to do with the pie, the pig, and the wine, I knew not, so was constrained to leave them as they were, hoping we might not allow the enemy to penetrate so far. I then moved off the baggage, and, directing the servants who had charge of it to proceed up a lane which carried them towards the rear, I moved on and joined the battalion. Just as I reached the plateau, or high ground in front of the church of Arcangues, I met an officer of ours to whom I had lately lent a fine young mare, for which I had not food sufficient ; and he having no horse himself, I thought he would take care of her ; but here I met him going into the fight riding on the poor animal, although scarcely able to drag one leg behind the other. I remonstrated with him, but he did not mind me. The result was as might have been anticipated—she soon after dropped down, unable to move farther, and died ; thus I lost L.35 more, which she had cost me. By this time the enemy had driven in the regiment which had been on picquet, and one or two of our companies were sent forward to cover their retreat to the church behind us, where they were ordered to take post, it being a high and fine position, and had by this time been partly fortified. My people retired gradually before the enemy, who now advanced in great numbers.

Our 1st battalion were not so fortunate in effecting their retreat. An officer and some men having got into a hollow way, were surrounded by the enemy and taken; another was killed; and another, with his section, had to force their way through a strong body which had got in his rear. My battalion did not fall into any scrape of that nature, but sustained a considerable loss in killed and wounded, from the vast superiority of the enemy in point of numbers, who, no doubt, did not escape with impunity. We held our ground at the bottom of the hill on which the church is built, the French not being able to force us farther back; the 1st battalion, at the same time, holding the fence and ditch in front of the Chateau, as well as that building itself. But a rather unpleasant occurrence took place at this time. When the enemy appeared on the plateau before mentioned, a regiment behind us, without orders, I believe, opened a heavy fire upon them, several shots of which struck among our men. One of them went in at the back of one of our soldiers, and killed him on the spot; another penetrated the back window of a house into which a party of ours had entered for defence, and very near struck an officer, who was in the room at the time. These shots must have been fired either by young soldiers, who scarcely knew how they pointed their muskets, or they must have taken our people for the enemy, from which, indeed, they were not far distant. I am confident it was purely accidental, for no two corps could be on better terms

than that regiment and ours always were. The skirmishing continued till dark.

This was one of a series of masterly movements between
the two contending generals. Lord Wellington having
sent a pretty strong force across the Nive, as before mentioned, Soult imagined he had so weakened his force on the
left, as to render it probable he might penetrate it, and thus
cause his lordship to withdraw his troops again from the
right bank of the Nive ; but he was anticipated ; for Lord
Wellington had no sooner established himself on the other
side of the Nive, than he brought one of the supporting
divisions of that movement to support us at the church of
Arcangues, it being an important post to hold; so that, when
we looked behind us, after we retired into position, we saw
innumerable bayonets glistening in the sun, and ready to
move forward whenever they should be required ; but they
never were wanted here, the light division being quite sufficient to sustain any attack the enemy had yet made on
them. This, however, showed the provident care of his
lordship, and how completely he had penetrated Soult's
design.

This night two or three battalions of the Nassau and
Frankfort regiments came over and left the French. They
had heard that the Dutch had declared against Bonaparte,
and wished to be transported to Holland, with all their
arms and appointments, which they brought with them.
We remained in bivouack on the ridge extending between
the church and chateau of Arcangues all night, our picquets
remaining in possession of the houses and hedges at the
bottom of the hill, where we stopped the French in the
morning. I visited the picquets at night, in company with
my commanding-officer, where we found all well, and alert.
The next day, there being no firing between us and those

in our front, three French officers, seemingly anxious to prove how far politeness and good breeding could be carried between the two nations, when war did not compel them to be unfriendly, took a table and some chairs out of a house which was immediately in our front, and one which we had lately occupied as a barrack; and bringing them down into the middle of the field, which separated the advance of the two armies, sat down within 100 yards of our picquet, and drank wine, holding up their glasses, as much as to say your health, every time they drank. Of course we did not molest them, but allowed them to have their frolic out.

During the day, also, we saw soldiers of the three nations, viz. English, Portuguese, and French, all plundering at the same time in one unfortunate house, where our pie, our pig, and wine had been left. It stood about 150 or 200 yards below the church, on a sort of neutral ground between the two armies; hence the assemblage at the same moment of such a group of these motley marauders. They plundered in perfect harmony, no one disturbing the other on account of his nation or colour. There were a great number of apples in it at the time we left it, belonging to the owner of the house, but when we returned, two or three days afterwards, the desolation was complete. Our once comfortable quarter contained nothing now but filth and dirt. One poor girl had remained in it all the while, but she could not save one article; indeed, in such a case it would have been a service of danger to attempt it.

At night one of our sergeants played the French a trick. He took with him a few men, and, knowing the ground well, they passed the French sentry unobserved, having reached the house at the top of the field out of which they had brought the table, &c., where their picquet was stationed. He made a rush at their arms, which he found piled in front of the house, and set to work and broke them before the French had time to recover from the consternation into which they were thrown by so unexpected an assault. He and his party then came running off without sustaining any injury. He was a most determined brave soldier this, but afterwards lost an arm at Toulouse, and was of course discharged with a pension.

On the 12th, the enemy made a mighty show of attacking our position, having greatly increased their force in front of us, and had, some way or other, found the means of spreading a report in our lines that 1800 grenadiers had been chosen to lead on the attack. They also traced out batteries, and cut embrasures, apparently with the intention of burning or knocking down the chateau of Arcangues, the owner of which remained in it all this time, and was rather suspected of holding correspondence with his countrymen. It is not unlikely it was by his means the report above alluded to was propagated. Every thing now wore a serious aspect, and of course every thing was done to render their attack abortive. All were animated with the best disposition to defend the post to the last extremity; but while the generality believed all these preparations were serious, there were others who thought it only a *ruse de guerre;* indeed, had our friends, the German hussars, (with whom we had often acted in concert,) been here at this time, it is more than probable they would have been strongly inclined to the latter opinion, for they scarcely ever saw the French make a great bustle and noise, as if about immediately to advance and attack, but they would coolly say, after eyeing them awhile, " Oh, he not come to-day!" " He go away!" and were generally certain of being right. So full of trick and artifice are our French antagonists, that they generally act in quite a contrary manner to what appearances indicate. But they began to be known; hence the scepticism of some of our people on the present occasion. Accordingly, about midnight, when the attack was to have been made, away they went, and retired nearly into their lines, leaving only a few to keep the ground.

At daylight next morning we again moved forward, on which there was a good deal of firing between the Portuguese battalion that had followed them and their rearguard; but when our people advanced to our old post on the ridge, I, happening to be first, took off my cap, and, putting it on the top of my sword, held it up, which the French taking for a signal of peace, as it was intended, the firing on both sides ceased, each party taking up the post they held previous to the late movements. We wondered why the French had retired, but presently heard a tremendously heavy firing in the direction of the Nive. Soult, it seems, had withdrawn nearly all his troops from our flank, and marching rapidly through Bayonne, had attacked General Hill, who commanded on the other side of the Nive, with great impetuosity, thinking Lord Wellington had weakened that force to strengthen us; but here again Soult was outwitted, for he found on that side quite sufficient to give him as sound a drubbing as he ever got; the Portuguese on this occasion, I understand, performing wonders.

These five days' fighting (for on every day there was firing, more or less, in one part or other of the line) were called the Battle of the Nive. We had had three days' work of it—they on our right two—and Sir John Hope's people, on our left, four, I believe, and they not trifling ones. In every thing Soult undertook, he was completely foiled—all his schemes having been clearly seen through by his more sagacious opponent. Indeed he had inflicted a heavy loss on

M

our left wing, commanded by Sir John Hope, where the fighting had been most severe, but no doubt he suffered equally, if not more severely than they did. I am told that the enemy's light troops were most insolent and annoying to our heavy regiments on the left, on this occasion. What a pity that they could not have been opposed by troops of a similar description!

It may be remembered the civil officer of whom I made mention, as having rode away with the greater part of his wardrobe hanging about his horse; he was more fortunate than we were, for the things which he left, his kind land-lady took care of, and hid in some snug corner till the business was over, and on his return restored them all to him. He said the cause of his going off in such a hurry arose from a cannon-shot having struck the lintel of the door or window of his house while he was in the act of shaving, on which he bundled out with whatever he could scrape together, and set off.   I verily believe it must have been the effect of imagination, for I remained behind him at least a quarter of an hour, and although our houses were close together, I did not either hear or see a shot fired in that direction till we had reached the hill, nearly an hour after; but he constantly maintained that it was so.

We again took up our old quarters in front of the church; but oh, how changed were they now from what they had formerly been in point of comfort! nevertheless, they still afforded us shelter from the inclemency of the weather. Soon after dark on this evening, a rather unpleasant affair occurred at the left advanced post of our division. An officer and two men coming from the French advance, with what intention is not known, were observed by the corporal who was stationed at our abatis, who immediately took out his rifle and shot the officer through the body, on which his two men lifted him up and carried him into their picquet-house. We were apprehensive this would put an end to that good understanding which had hitherto subsisted between the picquets of the two nations, and much regretted the circumstance. It is more than probable the officer was coming as a sort of patrol, to ascertain whether or not we had left the post, which, being a military undertaking, subjected him to all the chances of war attendant thereon. This is the more probable from his having two soldiers with him armed, as I understand they were; but if it was meant as a friendly visit, as formerly sometimes took place, it was greatly to be lamented; however, they did not, on account of this occurrence, manifest any soreness or ill-will afterwards, and the mutual good understanding continued to subsist between us.

While we remain at rest here a short space, I will endeavour to put the reader in possession of the character of the inhabitants, among whom we have been sojourning for a few months past—I mean the Biscayans. From the time we crossed the Ebro, a wonderful change took place in the appearance of the natives; and I believe the same description of people extend considerably into France, although under another government; they, I understand, still retain their ancient customs, dress, and language; they are denominated Basques, from the name of the province, I apprehend, which is called Biscay. They speak a different language from either the Spaniards, who border them on one side, or the French, on the other; and some of our officers who spoke Welsh, said they could understand a few of their words; it is denominated the Basque language. They generally wear cloth of their own manufacture, which is commonly blue, in some parts red or brown; in the neighbourhood of Pamplona, almost always the latter. The men wear a sort of Scotch bonnet, with a short jacket and trowsers, and are an amazingly athletic and active people. The women wear a short jacket also, of the same colour with their petticoat; and with their hair, which they encourage to grow to a great length, plaited in one large plait, and tied with a small piece of ribbon; it is allowed to hang down their back, and almost in all cases reaches to, or below their middle. They wear a handkerchief tastefully disposed upon their head. They are a fine, tall, and handsome race of women; but they have a custom of compressing their breasts, so that they appear as flat in the bosom as the men, which, to an English eye, is not becoming. The women do the same kind of work as the men, that is, they plough, and labour at all sorts of husbandry; but what seemed most remarkable to us, was their sole management of the ferry-boats about Passages and St Sebastian; they row as well as any men, being amazingly strong and active; they seem content with their lot, and always appeared cheerful and happy. I believe they are strictly virtuous; and although very handsome in general, they did not seem so fond of admiration as the females of many other countries are; upon the whole, I think they resemble the Welsh more than any other people with whom I am acquainted; their countries are exceedingly similar, being mountainous, and in general not over fruitful, so that constant labour seems to be rendered absolutely necessary to insure to them the means of subsistence; hence they are industrious and frugal, and, upon the whole, an interesting and moral people.

CHAPTER XIII.

The Author's Battalion quartered in Aurantz on 3d January, 1814—
The Cantonments at Aurantz broke up on 16th February, and the
Campaign of 1814 commenced—Farther Advance into France—Skir-
mishing with the Enemy—Military Manœuvres—Battle of Orthes—
Defeat and Pursuit of the Enemy—Succession of Attacks on them—
They are driven from their Position in and near Tarbes—Skirmish-
ing at Tournefoile—The Enemy retire towards Toulouse.

On the 3d of January 1814, we were ordered to quit a
part of the country, which, from the various occurrences
that had taken place since we first arrived in it, had, in
some measure, rendered it interesting to us. We moved a
little to the right, and crossed the Nive, and again moved
in advance about a league or more. This movement was
made in support of some operations which Lord Wellington
was conducting in the direction of the Adour, which being
completed, we returned to the Nive, and took up our cantonments in the villages of Ustaritz and Aurantz. About
this time, nearly the whole of the peasantry, who had fled
on our entering France, were now returning to their habitations, all fear that we should murder them, and eat their
children, having by this time been completely dissipated.

Indeed we were often told after this, that they would much prefer having a British army among them, to their own people, for they were always haughty, they said, and overbearing, and never scrupled to take whatever they had a mind for, while we were orderly and quiet, and never took an article without amply repaying the owner for it. Indeed I am well convinced the change the poor people had made in their lodgers was greatly for the better to them.

My battalion was quartered in the village of Aurantz, from which we often took a stroll, to look at the scene of our late operations. The French having, in consequence of Lord Wellington's movements near the Adour, strengthened their army in that direction, which of course rendered it necessary they should contract the limits of their front on the side towards Spain, they had consequently withdrawn their advance considerably within their former lines. We now also had plenty of opportunity for shooting, but were but ill supplied with fowling-pieces, or we might have killed an abundance of woodcocks, every thicket in the neighbourhood being filled with them.

The weather now was extremely bad, and the roads impassable, except by yourself wading up to the knees, or having your horse almost continually nearly up to his belly. In consequence of the difficulty of communicating by dragoons, on account of the roads, telegraphs were established all along from the right of the army, on the banks of the Adour, to St Jean de Luz on our left, the head-quarters of the army. While in these cantonments, an account arrived of our gallant Major-general (Kempt) having been appointed to the colonelcy of the 8th battalion of the 60th regiment, which had just been raised. At the recommendation of my commanding-officer, now Major Balvaird, the general kindly transmitted my name to the War Office for the appointment of paymaster of his battalion; but unfortunately for me, before my name arrived, his late Royal Highness the Duke of York, as Colonel-in-chief of the regiment, had nominated another person to the situation. It had always hitherto been customary for Colonels-commandant, and not the Colonel-in chief, to nominate their own staff, but on this occasion another rule was adopted, which, of course, was a great disappointment to me, as I had, with considerable trouble, got all my sureties, &c. prepared, although they were now not needed.

I had, during our stay here, one or more trips to the paymaster-general for money, for although the paymaster of the battalion had by this time arrived, I had several months' pay still to draw, the army being considerably in arrear in their pay. I had thus an opportunity of visiting St Jean de Luz, and all the enemy's late fortifications and position in that neighbourhood, and amazingly strong they had indeed rendered the ground in front of that town. It was a considerable and well-built town, partaking a good deal of both the Spanish and French character of course, it being the first French town next to the frontier; and, as I said before, there being very little difference between the Basques on either side of the Bidassoa, the change of countries in respect to inhabitants was not very observable except among the better orders.

On the 16th of February we broke up from our cantonments in Aurantz, and commenced the campaign of 1814, crossing the Nive at Ustaritz, and moving on in the direction of La Bastide de Clarence. We encamped on a wild heath, without any village or town being near us, and again the next morning continued our route to the place above-named, which we reached about noon, and encamped on a hill beyond it.

On the 22d we advanced to St Palais, having passed other villages, the names of which I have forgot, in the intermediate days. Nothing, however, of any note occurred in that period. On the 23d we encamped near La Chere and Charrette ; on the 24th we crossed two rapid and deep streams of the Bidowse. The first we got over with considerable ease,—it was the Gave de Mauleon, which we crossed at Nabes ; but the second, the Gave d'Oleron, was not only both deeper and more rapid than the other, but the passage seemed intended to be disputed with us ; some French cavalry having made their appearance on the opposite bank, as we approached the river. The resistance they could offer, however, seemed very trifling, for, on our bringing up some guns to the bank, and a few shots having been fired from them, and from a company of our second battalion, they withdrew.

We now prepared to go over ; accordingly, every man was ordered to take off his pouch and buckle it on the top of his knapsack, the ford being so deep as to take the men up to or above the middle. On this occasion I had I know not how many of the poor men hanging about me and my horse. Some were holding by the stirrup, some by the tail, and others by the mane, or wherever they could lay hold, for the stream was so rapid as to nearly sweep them off their legs. Indeed I understand several of those who followed us were actually swept down, and perished.

On reaching the farther bank, we found the French had endeavoured to render it impassable, by throwing harrows, &c., with their spikes upmost, in the only places where you could ascend from the river. I believe a trumpeter of the French was all who fell on this day.

We passed through Ville Neuve, and formed in a field beyond the village, till the whole division had got over. It was in this village where the scene between the mother, the child, and some of our officers, took place. When joined and formed, we moved on to a high and ugly common, not far in rear of the village of Orion, where we bivouacked for the night. It was most uncomfortable.

Before we reached our ground this evening, we observed, at a short distance to our left, a body of about 200 French infantry moving on parallel to us, but apparently making all haste to get away in front of us. Some suggested the idea of attacking and taking them prisoners; but as they were rather before us, it could not have been done without setting one of the battalions at them in double-quick time, and which would not have been an easy operation, after a long and fatiguing march, and fording two rivers. Besides, as our Quartermaster-general said, it was certain they could not be far from their support; consequently it would only bring on an affair, which it was not the General's wish to do at that time, for there was none near to support us should the enemy send a force against us. This day General Picton's division had a sharp affair at Navarreins, where they forced the passage of the Gave we had crossed.

On the 25th, we moved forward early in the morning, and on reaching the village of Orion, we found that Soult had had his head-quarters the night before, with a consider-able portion of his army, in and around the village; it was therefore fortunate we did not attack the French detach-ment before mentioned, for we should certainly have had Soult, with all his people, upon our single division. A French band had remained in this village till our arrival, having deserted in a body from the regiment to which they belonged, or they, seeing they could not make their escape, pretended to desert and join our army.

We bent our course towards Orthes, which was now only

a few leagues in front of us. A man brought a cask of
excellent wine to the road-side, with the intention of giving
every man of the division a drink, but we could not wait,
and were consequently obliged to leave the good man's gift.
It showed that either good-will or fear had prompted him
to this act. I rather think the former was the cause, as he
lived some distance from the road. We had not continued
long on the march, till we heard a loud and thundering explosion in front of us, which, as it was expected, turned
out to be the bridge of Orthes, which the enemy had
blown up. A short while after we came in sight of the
town, and one of our Portuguese Caçadore regiments being
sent forward, a smart skirmish commenced between them
and the French, who had been left on and about the bridge
to prevent our repairing it. I foolishly went down to see
what was going on, and had nigh paid for my curiosity.

We took up our ground behind a height which overlooked the town, through which the enemy were passing in
large columns. In consequence of this, we got some guns
into a field in front of our hill, and commenced a cannonade
upon them, which, we could observe, made them hurry
their pace considerably. They also brought some heavy
field-guns to bear upon us, and fired some shots, but without doing us much injury. Throughout the whole of the
road by which the French had come before us, desolation
and misery marked their footsteps ; and in the village of
Orion, where Soult himself had slept the night before, nothing could exceed the despair and misery of the few remaining inhabitants, who told us they had been literally
stripped of their all ; indeed, they appeared most forlorn
and wretched beings ; and, as might be expected, poured out
the most heavy and bitter complaints, not unmingled with
imprecations, on the heads of their plundering countrymen.

I went into a poor weaver's house here, where, if I mistake not greatly, the marauders had actually cut the web he was weaving out of the loom, and carried it off with them.

We remained on this ground all night, and the next morning his lordship was intently occupied for a considerable time in reconnoitring the enemy's position. At length, as if he had fully made up his mind how to act, he ordered our division to fall in, which was promptly obeyed; then, sending his staff with directions, we were ordered to file to the right, and to move down towards the river, apparently with the intention of crossing a little above the bridge, which had been destroyed. On the other side, immediately opposite what appeared to be the ford, were large bodies of infantry, together with a great quantity of artillery.

I recollect my battalion was leading the division, and it appeared at this moment as if we were going to be engaged in a most arduous and hazardous undertaking; for the enemy's artillery would have swept us off the face of the earth before we could possibly have reached the farther bank; however, this was only a *ruse de guerre,* and a most deep-planned and well-executed one it was; for while we were moving down towards the river, a staff-officer came riding, and ordered us all to hide as much as possible from the view of the enemy, by crouching down, &c. as we moved along. It may seem rather paradoxical to be ordered thus to act, at the same time that we wished the enemy to observe our movement; but the fact is, there were probably a thousand eyes fixed on us all the time we lay here, and who watched most closely our every movement; consequently, we could not stir without the enemy being aware of it; and if on this occasion we had made a show and a parade of our movement, it would have been suspected as only a feint at once, as the French themselves, from often practising this stratagem, would have penetrated immediately our object. But our Chief went a step too deep for them, adepts as they are in all the arts of this kind; for he made a pretence of hiding from them his movement, knowing well that we were observed; and this completely deceived them. This threat of crossing here was made in order to favour the construction of a bridge about eight or ten miles down the river, and the crossing there by another division, as they were thus enabled to guess where the principal force for opposition would be required. I believe a better planned or more successful stratagem was never practised. But I own, when we were marching down to the river to cross in front of the immense masses which we saw ready to oppose us, I believed that few would survive to tell the tale hereafter.

The moment when we were just opening from the covered ground to plunge into the river, we were instantly countermarched with all expedition, and moved down the river at a quick pace till we reached the pontoon bridge which had been so successfully constructed and thrown over at the village of Sala. This being now perfectly safe, we encamped at the village for the night.

On the morning of the 27th, we early crossed the river called the Gave de Pau, and moved forward in the direction of the town of Orthes by the great road. On the right bank of that river, when we came within about two miles of the town, we were moved more to our left, ascending the high ridge which runs parallel with the river, and on which the French had taken up a strong position, and were said to be between 30,000 and 40,000 strong. One division had been ordered to move along the summit of this ridge, on which ran the great road to Peyrehourade, and to attack the enemy on that flank, while our division communicated with that and the 3d division to our right. When the action was commenced, the 2d division had been directed to ford above the bridge, where our feint had been made the day before, and passing through the town, to attack on the opposite flank, and thus cut off their retreat towards the Pau. The enemy's position proved to be exceedingly strong, and difficult of access by us.

The action commenced by the 4th division attacking on the road leading along the ridge, where an obstinate and bloody conflict took place, without our people being able to make any impression. The attack of the 3d division, on our right, also commenced immediately after; but such was the nature of the ground on this side, being mostly in long pointed ridges, running out like the rays of a star, and which were exceedingly strong, that no efforts were able to force them from this ground.

General Hill had by this time got over the river, and was approaching the position. My division, having been deprived of two of its regiments, which had been sent, previous to the commencement of our operations this spring, to receive their clothing at St Jean de Luz, being rendered weak in consequence, it was kept in reserve, as I before mentioned. During this unsuccessful attack, our gallant Chief was for a considerable time immediately in front of us, watching with the most anxious care every motion of both armies. He appeared to me to be extremely thoughtful and serious on the occasion, as our troops did not succeed in forcing this stronghold of the enemy. The firing at this time was extremely animated, particularly on the ridge to our left, where great slaughter was made on both sides. And the French having discovered where he and his staff were assembled, opened a smart cannonade on the group, but without doing any mischief, I believe, and without being noticed by him. Their shots generally fell about our division, which was formed immediately behind the hill on which he stood.

At length, whether from the request of Colonel Barnard, who was at this time by his lordship's side, or whether by his own direction, I know not, but the Colonel was ordered to take on the 52d and 1st Portuguese belonging to the Caçadores, our 2d brigade, and endeavour to force a passage through the French line, by the gorge of the valley, which lay immediately in his front, and they would thus, if successful, penetrate into the centre of the enemy's position. They accordingly moved up the valley in column of companies, sustaining all the time the most galling and destructive fire, for the enemy were thus on each of their flanks, as well as in front. When they reached within a short distance of the centre height, they formed line, and moving on at a brisk pace and carrying every thing before them, they drove the enemy from the plateau, and thus penetrated into the very heart of their army. This was a most daring and intrepid movement, for although assailed by ten times their force, and nearly surrounded by the enemy, these gallant corps hesitated not to push on, although the very elements seemed as it were to fight against them ; for on the brow of the enemy's position the fire had been so heavy and so incessant, that the very furze bushes and herbs of all kinds were in a blaze along the front, through which, with innumerable foes behind it, these gallant men forced a passage at the point of the bayonet.

This movement had the effect of at once deciding the fate of the day, for Soult seeing his very centre and strongest position carried, which separated between his wings, at once ordered a retreat of his whole force. The remainder of our division were now despatched with all speed in pursuit of the flying enemy, but they never attempted after this to make a stand, and nothing was left for us to perform but to give chase to the fugitives. When we reached the enemy's centre position, we found that every thing had been cleared away which could in the least impede his movements ; every hedge and ditch had been completely levelled, so that nothing remained but a beautiful plain on the top of the ridge, except where works of defence had been thrown up. We were not successful in capturing any of the enemy, except the wounded, who had necessarily been left on the field, and we did not lay hold of any of his materiél, except a few guns which he had been obliged to abandon in a swamp below the position.

I have related only such things as fell within my own observation, but no doubt many were the heroic and gallant deeds that were performed in this hard contested battle, besides what I have detailed. As might be expected, the gallant 52d and its supporting corps, the 1st Portuguese Caçadores, suffered dreadfully, leaving probably one-fourth of their numbers on the field. But I must not omit mentioning one trait of gallantry which attracted the admiration of the whole army. Lord March (now the Duke of Richmond) had for some time been on the personal-staff of Lord Wellington, where his services had been most efficient. He also was at this time a captain in the 52d regiment, but from his high civil rank had never served as an infantry officer with his regiment. He was determined to know and practice his duty in every situation, and therefore requested leave from his lordship to be permitted to join his corps as a captain, which was granted of course, and this was his first debut in the character of an officer of foot. It was no doubt a sharp trial ; and poor fellow, while bravely leading on the company which his Majesty had intrusted to his command, he fell dangerously (then supposed mortally) wounded. This was a noble example to set our young nobility, and they cannot do better than to follow such a precedent. I understand he has been heard to say, "that the chance of a staff-officer being hit in action, is not near so great as that of an officer of infantry, who must quietly brave all that comes against him, while a staff-officer, being well mounted, can quickly get out of danger; and that if a gentleman wishes truly to learn his profession as an officer, he ought to serve for a time in the infantry whilst engaged in operations fh the field."

This was a most decided, but withal an unfruitful victory, and only tended to establish more firmly the superior skill of our commander, and the superior bravery of the British army. We had heard of the proceedings of the allies in the north, and of a number of the French generals having deserted the cause of their once potent, but now fallen master. And I verily believed that Soult had collected his whole force together here for the express purpose of either allowing himself to be surrounded, and thus make a show of being compelled to surrender, or of inducing his whole army to come over at once to the side of the Bourbons, but in all these conjectures I was completely mistaken; for whatever may have been Soult's faults as a man, he has always shown himself a consistent and an able defender of the cause he first espoused, and as such is certainly respectable.

We pursued the flying columns of the enemy for about two leagues beyond the field of action, crossing in our pursuit the river Luy de Bearne, and at night took up our abode in bivouack, near the village of Bonne Garde. The night proved extremely cold and frosty, for in the morning

1

when I intended to arise, I found my cloak frozen to the ground. We had no kind of covering. My commanding-officer had taken up his abode in a cottage close by, where there was no bed but what the people occupied. He therefore got into the kneading-trough, in which he slept very comfortably, but in the morning I remember he turned out like a miller.

We started soon after daybreak, and continued our march, crossing the small river Luy de France. Here I remember our assistant Quartermaster-general told us what great difficulty he found in obtaining information from the inhabitants as to the by-roads which run parallel to the great road from Orthes; for these good people could not conceive why he should be hunting after by-roads of this description, which were generally very bad, while the great road, which was always good, lay so near the line by which he wished to move, not knowing perhaps, or not understanding, that other divisions of the army were moving on the high-road, while we wished to make a corresponding movement on their flank. They would always, however, after directing him how to proceed for a while, bring him again on to the great road, which he wished to avoid for the reason before given.

The comfort and the efficiency of an army in the field depends more, I am persuaded, on the abilities and zeal of officers in the Quartermaster-general's department, than on any other branch of the service; for if they are remiss or unacquainted with their duty, the marches and counter-marches, the halts, and the changes of direction, are so numerous and annoying, that the spirits and strength of the troops are soon worn out, and of course dissatisfaction and inefficiency soon follow. But to the credit of the officers of this department at the period of which I am writing, I believe never army possessed more able, more zealous, or more active staff-officers, than we did, and that principally owing to the excellent example set them by the head of this department, than whom a more able conductor of an army does not exist. On one of these occasions when our assistant Quartermaster-general had occasion to wait upon the authorities of a village, he jokingly asked them for passports, as is customary in France, to proceed into the country. " Ma foi," says the worthy Mayor, " you obtained your passports at Vittoria, you need no others now."

We halted for the night near the village of Duerse. In the morning, we forded the Adour near a small village, the name of which I forget, and making a long and rapid march, we took possession of the city of Mont de Marsan, where we found immense magazines of provisions, which had been collected by the enemy. This was the most valuable capture that had been made by the British army since its arrival in the Peninsula; for although a great deal of treasure was obtained at Vittoria, yet a considerable portion of that fell into the hands of individuals; but this was secured for the benefit of the whole army. The enemy had abandoned the city previous to our arrival, consequently it was a bloodless conquest, which rendered it the more valuable. Mont de Marsan is what may be termed a fine and an extensive city, containing about 3000 inhabitants.

The people received us kindly upon the whole, and showed us great attention. Here we had superb quarters, and the change from what we had lately been accustomed to, produced a rather uncomfortable feeling; for our clothes and all our equipments so little corresponded with the magnificence around us, that we should have preferred less stately mansions, if comfortable, as more congenial with our respective establishments. But we did not long enjoy our splendid lodgings; for, having secured the booty, we left the city, and returned to the banks of the Adour. The march both to and from this city had been along straight flat roads, cut through an immense pine forest, with which this department is almost completely covered. The roads had been for some time much traversed, and having a sandy bottom, were consequently very bad at this season of the year; added to which, a violent storm of snow and sleet assailed us all the march of this day, which made it a rather uncomfortable business. We halted for the night in a village named, I think, St Maurice, and the next day were moved into St Sever, a considerable town on the left bank of the Adour, in which Lord Wellington had taken up his head-quarters. Here we remained some days, doing duty over his lordship, when we crossed to the right bank, and moved up the river, halting at the town of Grenade. We next morning continued our route up that bank till we reached Barcelonne, a considerable town some little distance from the river, and nearly opposite Aire, a large town on the left bank, and near which General the Hon. Wm. Stewart, with the 2d division, had had a smart brush with the enemy on the day we captured Mont de Marsan.

On the evening of the 10th we halted at the village of Arblade, and, on the 11th, entered Tarsac, where we remained for the night. We were next morning pushed on to a village in front, about a league distant, but were allowed to remain there only for one night, for the enemy now began to appear in our front in considerable force. We were consequently withdrawn, and, passing through Tarsac, the division formed in a wood about halfway between that and Aire. We expected something serious was about to occur, but, from what cause I know not, the enemy again retreat-

ed, leaving a body of cavalry on the road about half-a-league
beyond Tarsac, to which we again returned and took up our
quarters.

On the 16th, as these fellows still continued so near us,
although evidently without any infantry to support them,
it was determined either to drive them away or take them
prisoners. I must observe, our 15th hussars were at this
time occupying Tarsac with ourselves, and one squadron of
them were selected for this service. The advance of the
French consisted only of one squadron, the remainder of
their regiment being at some distance in rear as supports;
consequently it was but fair that an equal force should
attack them. Captain Hancox's squadron (in which was
Captain Booth, with his troop) was pitched upon for this
affair. The remainder of the 15th were drawn out to support them, if needed, but were not to take any part in the
combat. Every one of course went out to see the fight.

Accordingly this squadron moved on to the front, and
steadily advanced upon the enemy, who seemed determined
to stand the charge, as they put every thing ready to receive our gallant dragoons. When within a proper distance
the word " trot" was given, and soon after " gallop," and
then " charge," when our fellows dashed in among the
French, upsetting them in all directions, and cutting many
of them down to the ground. In a few minutes the business was settled, for our people returned, bringing in with
them the captain commanding, (and who, I believe, had
been personally engaged with Captain Hancox,) with about
twenty-five men, prisoners. The rest made their escape.
The French captain, and the greater part of the twenty-five
men, were wounded, and some were left dead on the road.

I shall not soon forget the little wounded captain. He,
I believe, was either a native of Tarsac, or somewhere near,

and had been determined to show his valour to the utmost; hence his standing, when he ought to have retired; but all the way, as they were bringing him along into the village, and after he reached the house where he directed them to take him, he kept crying out, " I'm as brave as a lion!— I'm as brave as the devil!" and could scarcely be got to hold his peace while the surgeon was dressing him. Most piteous moaning was made by many of the inhabitants, to whom it seems he was well known.

We understood afterwards that this regiment, the 13th French hussars, had fallen rather under the displeasure of Soult, for some ill conduct on a former occasion, and that they were thus determined to wipe off the stain and retrieve their character; but they would have shown more sense, and have rendered more service to their country, had they retired when they saw it was determined to drive them away.

On the 18th, we again advanced by the road the French had taken, and, crossing the Adour at the bridge and village of La Row or Arros, we pursued our route till we reached the town of St Germain's, where we halted for a short space, and thence to Plaisance, a good town, where we remained for the night. An unfortunate circumstance occurred in or near this town, which might have produced the most disastrous consequences :—A man, who most likely had been resisting the plundering of his house, was basely murdered by some soldier or soldiers of the division; but although every endeavour was made to discover the perpetrators of this vile act, they could not be found out; but a subscription was set on foot among the officers of the division, and 100 guineas were collected and paid to the unfortunate widow, who, though grieved for the loss of her husband, was thankful for the money. I strongly suspect my friends the Portuguese were the culprits on this occasion.

On the 19th we again moved forward, and, passing Obrigort, halted for the night at the village of Aget. Towards the close of this day's march, we both heard and saw smart skirmishing, down on the great road which runs parallel to the ridge on which we were, and from Auch to Tarbes, along the plain on our right, and passes through Vic Bigore. Near this town the firing was very brisk. We understood it was Picton's division driving the French before them.

The next morning we started early, and, continuing our march along the ridge of the height on which our last night's quarters were situated, we reached pretty soon the town of Rabasteins, where we learnt that the enemy had taken up a position in and near the town of Tarbes. We, accordingly, changing our direction, moved to our right, down the road leading from the former to the latter place. We passed on this road the sixth division, which, it seems, was ordered to keep on the flank of the enemy, which, should he make a stand, this division was to turn. When we got within about a mile and a half of Tarbes, we discovered the enemy posted on a strong woody height on the left of the road, with a windmill on its highest and most distant point.

The whole of our 95th people were accordingly ordered forward, to endeavour to drive them from this position. My battalion formed the right, the 2d battalion the centre, and the 1st battalion the left of our line of skirmishers. We found them covered in front with a great number of light troops, which occupied us some time in driving in, and in which service we suffered considerably, for they occupied the hedges and dikes on the high ground, from which it was necessary we should dislodge them. We had also a considerably-sized brushwood to pass through before we could get at them. At length, after much smart skirmishing, we gained the height, but found the whole of their heavy infantry drawn up on a steep acclivity, near the windmill, which allowed them to have line behind line, all of which could fire at the same time over each other's heads, like the tiers of guns in a three-decker. We continued, however, to advance upon them, till we got within a hundred paces of this formidable body, the firing from which was the hottest I had ever been in, except perhaps Barossa. At this moment I received a shot through my right shoulder, which compelled me for a moment to retire ; but meeting the main support of my battalion advancing with Colonel Ross at its head, and finding my wound had not disabled me, I again advanced with him, until we got close under the enemy's line, and took post behind a hillock, which protected us from their fire.

We here found Colonel Norcott, who then belonged to the 2d battalion, riding about on his large black mare ; but he had not ridden long till he also was wounded through the shoulder, from which he still suffers. While we were in this situation, a shot struck a captain of ours in the side where he had his drinking-horn slung ; in fact it struck both the horn and his side ; but, from some cause, it did not pe- netrate the flesh, but bruised it sore, which is generally painful. The captain, and those about him, thought he was shot through the body ; they accordingly picked him up, and were carrying him off to the rear, when he cried, " Stop, let me feel," and putting his hand down to the place, and finding no wound, he sprung out of their arms, and, with the most ludicrous appearance possible, returned to his post again. No one present could refrain from laughing at the ridiculousness of this occurrence, although at the moment

the men were falling fast around us.   At this time also, a
spent shot, one which I imagine had first hit the ground,
struck me on the left arm, but did not injure me.   I now
thought it better to go to the rear to get my shoulder
dressed, immediately after which I became quite faint
from loss of blood.   The firing still continued most animated on both sides ; but before an hour had elapsed, the
French were driven completely from every position they
held on this very strong hill ; and as I returned, (after having been dressed, and having swallowed some spirits to
remove the faintness,) I found them posting away with all
expedition to the plain below, some guns, which had just
arrived, giving them an occasional shot, but from which
they did not suffer much, they marched with such rapidity.
We immediately followed them down to the plain, on
reaching which, we perceived a body of French troops
coming apparently from the town of Tarbes, pursued by the
3d division, with whom they had been engaged, and which,
with some exertion, we thought we could intercept and cut
off ; but they, perceiving our intention, inclined considerably
to the right, and marching with all speed, they got away
before us.

The enemy now having all retired across the plain, began
to take up a strong position on a height at its extremity,
towards which we continued to advance ; but Lord Wellington having expected that the 6th division would by
this time have reached their position, and, attacking in
flank, have rendered our attack in front more likely to
succeed, and they not making their appearance, although
it was now nigh dusk, he ordered the divisions here to
halt, and bivouack for the night on the plain.   I never
saw any one more disappointed, or apparently more annoyed
by this last order, than our Adjutant-general, the lamented

Sir Edward Packenham; he was for attacking them at once; but this could not have been done without a great sacrifice of excellent troops, as all those were who now filled the ranks of the British army, having by this time been completely seasoned, and become almost invaluable. In reviewing the operations of this day, I need say little, as facts speak for themselves. The enemy had on the Windmill hill, as it was vulgarly called, or more properly the hill of Oleac, I believe a whole division, consisting of at least 5000 or 6000 men, while not a shot was fired by any but by the sixteen companies of my regiment, amounting probably to 1000 or 1100 men; it is true the other regiments of the division were drawn up in rear of us, and would have supported us had we been repulsed. But it is not so much to the driving away of this so much stronger force, that I would draw the reader's attention, as to the great loss the enemy sustained, and solely from our fire. I believe I shall not be far from the truth, if I state their loss in killed and wounded as equal to the whole strength of our sixteen companies.

Lord Wellington, in his dispatch, mentions the destruction caused in the enemy's ranks as unusually severe; hence the advantage of rifles over the common musket, or else the superior mode of using our arms beyond what is practised in the line. The Americans tauntingly tell us, our soldiers do not know how to use the weapons that are put into their hands; and, truly, if we are to judge by the awful destruction which they have occasionally inflicted upon our brave soldiers, we should be led to suspect that they understand this science much better than ourselves. It might, however, be easily remedied, if more attention were paid to the instruction of the recruit in this most essential qualifi-

N

cation, and more time and ammunition devoted to target practice; but, at the same time, every officer should be made to know something of projectiles in general, or he will, as at present, be incapable of instructing his men. I will venture to assert, that eight out of ten of the soldiers of our regular regiments will aim in the same manner at an object at the distance of 300 yards, as at one only 50. It must hence be evident that the greater part of those shots are lost or expended in vain; indeed the calculation has been made, that only one shot out of 200 fired from muskets in the field takes effect, while one out of twenty from rifles is the average. My opinion is, that our line troops ought to be armed with a better description of musket. If five shillings more were added to the price, it would make a great difference in the article, and be very trifling to the public. Our army has always been too sparingly supplied with flints, which may be had almost for an old song; but if wanted in the field, nothing can supply their place. Many a brave soldier has fallen while hammering at a worn out flint. It is true we can, with the weapons we have, drive any other army out of the field, but not without occasionally sustaining an overwhelming loss, particularly when opposed to the Americans; and could we meet them with the same advantages they possess in point of shooting, our chances of victory would be greater, and at less expense. These are my private opinions only, and are deduced from the experience I have had, both as a heavy infantry soldier and a rifleman. I am now firmly persuaded, that of the near 200 shots I fired on the 2d of October 1799, in Holland, not one took effect, from my total want of knowledge how to aim. What an useless expenditure this was of both time and ammunition! Much indeed has lately been done by Sir Henry Torrens, to supply the deficiency of which I have been speaking, but still not sufficient, in my opinion, to remedy all the evils attendant thereon.

Our loss on this occasion was very heavy, being about 100 men and eleven officers killed and wounded; the proportion of officers being nearly double what usually takes place. The regiments which supported us also had some casualties, arising from the shots which passed over our heads striking among them; but they were not considerable. My servants having heard I was wounded, went to Tarbes, (where all the wounded were collected,) with my baggage. I should consequently have been very ill off, had not my kind friend and messmate, Major Balvaird, lent me his tent and bed, as he himself had been ordered on picquet. Immediately after nightfall, the enemy had all retired from the position in front of us. We accordingly next morning continued the pursuit, and halted at night at the village of Lannemazen, not far from the borders of the Pyrenees, towards which, in their retreat, they had been inclined. This day and night, my shoulder had become extremely painful. We started again in the morning; but leaving the Pyrenees, we turned our faces more towards Toulouse, and took up our abode for the night at a considerable-sized town, called Castelnau; here the inhabitants received us very kindly, and we had excellent quarters. However, on the following morning, we were obliged to continue our march, and passing through several villages on the road, halted for the night at L'Isle, in Dodon. During this day's march, my poor old horse played me a sad trick. He was one which I had been compelled to purchase as soon after I lost my little Portuguese one by the bad shoeing of the blacksmith at Sumbilla, as I could fall in with one for sale. He was a very tall grey horse, rather old, and whose mouth had not been well made in his breaking ; he was withal rather stubborn, or more properly speaking stupid, consequently he did not always obey the rein as he ought. The roads were excessively deep and dirty, and as I was riding at the head of the battalion, and had occasion to pull him a little to one side, for some purpose or other, he either would not, or could not, obey the pull of the rein ; and as I had but one hand, he took advantage of it, and sat down completely on his haunches, in the very deepest of the mire. Of course I was tumbled right over his rump, and rolled in the mud, and after extricating myself as well as I could, I crawled out, as pretty a figure as may well be imagined. This, as might be expected, raised the laugh of all who saw it, at my expense; but, uncomfortable and ridiculous as my situation was, I was not hurt, the mud being sufficiently deep to protect me from any injury by the fall. In this village I fell in with a Frenchman who had just come from Toulouse, towards which he understood we were bending our course. He gave me such a flaming account of the " belle position" in the neighbourhood of that town, and of the impregnable works which Soult had caused to be thrown up, and of the superb artillery which were stationed there, and which, he said, were those who had served in the famous battle of Austerlitz, and of the utter improbability of any impression ever being made on them by an enemy, that if I had given credit to the half of what he told me, I might have been filled with fear lest all our laurels might here be tarnished. From what motive this rather exaggerated statement was made, I know not, but am inclined to think it was merely an inclination to indulge in a trifling gasconade. On the 25th we reached Mont Ferrand, where we halted for the night.

On the 27th, in the morning, we were moved forward to the village of Tournefoile, where it seems some of our cavalry had been quartered the night before, but who had had their quarters beat up during the night by a body of the enemy, who still held the ground beyond the village. My battalion, and a Portuguese battalion, were sent forward, the remainder of the brigade following. We found the enemy occupying the road leading from the village to a bridge about half a mile distant, together with the hedges and enclosures in the vicinity. My people extended to the left, while the Portuguese battalion kept on the road. A smart skirmish now commenced, during which the enemy gradually retired towards the bridge; but at this time a most remarkable occurrence took place. One of our men (the servant of a friend of mine) received a shot in the mouth, which struck out several of his teeth. One of these was propelled with such force by the blow that it flew at least twenty yards, and, entering the left arm of one of the Portuguese on the road, inflicted a deep and severe wound. When the surgeon of the 43d, who was the nearest to this man at the time, came to dress the wounded Portuguese, he, instead of a ball as every one expected, extracted a tooth, at which, no doubt, both he and all about him were quite astonished; and a report was immediately set afloat that the enemy were firing bones instead of balls. This most extraordinary circumstance was not cleared up till they were informed of our man having had his teeth knocked out, when, after comparing the relative situations of the two men, it became quite evident how this most uncommon wound had been inflicted. If any thing like a joke might be permitted on such an occasion, it may with great propriety be said, the Frenchman who fired the shot had killed two birds with one stone. I happened to be near our man at the time, and besides seeing him wounded, I enquired minutely into the circumstances, or I own I should have hesitated before I gave implicit credit to the story; so it may probably be with my reader. Poor fellow, he had afterwards nearly all his intestines torn out by a cannon-shot at the fatal attack near New Orleans, and where I saw him writhing in the agonies of death; his name was Powell, and he was, I believe,-a Welshman.

Not long after the commencement of the skirmish, the artillery on both sides was brought into play; but the enemy kept gradually retiring till they crossed the bridge, and as we did not pursue them, they quietly walked off, taking the road towards Toulouse. I cannot conceive for what purpose this body of troops had been sent here, unless it was intended as a reconnoissance, to ascertain whether any, and what description, of troops had arrived at this point, as their waiting, after driving out our cavalry, to see whether any infantry approached, would seem to indicate. Major Balvaird was conspicuously brave on this occasion. The loss on either side was but trifling.

CHAPTER XIV.

The British Army cross the Garonne—Advance on Toulouse—Prepare for the Attack—The Attack—Spaniards driven back—Battle very hot—French completely defeated—Soult evacuates Toulouse, and tardily adheres to the Bourbons.

On the 28th or 29th, we were moved forward, and after a short march we reached a beautiful plain, with Toulouse appearing most magnificent in the distance. Here we went into cantonments, in the different villages and chateaux in the neighbourhood, the greater part of which were completely deserted, and many of them most wofully sacked and plundered, which could have been done only by their own troops. A noble and stately mansion, belonging to a Mr Villeneuve, stood immediately in front of our outposts, which had shared the same fate with all the others, every article of furniture having been entirely destroyed. The cloth had been torn from the billiard-table, the splendid pier-glasses shivered into a thousand atoms, and, in short, every article of luxury or splendour which a man could wish for, might have been found in this princely habitation previous to its desertion by its owner; but now devastation

and destruction had laid its unhallowed hands on all in which
its possessor had formerly delighted. I, with my messmates, took the liberty of visiting Mr V.'s fish-ponds, where
we found some fine-looking carp; and having some hooks by
me, we caught a considerable quantity, which we imagined
would be a great treat to our messmates; but we found
them excessively muddy, and not worth eating. Here also
we rejoiced in being able to procure some good provender for
our still half-starved horses and mules. The grass and cinque-
foil which we found in this beautiful and luxuriant plain,
in a few days began to make a wonderful improvement in
our poor fellow-travellers. I know not a more gratifying
feeling than we experienced in thus being able to feed the
hungry; for although they were but of the inferior creation,
yet so much did our own comforts, and, indeed, efficiency
for service, depend on their being capable of performing the
task allotted to them, and so much did the circumstance of
our having passed through trials and dangers together at-
tach us to them, that I very frequently would have preferred
getting them a meal even at the expense of wanting one
myself. Here my little Portuguese horse, which I had
originally brought from Lisbon, and who had been my companion in all my wanderings, (except when he was left for
a while owing to his bad foot,) began to look quite brisk
and lively again; for hitherto his spirits had been very low
indeed since he happened by his misfortune, and had been
literally starved into the bargain.

A pontoon bridge having been constructed some distance
above the town, and which our engineers had been able to
accomplish on account of its being thrown over above the
junction of the Ariege with the Garonne, on the 31st we
moved down towards this point, and crossing it, my battalion
was left as its guard in a village on the bank of the river.

The remainder of the division, and the —— division,* moved up the Ariege river with the intention of crossing, and thus approaching Toulouse in that direction; but, from the heavy rains, the river was too much flooded, which, together with the dreadful state of the roads, these troops were unable to effect this operation, and were consequently recalled.

By the 2d of April the whole had recrossed the Garonne, when we again went into our cantonments on the plain, but now farther down the river than before. We remained here a few days, and I cannot help recording a remarkable circumstance which took place at this time. For want of dwelling-houses we had been obliged to put a certain number of the men of my battalion into a sort of wine-house; it was not a vault, for it was above ground, but had a considerable number of barrels of wine in it, amongst which the men were obliged to sleep. It will scarcely be credited, but not one of these men ever appeared the least intoxicated during the whole time they lay there. Whether they were completely tired of wine, or whether their having been placed in such a situation produced a feeling of honour and pride among them, I know not, but I verily believe less wine was drunk by these men during the time they remained here, than would have been had they had to pay most exorbitantly for it. With soldiers I believe it is as with mankind in general; what is prohibited always appears more valuable or more pleasurable in our eyes, than what we may with freedom enjoy.

On the 6th we moved down the river till within a short distance of Grenade, about twelve miles below Toulouse. We halted near a small village, and encamped. A pontoon bridge had been thrown over the Garonne here, and one division (I believe the 3d) had crossed; but now, owing to

* Some obscurity is occasioned here and elsewhere, by blanks being left in the MS., which the death of the good-humoured and kindly author has rendered it now impossible to fill up.—ED.

the swollen state of the river, together with several attempts which were now made by the enemy to destroy the bridge, by floating down trees, &c. which might eventually carry it away, it loosened at the farther end, and the anchors being taken up, the whole was allowed to float down to our side of the river, keeping fast the end next our own bank. We remained in this situation for several days, one division only being on the opposite side, with which it was impossible to communicate, or, if attacked, to afford it almost any support. Now was the time for the enemy to bestir himself; for had he marched out of Toulouse with half his force, and been met at this place by the force he had at Montauban, they must have annihilated this division, or taken them prisoners. It is true we might have rendered them some little assistance by our artillery from the bank we occupied, but the distance was so great that a determined enemy would not have held back from the dread of it.

I took a trip from hence to Grenade, where the paymaster-general had established the military chest, as I had not yet quite finished my paymaster's duty. It is a good-sized town, but contains nothing remarkable, only here I remember I got some excellent wine of the Champagne kind, and which my friend poured out of an immense magnum bottle. I understood our Chief was most anxious to have the bridge re-established by the 9th, which was Easter eve, the weather having now somewhat taken up, and the river of course had fallen; but although the engineer thought he could effect it, and had promised his lordship it should be ready by that time, it was not passable till the morning of the 10th. Early on that morning, my division crossed to the other side, together with the 4th and 6th divisions, and a whole host of Spaniards.

I omitted to mention, that these latter gentry, on their entering France, had behaved most wantonly, and had com-

mitted numerous atrocities; on which, his lordship, as Gene-
ralissimo, had ordered them back to their own country again;
but upon the promise of good behaviour, and an anxious desire to participate in the honourable achievements of the
allied troops, he had granted them permission to rejoin the
army, and they were to have a post of honour assigned
them at the ensuing battle. Such was the current report
which prevailed among our army newsmongers: be it as it
may, however, they were here in number, I should think,
about 6000 or 8000. The whole army now present having
crossed, except General Hill with the 2d division, advanced
upon the town of Toulouse. We here found a beautiful
country and excellent roads, along which we got on rapidly. The town stands close to the right bank of the river,
along which there are numerous quays, and over which
there is an excellent bridge, communicating with the
suburb on the opposite side, called St Cyprian. From the
river on the north side of the town runs the famous canal
of Languedoc, with which it communicates by locks, and
which, encircling the town on that and on the east sides,
with the river on the west, almost entirely encloses it. On
the east side of the town, and just beyond the canal, a considerable eminence arises, forming a sort of chain or ridge,
on the top of which numerous redoubts and batteries had
been constructed, and which, both from the nature of the
ground and by the great labour bestowed upon them, had
been rendered, as the Frenchman told me, nearly impregnable.

The 6th division, supported by the 4th, had been ordered to move considerably to the left, and, after crossing
the Garonne, to attack this formidable position on the
outer side, while the Spaniards were to attack it immediately in front. My division was ordered to communicate

with the right of the Spaniards, and, extending down to
the great Montauban road, was to press upon the town in
this direction, in order to aid the attack upon the height before mentioned. The 3d division joined our right at the
Montauban road, and extended from thence down to the
river, and were ordered to act similarly to us. The 2d
division, under General Hill, remained on the other side of
the river, and was to co-operate by attacking the suburb
before mentioned, together with the works for the protection of the bridge, and for the same purpose of our attack,
namely, to keep the troops in these parts of the town employed, while the 6th division and Spaniards attacked the
height. Immediately in front of our division, we found
considerable bodies of troops, at some distance from the
town, occupying the houses all along the road, and which
it took us a considerable time to drive in. They had
also constructed a battery on the bridge over the canal,
where the great road passes, and from which they kept up
an almost incessant fire. At the hither end of the bridge
also there stood a very large convent, which they had fortified in a very strong manner, having loopholed the whole
of the surrounding wall, which was twenty feet high, and
had also looped the upper part of the convent, which contained a garrison of probably 1000 or 1200 men.

We commenced operations in conjunction with the 3d
division on our right, in driving these people in, and with
whom a smart firing was kept up during the whole day.
The French had also other troops beyond the canal, and
on the Moorish or Roman wall which encircled the town
inside the canal, and both of which they had fortified; so that,
had it been intended we should force the town on this side,
we should have found it a difficult undertaking: we were,
however, merely (as said before) to press upon them with-

out committing ourselves ; but unfortunately, in the eagerness of some of our people to push forward, they got
immediately under the muzzles of the pieces of the men
who were defending the convent, and from the loopholes
several of our poor fellows were shot without being able to
see their antagonists. A good number fell here ; for it was
not more than thirty yards distant where they had taken
up their post, and an unpleasant one it was as well as dangerous ; for they were obliged to stand in a drain which ran
from a jakes, and which of course emitted no very desirable
flavour ; or, if they had left it for a moment, they were immediately shot. Our adjutant escaped here as by a miracle,
the bole of a very small tree having stopped the ball that
would have pierced his body. When, however, we had got
them fairly driven in, we had then time to look about us,
and the first thing we saw was the Don moving on to the
attack of the height with all due ceremony. They gained
the first or lower ridge without much opposition, and here
getting up some artillery, a pretty heavy fire was opened on
the enemy ; but the French remained quite passive, not offering to resist the approaching Spaniards till they got within a certain distance of their works on the top of the hill.

The Spaniards, elated by having gained the first ridge so
easily, pushed on too rapidly, and without having taken time
to re-form their columns after the first conquest. They
were not aware either that a rather deep ravine separated
them from the enemy's works ; however, on they pushed,
in a very disorderly manner, till they reached the point the
French intended they should reach, when a fire was opened
out upon them, such as they had never witnessed before.
Few troops would have remained unshaken by such a reception, but to the Spaniards it was intolerable ; consequently they broke into a thousand parties, and, turning

5

tail, it was who should be first away from such unpleasant doings. I am told that Lord Wellington at this moment could scarcely hold his sides for laughing, and cried out he " wondered whether the Pyrenees would bring them up again, they seemed to have got such a fright." He did not indeed depend on their valour, or he would have made a bad winding up of his Peninsular campaign. The moment they left the height, every man took the way that seemed to him best, and they soon after literally covered the whole plain, and set to work with all expedition to plunder at least, if they would not fight. Some of the villains had the audacity to come and take a poor man's horse out of the stable of the very house which we were then, as it were, defending, and had nigh got off with it; but having been perceived, it was taken from them, and restored again to its owner.

The left of our division was now obliged to be moved up to fill the space vacated by these vagabonds; and in doing which a good deal of hard fighting took place. This also made the people in front of us rally again, and coming out in great numbers hurraing and shouting, we had something to do to drive them back. But by this time we heard, in the distance behind the hill, a dropping and now brisker fire; by and by, approaching the summit, it became quite animated. We could plainly perceive now the different appearance which the French assumed; they no longer lay supine and passive till their enemy approached their works, but fought for every inch of ground, and all was now animation and bustle among them, hurrying to the support of those troops who defended the redoubts, &c. on the point assailed. The battle now raged with great fury, each party with all their might for the mastery, and the French, we could perceive, when compelled by sheer force to yield ground, did it with the utmost reluctance. At length, we saw the British colour waving on the summit of the hill, with the most deadly warfare raging on each side of it; but every move we saw was in favour of the British.

The 42d regiment had by this time gained possession of the principal redoubt, which they held till their ammunition was all expended, and which the enemy perceiving, or suspecting, again advanced, and gained possession of it. Things did not now wear quite so favourable an aspect; but being promptly supported by other troops behind them, a movement was again made in advance, and again the French were expelled from the redoubt. Great was the slaughter in and about this place, as I saw next day when I visited it.

The enemy were now reluctantly compelled to yield up all those famous works, on which so much time and labour had been expended, and on which they so much relied, and were obliged to abandon (slowly indeed) this long disputed ridge; but they fought till they were fairly forced down into the town, where they still kept up a feeble fire; at length it gradually subsided. This was the principal part of the drama; but it had many subordinate plots. On our right, General Picton, with that ardour which ever characterised him, was scarcely well satisfied to play an under part on this occasion; and, instead of merely keeping his opponents in play, as I before hinted, he was for effecting a forcible entry into the town. He accordingly attacked with his division a strong and well-secured battery, near the canal, in doing which his brave Connaught Rangers, who had scarcely ever hitherto known a reverse, met with a severe and bloody repulse, in which they lost a great number of excellent officers and men. The other corps of his division, who co-operated, also suffered greatly. General Hill strictly obeyed his instructions, and, as he always did, effected every object at which he aimed.

In this action I had another opportunity of witnessing the effect of presentiment. Early in it I was sent forward by my commanding-officer with some orders to a company of ours, which was in front skirmishing, and which had taken possession of a house, which partly screened them from the enemy's battery on the bridge. Behind this house, one of the men was sitting on a heap of stones with the most woe-worn countenance possible. He had separated from the rest of the men, and was sitting here apparently ruminating on his fate, and appeared to be quite absorbed in his meditations. I remarked him most particularly, wondering what could render him so different from the rest of his comrades, who were all life and animation, and from what he had formerly been himself in action. He presently went forward with some of the other men, and soon after fell to rise no more. The poor man's melancholy look made a deep impression upon me at the time, together with his fate soon after.

Thus terminated the battle of Toulouse; our troops maintaining the ground they had gained, while the enemy had retired into the town completely beaten. Soult seemed undetermined how to act, whether to endeavour to hold the town, (which indeed he might have done for a day or two perhaps,) or to leave it by the road towards the south, the only one now open to him. We rested on the field all night, the enemy sending an occasional shot or shell in the direction of our camp. Next morning we still found the enemy retaining possession of the town; and nothing being likely to be done, I rode up with another officer to see the bloody field, with all its redoubts and batteries, and also to

see, if I could, in what situation the enemy now appeared.
Just as we reached the summit, a cry was given by the 42d
sentry, " Turn out the picquet." There was a good deal
of firing going on in the suburbs nearest to the position,
which this Highlander thought it right to apprize his people
of. We looked a considerable time with our glasses, and
observed a good number of troops on a green and open space
in that part of the suburbs, and who every now and then
would fire their muskets. I thought it must either be a
sort of *feu-de-joie*, or a funeral, and it turned out to be the
latter. They were burying a general officer, who had fallen
the day before, and to whom they were paying the last
melancholy honours ; but it was conducted in a quite different manner from our military funerals, for they did not
fire in volleys like us ; but every few minutes apparently a
few men only fired, and by and by some others. This had
the effect, however, of turning out our whole line in the
neighbourhood of the position ; and as I was afterwards
returning, I met Colonel Barnard and Colonel Colborne
(than whom there were not two better officers in the army)
riding up to see what was the matter. Colonel Barnard
asked me what it was. I told him what I thought it was.
He said the whole line had fallen in, thinking it was an
attack.

Towards evening we heard that the inhabitants of the
city had been most urgent on Soult to withdraw from it ;
and that he had promised to do so. Indeed, had he not,
Lord Wellington might, if he chose, have soon reduced the
town to ashes ; for the heights we had taken were not 500
yards distant from the city, and completely overlooked it.
On the morning of the 12th, therefore, Soult marched out,
and was not molested by our troops. He took the road to
Villefranche and Carcassonne, up the canal of Languedoc,

N 2

our cavalry following their track. Now all the loyalists came rushing out of the town to meet and welcome us: every one wearing white scarfs or favours to denote his attachment to the Bourbons. Now all was joy and festivity, and nothing but shaking of hands and embracing was to be seen in all directions. This day also arrived Lord Stewart from Paris with the account of Bonaparte's abdication, and of the Bourbons having been reinstated. It was also rumoured that Soult had received this news previous to the battle; but not being inclined to yield obedience to that dynasty, he had allowed the warfare to proceed. Indeed, what almost puts this beyond a doubt, was his still continuing for many days after this to refuse sending in his submission to the Bourbon government. We also heard afterwards that the courier bringing the official information of Bonaparte's fall, &c. had been detained by the postmaster of Montauban by Soult's direction; for although he had had private intelligence of the fact, he imagined the detention of the official information might screen him hereafter. Such are the surmises of the wise heads respecting this affair, which, as it turned out, is to be regretted; for the sacrifice of so many valuable lives on both sides was a thing of no trifling importance; but I believe Soult felt sore at his having been so often worsted, and hoped here in some measure to retrieve his lost honours; for it cannot be doubted, I believe, that he expected to be able to repel our attack at least, if not to force us to retire from Toulouse.

On the 13th, the divisions marched into the town; my battalion having the fauxbourg adjoining the lately disputed position assigned to it, and in which we found very comfortable quarters. To show that the French people of this place took Lord Wellington either for a very generous person, or a great fool, a man who owned a house on the border of the position, and which the French had fortified by loopholing it, and otherwise rendering it unfit for occupation by its owner, sent in a memorial to his lordship, praying him to order that he might receive out of the military chest a sufficient sum to enable him to put his house in its former state ; and this, although it had been done by his own countrymen. I suppose his lordship would laugh at it when he saw it. I should have been inclined to be angry with the fellow. The man showed the memorial to the adjutant and myself before he sent it in—a step which of course we dissuaded him from taking.

Notwithstanding it was notorious that Bonaparte's career was at that time finished, Soult still made a show of holding out for him ; in consequence of which the army was again put in motion to compel him either to send in his adhesion to the new government, or to resign his command of troops who had not now a master. He had taken up a position near Villefranche. Accordingly, we marched, I think, on the 15th or 16th, the which rather alarmed him ; and in consequence he despatched Count Gazan with terms to offer to his lordship, the which, after some alterations, were finally agreed upon, and the army returned once more to Toulouse, where we resumed our former quarters.

Thus finished the Peninsular War, the last campaign of which had been the most active probably that is recorded in history. In ten months and a half we had marched from the frontiers of Portugal, had completely traversed Spain, which we had cleared of its long troublesome and insidious invaders ; had penetrated far into the interior of that country, which three years before gave law to most of the continental nations ; and had worsted, in various actions, those troops, which, except when encountering the British, had been accustomed almost invariably to conquer.

CHAPTER XV.

Author's happy state during 1813 and 1814—Character of the veritable
French—British distributed over the Country—Civility of the Inhabitants of Grissolles—Amusements in quarters—The British prepare
to quit France.

WHEN I look back on the events of 1813 and 1814, I
cannot but deem that the happiest period of my life, for I
had been actively, and, as I believed, usefully employed.
My mind during this time was tranquil, and I was, with a
few exceptions, prosperous in my outward circumstances.
All those among whom my lot was cast were now sincerely
friendly to me, and I believe I may with confidence affirm
that I had not (with the exception of the person before
mentioned, and who was now far removed from me) a single
enemy in the world. It is true my occupation had not
been, strictly speaking, of a Christian character, but I believed I was fulfilling my duty ; hence the peace of mind
which I enjoyed. I have since learned certainly, that a
Christian, to resemble his Master, should be more ready to
save than to destroy men's lives ; but, at the same time, I
cannot see why a Christian soldier should not be as zealous

in the defence of his king and country, as those who are
actuated by other motives; and it is certain, I believe,
although I once doubted whether there was such a precept,
that in whatever calling or occupation a man is in when
called to become a Christian, that therein he should abide,
1st Cor. vii. 17, 20, and 24.   But I attribute the peace of
mind I then enjoyed as much to the constant employment
which the nature of our services entailed upon us, as to any
other cause.   Be it remembered, I was doing the duties of
both paymaster and quartermaster during this period, and
my battalion had been as often called into action as any in
the army, having been engaged in battles and skirmishes
no less than sixteen times in less than ten months.   This
naturally left little time for reflection.   But, above all, I
am bound to render thanks to where alone it is due, to that
gracious and beneficent Being, who not only watched over
me during this period, and protected me from harm, but
who poured his choicest blessings upon me, even the blessings of a cheerful and contented heart, together with the
means of retrieving my sadly deranged finances; for had I
not been appointed acting paymaster, I might have gone to
prison on my return to my native country, from the unavoidable losses I had sustained, and which I shall mention
by and by.   Another cause of comfort and cheerfulness
arose from our operations against the enemy having been
invariably successful; for we never, from the time of our
leaving the frontiers of Portugal, till we took possession of
Toulouse, met with any thing like a serious reverse.

Most of my readers no doubt know that the city where
we had now taken up our quarters is one of the largest and
finest in this part of France; but as it has been so often
described, I shall content myself with merely informing my
readers, that the people among whom we now resided were

truly and veritably French. The character of the inhabitants, since we left our poor friends the Basques, had materially changed ; that kind, but rude and simple hospitality, which had on most occasions been displayed by those honest mountaineers, had now given place to all that imposing, but less sincere politeness of the real French character. We were, indeed, treated here with every degree of respect ; and perhaps more, or at least an equal degree of attention, was paid to our convenience and comfort, as they would have shown to their own troops. We had every reason, therefore, to be perfectly satisfied.

In this part of the country there are a great number of Protestants, which, of course, permitted us to live on better terms with them than had they been all such stanch and ' bigoted Catholics as we met with in some parts of the Continent, and where our heretical presence was frequently looked upon as a contamination ; for I remember well in the small village of Zalada, where we lay for some time, near Astorga, we never left the village, as they supposed, for a permanency, but the joy bells were rung for our departure. It was our lot, indeed, to be frequently quartered in this village, and such was their invariable custom. It is true the Padre and people of the place only expressed openly the feeling that was covertly, but universally, entertained throughout Spain and Portugal respecting us ; for although the monks and priests made great pretences of friendship and good-will towards us, while we were upholding them in their iniquitous dominion over the minds of the people, yet secretly they cordially hated us, and were glad when at last our successes contributed to rid their country of both the invaders and their conquerors. One noble Spanish lady, (I remember well,) when I was quartered at Cadiz, made use of an expression which I am sure would shock and horrify my simple and delicate country-women. She said, " She should rejoice to see all the French then in their country hung up in the intestines (las tripas) of the English, who had come to drive them out." Thus they should get quit of both. This lady, as might be supposed, was a most depraved and abandoned being, yet even she, it seems, looked upon us in the light of a curse or plague sent upon their country, rather than as a generous and gallant people, who had not hesitated to sacrifice much, both of blood and money, in freeing them from their French oppressors. But such, I fear, is the too general feeling in that country ; for while the innumerable religiosos which overrun that nation maintain their cursed dominion over the minds of the other classes, an English-man will always be looked upon by them as a dangerous and hateful being, uniting in himself both the mortal sins, first, of having totally cast off the Pope's authority, and being the subject of a free and popular government—than either of which, not even Satan himself could be more odious to them.

We were not allowed, however, to remain long in Tou-louse, but were distributed over the country in the neigh-bourhood, lines of demarcation having been pointed out which were to separate the French and British armies. My division was sent down the right bank of the river, and occupied Castel Sarazin, Grissolles, and Castelnau, &c. My battalion was stationed at Grissolles. During our stay here I had two or three opportunities, in company with others, of going to see Montauban, the seat of a Protestant college, and famed in romantic lore. The people were kind and obliging, and showed us every attention ; but unfortunately a French garrison was quartered in it, the officers of which took every opportunity of quarrelling with ours. Indeed we had no business there, and were consequently obliged to put up with more than we should have otherwise done, for we were strictly forbid to enter any place within the French lines ; but we did not conceive that those fellows, who had shown themselves so friendly and polite near Bayonne, while we were avowedly in arms against each other, would now turn round upon us when peace was made, and endeavour to engage us in quarrels and duelling.   But I believe they felt a degree of soreness at our acknowledged superiority as soldiers, (for even the inhabitants of Montauban, where they lay, did not hesitate to express it,) and thus wished to be revenged for the many victories we had gained over them.   Indeed there was a sort of recklessness about them which is not easily accounted for, unless they supposed their occupation was gone, and cared not what became of themselves ; but they did not succeed, I think, in any instance in obtaining their wishes, for they would not fight with pistols, the only weapon which gives each a fair and equal chance, but insisted upon using the sword,—a mode of fighting to which the English in general were utter strangers.   The people uniformly gave us warning as soon as ever they learnt that a plot was laid to insult us, on which we generally came away without subjecting ourselves to it ; and when their designs became too evident, we refrained from going there.   It was only a short distance from our quarters.

During our stay here, also, the Marquis de Pompignan, a gentleman residing between Grissolles and Castelnau, and where our Major-general had taken up his quarters, gave to the officers of the brigade a splendid fête.   I know not exactly how to denominate it, for it was a sort of dramatic medley, part of it being performed in the garden and part in the house, where a private theatre had been fitted up ;

that in the garden, it was said, was intended to represent some military event,—I think it was the burning of Moscow, and in which the Marquis's beautiful daughter bore a part.

This young lady was said to be greatly enamoured of an honourable gentleman, aide-de-camp to the General, who was quartered in their house, and between whom it was expected a match would have taken place. She was extremely beautiful and engaging.

We sometimes went a-fishing while we remained here also, but were not successful, there being none other than lake-fish, such as perch, &c., in the neighbourhood, which were scarcely worth taking.

Here, also, for want of better occupation, some of our young gentlemen amused themselves by hunting and lashing the Spanish muleteers as they were returning, after having delivered in their loads at the commissary's stores. They always rode one mule, (sideways, like a woman,) and led one or two more, and were most dexterous in handling the long shank of the halter, with which they sometimes soundly belaboured their pursuers ; and had they not been set on by two or three at a time, they would not have liked better fun than to fight one of our gentlemen with his whip, for they saw that it was only for amusement, and generally took it good-naturedly ; but our young gentlemen, as they generally do, carried the joke too far, and it was consequently put a stop to. Of course none but the young and idle took any part in this exercise.

We had, while we lay here, also several little balls and hops ; and here, for the first time, several of our young men began to dance quadrilles ; in short, there was no want of amusement among this gay and lively people, who are ever intent upon pleasure themselves, and who of course

o

found our wild and thoughtless young fellows ever as ready to second their endeavours to get up something new and entertaining. Certainly their morality is not the highest in the world, but their vices are most of them divested of that coarse and disgusting appearance which similar vices carry on their front in England ; and thus, while they are generally more pleasing, they are the more seducing, and consequently the more dangerous. However, as no person is compelled to enter into these scenes of dissipation and voluptuousness which they rejoice in, I found it, upon the whole, a very comfortable country to live in. The people were kind and civil, and were always good-natured and polite, and, as we now had plenty of the good things of this world at our command, I spent two months here very contentedly. It is true we had none of those excellent privileges with which my native country abounds, and which I have since learnt highly to prize,—I mean the privileges of the gospel,—the food for the nobler and never-dying part ; but I was then ignorant of their value, for although I had been convinced and convicted, I had not been converted. I was still in darkness respecting the way, the truth, and the life, and yet my foolish and . carnal mind whispered peace ; hence my contentedness in this situation. No! it was not till some years that I discovered that there is but one way to real happiness, but one true foundation on which to build our hope,—even that which is laid in Zion.

But the time had arrived for us to move down towards Bordeaux, preparatory to our quitting France. Accordingly, on the 3d June, we forded the Garonne, and stopped all night in Grenade, a place I formerly mentioned. We next day reached Cadours, a village near Cologne, where our 2d battalion was that evening quartered. In the afternoon of that day, a storm collected in the north, which I think had the most frightful appearance I ever witnessed. It was actually as black as night in the direction in which we saw it. It did not reach us, but it alarmed the inhabitants of our village so much, that they set on ringing the church bells with the utmost fury imaginable. We could not account for this strange proceeding till we enquired of them why it was done. They told us the devil was in the storm, and the bells being holy, he durst not, when he heard them, proceed any farther in that direction. Indeed they had ample reason to be in dread of its reaching their village; for the next day, as we passed along the country where it had raged most furiously, the whole face of the country was desolated. It had been a hail-storm such as I never before witnessed. The hailstones were still lying, some of them larger than a bullet; the vines had been all destroyed; the crops of corn completely swept from the face of the earth. Trees knocked down, birds killed; in short, nothing could equal the appearance of misery and woe which this awful hail-storm had inflicted upon the unfortunate inhabitants, many of whom were going about wringing their hands in all the bitterness of heart, which a consciousness of being deprived of every hope of subsistence for the year to come would naturally inspire. Indeed most of them were literally stripped of their all.

On the 6th we marched into Lectoure, a fine town on the river, and famous for having given birth to Marshal Lannes, one of Bonaparte's best generals. It stands on a high ground near the river, and overlooks one of the richest and most beautiful plains I think I ever saw. Here I experienced another misfortune in my steed. My little Portuguese horse (which was now in high condition, and being an entire horse was apt to fight) quarrelled with a large horse belonging to one of our officers, while I was

serving out the billets; and although we were both mounted at the time, the quarrelsome animals reared up against
each other, and fought most desperately; but his, being the
strongest, pulled mine and myself down to the ground. I
luckily fell clear of him, and was not hurt; but he by some
accident got a kick in his hind leg or foot, which completely lamed him, and I could not ride him any longer.

We passed through Condom, another fine town, and
Nerac, also a good town, and nearly full of Protestants.
We next day halted at Castel Jaloux, where I was quartered
on a house of religeuse. Here my poor little horse was so
very ill that I could not drag him any farther. I was consequently obliged to leave him with those good dames, to
whom I made him a present, and parted from him in the
morning with sincere regret. They promised to take care
of him, which I hope they did. We next reached the town
of Bazas. Here there was to be another parting scene exhibited. The Portuguese were ordered to leave us here, and
proceed towards their own country. The Spanish and
Portuguese women who had followed the men were either
to be sent home from hence, or their protectors were to
consent to marry them. Some adopted the latter alternative, having had children by them, and some others who
had not, and the remainder, of course, were compelled to
separate. Our division drew up in the morning they marched,
and honoured the brave Portuguese (for indeed they had
always behaved well in the field) with three cheers,
as they turned their faces towards Portugal. Many were
the heavy hearts in both armies on this occasion; for it is
not easy to conceive how the circumstance of passing through
scenes of hardship, trial, and danger together, endeared the
soldiers of the two armies to each other. It was perhaps
never before felt so fully how much each was attached to

the other; but the departure of the poor women caused many heavy hearts, both among themselves, poor creatures, who had a long and dreary journey before them, and among those with whom they had lived, and who had shared in all their good and bad fortune; but among these, several on both sides were not oppressed with too fine feelings.   A friend of mine, who was an officer in the Portuguese service, told me afterwards that the women marched down to Spain and Portugal at the same time his regiment did; that they formed a column of 800 or 900 strong; that they were regularly told off into companies; and that the commanding-officer, a major, and all the captains, were married men, who had their families with them—all excellent arrangements; but that they were the most unmanageable set of animals that ever marched across a country.   The officers had to draw rations for them all the way; but many of them, he says, left the column and went wherever they pleased. Few reached Portugal in the order in which they started.

We reached Langon on the 12th, and Barsac on the 13th June.   This latter place is famed for a fine white-wine, something resembling sauterne.   The adjutant (who had now been my chum for some time) and I were here quartered in a fine old baronial castle, the inmates of which showed us great attention.   A ball was given in the evening to the officers of the brigade.

On the 14th we halted at Castres, and on the 15th entered Bordeaux.   This was the finest town we had seen since we entered the Peninsula, except Lisbon and Madrid.   This town had been occupied by the British for some time, a division of the army having been sent by Lord Wellington to take charge of it in the name of Louis XVIII.

We were not, however, destined to be quartered in this southern capital of France, but marched right through it, on

the road towards the village of Blancfort. On the road the
division was formed, and very minutely inspected by our
gallant Chief, who was dressed in all his finery, his orders,
and medals, and ribbons, &c., which he wore for the first
time that ever I had seen. He looked most splendid indeed,
and right proud were we to see him in them. After inspection we moved on to the camp at Blancfort, where we
found a great part of the army assembled, waiting for the
arrival of shipping to carry them off. Some had sailed a
considerable time before our arrival. Besides our tents, the
adjutant and I had got a cottage close by, in which our servants and our baggage were put. We had not been here
above two or three days, I think, till his two servants, that
is, his servant and groom, took it into their heads to desert.
This was not the first instance of desertion that had taken
place lately; for as we drew near the time of departure
great numbers ran off into the interior, mostly bad characters. However, on this occasion, these worthies were determined to have something to carry them on the road, and,
without hesitation, broke open their master's panniers, or
boxes, and took away all the money he had, which did not
indeed amount to any great sum, for it was only 40 dollars,
(about L. 10 British,) but it being all he was worth it was
a great loss to him.

I have reason to be thankful to Providence for my escape
on this occasion. My paymaster's chest was standing close
to the adjutant's panniers when they broke them open, and
they did not touch it, although it contained about L.400
worth of gold. Had they taken that I might have gone
after them. I of course expressed my thankfulness for this
lucky escape, and told several people of it. I fancy some
person (my groom, I suspect) overheard me telling what a
lucky escape I had been favoured with, and determined in

his own mind that I should not always come off so well. The sequel will show : A few days after this I had occasion to go into Bordeaux to draw some money from the Commissary-general. The amount was 600 dollars, or about L.150. As I could not conveniently carry them out to the camp, I requested Major Balvaird, who had a quarter in town, to allow me to put them in his portmanteau till I had an opportunity of getting them sent out. His servant had overheard this conversation, and made up his mind at once to desert and take this money with him ; but providentially again I escaped. I found the means, before night, of carrying it out to the camp, and the Major gave it me unknown to the servant. That night he broke open the portmanteau, and, taking every thing worth carrying away, (among which was a gold watch of mine,) deserted, and got clear off. This money, also, had it been taken, would have sorely crippled me, although I might perhaps have overcome the loss.

We marched in a few days after, passing through the district of Medoc, famous for Bordeaux or claret wine, and halted for the night at Castelnau de Medoc. The next day we passed through Chateau Margaux, where the best and most expensive of the claret grows, and again encamped at Pauillac, from whence we were to go on board.

Now was the time for the person who had overheard me speaking about my escape with the L.400, to make his grab and start off, or he would be too late. Accordingly, after dark, he or they lifted up a part of the tent where the box was standing, and, pulling it out, set off with it bodily. But, again directed by Providence, I had taken the money out of the box, and given it into the hands of a gentleman, to take care of for me ; and there remained in the box my papers and books, public and private, about L.19 in money, an old silver watch, and, among other things, the half

doubloon which poor Croudace had given me to take care
of for him on the evening previous to his death at Badajos,
and which I was preserving as a memorial for his afflicted
friends.

As soon as the box was missed I instantly raised the hue
and cry, and, reporting the circumstance to my commanding-officer, he ordered the rolls to be called, to see if any
man had deserted ; but no, they were all present. I then
offered a reward of forty dollars to any one who would
bring me the box and papers, and did not regard the money.
Instantly the whole camp was in a move to find the box,
and search was made in all directions. I of course was not
idle myself on the occasion ; and having a man or two with
me, I actually discovered where the box had been opened,
for I found the inkstand, that had been in it, lying near a
heap of wood close to the bank of the river, into which,
after plundering it, no doubt they had thrown it. I now
went down to the town and waited on the mayor, offering
the same reward to any of his people that would try to find
it in the river ; but, unfortunately, just as there was the
best chance of recovering it, the order came for us instantly
to go on board.—Thus was I deprived of every document I
possessed, both Paymaster's, Quartermaster's, and private. I
had fortunately got my Paymaster's accounts made out up
to the very latest period, and transmitted to the War-Office,
or I know not what I should have done ; but my duplicates
were gone, and when afterwards objections were made to
some of the items in the charges, (as is always the case,) I,
being unable to answer them, was obliged to submit to the
loss of them. I had also several private accounts unclosed,
on which I lost considerably, so that altogether I calculate
this loss fully amounted to L.100, besides the vexation of
not having my papers to refer to when wanted.

I had been obliged to part with all my remaining animals for next to nothing, for when the French people found we were obliged to leave them, they offered us the most shameful trifles possible, but which we were compelled to take or give the animals away: One I did actually make a present of, besides my little Portuguese horse before-mentioned. I made a close calculation, and found that my losses in horses and mules, from the beginning of 1812 to June 1814, did not amount to less than L.150, besides sums that I lost by officers who died. By one I lost L.84, and another L.74 odd, so that, as I said before, had I not fortunately been appointed Acting Paymaster, I should have been so much involved, that at this time I durst not have returned to my native country. I do not complain, for most of my losses were sent by Providence, who saw best what was fitting and good for me; but never, till the Peninsular campaigns, were officers obliged generally to provide and keep up their own baggage-animals, and from the loss of which I had suffered so severely; and I cannot but think that rule, always acted upon till these campaigns, ought to be continued, and that subalterns at least ought to have their baggage always carried at the public expense.

CHAPTER XVI.

Author's Battalion embark for England—Land at Plymouth—Expect to be again ordered on Foreign Service—Order received—Embark, with other troops, for America—Land at Pine Island.

WE embarked on the 8th July on board his Majesty's ship Dublin, of 74 guns, commanded by Captain Elphinstone, which took the five companies of my battalion, with two companies of the 43d. We sailed the next day, I think, and had generally fine weather during our voyage, which lasted till the 18th, when we arrived at Plymouth. She was but a dull sailer, or we ought not to have occupied so many days in so short a passage. During our voyage, as remarkable an instance of heroic fortitude and bodily strength was exhibited by a sailor of this ship as I ever remember to have witnessed. He was doing something on the fore-yard, and by some accident he was precipitated into the water, but in his fall his shoulder came in contact with the flue of one of the anchors, by which it was deeply and severely cut. The ship was going at about five knots an hour, and it took

near half an hour before she could be brought round and a
boat sent to his assistance ; and notwithstanding the severe
cut he had received, from which the blood was fast streaming, he not only contrived to keep himself from sinking by
buffeting with a heavy sea, but actually stripped off his
jacket in the water, as it seems it had been an encumbrance
to him. When the boat reached him, the poor fellow was
nigh exhausted, and a few minutes more would have deprived the ship and the service of an excellent sailor, but
having been got into the boat, he was brought on board
more dead than alive, where every attention being paid to
him, he soon afterwards recovered.

We landed at Plymouth on the 18th, and occupied one
of the barracks. We did not exactly know what was to
become of us. Kent being our regimental station, we expected to be ordered to march and join the left wing in that
county, but were still kept at Plymouth, where we met with
great kindness and attention from the inhabitants in general, who are upon the whole, I think, an excellent and a
moral people. We also fared sumptuously here, every description of food being both cheap and good. Fish in particular is most abundant and excellent. In short, we were
here as comfortably and as well quartered as we could desire, and every thing tended to make us perfectly satisfied
with our lot. We relaxed by attending the theatre occasionally, which is one of the best provincial ones in the
kingdom, and at this time could boast some very good
actors. There were a variety of other amusements, such as
fishing, &c., which of course we indulged in occasionally.
From hence I was called up to London to meet our Colonel,
the Hon. Sir W. Stewart, to arrange our battalion concerns,
&c. for the few latter years of hurry and confusion, and
which was at last got done to the satisfaction of all con-

cerned. Here also we began to replenish our wardrobes, which. it will easily be imagined, were not the most magnificent in the world on our first arrival.

But we were not long permitted the enjoyment of English society or English comforts, for we had scarcely been a month at Plymouth till we received an order to prepare again for foreign service, and the nature of that service being kept a profound secret, we scarcely knew what necessary articles of equipment to prepare. The general opinion, however, was, that our destination was some part of America, consequently we endeavoured to meet all contingencies by preparing both for a warm and cold climate. All hands of course were vigorously set to work, in order to be ready when the summons arrived, which we knew might be very soon expected. An alteration was made in the arrangement of our battalion. The staff was ordered to proceed to join the other wing at Thorncliffe, which of course included myself, but Major Mitchell, who was now appointed to the command of these five companies, was anxious to take me out with him in the capacity of acting paymaster, and to his friendly and earnest endeavours, added to the kindness of Captain James Travers, who had at first intended to apply for that situation himself, but renounced it on my account, I am indebted for again having an addition of 10s. per diem made to my regimental pay during the continuance of service on this expedition.

At length the order arrived for our embarkation, and on the 18th September, just two months from the day of our arrival in England, our five companies were sent on board his Majesty's ships Fox and Dover, both frigates of the smaller class, and which had been prepared for the reception of troops, by having a part of their guns taken out, and being, as it is termed, armed " en flute." The commanding-officer, with the staff and three companies, were put on board the Fox. We laid in an immense sea stock of provisions, &c. not knowing how long we might be on the water, but unfortunately for us we had scarcely put foot on board, when the order was given to weigh and proceed to sea forthwith, so that no time was given for the stowing away of all the stock, which had cost us about L.24 per person ; the consequence was, a great part of it was lost or destroyed, from its being knocked about the deck in the midst of the confusion and bustle consequent on the crew and the soldiers (strangers to each other) being set to work to weigh anchor and make sail in such a hurry. Little assistance was afforded us from the ship on this occasion. We thus lost nearly the half of what we had been at so much pains to provide ; but such things being common occurrences in a life like ours, it was therefore vain to fret.

The force that embarked at the same time with us, consisted of the 93d Highlanders, a company of artillery, some rocketeers, a squadron of the 14th light dragoons, without horses, and our five companies, the whole under the command of General Keane. The good people of Plymouth, as is customary, cheered us as we left their shore, wishing us the most ample success and good fortune, and which we, who had for so long a time been in the habit of conquering, did not for a moment admit a doubt of being fully realized.

We sailed, as I said, on the 18th September, and stood down the channel with a pretty fair breeze, till we reached what are commonly called its "chops," where we encountered adverse winds, and blowing a succession of gales (equinoctial, I imagine) which detained us beating off and on for seven days. This was as uncomfortable a beginning of our service as could well be imagined. High winds, with rain, and contrary to the way we wished them, were cer-

tainly rather trying to the patience of us landsmen, and
there was something in our situation on board this ship
which did not at all tend to alleviate our discomfort.   In
fact, we wished our fortune had placed us on board a transport rather than where we now found ourselves.   All the
discipline and strictness of a regular man-of-war was enforced,
without any of the countervailing comforts and conveniences usually found on board such ships ; and to such a length
was this carried, that because our officers sometimes stood
on the quarter-deck, holding on, in the rolling of the ship,
by the hand-ropes which surround the companion, not only
these, but the ropes which were stretched to prevent people falling out at the gangway, were ordered to be removed,
that nothing should remain by which lubbers like us might
hold on in the heavy rolls to which the vessel was subject
in gales like those I have been describing. We were no less
than twenty-four people in the cabin, twelve of our officers
and twelve gentlemen of the commissariat department, so
that we were sufficiently crowded, besides being in several
other respects ill provided. But all this would have been borne
with cheerfulness and good-will, had we not experienced
such a total want of kindness and urbanity from a quarter
where we least expected it, and from which that unkindness
could be made most effectual.

We lost the fleet during the continuance of these gales,
but sealed orders having apprized our commander where to
rendezvous, we made sail for the Island of Madeira, which
we reached on the 9th October, and where we found the
fleet.   Some of the wags of our other two companies on
board the Dover, pretending to think we must have been
cast away and lost, had erased all our names from the army
list as defunct. This rather annoyed some of our folks, but

it might have been easily seen it was only a little waggery in which they had been indulging themselves.

A day or two before we reached Madeira, we fell in with a strange sail, to which we gave chase, and brought her to; she proved to be an English merchant brig. It was said our commander wished to have a little independent cruise, which caused him to part from the fleet, and that there was a famed American privateer called the Wasp that had made a great number of captures, and which he was anxious to fall in with that he might take her. Had such a thing occurred as the Wasp appearing in sight, and we had given her chase, I could have compared it to nothing but to a vulgar simile which I have sometimes heard used, that of a cow endeavouring to catch a hare, for indeed she was, I believe, one of the fastest sailers that had ever been known, while we, on the contrary, were in comparison just like the cow to the hare. This also must have been a piece of waggery on the part of those who first set such a report afloat, for no man in his senses would have ever thought of chasing privateers with the Fox frigate at the time of which I am now writing. I regret I did not go on shore on this beautiful island, the town and scenery of which were most inviting, but as our stay was only to be so very short, it was scarcely worth while.

We sailed again on the 11th, after having first got a cask of excellent Madeira wine from the house of· Messrs Gordon and Co. This was the best, I think, I ever drank. We stood almost due south, passing pretty close to Teneriffe and the other Canary Isles, until we fell in with the trade-winds, when we kept more away towards the south-west. Our voyage now became delightful, for a gentle and refreshing, but constant and steady breeze, carried us on at the rate of about five or six knots an hour, without having occasion hardly to alter a sail or rope. We passed to the tropic of Capricorn on the 15th October, when our sailors prepared to indulge in the same innocent but amusing ceremonies that are adopted on crossing the equator. Neptune, with his Amphitrite, got dressed in full costume, and every other appendage being ready, it only now remained that the commander's sanction should be obtained to their commencing the imposing ceremony; but no! his godship was dismissed in no very courteous manner, and told to go and attend to his duty. Thus the fiat of a greater than Neptune, even in his own element, reduced him from the godlike rank he held to that of a mere forecastle sailor; and thus were all our expectations frustrated. In all the other ships of the fleet the amusement was carried on with the greatest good humour, as we could plainly perceive with our glasses.

On the 18th, we passed pretty near the Isle of St Antonio, the westernmost of the Cape Verde Isles, and then bearing off still rather more to the west, we kept our course generally at about 12 or 13 north latitude, and in this manner crossed the Atlantic.

From the time that we had entered between the tropics, we had seen numerous shoals of flying fish, some of which, when closely pursued, (by the dolphin generally,) actually fell on board our ship. A very accurate drawing of one of these was made by one of our lieutenants, a friend of mine, who, I believe, has it to this day. They were generally about the size of a herring, and much resembling that fish in shape and colour, with two fins projecting from behind their gills, nearly as long as their body. These are their wings, with which they can fly generally for 100, or 150, or sometimes 200 yards, when they fall again into the water. We also caught a dolphin about this time, our carpenter having harpooned it from the bow of the ship; but I was

6

considerably disappointed in finding it did not exceed from twenty-four to thirty inches in length ; and the hues of it, though beautiful when dying, by no means answered my expectations.

On the —— November, we made the island of Barbadoes, and anchored in Carlisle Bay, off Bridgetown, the capital of the island. It is not easy to describe the effect which is produced on an European the first time he beholds the beauties of a tropical country, and which, I think, he does in the greatest perfection while they are yet distant from him. Robertson's description of Columbus's first view of a West India island is, I think, as correct and as beautiful as any thing can possibly be ; and his feelings for the moment (heightened indeed by the circumstance of his having at length attained to his long-looked-for Western India) will describe pretty nearly what every one must feel, who has not before beheld the productions of a tropical climate. But oh ! how is the scene changed when you get on shore ! Nature indeed is still beautiful and rich beyond the conception of a northern native ; but man—how fallen ! Here (I think I shall not far err if I say) you behold man in his lowest state : the savages of the woods are, in my opinion, much higher in the scale of being than those whom our cursed cupidity has introduced to all our vices, without one alleviating virtue to counterbalance the evil. But how could the poor Africans learn any thing that is good from those who do not practise good themselves ?

One of our people while here said, " he thought the men were all rogues, and the women all unfaithful." Of the slave population the latter is certainly a correct description, almost universally, in Bridgetown ; for, with shame be it spoken, their masters and mistresses calculate upon their worth as if they were brood-mares, by the number and the description of wretched beings which they can bring into this world of misery. What indeed could you expect from those who can thus act, and those who sanction such conduct, but the like treatment that Mr Shrewsbury met with, if you endeavour to show them to themselves or to others in a true light? While the strong man armed keepeth his castle, his goods are in peace ; but let another endeavour to bind this strong man, and take his goods from him, and oh, what a resistance may not be expected! Let the West Indians have slaves whom they may treat as cattle for their own gain and profit, even if it be at the expense of the souls of the poor wretches whom they thus destroy ; but endeavour to show these degraded human beings that they are capable of being raised to a level with their unfeeling and avaricious masters, and you may shortly expect the fate of a Smith or a Shrewsbury, so regardless are these dealers in human flesh of their duty as men who must soon render an account of all their actions.

It may be said, that I saw little, while here, but the very worst of society, and this may in a great measure be true; but it is evident that such things were done and sanctioned at Bridgetown when I was there, in 1814, as led me to pray that my lot might never be cast among such people.

I now gladly turn from this scene of vice and misery, and pursue my narrative.

In the bay at this place a hulk was stationed for the reception of prisoners of war. Our boats usually passed pretty near it on going on shore for water. A number of Americans were on board as prisoners. On one occasion, or more, I believe, they called out to our fellows as they passed under her stern, " So you have come out from England to attack our country, have you? I hope you have brought your coffins with you, for you will need them before you return." And, in truth, many of those fine fellows to whom this insolently coarse but patriotic speech was addressed, did indeed require coffins before the business we were going upon was finished.

We left Barbadoes on the —, and, passing down through the midst of the islands, we left St Lucia on our left and Martinico on our right hand. We also passed close to Dominico and Guadaloupe, with several smaller islands which I do not recollect, and, keeping to the southward, passed St Christopher's, Santa Cruz, Porto Rico, and St Domingo, having a fine view of the whole as we moved delightfully along. This latter large island took us more than two days in passing; but on the 21st we came in sight of Jamaica, the chief of our West India possessions. We stood off and on near to Port-Royal till the 23d, when we made sail to the westward, and on the 25th came to anchor in Negril Bay, at the extreme west end of the island of Jamaica. Here we found several sail both of men-of-war and transports, having on board the troops which had been engaged in the operations against Washington and Baltimore, &c., and consisting of the 4th, 21st, 44th, and 85th regiments, with some artillery. They were not strong indeed, having been considerably reduced by their late arduous services; but their numbers, added to ours, we thought quite sufficient to enable us to make a descent upon the American coast near New Orleans, which it was now whispered was our destination : indeed this had been conjectured from the time we left England, but nothing certain was known, and even now it was not officially made public. A day or two after our arrival here, two of the West India regiments also joined us, the 1st and 5th, at least a part of both ; so that we now mustered a respectable force. Admiral Sir Alexander Cochran commanded the naval part of the expedition, he being here on our arrival on board the Tonnant 84; several smaller vessels also, with stores, &c. &c. joined us from Port-Royal. When the whole were collected together, we felt proud of our fine force, which we vainly imagined nothing we should have to encounter could withstand for a moment : but the battle is not always to the strong; and we were shortly after painfully reminded of this truth. But I must not anticipate,—evil always comes early enough.

During our stay here, I went on shore for a few hours, and visited some of the farms or plantations. Indeed, while we remained, the place where we landed was generally like a fair ; for the inhabitants had assembled in great numbers, bringing with them live stock and poultry and vegetables, &c. for sale, all of which were greedily bought up at prices high enough, I warrant you. The vegetation at this place was most luxuriant, even in this the middle of winter almost ; but I apprehend this was the finest season of the year, for it was not at all intolerably hot, and every thing had the appearance which our country assumes in the height of summer. An accident occurred whilst we continued here, which had nigh proved serious. The Alceste frigate, one day, in shifting her berth, run with her head right on board the Dover, where our other two companies were on board. She cut her up from the stern into the cabins, not less I am sure at the top than ten feet. Two of our people were in the cabin at the time playing at backgammon, and were not a little astonished to see the prow of another large vessel tearing its way right into the very place where they were sitting.

On the 29th, signal was made to weigh, when the whole got under way, and started in fine style ; our now gallant fleet covering the ocean for many miles. We kept along

on the south side of Cuba, and on the 3d December made
Cape St Antonio, the westernmost point of that large island.
From hence we now stood to the northward, crossing right
athwart the Gulf of Mexico. During our stay at Barbadoes,
we had purchased a live sheep and a pig, as we feared our
stock might run out before we landed. The sheep was productive of great amusement to our messmates, at the expense of the poor caterer. In all hot climates, I believe,
the wool of the sheep becomes in course of time more like
the hair of a goat than what it really is. This was the
case in the present instance, most of our people declaring
they would not eat of such an animal, which was, as they
conjectured, a sort of mule bred between a sheep and a goat;
while the poor caterer was like to have the sheep thrown
on his hand. This produced many a bickering, even after
it was known that such was the case in warm climates; for
they kept up the fun as long as possible, always trying to
keep the unfortunate caterer in hot water about it. The
sheep was killed, and produced excellent mutton—not fat
indeed, but eatable. We were not so fortunate, however,
with our pig; it appears it must have been diseased—what,
I believe, is usually termed measly. It was dressed without this being known, and eaten; and the consequence was,
all the twenty-four of our mess, except myself and another
were literally poisoned. In the middle of the night, when
it began to take effect, the most distressing scene took
place imaginable, and the medical men were kept busily
employed for a considerable time afterwards preparing and
administering emetics, which providentially had the desired
effect on all, for in a short time the whole recovered; but
had medical assistance not been promptly administered, the
chances are some of them would have suffered. Its effects

were something like cholera morbus, working both up and down in the most violent manner.

On the 10th December we made the American coast off Mobile, where we fell in with a vessel, on board of which was Colonel Nichols of the marines, with three or four Indian chiefs of the Creek nation, to which people he had been for some time previously attached, they being then at war with the Americans, and consequently our allies. They came on board our ship, and were shown every thing curious ; but their reason for visiting us was, that they might see our rifles, for they considered themselves good shots, and wished to examine our arms, with which they did not express themselves over-satisfied, as they had been accustomed to see no other description of rifles than those used by the Americans, which are both much longer and heavier, but carry a much smaller ball. Indeed they had never seen any military rifles, but only such as the above, and which are constructed solely for the purpose of killing deer and other game. The gallant colonel endeavoured to amuse us a little on this occasion with the wonderful feats of his protegés. He told us, that they being generally very short of balls, were always very careful how they expended them in hunting ; and that their rule was never to fire at a deer, until it was in the act of passing between them and a tree, that, should the ball go through its body, as it sometimes did, it might lodge in the tree on the other side, and they would then go and pick it out, and recast it. We thought he ought to have told that story to his own corps the marines ; for I believe he did not get many of us to give implicit credit to so wonderful a tale. They were most grotesque-looking figures ; most of them were dressed in some old red coats, which they had got hold of by some

means, with cocked hats of the old fashion.   These I believe had been given them by some of our people, for they
were English manufacture.   But they had tremendous
large rings, &c. hung in their ears, the laps of which were
stretched nearly to their shoulders ; some of them also wore
rings in their noses ; and some of them were without any
sort of lower garments, having nothing but a sort of cloth
tied round their waist, which passed through between their
legs and fastened before.   These people it was intended
should bring their warriors to join us near New Orleans ;
but, owing to some cause with which I am not acquainted,
none but these three or four chiefs ever came near us.

On the 11th we anchored near the Chandeleur Islands,
at the entrance into Lake Ponchartrain.   But it was discovered that the Americans had some gun-vessels, which,
on account of their drawing only little water, had been
stationed in this lake for its protection, and on our appearance had retired nearer to New Orleans.   It was necessary
that these should be previously disposed of in some manner,
before the disembarkation of the troops could with safety be
effected.   None of our ships could follow them on account
of the shoalness of the lake.   An order was therefore issued
for all the men-of-war to prepare their boats for an attack
on these vessels, the chief command of which was given to
Captain Lockyer of the Sophia gun-brig.   On the morning
of the ——, they therefore assembled for this purpose, and
pushed up the lake in search of the gun-vessels, which were
discovered moored near some islands called by the natives,
" Les Isles Malheureuse," or the " Unfortunate Islands,"
and which form the entrance from Lake Ponchartrain
into Lake Borgne, or Blind Lake.   No time was lost in
attacking this formidable flotilla, consisting of vessels carrying from five to six guns each, and commanded by a lieu-

tenant of the American navy, named by them Commodore Jones. A most determined and gallant resistance was made by the Americans; but superior numbers, with equal, if not superior courage and seamanship, prevailed, and in a short space of time the whole were captured. Both the commandants were severely wounded, with a great number of officers and men killed and wounded. Nothing could exceed the gallant intrepidity, I understand, with which our boats advanced to the attack; for, from experience I am well convinced, the fire from those gun-vessels must have been most destructive; for better shots, either with artillery or small arms, do not exist than the Americans. Orders were now issued for the army to prepare to land; but the distance, from where we had been obliged from shoal water to stop to the town, being so great, it was determined to form a sort of depôt on a small island, near the mouth of the Pearl River, called Pine Island; and farther to facilitate the transport of the troops, small brigs, &c. were sent as far up the lake as possible, into which the troops were put successively from the larger vessels, and from which they generally took their departure for the above island.

On the 15th our people left the Fox, and were moved up the lake into one of the brigs before noticed, where we were packed in as tight as herrings, there being near 400 men on board a little thing scarcely calculated to contain the fourth of that number, and where there was not literally room to lie down. But, on the 19th, we were relieved from this rather close confinement; and being put on board of long boats, we pushed off for the island, which lay at a considerable distance, notwithstanding the measures that had been adopted to shorten our voyage. The weather proved extremely rough and unpleasant, which rendered our trip neither over-safe nor comfortable ; and to mend the matter, the seamen on board our boat were rather in the wind, and did not manage her so well as was desirable ; for, poor fellows, they had been engaged in this fatiguing service for several days, (a considerable number of the troops having been previously landed,) and were consequently the more easily prevailed upon to indulge when grog came in their way. Our middy too was quite worn out with fatigue, and slept nearly all the time we were on board. Our boat was several times on the point of being swamped, for the water came in quite plentifully on occasions of her being laid down by sudden squalls. Another boat, which accompanied us, had her mast carried away.

We landed on the island before mentioned in the evening, and of course looked out for the best shelter we could find. But it was a complete desert ; nothing but reeds grew on it, except a few stunted and scrubby bushes at the lower end of it. It came on a most severe frost during the night, which I understand caused the death of several of the sailors, who had indulged perhaps a little too freely, and had lain down without any covering. Some of the poor blacks also, I understand, suffered in consequence of the severe cold, a thing with which they were totally unacquainted, and against which they were ill provided, having nothing but their light and thin West India dress to keep it out. It was laughable the next morning to see them examining so intently the ice which had been formed on the pools near our bivouack. They could not conjecture what it was ; some of them asserting it was salt ; while the greater part were totally at a loss respecting it. I had by great good luck got into a sort of hut belonging to some

P

of the officers who had previously landed; but I do not remember in all my campaigning to have suffered more from cold than I did this night, and was extremely glad when daylight appeared, that I might be able to move about.

CHAPTER XVII.

Proceed to attack the Enemy, and capture one of their picquets—Advance in search of a Bivouack—Alarmed by shots in front—Fired on by an American schooner—Captain Hallen severely attacked—Manœuvres on both sides—Ruse of the Enemy—Fighting continues—Enemy repulsed at all points—Courage of the British—A British Battery brought into play—Activity of the Enemy.

By the 21st, the whole army had been landed on this island, when they were told off into brigades, and inspected by the General. During our stay here, about five or six French Americans, (the natives of New Orleans, or neighbourhood,) arrived as friends, and told us that there were scarcely any troops in the district; so that we had nothing to do but to land on the opposite side, and march right on to the town, and that the inhabitants would welcome us most cordially, and that no resistance might be expected. I did not, I confess, put much confidence in their information, and believed at the time, that they came more as spies than with any view of befriending, as they pretended, our cause. More correct information was obtained from Spanish fishermen, who had been following their occupation at the mouth of a creek on the New Orleans side of the lake, and who had come across, I believe, at the suggestion of Major Peddie, our assistant Quartermaster-general, who had been despatched to find out a suitable landing-place for the army. From one of them, I learned afterwards that there were troops in the town, commanded by General Jackson, and that a battery of two guns had been erected on the road, by which we must advance. What they told the General, I do not know, but fancy he saw no reason to alter his plans, from the information of either party. Every thing being ready by the morning of the 22d, the advance guard, commanded by Colonel Thornton, and consisting of the 85th and 95th regiments, with two light three-pounders, some artillery and some rocketeers, accompanied by a few artificers to repair bridges, &c. embarked on board the boats, that had been assembled for the purpose—two companies of the 93d followed us ; these troops occupying the whole of the boats that could be mustered in the fleet, consequently the remainder of the army had to remain where they were till the return of the boats. The distance was not less, I should think, than from thirty to forty miles. We pushed off about two o'clock P.M., the wind being favourable for a considerable part of the way, but it failing, the men were obliged to commence with the oars. We were completely wedged in, so that there was no moving, let the call be ever so urgent. I suffered much from a severe pain in my side, from being obliged to remain so long in the same position ; but we endeavoured to divert the tedium in the best manner we could by amusing stories, &c. My luck placed me on board the Bang-Up, a fine cutter belonging to the admiral, and commanded by a countryman of mine, a Lieutenant Foster of that ship. We did not reach the mouth of the creek, or bayou, as it is called by the natives, till a long time after dark. As we approached it, some light boats were sent forward with Captain Travers of ours and his company, to endeavour to surprise a regiment of the enemy, which we knew were stationed in some huts at the mouth of the creek, and which huts belonged to the Spanish fishermen before mentioned. From the information they gave, the best arrangements possible were made for effecting this; for Travers, moving silently on, and landing his men at the opposite ends of the hamlet, there remained no way of escape open for the troops in the houses. As soon as all was ready, they rushed forward and secured the whole picquet without a single shot being fired, with the exception of two men, who preferred venturing into the marsh, in rear of the huts, where it is not improbable they perished. The duty was conducted so quietly, and so expeditiously, that very few of the other troops knew any thing of the matter; but this alone secured us a landing without opposition, for had a firing been begun on either side, it must have alarmed the American army, who, no doubt, would have used their endeavours to oppose our landing.

We soon after began to enter the creek, but such was the darkness of the night, and the shoalness of the water, and such the uncertainty of the way by which we had to proceed, that very little progress was made during the remainder of the night; daylight, however, enabled us to move forward at a brisker pace, but from the obstacles that had presented themselves in the dark, the squadron of boats was sadly dispersed; and when we reached the head of the creek, only two or three of the light boats, with the staff and naval officers, had arrived, and considerable intervals of time elapsed between the arrival of the different boats with troops; so that had the enemy been aware of our intention, and had they had a force of a few hundred men hid in the high reeds which grow in this marsh, they might, I am persuaded, have cut us off in detail, for from the causes before mentioned, no two boats were sufficiently near to assist each other.

We got on shore about an hour after daylight; and right glad was I to be enabled to stretch my legs, which had been kept motionless for the last sixteen hours. As soon as the whole advance-guard had landed, and a few planks had been thrown over a deep rill which we had to cross, we moved forward towards the high ground, Captain Travers' company leading; and, in order to magnify the appearance of our force, should any concealed American be looking on, we extended our files to double the usual distance, and thus passed through a wood which skirted the swamp, and which it was necessary to traverse before we could reach the open country, which we did about six miles below New Orleans. As soon as our advance cleared this wood, they observed a good-looking farm onstead, towards which they moved in double quick time, and arrived just in time to seize and make prisoner a Monsieur Villerey, a major of the militia, just then setting off to join his people. We heard (but I will not vouch for the truth of the report) that a considerable body of the enemy had been assembled on the high-road, near to Monsieur Villerey's house, but on learning that we had landed, and were moving rapidly forward, they separated, one part retiring towards the town, while the other went down the river. Our advance now moved on with celerity, and dashing on to the different farm-houses in the neighbourhood, seized several groups of arms at each of them, which it seems had either been abandoned by the troops to whom they belonged, or had been collected there for some military purpose. They captured at some of these farm-houses to the amount of twelve or twenty stand; and in all not less than fifty.

Monsieur Villerey unfortunately contrived to make his

escape, through the too great leniency of one of our lieutenants.   I think the most probable opinion respecting the
arms and the troops assembled near Monsieur Villerey's is,
that it was the militia of the district just at that moment
assembling, which will not only account for the arms being
found in such numbers, (under the verandas of the houses,)
but also for Monsieur Villerey himself being then on the
point of setting out in his warlike costume, and the number of men which were observed near his house.

About twenty militiamen were also captured in and
about these houses.   Except there, the whites had all abandoned their houses; but a considerable number of black
slaves remained at each, whether of their own accord, or
left to protect the property, and occasionally convey information to their masters, I know not.   As soon as our advance
had sufficiently reconnoitred the adjacent houses, &c. the
whole of the troops moved on past the house of Monsieur
Villerey, and turning to the right, followed the great road
to New Orleans for about half a mile, till a suitable piece
of ground presenting itself in the neighbourhood of some
other farm-houses, the whole turned in to a green field a
short distance from the road, and forming into close columns of battalions, commenced bivouacking for the night.
The road ran partly on, and partly alongside of the river
dike.   Immediately between the troops and the river, this
dike was perhaps about three feet high.   On our right was
a farm-house, and a little to the right and front another—
the latter a pretty large one—all these, and indeed all the
farm-houses in this neighbourhood, are surrounded at one
end by the huts of the slaves, and generally on the other
by barns and other out-buildings, and in the rear a garden
or orchard.   The ground in all this country, which is perfectly flat, apparently of alluvial formation, is divided into

fields, &c. by wooden paling of the common description, very few hedges being to be seen.

The situation in which the troops were placed, was as follows, viz. The artillery and rocketeers in one line; immediately behind them, my battalion and the 85th, in close column; the 4th in rear of us, and the 93d two companies in rear of the 4th; the whole in close columns. The men, as soon as dismissed, instantly set about cooking, for they had had nothing from the morning before, and it was now considerably past mid-day. Captain Travers' company, which had formed the advance-guard, still remained in front as a picquet, and occupied a post on the great road, about a mile in front of the division.

About three o'clock P.M., we were all alarmed by some shots at the advanced picquet; and, on enquiry, found that an American staff-officer, escorted by about thirty cavalry, had come galloping down, no doubt for the purpose of reconnoitring us; when within distance, our people instantly fired, one of which shots wounded the staff-officer, and another killed a horse, but they contrived to get him off. This caused the whole of the troops to fall in till the cause of alarm was ascertained, after which they set about their cooking again with great glee. Considerable discussion now began to take place amongst the knowing ones, as to the merits and demerits of our situation, in point of security; and of course various opinions were given on the occasion. One officer of ours, a particular friend of mine, did not hesitate roundly to assert, that we were in a most unprotected and dangerous situation. I do not remember exactly the reasons he assigned; but certainly, could he have foreseen what yet remained in the womb of time, he would have had much stronger reasons for his opinion. Another company of ours, (Captain Hallen's,) and one of the 85th, were ordered to

prepare at dusk to relieve the picquet in advance ; and as
I messed with Captain Hallen's company, I accompanied it
on this duty. I did not go with the main body of the company, there being no house at that post, but with one section, commanded by Lieutenant Forbes, and we occupied a
small house to the right, and a little to the rear of Captain
Hallen's party, which was stationed on the great road. The
company of the 85th occupied the large farm-house before-
mentioned, a little to the right and front of the column.   I
had purchased an excellent turkey on our arrival at Monsieur Villerey's house, which we had dressed at this little
house, and made a most hearty meal indeed, after which we
took each a tot or horn of grog to comfort us.

We had not long finished our comfortable meal, when we
were astounded by the report of heavy ordnance, apparently
close to the bivouack of the column, and which reports followed each other in quick succession.   A cheer was also
given, but by whom, or what the occasion of the firing was,
we were totally at a loss to conjecture.   I at first imagined
it was some of our men-of-war that had been able to pass
the forts down the river, and that they were firing a salute
and cheering in consequence ; and yet this seemed a strange
conjecture ; but we did not long remain in suspense, for we
were soon after informed of the real state of the case, that
it was a large American schooner, with at least fourteen guns,
and which she had been enabled to bring to bear upon our
unfortunate bivouack with the most deadly precision, great
numbers having fallen at her first broadside. The troops of
course dispersed in some measure, leaving their fires, which
had too well served as a direction for the fire of this terrible
schooner. But the time was not far distant when we should
have other enemies to encounter ; for by the time the
schooner had fired a dozen broadsides, a noise was heard in

our front; and just at this moment an American was brought in by a man from Captain Hallen's post, who had foolishly come right into the centre of his picquet, and asking if they could tell him which way the regulars had gone. This showed that he was a young soldier, who did not know our troops from his own; but it also showed that the regulars which he was seeking could not be far distant; consequently, every thing was got ready to give them the best reception possible; but as the people we had heard in front of the post where I then was appeared to be rather to our right, I feared lest they might get unawares upon the company of the 85th, which was stationed in the farm behind us. I consequently set off with all dispatch to give them timely warning, but when I arrived there, I could not find the officers, nor could I see where the picquet was posted; I therefore thought they must be on the alert at the bottom of the garden, which lay in the direction in which we heard the noise; and meeting here an officer and several of our men, who had moved in this direction, from the fire of the chooner, I told him I was certain that Hallen would be shortly most vigorously attacked, from the information I had learnt respecting the regulars, and advised him to collect all the men he could, and proceed forthwith to reinforce him at the advance. This he instantly did, and it was well, for by this time the firing had commenced in volleys at that post. I then returned to the picquet-house, where I had previously dined, and found the officer was going round his sentries; but as the firing was going briskly on at Hallen's post, I expected every moment to be attacked here, and began, in the absence of the officer, to post the men as advantageously as the nature of the ground would admit.

The house stood on a little path, or bye-road, running

across the country, from the river towards the wood, and which, before he could get into, the enemy would have to clamber over a railing which lay on the side from which they were advancing. On the hither side of the road was a ditch, with a hedge, almost the only one to be met with, and a little copse of small trees. Into this copse I put the men, extending them along the inside of the hedge, which would not only keep them from the view of the enemy, but be some little protection from their fire, and would leave them the more at liberty to retreat when overpowered by numbers, as it was certain they must shortly be. But all my labour was in vain, for when Forbes came from visiting his sentries, he did not approve of my disposition, but took them all out, and formed them on the open road, without any cover, and with a hedge and ditch in their rear, both of which they would be compelled to pass the moment the enemy pressed upon him. I felt annoyed, not only at his want of courtesy to me, but that he would thus expose his men to almost certain destruction, without being able to effect any thing against the enemy, or at all check his advance. I accordingly left him in a huff, and went again to try to find the picquet of the 85th in the house behind us. I was determined to make a more close and thorough search than I had done before, and for this purpose went over the gates, &c. into the yard behind, when lo, I found myself within a yard or two of a strong body of the enemy, which had got into the garden at the lower end, and were just advancing to the house. I crouched down, and hid in the best manner I could, and luckily was enabled to creep off without their discovering who I was. Just as I reached the outer gate, I found a sergeant of ours there, to whom I said, we must set off with all possible speed; and accordingly we both took to our heels, and ran like heroes; the noise of which brought the fire of twenty or thirty rifles after us, but luckily without effect.

I now made the best of my way towards where I judged the main body of our people were, on the great road, in order to inform Colonel Thornton of what I had seen, of this column of the enemy having got possession of the house and garden I had just left, and by doing which they had nearly separated the advance picquet from the main body. He said he had sent two companies of ours, and two of the 85th, to the house immediately in the rear of this I speak of, and in a short time afterwards they and the Americans came into close contact, for they immediately commenced firing ; and where as strange a description of fighting took place as is perhaps on record.

The enemy soon discovered from some men, whom they had unfortunately taken, what the regiments were that were opposed to them—and with all that cunning which the Yankees are famed for, instantly turned it to the best account—for in several places they advanced in bodies, crying out at the same time, " Come on, my brave 85th !" or " My brave 95th !" and thus induced several of our small detached parties to go over the rails to them, supposing they were some of our own people, when of course they were instantly made prisoners. This *ruse* did not always succeed, however, for some of the parties turning restive on their hands, refused to surrender, and thus a fight hand to hand took place, and in which they generally had the worst of it.

On one occasion of this kind our people made a body of them prisoners. The men and officers being requested to lay down their arms, the officer, after surrendering, when he saw there were not many of our people, drew a sort of dirk or knife, and made a stab at the officer of ours who had taken him. We instantly cried out to the men near him, one of whom took up his rifle and shot the villain through the body. They had before this time brought two of their regular battalions close in front of our advance, which did not consist of more than 100 men, and were pouring in dreadful volleys into that small but gallant detachment; but even in this they showed themselves young soldiers, for they formed up the two battalions in line at about forty or fifty yards in distance from the post, and gave the words " ready—present—fire," with all the precision of a field-day; but being so near, of course every word was heard by our people, who, at the critical moment, always took care to cleave as close to the ground as possible, by which they escaped most of their shot. They then up and at them, and, pouring in a desultory but most destructive fire, brought great numbers of them to the ground. Their force, however, was too great to be opposed successfully by such a handful of men, and these brave fellows were at length compelled to yield a little ground; but it was not more than just to enable them to cover themselves, and form again in proper order; and from this time all the efforts of these two battalions were unable to remove them. Indeed, not long after, our people became the assailants, and, advancing again, retook their original position. Poor Hallen was severely wounded on this occasion, and lost about forty of his men.

Two or three naval captains came also to see the fight at Hallen's post, one of whom soon fell severely wounded. The other, the gallant captain of the Dover frigate, with whom part of our people went out, and with whom we all came home, behaved most nobly. Whenever the enemy had fired their volley, he cried, " Now, my lads, up and give them another broadside!" and thus contributed, by his animating conduct, to inspire all around him with confidence.

Poor Forbes just met the fate that I expected. He stood upon the road, and opened his fire upon the enemy as they approached ; but they being perhaps more than twenty times his number, he was instantly compelled to give way, after being himself wounded, having his sergeant killed, and losing nearly the half of his men. The schooner all this time kept up a most galling and incessant fire. Some attempts were made with our light three-pounders, and with rockets, and even with small-arms, to compel her to sheer off, but they were all in vain. Her men, protected by her stout bulwarks which surrounded them, defied all our efforts, and continued to pour in both round and grape wherever they judged, from the direction of the fire, our people were stationed. Luckily the darkness of the night rendered her fire less destructive than it would otherwise have been.

A considerable body of the enemy had penetrated to the house immediately on the right of our original bivouack, where the firing was kept up between them and the parties opposed to them with great spirit for a long time ; but the General, having detached the 4th regiment to form line a little to the rear and right of that house, completely secured that flank from being farther turned. Notwithstanding this, the skirmishers of both armies extended to the wood, some of whom we found lying the next morning almost touching each other. The firing now began to slacken, the enemy having been repulsed at all points, and, towards three o'clock in the morning, it had completely ceased,.when they retired, leaving us in possession of the warmly-contested field.

My battalion had been extremely unfortunate in this action ; for almost at the very outset, when the attack on

Hallen's picquet commenced, Major Mitchell, our commandant, had taken a party of about twenty or thirty men, and advanced for the purpose of supporting that post. Between the bivouack, however, and the point he intended to reach, he unexpectedly fell in with a large body of Americans, (for it was so dark he could not distinguish who they were,) when both himself, and all the men he had with him, were made prisoners. The loss of our five companies in this action was about 120 men; that of the 85th more, I believe; and in all, I think, it amounted to about 300 men. The loss of the enemy must have been considerably greater, if we are to judge from the number of dead they left on the field, and, which is a good criterion, the general average being about ten wounded for one killed.

Nothing could equal the bravery of the few troops we had in the field on this occasion. Their numbers certainly did not amount to 1800 men; while the enemy could not have had fewer than from 4000 to 5000. They had two regular regiments, the 7th and 44th; they had a large corps of irregular riflemen from Kentucky, and another stronger corps from Tennessee, with all the militia of New Orleans and its neighbourhood, every man who is able being compelled to bear arms in case of invasion. They had about 300 irregular horse, whether militia or not I cannot tell, but think it likely they were in all at least 4000 men— with the great and effectual assistance of the schooner, which did us more mischief than 1000 men could have done, probably not so much by the loss she occasioned us, as, by being able to fire on our flank, and even in our rear, she rendered the enemy the most essential service, besides the fire of the ship on our advanced picquet.

We were thus completely surrounded on three sides, and had not the troops behaved with the most determined courage and intrepidity, we must have been driven back, and eventually the greater part would have been taken prisoners; for the path to the water was quite narrow, and even should we reach the head of the creek where we landed, the boats had probably all left it by this time to return for the other troops. Indeed it was reported afterwards, that the arrangements of General Jackson were such, that we were to have been attacked in the rear at the same time as in front, and by the schooner; but the troops for that purpose either not being in readiness, or being too distant to arrive in time, were too late to take part in the action, but arrived about three o'clock in the morning, when they met with a half-drunk artillery-driver of ours near Mons. Villerey's house, as he was returning from the field, and who, seeing a large body of men, which he took for some of our other regiments that had landed, cried out to them, " Come on, my lads, for the Yankees never got such a licking in their lives!" This, it is said, had the effect of frightening them back, without proceeding farther.

I will not vouch for this being fact, but such was the report the next morning; and indeed it is feasible, from the number of people (apparently going with orders, &c.) which we saw galloping down on the other side of the river in the afternoon; and it is certain that a considerable body of militia must have resided down the river, setting aside the report which I mentioned, of some troops having retired in that direction in the morning, when we first advanced; and nothing would have tended more to our complete overthrow than such an attack on our rear, could it have been accomplished.

I might here mention, that Captain Hallen saw the schooner as she passed his picquet, on her way down from New Orleans, on which he instantly despatched a man with

3

the information; but she having the current in her favour, sailed much quicker than the man could run, consequently his information came too late.

I omitted to mention also, that a large ship of 20 guns came down the river at the same time with the schooner, but being less manageable than that vessel, she had anchored abreast of Hallen's picquet; and that he had to sustain her fire, as well as that of the troops in his front, during the whole of the attack of the 23d. She remained at that spot without moving.

I will here also notice another circumstance which took place at this post. An American rifleman fell into the hands of some of Captain Hallen's people, who, when he was brought in, were desired to take his arms from him. These he seemed reluctant to part with, and said to the officer, " Recollect I shall hold you responsible for that rifle, if you take it from me !"—on which the officer took hold of it by the muzzle, and flung it right into the river. I daresay the poor fellow thought they were a strange sort of people he had got amongst ; and I doubt not he had set a great value upon his rifle.

Another officer and myself had a providential escape the next morning, for we had scarcely left a little wooden hut, behind which we had taken up our abode, and slept for a few hours after the fight, when bang comes an eighteen-pound shot right through the house, just at the very spot where we had a minute or two before been sitting. It seems the captain of the schooner, which still lay abreast of us at about 800 yards distance, and from which this shot had been fired, was determined we should not occupy any of the houses in the vicinity, for, beginning with our hut, which was nearest to him, he fired into every house within reach of his guns, although he saw as plainly as we did that most of them were filled with the wounded ; nay, he carried his savage cruelty so far, that he actually fired on a party of the 85th as they were removing one of their wounded officers. It could not be pleaded that he did not know what it was, for, being only half-a-mile distant, and much elevated above our level, with a glass he could see as well as we could what they were doing, for they were carrying the poor fellow on a bier, on their shoulders. He continued this cruel work all the next day, the ship also giving us an occasional shot.   One shot which he fired went through the front of a house in which some of our wounded men were lying, and, striking low, it carried the knapsack out from under the head of a man of ours named Rayour, which he had put for a pillow, without doing him the smallest injury.   I could not credit the story till I went and actually saw the hole by which it entered, the knapsack and the shot lying near the fire-place. After this I went to view the house where I had fallen in with the column of the enemy the night before, and where the 85th were now stationed ; but the fire of the schooner still continued, one shot from which we saw was directed towards us.   It fell right in among the 85th, and, striking a corporal about the breach, as he was endeavouring to get out of its way, it passed out at his breast, on which he gave himself a sort of shake, and fell lifeless to the earth.

Nothing could exceed the great annoyance this mischievous schooner continued to be to us all that and the next day, for they not only saw every thing we did, but we could not move in any number without being saluted with an 18 lb. shot, and we had no means of retaliation.   But during the 25th, efforts were made to get up some heavier guns from the fleet, and every thing having been settled as to the plan, &c., a battery was constructed as close to the

water's edge as possible in the river dike, and a number of
gun barrels having been collected from those broken, &c.
during the late fight, a sort of furnace was erected for the
purpose of heating shot, with which it was determined to
give her a salute the next morning. Every thing succeeded
admirably. The battery was constructed, embrasures cut,
and shot heated, and all ready by daylight on the morning
of the 26th; of course we were all looking out to witness
the effect, and most noble it was, for when the guns opened out upon her, the people on board seemed quite thunder-
struck, and although they attempted to return our fire, it
was only like the blows of a man beat blind by his antagonist, for her shot fell in every other direction but that in
which she should have thrown them. However, they could
not stand to fire more than one round, as our hot shot rendered their situation very soon untenable, and taking to
their boats, they made their escape to the opposite shore
with all expedition.

The distance from the battery to the schooner had been
so accurately measured by Major Blanchard, who superintended the construction of the work, that almost every shot
and shell penetrated the hull of the vessel, and in a short
time after her crew had left her, she broke out into a blaze
of fire, which soon reaching the magazine, she blew up with
a loud explosion, to the great comfort and joy of all our
army. This of course deserved and obtained three as hearty
cheers as I believe were ever given by Britons, and no doubt
the Americans were greatly chagrined at the loss of their
fine and exceedingly useful vessel. A shell or two were
directed towards the ship, but she having seen the fate of
the schooner, got out her boats, which, taking her in tow,
she set off up the river in all haste. Could a battery have
been constructed to fire upon her at the same time, it would

have saved us some hard knocks afterwards. She, however, effected her escape, and we now remained in peace for a few days at least.

On the 25th, Sir Edward Packenham and General Gibbs had arrived; the former immediately assumed the command, and they both set off to the front to reconnoitre the enemy and the kind of country around us.   Every night since our arrival the enemy had been incessant in their means to harass and annoy us, as in truth they had a right to do if they pleased, but it was exceedingly distressing to the troops, and therefore I mention it.   They seldom let an hour pass during the night, that they were not firing at some of our out sentries, and on some occasions they brought the body of irregular cavalry, before mentioned, immediately in front of our outposts, and fired volleys, which, although it did not do much injury to our advanced picquets, had the effect of turning out the whole line, and that often repeated, with the annoyance from the schooner, certainly did not leave us much time for comfortable rest. They frequently lay in ambush for the reliefs of our sentries also, and patrols, and fired upon them sometimes with effect.   In short, they did all they could to annoy and weary us out, but of which we ought not to complain, as they were defending their own country, and allowances ought to be made in such a case that would not be tolerated in an army having no interest in the soil. I trust Englishmen will be equally zealous and bitter to their enemies should our country ever be invaded.

CHAPTER XVIII.

British Army told off into Brigades—Advance, and are hotly received—
Heroism of a young Artillery Officer—We take up a fresh position—
The Enemy work incessantly in raising an extensive breastwork—
Two Batteries erected, from which our heavy Ship Artillery are
brought to bear against it, but without effect—The Enemy also place
their Ship Guns on Batteries—Colonel Lambert arrives with the 7th
and 43d regiments—Preparations for a grand attack on the Enemy's
lines, which entirely fails, and the British are repulsed with great
loss.

THE remainder of the army all arrived during the 24th,
and were put in bivouack in an oblique direction, with
their front to the late field of action, their right thrown back
towards the wood, and their left towards Mons. Villerey's
house. The 93d formed line in advance at an angle of the
wood, as a sort of outpost, while the 85th and ours were
stationed in and around the house, to which I have so often
alluded, *i. e.* where I fell in with the column of the enemy.
Our advanced picquets remained the same as before the
action. If I might here be permitted to hazard an opinion,
I should say that had we advanced upon New Orleans the
morning after the fight, I think there is little doubt we
should have been successful; for when an irregular and un-
disciplined body of troops once meet with a reverse, it is
difficult to bring them into action again with that steadiness
and determination which they often evince in their first
essay.

I understood General Jackson had some trouble in keeping them together after their defeat on the night of the 23d,
and the only mode in which he could get them to form was,
in planting the first who retired in line near the road, and
as each successive detachment arrived from the fight, they
were made to form on their left, the whole line sitting or
laying down for the remainder of the night.   It is easy to
perceive that they would have been quite unmanageable
should they have been seriously attacked, while their spirits
were depressed by their recent failure, and as the works
which we afterwards encountered did not then exist, at
least only in part, I think they would have retired after a
very slight resistance indeed.   I had the information as to
the manner in which they formed, from some of those who
were made prisoners, and who witnessed it. All this, however, is merely the opinion of a private individual, who
judged from appearances only, and it is not in the nature of
things probable that I should be able to form so correct a
one as those who possessed more ample information.

After the arrival of the two general officers before mentioned, the army was told off into brigades as follows, viz.
the 1st brigade, commanded by General Gibbs, consisted of
the 4th, 21st, and 44th British, and 5th West India regiments ; the 2d brigade, commanded by General Keane,
consisted of the 85th, 93d, and 95th British, and 1st West
India regiments, (observe, the West India regiments had
by this time become exceedingly reduced in point of numbers from cold and hardship, which they seemed unable to
bear, and very soon after almost ceased to be regiments, so
many of them were sent away sick ;) the artillery was
commanded by Colonel Dickson, an excellent officer ; the
squadron of the 14th light dragoons not being able to get

mounted, formed the guards at the hospitals, and at head-quarters, &c.

Every thing having been previously arranged on the morning of the 28th, we advanced in two columns, the right near the wood commanded by General Gibbs, and ours on the left by the great road near the river, commanded by General Keane. The enemy had all along kept possession of those farm-houses which lay at some distance in front of our picquets. They were consequently driven from these as we moved forward, which we did, I should imagine, to the distance of about three miles, their picquets retiring gradually before us. We here discovered that the enemy had thrown up a strong fieldwork, which extended from the river to the wood, and which consequently shut up every avenue to our farther advance, without fighting. We also found that their numbers had considerably increased, as we could perceive by the immense bodies of troops be-hind their works. As we pressed upon their picquets as they retired, we got a shot or two at them with our field-guns; but every thing remained quiet within their lines till we had arrived within about 400 yards of them, when they opened out on the head of our columns as destructive a fire of artillery as I ever witnessed. One shot struck in the column of the 85th, which knocked down two officers and about ten men. My battalion was leading, and being partly extended skirmishing, they did not offer so fair a mark for artillery as a solid body, and consequently escaped this.

The ship also, which was anchored a little in advance of their work, opened her broadside on the columns on the road at the same time. Our gun and howitzer, the only two pieces we had there, endeavoured to return the fire of the ship, but without doing her much injury. When the fire was found to be so galling, the troops were moved off the road into the fields on the right, and my battalion advancing about 100 paces farther, was ordered to lay down in a sort of ditch which was there, and to shelter themselves the best way they could. The 85th and 93d formed also more to the right, and secured themselves as well as the nature of the ground would admit. It was only intended as a reconnoissance, consequently the troops did not advance farther, as soon as the nature of their position was ascertained. It appeared to be a high dike of casks, formed as a breastwork, with a considerable quantity of artillery mounted on it, and with a sort of canal or wet ditch in front of it.

Of course, all this took some time to ascertain, during which they kept up an incessant cannonade, both from their works and from the ship. The latter poured in an immense quantity of large grape, which rendered the situation of those exposed to it extremely unpleasant. Our two fieldpieces were very soon silenced by the superior fire of the enemy, and in an hour after our arrival at this point, there was not a man left with them but the officer, who was quite a youth, but yet stood as steady as if he had been on a common parade, although all his men were knocked down about him. I never witnessed more devoted heroism than this fine young man displayed. One shot, nearly towards the last, struck off his sergeant's head, and sent his cap spinning over a ditch, where another officer and I had taken up our post. Some rockets were also tried from this point, both against the ship and the enemy's works, but those directed against the vessel flew quite wide of the mark, and totally failed. Some of those fired into the works, we saw pass over the heads of the men posted in them, but whether they produced any effect we could not see.

The enemy either had set fire to the houses near us before they retired from them, or they had fired heated shot with a view of producing that effect; but we had not been long here ere the whole of the houses in the neighbourhood were in one grand and terrific blaze of fire. I do not exactly know what was done on the right, for we could not see distinctly for some trees which grew in the garden of the farm in that direction, but imagine they encountered something similar to ourselves, as the play of artillery from the enemy's line in front of them was equally unceasing with that in our front. Not a man showed himself out of the enemy's works.

When every thing was ascertained that could be, the troops began gradually to draw off, but this was obliged to be conducted in a very cautious manner, or the loss from their fire would have been severe. The 93d retired first, by separate wings, afterwards the 85th, but ours did not leave their ground till after dark, when, I believe, some of the Yankees began to advance in a rather triumphant and bullying manner, but were taught to keep at a respectful distance by a few shots well laid in among them. A party of sailors had been sent forward to bring off the two field-pieces, there being no artillerymen left to do it, and we had no horses. They undertook and accomplished this task most cheerfully and effectually, without a man hurt I believe.

The loss of my battalion on this occasion was not great. The army now took up a fresh position in which to bivouack, at about a mile and a half distance from the enemy's line, but which they could easily reach with the shot and shells of their larger pieces. The head-quarters were removed from Monsieur Villerey's house to a large farm or chateau behind our new lines, and which were formed in the following manner, viz.:—the 4th and 44th composed one line, with their right near the wood. The 21st formed on their left, but with an intervening space between them. The 85th and 93d formed one line on the left of the 21st, with an interval between their line and that regiment. This latter line was rather in an oblique direction, with its front towards a farm-house in advance and to the left, and where my battalion was ordered to take its station. This latter post was more exposed to the enemy's shot than any of the others ; it being a good deal advanced, and being close to the river, the guns from the opposite shore ceased not firing on it, generally with hot shot. The men were put into a sugar house belonging to this chateau, the floor of which being sunk a little below the surface of the adjoining earth, protected them wonderfully ; but on occasions they had their very cooking utensils knocked off the fire by the enemy's shot, in consequence of the exposed situation of this house. The acting quartermaster and myself being deemed civilians, and having no inclination to be deprived of our natural rest at night, as long as we could be allowed to obtain it, took up our abode in one of the outhouses at head-quarters, which we found unoccupied, and where our respective duties could be carried on with as much facility as if we were in the same house with the battalion, the distance between them being only about half a mile.

Here, also, the sick and wounded were brought, where they could enjoy more comfort than in the sugar-house, till an opportunity offered of sending them down to the shipping. To secure our front a little more, and to protect the troops against the shot from the opposite shore, a redoubt was thrown up about half a mile in front of the right, and pretty near the wood ; while batteries and breastworks were constructed on the road, to fire on any vessels of the enemy which might come down the river. These latter were principally constructed of hogsheads of sugar, which were found in the sugar-houses of the different plantations in the neighbourhood. But nothing could have answered worse than they did for this purpose, the enemy's shot going quite through them, without being at all deadened almost by the resistance they offered. In front of the left also, inside the road, a breastwork was thrown up, which secured the persons of a corps of marines and sailors, who occupied that part of the line. This body was, soon after the 28th, landed from the fleet; and the latter, having brought small arms on shore with them, acted as a small battalion.

It is evident the enemy must have worked incessantly, from our first landing, to complete the work they occupied; for, from the information I before mentioned, as given me by one of the Spanish fishermen, it is clear they had only two guns, mounted on something like a battery, on the great road. But now that work extended even into the wood, a distance of at least three quarters of a mile, and at this time there could not be less than ten or twelve pieces of heavy ordnance mounted on it. We were told by the slaves who had remained in the houses, that the ditch behind which they had constructed this work was a sort of small canal, which the gentleman who owned the property used for the purpose of transporting the produce of his farm from thence into the river. From this time we could plainly perceive great numbers of men continually at work upon it, mostly blacks, of which they would, of course, have abundance; but their white people also (the army, we conclude) were constantly employed upon it. We could see distinctly that they were widening and deepening the canal in front of the work, and raising the parapet to a considerable height.

It was now determined to try what our heavy ship-artillery would do against this work. Accordingly, the greater part of the army were employed in bringing up these unwieldy machines, and to effect which required no slight power and perseverance, as we had no means of transport but the sheer strength of a number of men combined, to drag them successively through the deep soil. A sufficient number of them having been brought up by the 31st, strong working parties were employed all night in erecting two batteries, as near to the enemy's works as they could with safety venture, and getting the guns, carriages, and ammunition, &c., into them. These were formed principally of casks, &c., filled with earth; and I am not sure that some sugar hogsheads were not used on the occasion. However, at daylight on the morning of the 1st Jan. 1815, the whole of the troops were ordered under arms, and moved forward to nearly the same points they occupied on the 28th ult.

This morning there was an extremely thick fog, which greatly favoured our movements, the Americans being, I believe, totally ignorant that any alteration had taken place in the situation of our army. As soon as the fog cleared away, our artillery opened out a tremendous and thundering cannonade upon the enemy's line, which so completely astonished them, that there was not a shot returned for twenty minutes at least, so little did they expect heavy artillery there. Nay, we heard afterwards that a great number of the irregular troops were so alarmed, that they actually quitted the lines without orders, and were posting off to New Orleans, and were with great difficulty brought back again. As soon as they perceived, however, that nothing more than a cannonade was intended, and that our troops did not advance to the attack, they commenced gradually with their artillery against ours, the fire of which increasing as their confidence increased, they were not long in silencing our guns, and in dismounting some of them. The fact is, our works had been thrown up in such haste, that they were not nearly so strong as they ought to have been made, had there been more time; the conse-quence was, their shot penetrated into every part of our works, and caused us not only considerable loss in artillery-men, (with one officer killed,) but, as I said before, actually dismounted a great many of our guns. This consequently entirely failed of having the desired effect; but with such a very favourable opportunity as this morning's fog pre-sented, together with the alarm and terror with which the enemy were struck on opening our artillery upon them, there is not the most distant doubt that we should have at once got possession of their lines, had we but advanced to the attack. It is true, we were not prepared for passing the ditch, having no fascines or other necessaries for that pur-pose; but the resistance, in my opinion, would have been so slight, that we might almost have chosen our own place to cross it; and it was not very deep at any place. The battalion of sailors were quite annoyed at being kept look-ing on, while so fair an opportunity, as they thought, offer-ed, and were crying out one to another, " Why don't we go on? what is keeping us back?"

'Tis not to be doubted that the first effect of any new thing in warfare is always the most certain of producing success, particularly against inexperienced troops; but let them see and know the whole of the effects that such a thing is calculated to produce, and the alarm wears off, and confidence and courage return with wonderful rapidity. So it was here; the first fire of our guns struck them dumb with amazement and terror—But mark the contrast! Both the latter part of this day, and on the 8th, at the general attack, how little they seemed to care for all the artillery we could bring against them! Their gun, a 32-pounder, was a most bitter antagonist to our principal battery. This happened to be erected nearly in front of that part of the line where this gun was situated, and when it fired, its shot always struck the battery at the first bound, and then it ricocheted into the redoubt where I had taken up my post. General Keane, with a part of his brigade, was in this latter work, and some of them narrowly escaped the effects of the numerous balls thrown from this gun. We were told the captain of the schooner, after having been deprived of his vessel, had been appointed to the charge and management of this gun, with some of his crew to work it; and indeed it seemed very like the bitter and determined manner of our former opponent, for any of the other guns seemed like children's play to the unceasing and destructive fire of this heavy piece of ordnance. I could distinctly see that they were sailors that worked it—one of whom, a large mulatto, with a red shirt, always spunging her out after firing.

In what I am going to relate, I know I shall incur the risk of being deemed a *traveller* by some of my readers, but that shall not deter me from telling what I plainly and repeatedly saw with my own eyes, assisted by a glass. At the distance of three quarters of a mile, I could distinctly perceive the ball from this gun every time it was fired, it appearing like a small black spot in the midst of the column of white smoke, and which gradually grew larger in appearance as it approached us. In many instances I was providentially the cause of saving some of the men who were in the redoubt with us, because, seeing which way the ball was coming, I told them when to lie down; and on one occasion was the shave so close, that it actually carried away one of the men's packs as he lay on the ground. Another shot struck about three feet above our heads, and carried away part of a piece of timber which supported a shed just behind us.

I forgot to mention, that, after the 28th, the Americans, conceiving that the guns of the ship would be of more use if taken out and placed in batteries, this was accordingly done; the greater part of them being planted on the other side of the river, and being completely on our flank, were enabled to annoy our people considerably, who were posted near the great road.

About two or three o'clock in the afternoon of the 1st, the army began again to retire to its bivouack, leaving covering parties to protect the batteries; and after night, the whole having formed, working parties were sent to bring off as many of the heavy guns as possible. Some of these, however, they were obliged to bury in the earth, not being able to drag them away before daylight next morning. This work seemed more oppressive and fatiguing to the troops than the bringing of them up did, inasmuch as they were animated in the latter instance by the hope of their being able to effect something against the enemy through their toil and labour; but now disappointment added poignancy to their sufferings. However, although things began to assume not quite so favourable an aspect as formerly, yet every thing was borne with the greatest good-will, as they were still confident of all their laborious services being ultimately crowned with success. In all these fatiguing services, the sailors bore an ample share, and were of the very utmost benefit to the whole army, for they could readily contrive the means of moving those immense masses of metal by purchases, &c., which to a soldier would be utterly impossible. Indeed, throughout the whole service, the gallant tars deserved the very highest praise, for they were equally brave as laborious and willing.

All hands, both soldiers and sailors, had been up the whole of the night of the 31st, and now up again all night of the 1st. This was very trying, no doubt. If any thing like dissatisfaction was evinced, this incessant toil and want of rest in encountering it, arose more from a desire to be led on to the attack, than from any wish to be rid of their labours, however painful these were. As this attempt had failed, no other scheme now appeared to present itself, but a vigorous and well sustained attack on their line; for several efforts had been made to penetrate through the wood, to endeavour to ascertain whether it was possible to turn their position at that point, but all these efforts had failed. The last that was attempted was conducted by Lieutenant Wright of the engineers, but both himself and nearly all his party perished; for it seems they fell in with a body of American riflemen, who, being much better accustomed to travelling in woods than our people were, fell on them, and, as said before, nearly cut off the whole party; yet it is evident it was not utterly impassable, or the two parties could not have met.

I do not recollect to what regiment the men belonged who accompanied Wright, but think it probable they were altogether unacquainted with that description of service, which led them into the fatal snare in which they fell. I am confident I saw blacks, who passed and repassed by the wood, but it is certain that no attempt upon a large scale could be made in that direction to turn their position; and it was probably the better plan to abandon the idea altogether. A very excellent expedient was however devised, for the purpose of turning the right flank of the enemy; it was certainly a bold and vigorous idea, and one which, if successful, would no doubt have secured to us the victory and the possession of New Orleans. This was no less than cutting a canal, in order to unite the Mississippi with the lake by which we had arrived, and by getting boats out of the latter into the river, to transport a sufficient number of men to the opposite shore, for the purpose of making a diversion in aid of the principal attack on this side.

Nothing could exceed the grandness of the conception. Accordingly, all hands were set to work to widen and deepen the rill of water which flows into the creek at the landing-place, and, continuing it up past Monsieur Villerey's house, to let it enter the river a little above that point. This, as may easily be conceived, was most laborious and dirty work ; and, lest the health and spirits of the troops should suffer from such incessant fatigue, they were told off into four watches or spells, each of which followed the other in regular succession, so that the work never stood still. When it had reached near the house and high-road, screens were put up on the latter, to prevent the enemy on the opposite bank of the river from seeing what was carrying on ; but as the blacks were passing and repassing almost continually by the wood, as I before mentioned, no doubt the Americans were well acquainted with what we were doing.

On the —— General Lambert arrived with the 7th and 43d regiments, to our great joy, two finer regiments not being in the service. Consequently every eye now sparkled with hope, that our labours and privations would soon terminate, as every one confidently anticipated a favourable result, and seemed still inclined to despise that enemy who had shown us that we could not do so with impunity. We were glad to meet many of our old Peninsular friends in these two fine corps, and of course welcomed them to the

New World in the best manner we were capable of. They took up their ground a little in front of the canal which was cutting, there not being room sufficient for them in the line of our bivouack. We were now about 7000 effective troops, and all beginning to cheer up again, imagined nothing could withstand us.

By the 6th the canal was finished, and the boats brought up into it. There was obliged to be a lock in it at the entrance from the river, for the strength of which Sir Edward, our Chief, I understand, expressed his apprehensions, but was assured by the engineer that there was not the slightest danger. I give this merely as report.

On the 7th the arrangements for the attack next morning having been completed, orders were issued to that effect. The arrangements were as follows, viz.—a corps consisting of the 85th regiment, with 200 sailors and 400 marines, and the 5th West India regiment, with four light fieldpieces, the whole under the command of Colonel Thornton, was to embark in boats by twelve o'clock, and to be all across the river by daylight next morning. This force would amount to about 1200 or 1300 men, and were destined to attack and carry the works on the opposite bank, getting possession of the guns without allowing them to be spiked if possible, when they were to be turned upon the right flank of the enemy's position, on this side the river, to favour our attack. It is clear, then, that this movement should precede that of the grand attack by a considerable space of time. In the grand attack the troops were to be disposed as follows, viz.—The right column, under General Gibbs, was to consist of the 4th, 21st, 44th, and three companies of my battalion, which latter were to extend as close to the enemy's work as possible, previous to the advance of the column, and, by maintaining a constant fire, were to endeavour to keep the enemy down as much as possible. The 44th was to be divided; one-half of that corps was to carry fascines, &c., which they were to throw into the ditch on reaching it, in order that the remaining regiments of that column might be able to pass it. These fascines were to be had in the redoubt I before mentioned. The other wing of the 44th was to lead that column, followed by the 21st, and then the 4th, regiments. This was to be the principal attack. The left column, commanded by General Keane, was to be composed as follows, viz.—one company of the 7th, one of the 21st, one of the 43d, and two of ours. The whole to be supported by the 93d regiment. These were to make a feint attack upon the half-moon work which the enemy had constructed near the river, and if opportunity offered, to turn it into a real attack, and penetrate the enemy's line, co-operating with the other column. Our two companies were to act here in the same manner as the other three with whom they were to form a junction, thus covering the whole front of the enemy's work. Some blacks of the 1st West India regiment were to enter the wood on the right of our right column, and to keep up as much noise as possible by firing and sounding bugles, &c. to induce a belief that a large body of troops was moving in that direction. The reserve, under General Lambert, was to consist of the 7th and 43d regiments, and was to be so stationed as to be able to render aid to either of the attacking columns. Strict orders were given that no obstacle was to be permitted to retard the advance of the columns, but that they were to press forward and endeavour to overcome every hinderance that might present itself.

As far as I recollect, and from the information I have since gained, these were substantially the orders issued, and arrangements made, on this occasion. The commanding-officers and heads of departments were also assembled, and each told the part he had to perform; on which occasion, I understand, the commanding-officer of the 44th expressed himself in terms which I could scarcely conceive it possible could fall from the lips of a soldier, which were, that " it was a forlorn hope with the 44th." In all my campaigning I never yet heard a commanding-officer who did not look upon the post of danger as the post of honour, and who did not rejoice, as if a favour was conferred on him, when appointed to an arduous or hazardous duty. Had the commanding-officer of the 44th served in the Peninsula under our illustrious leader there, he would, I am confident, have been animated by a quite different spirit. After dark I went with my commanding-officer and adjutant to view the ground over which our battalion was to march next morning, and to find out the wooden bridges, &c. over some ditches which lay in the way, that no delay might take place when they were to be called upon to act.

I was sadly disappointed at our not meeting with any other commanding-officers engaged in this most necessary duty, and at the time I expressed my apprehensions as to the result. I pointed out to him the different manner in which the business had been conducted previous to the assault of Badajos, and previous to the attack on the enemy's position on the Nivelle, where every commanding-officer, or others, who had any particular duty assigned to them in the next day's operations, were brought to ground from which it was clearly pointed out to them how they were to move and act; but here all seemed apathy and fatal security, arising from our too much despising our enemy. This latter, I believe, was the principal cause of our not taking the necessary precautions, and consequently of our failure; particularly the commanding-officer of the 44th ought to have been brought and shown where the fascines were lodged, that no excuse of ignorance on that score might be pleaded. A rocket thrown up was to be the signal for the troops to advance to the attack, after they had been properly posted under the cover of night for that purpose. I own I did not at all feel satisfied with what I had seen and heard, and retired to rest with a considerable degree of despondency on my mind; and as I knew I could render little aid to the service in a case like the present, I determined I should not take any part in it, for I almost felt confident of its failure.

The whole of the troops were at their post by the time appointed; but, unfortunately, as the sailors, &c. were getting the boats out of the canal into the river, the lock gave way after only a very few had passed it. Thus the whole business seemed at one. blow to be totally ruined. Every effort was made to remedy the evil, but it was irremediable. They toiled, however, to get more boats into the river, but the delay had been so great that it began to draw towards dawn before they had effected any thing worth mentioning. Poor Sir Edward seemed like one bereft of his reason, for this failure had blasted all his most sanguine hopes; and as the troops were now close under the enemy's works, and could not be withdrawn before daybreak, nor without being perceived by the enemy, he thought it as dangerous to turn back as to go forward with the operation, consequently he ordered the rocket to be fired, although it was considerably past the time for the attack to take place, and no troops on the opposite shore. As soon as this was done, he galloped to the front. But the enemy had been quite prepared, and opened such a heavy fire upon the different columns, and upon our line of skirmishers, (which had been formed for some time within about 100 or 150 yards of the enemy's work,) as it is not easy to conceive. I was not in it as I said before, but I was so posted as to see it plainly. But the 44th, with the fascines, were not to be found. Their commanding-officer had taken them considerably past the redoubt where the fascines were placed, and when he bethought him of what he had to do, he and his men were obliged to turn back to seek them ; and thus, when he ought to have been in front to throw them into the ditch to allow the other troops to pass over, he was nearly half a mile in rear seeking for them. But I believe it would not have availed much had they been there in time, for the right column never reached the point to which it was directed ; but from the dreadful fire of every kind poured into it, some of the battalions began to waver, to halt and fire, and at last one of them completely broke, and became disorganized. Sir Edward seeing this rushed forward with his hat in his hand, and endeavouring to animate them by his presence, he cheered them on to advance again ; but at this moment he fell, after receiving two wounds, the last of which was mortal. General Gibbs also fell nearly at the same time mortally wounded, and was borne off the field. Thus was the right and principal column deprived of both its leaders ; and although one regiment gave ground, and could not be brought again to the attack, the other continued to keep in a body, although any attempt now must be hopeless, and they were losing such numbers of men that they must shortly be annihilated. They accordingly retired without effecting any thing.

The left column succeeded somewhat better ; but, as things turned out, it was only to enhance their own loss. They forced their way into the circular work before mentioned, in which they made all the men who defended it prisoners. But the canal still lay between them and the main work, which was passed only by a plank; and being so few in numbers, it would have been madness in them to attempt to go beyond where they had at present stationed themselves. Indeed, they were in a most critical situation; for, being within a few yards of the enemy's main body, they could not move without being shot through the head by their riflemen; and it was not till they had threatened to shoot the prisoners they had taken, that they induced the Americans to desist from attacking them; for by this time General Keane also had fallen severely wounded, and the 93d had been nearly cut to pieces; and General Lambert, with the reserve, had been obliged to advance and cover the retreat of the other columns. Colonel Dale, who commanded the 93d, fell early in the action, and the command devolved on Colonel Creagh; this officer, being unwilling to retire his regiment without effecting the object aimed at, although the men were literally mown down by the murderous fire of the enemy, and the other column had given way, still endeavoured to advance, but was at length reluctantly compelled to retrograde, taking care to keep his men together. This showed a fine and noble feeling in him, and is equally honourable to his gallant regiment; but unfortunately it tended only to swell the list of killed and wounded on this lamentable occasion.

My people were thus left to shift for themselves, and to get away in the best manner they could. But being extended, and not being so good an object for the artillery to fire at as the columns, they escaped with much less loss than could well be supposed. Some few of them reached the ditch when they saw the columns advancing, and which they say could have been passed with ease; but the columns never advanced so far, which had they done, and that rapidly, their loss would not have been half so great; for the enemy's troops in front of the right column were evidently intimidated, and ceased firing for some seconds as the column approached ; and there is little doubt, had they pushed on to the ditch with celerity, the Americans would have abandoned their line ; at least, such is my humble opinion. But the poor fellows on the left, who had gained the only work which fell into our hands on this bank of the river, were still detained there, unable either to advance or retreat ; and not one durst show his head above the parapet, or he was instantly shot dead.

Such was their confined and critical situation at this period, that an officer of the 7th, whose name I forget, being himself rather tall, and wearing at this time the high narrow-topped cap, could not squeeze in sufficiently close to cover himself completely by the parapet, the top of the high cap he wore sticking above the top of the work. This part of the cap, which was visible to the Americans within the line, had no less than four or five rifle-shots put through it while he lay there, but without touching his head. All this information respecting these three companies I had from Lieutenant Steele of the 43d, one of the officers who was in the work.

They were obliged at last to adopt a very singular but politic expedient, which was, to make one of the American prisoners embrace a man of the 43d, and thus to stand up together to see what was going forward ; for hitherto they were totally ignorant, from the causes above assigned. The enemy durst not fire in such a case, for fear of killing their own man. The news they now learned was most disheartening indeed, which was, that the whole of the British had retired, and that the Americans were coming out of their lines, and were moving in the direction of that work. Nothing now remained but to surrender, or to make an attempt to retreat, at the risk of being every man knocked down. The latter, however, they preferred ; on which Colonel Rennie, of the 21st, who commanded these three companies, was the first to make the experiment, and in doing which, the moment after he left the fort, he fell to rise no more. They thought it better for them all to go at once, and instantly the whole party made a rush out of the work. The greater part of them providentially succeeded in effecting their escape, although many a brave fellow fell in the attempt.

CHAPTER XIX.

Bravery and Success of Colonel Thornton—Negotiation for leave to
transport the Wounded across the River—Insult offered to the Bri-
tish—They retreat—Our Army embark, and determine to make an
Attack upon Mobile—Proceed in the direction of Mobile Bay—A
Brigade detached to reduce Fort Boyer—The Fort surrenders, the
Garrison becoming Prisoners of War—Intelligence of a Treaty of
Peace being concluded at Ghent—Cessation of Hostilities.

It now remains to detail the operations of Colonel
Thornton's party. It will be seen, that, although his
people were all ready at the appointed hour, they could not
get a sufficient number of boats to transport them to the
opposite shore. In fact, they did not get on board till it
was near daylight, and then only about one-half of the
appointed number. But, although at the risk of sacrificing
himself and the few men he took with him, he hesitated
not to make the attempt of fulfilling his orders. The signal
for the general attack, however, was made before he could
reach the opposite bank, and he had then to land, and after
making his disposition with the few troops he had, to advance and attack a corps of 2000 men, mostly covered by
works, some of which were extremely strong. He dashed
on, however, the advance of the enemy giving way before
him, till coming to their principal battery, he was obliged

to detach a part of his force through the wood on his left to turn their flank, while he with the remainder attacked in front. This was conducted in such a soldierlike manner, that, after a short conflict, the enemy gave way on all sides, and retiring with precipitation, abandoned to the victors batteries and works containing sixteen guns of various calibre.

But, alas! all this success came too late; for the principal attack had by this time ended in a total failure, attended with the loss of three out of four generals, and with nearly 2000 officers and men killed, wounded, and made prisoners. Had Providence prospered the work of the canal, and the troops could have been got across at the appointed hour, and in sufficient numbers, there is every reason to believe that the effect produced on the main body by such a powerful diversion, would have tended to the complete overthrow of the whole force before us; for so insecure did General Jackson feel himself to be after our establishment on the other bank of the river, and so alarmed at its consequences, that, in the evening of the fatal day, he would not consent to a cessation of hostilities, to enable us to bring off our numerous wounded, till General Lambert (who had now succeeded to the command) agreed as a preliminary to withdraw the force under Colonel Thornton from that bank; and this, although with great reluctance, the General was compelled from motives of humanity and other causes to consent to.

Before, however, a final answer was returned to General Jackson, I believe it was suggested to our General, that, with the possession of the other bank of the river, and with the 7th and 43d nearly yet entire, and with the remainders of the other regiments, our chances of success had not yet entirely departed, particularly as Jackson evinced

such eagerness for our withdrawing from that bank. General Lambert in consequence used means to ascertain the
feelings of the troops on this proposition, but without their
knowledge of his having done so ; but I regret to state,
they seemed utterly hopeless of ever being able to overcome such formidable difficulties as had presented themselves, particularly now that their means of overcoming
them had been so lamentably diminished.   The idea was
consequently abandoned.

In this negotiation between the Generals, which continued for some hours, Lieutenant-colonel Smith, our assistant adjutant-general, had repeatedly to pass from army to
army with flags of truce, before the matter could be finally
arranged.   This officer was most indefatigable in his exertions on this unfortunate expedition, and to him the army
is greatly indebted for his zeal, ability, and gallantry, on
this and every other occasion where they could be of service to his country, and by those in authority no doubt
they are duly appreciated.

Thus terminated the fatal attack on the lines of New
Orleans—a termination probably as disastrous in its consequences as any of modern date—not even excepting that
of Buenos Ayres ; for that, discreditable as it was to our
arms, did not cost the lives of such a number of fine soldiers ; and I fear we have not yet experienced the full consequences of this failure, for it is certain that the Americans are greatly elevated by it in their own estimation, and
it is not improbable they may be thence induced to maintain a higher tone in all their future negotiations with this
country.

One instance may be to the point, as showing the feeling
of individuals of that country on this subject.   A fellow in
the shape of an officer asked Colonel Smith, (I think it

was,) " Well, what do you think of we Yankees? Don't
you think we could lick any of the troops of the continent
easily?"—" I don't know that," says our officer.—" Why,
I'll prove to you," says Jonathan, " that we have shown
ourselves the best troops in the world. Didn't the French
beat the troops of every other continental nation? Didn't
you beat the French in the Peninsula? and haven't we
beat you just now?" This of course was conclusive, and
no farther argument on that subject could be advanced.

The remainder of the troops retired in the evening to
their sorrowful bivouack, worn out and sadly dispirited.
All that night was of course devoted to bringing off the
unfortunate wounded; but several of those who fell far in
advance had been taken into the American lines, and, I have
every reason to believe, were treated with the greatest humanity. Every effort was used, during the continuance of
the truce, to bring away the great numbers who lay wounded in the different parts of the field; and on this as on all
other occasions, the sailors with their officers, evinced the
utmost solicitude to render assistance to the army; a great
number of them were employed all night on this distressing duty. During the whole of that afternoon, both while
the negotiations were pending, and at other times, the
American officers were unceasing in their endeavours to induce our soldiers to desert and join their army. Too many,
I regret to say, listened to their offers, and accepted them.
To some they promised promotion, to others money or
grants of land; in short, they were more like recruiting
sergeants, I understand, than the officers of a hostile army.
My battalion did not quit the field till after dark, and it is
from some of them I have this information. A group of
two sergeants and a private of ours were accosted by an
American officer of artillery with a request that they would

enter the service of the United States ; that the sergeants should be promoted if they wished to serve, or that they should have grants of land if they preferred a civil life ; but that, if they chose to enter the army, he would ensure them the rank of officers. Our people listened to this harangue for some time, and then began, I regret to say, to give him some bad language ; telling him, at the same time, that they would rather be privates in the British army, than officers among such a set of raggamuffins as the Americans, and told him to sheer off or they would fire upon him. This so exasperated the cowardly villain, that he went off instantly into the line, they watching him all the while, and pointing the gun, of which, it seems, he had charge, it was fired, and knocked down the private, who was only wounded, however, by the shot. Innumerable attempts of this nature were made both now and all the time we remained before their lines subsequently, but which attempts, I am proud to say, as far as I have been able to learn, failed in every instance in the men of my battalion.

Much about the same time, an American soldier came within about 150 yards of our line, and began to plunder such of the killed or wounded men as he thought possessed of any thing valuable. He at length commenced upon a poor wounded man belonging to my battalion, which being perceived by a Corporal Scott of ours, he asked permission from his captain to take a shot at him. This being granted, (although a sort of truce had been established while the negotiations were going on,) he took up his rifle, and taking a steady aim, he fired, and tumbled the plundering villain right over the body of the poor wounded man.

The loss of our five companies in this attack amounted to seven officers and about —— men killed and wounded. Some of the other regiments, the 93d in particular, had suffered dreadfully, having lost more than half their numbers. The sad ceremony of burying such of the officers whose bodies had been recovered, together with attention to the wounded, occupied several days from this period, and sending the wounded, who were able to bear removal, to the shipping, kept great numbers of the remaining men continually employed; and the attention of all was now turned towards drawing off from this scene of our late disastrous attempt.

The General entered into a negotiation with Jackson about being permitted to send a portion of our wounded down the river in boats; for which permission some equivalent, which I forget, was to be granted on our part, and which, after considerable discussion, was eventually agreed to. The sick, the wounded, the stores of every description, were now despatched as fast as circumstances would allow; but the effecting of this occupied not less than nine days, during the whole of which time the enemy was incessant in his attempts to harass and annoy us. All their heavy ordnance was brought to bear on our bivouack; the sugar-house our people occupied, and even the head-quarters, did not escape; night and day they kept up a fire of shot and shells upon these points; but the distance being considerable, no very great mischief resulted from it, further than the continual state of uneasiness and alarm in which it kept the troops. On one occasion, however, a shell was thrown into the lines of the 43d, who had since the attack occupied a part of the general bivouack, and which, falling into a hut occupied by Lieutenant Darcy of that regiment, while he lay asleep, carried off both his legs as it fell. Poor fellow! he would thus be awakened in a rough manner indeed. I have since seen him in Dublin, the government having kindly compensated him by giving him a company, and I believe two pensions.

Several shells were thrown into the head-quarters pre-
mises, but providentially without injuring any one.   One
fell in the yard while a party of troops was halted there
for a short while, and which falling on one of the men's
knapsacks, which he had put off, it carried it, with itself,
not less than six feet deep into·the earth.   It did not
explode.   Some fell on the roof, which penetrated through
all the stories to the very ground.   Every night also the
picquets were kept in a state of agitation and alarm by the
continual attacks of small parties of our skulking enemy,
and my battalion, as did the others also, lost considerable
numbers by this petty warfare.   In short, the men's lives
began almost to be a burden to them.

There was another source of annoyance adopted on the
part of the Americans on this occasion, but which, affecting only the mental, and not the bodily powers of our
soldiers, was not so much heeded.   Every day almost
they assembled in large bodies on the parapet of their line,
with flags of various descriptions, some with " sailors'
rights" and numerous other devices, &c. painted on them,
using the most insulting gesticulations towards those who
were near enough to see them, a band playing Yankee
Doodle, and other national airs, all the while, and sometimes ironically favouring us with Rule Britannia.   Considerable numbers of our men deserted about this time.
Every encumbrance being removed, however, by the 17th,
orders were issued for the march of the army on the
following evening soon after dark, leaving the picquets as a
rearguard, which were not to march till a short while before daylight.   In retiring, some of the wounded, who were
unable to bear removal, were necessarily left in the houses.
where they had been collected ; but there were not many
so left, and no doubt the enemy acted humanely by them.

There were seven men of my battalion left, out of which three rejoined us after the conclusion of peace ; the other four, I believe, were very badly wounded, and died in consequence.   It was also necessary to abandon such of the guns as remained in the advanced batteries, because, both from their weight and their being so near the enemy, they could not be brought off without exposing our intentions of retreating.   Neither were these numerous, and most of them only iron ship-guns, which are of no great value.

The movement commenced according to the preconcerted plan, and being conducted with secrecy and regularity, every soldier was brought off, over a country almost impassable, and where, if followed and harassed by an enterprising enemy, great numbers must have either fallen into their hands or perished in the swamp.   But I believe, had the Americans even been aware of our intention, they would have hesitated before they came into collision with our highly exasperated army, and would scarcely have dared to attack us in the open field : they had had enough of that work on the 23d, to give them a specimen of what British soldiers could do when met fairly, front to front.

The marsh, it may be necessary to mention, extended from the lower skirt of the wood to the fishermen's huts at the mouth of the creek.   This creek we had sailed up on our advance, but this could not possibly be the case at present, both on account of our numbers being much too great for the number of boats, and of the danger to which it would have exposed the troops had they been attacked from the shore, but principally on the former account ; a sort of road had therefore been constructed by our artificers, by cutting down boughs from the wood, and laying them across such places as required something on the surface on which to tread.   This road extended, as nigh as I can judge, about

R

eight or ten miles, and in passing which numerous slips were made into the sloughs on each side ; but there being plenty of assistance generally at hand, they helped each other out : some men, I understand, were lost, however, in this night-march through the swamp.

Having arrived at the huts before-mentioned, the whole army set about forming such places of shelter as the desert swamp afforded. There were certainly reeds in abundance, but we wanted some sort of timbers for the support of the outward covering. We, however, did the best we could ; and now every exertion was made by the navy to bring the army off from this most uncomfortable place of abode, and regiment after regiment were despatched as fast as the boats and other small craft could go and return, the distance from hence to the shipping being about seventy miles. While we remained here, we who were fond of shooting found plenty of wild-ducks on which to exercise our sporting abilities ; but, alas ! we wanted shot, and were therefore seldom able to bring home a couple for dinner.

A considerable number of slaves, belonging to the estates where we had lately been stationed, followed us down thus far, some of whom would not return, but were afterwards sent on board of ship. These, male and female, often amused us with their native dances, the men generally having a number of rings or bells about them, which sounded as they kept time to the tune. Some of their dances were, however, far from decent, particularly on the part of the females, which, it may be supposed, highly delighted some of our young and thoughtless countrymen. Some were induced to return to their masters : for those who came on board of ship, I believe it was not till very lately that the two governments came to terms as to the remuneration which their owners claimed for them.

At length the turn came for my battalion to go on board, which we did on the 25th of January, when our whole five companies were put on board the Dover, the ship that had brought out two companies of the battalion, and which were then not much fewer in number than the five at present were; in fact, we had lost more than half. The whole army did not get embarked till ——, when the 7th Fusileers came on board. This regiment had been necessarily left alone at the fishermen's huts till the boats could return, as before stated, to bring them off, and yet even this single battalion the enemy, with upwards of 10,000 men, dared not come down and attack, although there were no works to protect it in this exposed situation. Nothing could possibly demonstrate more fully and clearly, that, notwithstanding the repulse they had unfortunately given our troops, they dreaded them in the open country; or else it must be attributed to the prudent sagacity of their leader, who, having gained a victory which he had previously scarce dared to hope for, now wisely resolved not to risk the tarnishing of his dear-bought laurels. It is not an easy matter to reconcile this cautious and timid conduct with their furious onset on the night of the 23d, and with their boasting speeches after our failure on the 8th instant.

Now, while we remain at rest for a short while on board of ship, let us take a retrospective glance at the late events. It is certain we were singularly unfortunate. Providence, which had smiled upon us in our late operations against the most formidable army in the world, the French, here taught us most painfully, that the victory is not always to be gained by strength or courage. Indeed it was but a just punishment for the contempt we entertained for our opponents, and which unfortunate feeling, I believe, was almost universal. I own I entertained it in a high degree; for I

judged it next to a moral impossibility that an army of un-
disciplined and unmanageable peasants, however numerous,
could for a moment withstand the attack of those troops
who had overthrown the victorious legions of Bonaparte.
But every soldier was a patriot, and they fought for their
country, and for a country of all others most suitable for
the operations of such troops; full of fastnesses, composed
of creeks, and necks, and woods, &c. of all which they did
not fail to take the utmost advantage.   For this work of
theirs, constructed on a spot of ground said to have been
pointed out by General Moreau, completely shut us out from
all approach towards the town, and compensated for every
disadvantage under which they, as irregulars, laboured; for
it was not only a formidable barrier to our army, but it gave
them, by the protection it afforded their persons, all the
steadiness of troops inured to combat, and permitted them
the full exercise of that superior skill as marksmen for
which they are famed, and which exposure in the open
field would have deprived them of; for here they were
covered up to the chin, and suffered comparatively nothing
from all our fire.

But I fear we have something for which to blame ourselves on this occasion.   It is certain, I believe, that they
had been timely apprized of the destination of our expedition, however secret we pretended to keep it ourselves, and
if rumour may in such a case be permitted to go for any
thing, it is said that information was conveyed from Jamaica
to New Orleans direct by a French ship, which left the former for the latter place some time before our arrival. How
she came into the possession of that information, I cannot
justly tell. It is certain, however, that the Americans must
have had timely notice, or General Jackson could not have

had the men from Kentucky and Tennessee to oppose us the first night we landed.

I before hazarded an opinion, that had we pushed forward on the 24th December, we should in all probability have proved successful. I will say nothing as to the point of debarkation being well or ill chosen, although many have said we should have been more likely to succeed had we attacked Fort ———, which, after carrying, would have allowed us to land behind the town, instead of three leagues below it. These things I am totally incapable of judging of, from my ignorance of the country. I also before expressed my opinion, that had we attacked on New Year's Day, when our artillery produced such an effect on the appalled Americans, we should have had a better chance of carrying their works.

Another thing in which I venture to differ from the plan adopted by our lamented commander, is, that I would have employed the 7th and 43d to the post of honour, instead of keeping them in reserve. They, it was well known, had each established a reputation for being the finest regiments in the service, and every reliance might have been placed in their executing whatever task was assigned them, if executable by human powers. Far different was it with those who unfortunately led the attack, for except one of the regiments of the attacking column, they had not any of them been conspicuous as fighting regiments.

It was, I believe, a well known maxim of Bonaparte's, always to put his best troops in front; if they were successful, their example served to stimulate the others to copy their example; if unsuccessful, their discipline and valour never permitted them to become so totally disorganized as to render the reverse irretrievable. The onset also of these better troops, must produce a far different effect on the enemy than the hesitating and dispirited attack of inferior ones. Had our troops on this occasion rushed forward to the ditch in double quick time, or at least at a quick march, I venture to affirm the work would have been carried with the fourth part of the loss of what they suffered. Reason itself must point out to any man, whether acquainted with military matters or not, that to move slowly under a galling fire is more trying and destructive to the troops so moving, than to rush at once to the point aimed at; but much more, to halt at the very point where every fire-arm can be brought to bear upon them with the deadliest effect, is of all other modes of proceeding the least likely to succeed. They were thus exposed for hours to as destructive a fire as ever was poured upon the heads of an attacking army, while, had they pushed on at the rate I mention, a few minutes would have sufficed to put them from under the fire of the artillery at least, for when close to the ditch, it could not be brought to bear upon them. Mark the mode in which the three companies on the left effected the task assigned to them. Before the enemy were aware almost that they were to be attacked, these troops were in possession of the work they were destined to storm; so quickly indeed that the defenders of that work had not time to effect their retreat, and were, as before noticed, made prisoners by the attacking party. This not only secured their safety while left there by themselves, but enabled them, in some degree, to effect their retreat with less loss than they would otherwise have been exposed to.

I have dwelt perhaps too long on this, but of all other causes I deem this to have been the greatest of our sad failure. It is lamentable, however, to be obliged to confess, that ill conduct on the part of some parties, but of one individual in particular, contributed in no small degree to our repulse on this melancholy occasion. For the rest, nothing could exceed the determined courage and patient endurance of hardship that the army in general evinced, and certainly nothing could exceed the gallantry of our leaders.

It was now determined to make an attempt upon Mobile, a town lying about thirty or forty leagues to the eastward of New Orleans. Accordingly, the fleet got under weigh and proceeded in the direction of the entrance into Mobile Bay, which is protected on the west side by shoals and Isle Dauphine, and on the east by a fort, built on a point of land called Mobile Point, and mounting about twenty pieces of heavy ordnance. Its name is Fort Boyer, I believe. Before our arrival in this country, an attempt had been made on this fort by one of our frigates, but which entirely failed, owing to her taking the ground on the shoals before mentioned. As she could not be got off, and as she lay under the fire of the fort, her crew were compelled to abandon her, but, I believe, not till they had first set her on fire ; her wreck lay here whenwecame. Until this fort was taken, no vessel of any size could enter the bay, consequently it became necessary to attack it in form. The brigade formerly General Gibbs's, consisting of the 4th, 21st, and 44th, was therefore landed a little behind the point, and proceeded without delay to invest it ; the remainder of the troops were landed on Isle Dauphine.

We were put on shore on the 8th February, and instantly commenced hutting ourselves by brigades. Some of the officers had tents issued out to them; the acting Quartermaster and myself had one between us. This island is almost covered with pine-wood, but in other respects it is nearly a desert, and without any inhabitants resident on it, save one family, a Mr Rooney, formerly from Belfast I understand, but now a naturalized American. He was married to a native of

Louisiana, a lady of French extraction. He had been a midshipman in the American navy, but had been dismissed for some misconduct, it was said, and banished to this island. He appeared to us to be no great things.

I omitted to mention that the 40th regiment had arrived from England before we left the banks of the Mississippi, but it being after the failure they were of no use, and were consequently not permitted to land. They were afterwards placed in our brigade, which now bivouacked near to the point of the island facing the bay. When we arrived, the island contained a considerable number of cattle, with pigs, &c. belonging to Rooney, but which had been permitted, as is customary in this country, to run wild in the woods, there being no danger of their leaving the island. These, however, soon fell a prey to such hungry fellows as we were, who had been for some time past on rather short commons. But they did not answer our expectations, being in taste, what may appear singular, quite fishy. This was attributed to their feeding so much on marine vegetables, there being little other pasture for them on the island.

A hoax was played off upon great numbers of our young hands respecting this fishiness. There was on one point of the island a considerable oyster-bed, and it was generally pretty near this that the cattle were found and shot, that being the most distant from our bivouack. It was therefore said the flesh of the cattle became of that peculiar flavour from feeding upon oysters. Some, without reflecting, credited this strange story, as the assertor generally said he had seen the cattle opening the oysters with their tongues. This oyster-bed, however, was a source of great luxury to us, for it not only afforded us the means of rendering the salt junk more palatable by having an excellent sauce to make it go down, but it even afforded a most wholesome and delicious meal upon occasions by eating them raw. We also made the best use of our time when not employed on military affairs, in endeavouring to catch as many fish as we could; and for this purpose, my mess purchased from one of the poor Spanish fishermen before mentioned (and who, for the information and kindness they had shown us, were obliged to quit their habitations and follow us), an excellent casting-net, with which the acting Quartermaster and myself occupied ourselves from day to day, generally bringing home a sufficient quantity of fish to serve our mess. I never laboured more assiduously in any occupation than I did in this, not only from a relish for such amusement, but because we really wanted something to eke out our scanty meals. We at length got a siene-net from one of the men-of-war, with which we were not only able to supply ourselves most abundantly, but always had a large quantity to give away to the soldiers. Wild-fowl also were very plentiful when we first entered the island; but from the number killed, and the constant shooting at them, they soon became scarce and difficult to get at.

Here also there were abundance of alligators, and on our fishing and shooting excursions we frequently started them from their lurking-places, which were generally among the reeds by the side of an inland lake, or rather creek of the sea. On these occasions we seldom saw them, for they always endeavoured to avoid us; but wherever they ran along the bottom of the water, they stirred up the mud so greatly all the track they took, that we had no difficulty in tracing them. I never remember to have seen a live one on these occasions, but a dead one once afforded us considerable amusement. One evening, on our return home from our constant occupation, there being three or four of us of the party, I was in front, and the acting Quartermaster and the others in the rear of me. On a sudden I was alarmed by the cry of " Oh stop, here's an alligator !" and before I could look round, a shot was fired apparently into the earth, close beside their feet. I went back to see what was the matter, and found indeed, as he had said, an alligator, but one which I suppose had been dead for several months at least. It was buried in the sand, and only a part of its body appeared; but whether he imagined it might have placed itself in that situation intentionally, with the view of enticing its prey within its reach, or what other thought he had, I cannot tell, but, to make assurance doubly sure, he fired his rifle right into the body of the half-rotten alligator. He was long and often severely roasted about this afterwards. A young one was caught alive, however, by some of the 14th dragoons, and brought home to England, and afterwards, I understand, presented to the British Museum. All this while the siege of the fort was going forward, but as we had nothing to do with it, we had plenty of time, not only to hunt for extra prog, but to amuse ourselves in any other manner we pleased.

The army, about this time, was inspected by our Chief, General Lambert, by battalions. My kind late commanding-officer, Captain Travers, who was severely wounded at the attack on the 8th, had rejoined by this time, although still very lame. During the inspection, the General said to him, " Travers, I am sorry to hear that your sergeant-major ran away on the night of the 23d, during the attack."—" That is impossible, General," said Travers, " for he fought as bravely as any man could possibly do, and was carried off the field near the end of the fight, severely wounded. But I have a guess what has given rise to this report. A sergeant of ours left his battalion, I believe, either during or after the fight, and having taken up his quarters near one of the houses where the wounded were carried, the surgeon pressed him to remain with him as hospital-sergeant. I made efforts to have him sent to his battalion, but could not get it done. This must have been the cause of such a story having got abroad."—" Ah," says the General, " I am sorry that the poor sergeant-major should have lain under a stigma, of which he was altogether undeserving; and, now since we have done him an involuntary injustice, and he is a deserving man, we must try what amends we can make him for it." He accordingly recommended him for an ensigncy in one of the West India regiments; and before that day twelvemonth, he had risen to the rank of lieutenant. Nothing could be finer than the feeling of Sir John Lambert on this occasion; indeed, he has always shown himself a most excellent upright man, and a gallant officer.

About this time, a Russian vessel was detained going up to New Orleans with a cargo of wine from Bordeaux; but although she would, I doubt not, have been a legal capture, for breaking the blockade, the master was permitted to dispose of his cargo to our army, and an excellent thing he made of it, for the wine, which he must have purchased for about one shilling or one and sixpence a bottle, he charged us in general about four shillings for; we were glad, however, to get it at any price, and a most seasonable supply it was indeed. On one of our shooting excursions, an officer of ours fell in with a sow and two or three pigs, in the wood; he instantly fired at one of the pigs and killed it; but when going to pick it up, the sow set upon him with such fury, that he was glad to abandon his prize, and retreat with precipitation.

When the army landed near New Orleans, the 14th light dragoons had taken their saddles and other horse equipments with them, in hopes of being able to get mounted in the

country ; and which, being bulky, required a good large
boat to bring off again. They were therefore put on board a
considerable-sized one, with an officer of the regiment and a
guard to protect them. On their way down towards the shipping, night overtook them before they could reach their
destination, on which they pushed towards the shore, whether of an island or the mainland, I cannot say, in hopes
of being more secure for the night ; they consequently put
on a sentry, and all lay down in the boat to sleep. Soon
afterwards, however, a boat came rowing rapidly alongside,
and before the sentry could discover who or what they
were, they boarded, and instantly made the party all prisoners. The officer, I believe, when called on to deliver up his
sword, was so annoyed at being trapped in such a manner,
that he threw it into the lake, as far as he could fling it.
The American officer who captured them was a lieutenant
in their navy, and went by the name of Commodore Shiel
(for every fellow is a commodore who commands even a
few boats). He was so elated by his success on this occasion, and, I believe, by having taken another boat with
stores, that he boasted to his prisoners, that he would take
even Admiral Cochrane himself yet, before he left the
country.

While we remained on Isle Dauphine, a commissary,
with a sergeant and party of our men, were sent on shore,
on the mainland, to shoot bullocks for the supply of the
army. They had landed, and the commissary, with the sergeant and I think two men, went off into the neighbour-
ing wood, leaving the two or three other men at the landing-place to protect the boat. Here again Mr Shiel made
his appearance, quite suddenly and unexpectedly, having
come round a jutting-point before the men were aware of
his presence ; he instantly, of course, made them prisoners,

and, taking their arms from them, he put them on board their own boat, then, sending a part of his crew on board to manage it, despatched it for the American harbour. He now with a few more of his people went in search of the commissary and his party, whom he soon found; and they seeing resistance would be vain, when their own boat was departed, were compelled at once to surrender. He instantly put them into his own boat; and taking the commissary into the after-sheets alongside of himself, the sergeant and the other men were put forward to the head of the boat. Whether any preconcerted scheme and signal had been agreed upon between the commissary and the sergeant, I do not know, but an opportunity soon after offering, the commissary gave the sergeant the wink, and instantly seizing Mr Shiel by the thighs, pitched him right overboard in an instant ; the sergeant, at the same moment, seizing the stoutest of Shiel's men, and serving him in a like manner. The others being attacked by the remaining two men, at once surrendered, and, I believe, suffered themselves to be bound ; and our people, having now resumed their arms and become masters of the boat, admitted Mr Shiel, who, I fancy, had clung to the boat to prevent his drowning, to come once more on board. What became of the other man who was thrown over, I know not ; whether he swam on shore, or was drowned, or was afterwards taken into the boat, I cannot tell ; but the result was, that the great, the boasting Commodore Shiel, was brought to the island a prisoner, ·where he landed like a drowned rat, and quite chopfallen.

The commissary, who was a fine, stout, and gallant young fellow, spoke highly in praise of Tom Fukes, our sergeant, for his bravery and good management on the occasion.

At length the works being all completed for battering

the fort, Colonel Smith was sent in with a flag of truce to demand its surrender.   The commandant was quite undecided how to act, and asked the Colonel what he, as a man of honour, would advise him to do.   " Why," says the Colonel, " do you not see that our guns are now overlooking your whole work, and that we could, in a very short time, knock it down about your ears ?   I have no hesitation in telling you, that the rules of war will fully justify you in surrendering to such a superior force, and when the siege has advanced to such a point as it actually is." His arguments, together with the truth of his statements, at length overcame the courage and determination of Jonathan, and he instantly agreed to surrender, the garrison, afterwards becoming prisoners of war, marching out and laying down their arms on the glacis.

Thus, on the 12th February, this important fortification fell into our hands, together with 400 men of the 2d regiment of the United States, and either one or two American colours.   This obstacle removed, every exertion was now made to advance up the lake to the attack of Mobile; but on the 14th, a vessel arrived with the unexpected, but cheering information, that peace had been concluded at Ghent between the two nations, and that it only required the ratification of Mr Maddison, the United States' president.   Of course, all further operations of a warlike nature were suspended for the present, till it was known whether the treaty would be ratified or not.   This ship also brought out the notification of our two Generals, Lambert and Keane, being appointed Knights of the Bath.   Some of our Colonels also were included in the list, viz. Blakeny of the the 7th, and Dickson of the royal artillery.

And now nothing was thought of but amusement, and making ourselves as comfortable as possible. But we began to get very short of provisions. Our people were therefore obliged to send to the Havannah, where they procured the strongest sort of beef I ever saw. It was not salted; but after the cattle had been killed, all the thin belly part had been cut round the whole bullock, in narrow stripes, of about two inches in width; this being laid, or hung up in the sun, which is extremely powerful in that country, it was dried without having the least offensive taste or smell, farther than a little rancidity, which was not by any means unpleasant; but when brought from on board, it had much more the appearance of coils of ropes (for it was coiled up in a similar manner) than provision for the use of man. An aide-de-camp of General Lambert's, then Lieutenant, but now Major D'Este, son of his Royal Highness the Duke of Sussex by Lady Augusta Murray, used frequently to join the shooting party of our acting quartermaster and myself; and, on one occasion, having obtained a canoe, a trip to the mainland was projected, for the purpose of shooting; accordingly we took two or three men with us, and started from the northernmost point of the island, that being the nearest to the main, which we saw before us, and not more than five or six miles distant. It was considered the best mode of proceeding for us all to get into the boat, except one man, who was a famous wader, (having often accompanied us in our expeditions around the island,) and who was to wade as far out into the sea as he could, dragging the canoe after him. This he could do very easily, for she was quite light, and the water was exceeding shallow for a great distance into the sea. He continued towing us in this manner for about half a mile, when, being fairly up to his chin, he and we thought it was high time for him to come on board; but, in doing this, he gave her such a cant as turned her right over, and pitched us all into the water. I luckily had my eye upon the man when he sprung to get into the canoe, and suspecting that she could not bear so rough a pull, was ready ; and accordingly, when I saw her going, leaped out, without being plunged overhead, as all the others were. But all our rifles, &c. were pitched out, and of course sunk to the bottom, to which we were obliged to dive before we could get them up. This accident put a stop to our excursion, and we waded out again, looking extremely foolish. Nevertheless we ought to have been truly thankful to Providence that it occurred before we got out of our depth ; for, with such a frail bark, it is more than probable some accident would have happened before our return, had not this prevented our further progress.

Innumerable were our adventures of this nature, for the water was delightfully warm, and having no military occupation at the time, we could not find any better amusement. A party, indeed, suggested the getting up of theatricals, which being approved on all hands, workmen were instantly set about erecting the theatre-royal, Isle Dauphine. This, of course, with the getting off of parts, occupied the managers and the other performers for some time ; but at length all being ready, most excellent entertainments took place, following each other in quick succession. At some of these parties, American officers, who now often paid us visits, were highly entertained, and paid us high compliments, not only as to the splendour and magnificence of our theatrical representations, but to our ingenuity as displayed in hut-building, which, they said, even surpassed the architectural abilities of the Indians in that branch of the art,—a high compliment indeed !

CHAPTER XX

Ratification of the Treaty of Peace—Exchange of Prisoners—Our Troops
embark for England—When off the coast of Ireland, receive intelligence of Bonaparte's escape from Elba—The Author and his Battalion reach the Downs, and proceed to Thorncliffe—Embark for
France—Arrive at Paris, and occupy the Champs Elysées—Review
of the Russian Guards—Russian Discipline—British Troops reviewed—Accident to Prince Blucher—Amusements in Paris—The Allied
Forces, except the Army of Occupation, leave Paris—The Author's
Battalion embark for England—Reach Dover, and return to Thorncliffe—He obtains leave of absence, and visits his Family—His Battalion ordered to Ireland—Sets out to join it, accompanied by his Wife,
who dies three days after they reach Dublin—His Battalion reduced
—Joins the first Battalion at Gosport, which is ordered to Scotland
—Arrive at Leith, and march to Glasgow—The Author returns home
in ill health—His Father dies—Joins his Battalion again—Winters
at home—His Battalion ordered to Ireland—Joins it at Belfast—They
occupy different stations during the Whiteboy Insurrection—Six
companies of his Battalion ordered to Nova Scotia, but the Author
remains with the other four companies—He is shortly ordered to
proceed to Nova Scotia—His health declines—Returns home in consequence, takes advantage of Lord Palmerston's Bill, and retires on
full pay.

On the 5th March, the ratification of the treaty of peace,
by Mr Maddison, arrived; and now all our thoughts were
turned towards our dear native country. On the 15th also,
all our poor fellows, who had been made prisoners by the
Americans, joined us at this island, an exchange in consequence of peace having of course taken place. Many of

these were strange-looking figures when they came among
us, most of them having been stripped of great part of their
uniforms, their caps particularly, and wearing mocassins, a
sort of Indian sandals, instead of shoes or boots, and being
so sunburnt as to be scarcely recognisable.

Major Mitchell told us that General Jackson had treated
him exceeding harshly, because he did not choose to give
the General such information respecting our numbers, &c.
as he wished. He also said he met with great insolence on
his way up to Natchez, where the prisoners were kept, from
the different parties of Kentucky men, and others, whom
he met on their way down " to take a shoot," as they
termed it, " at his countrymen." He met many thousands
in this manner, so that 10 or 12,000 is the very lowest
number that Jackson could have had for the defence of his
lines.

I do not remember that we ever had Divine service performed during the period of this expedition except once or
twice, and that about this time. Indeed the activity required of the army at all times, during the continuance of
hostilities, almost necessarily precluded it. At this time I
remember perfectly the preacher's text was, " My son, give
me thy heart." Alas ! how few of the hearts of his hearers
were given at that time to Him who only had a right to
demand them ! I confess with shame and sorrow, that
almost any trifle, however unworthy, possessed a greater
interest in my heart than He who had formed it, and who
alone is worthy of supreme regard.—The good Lord pardon
this neglect, for Christ's sake !

The regiments now began to go on board the different
ships, as fast as arrangements could be made to receive
them ; and when on board, they sailed at once without
waiting for the others, there being now no danger of falling

in with an enemy. The weather now began to grow exceedingly warm, which brought out alligators and snakes in abundance. The latter were extremely annoying, for they sometimes got into our very tents, and one on one occasion so frightened a captain of ours (who was not afraid of man) as to make him sprawl up the tent-pole to get out of its reach, roaring out at the same time most lustily for help. It was killed and put into a bottle of spirits, and I believe he brought it home. It was an exceeding small one, but with the most beautiful crimson, or rather pink-coloured wavy streak running down its back imaginable. We were told it was one of the most venomous of all the American reptiles, save probably the rattlesnake.

- The thunder and lightning also became very frequent, and the former, I think, the most awfully grand I ever heard. It appeared to roll along just on the very tops of the pine-trees, many of which indeed were scathed to the very roots by the latter.

On the 31st March our turn came to go on board, and we were rejoiced to find that the Dover, our old friend, was to be our principal ship, the remainder of the men beyond what she could hold being sent on board the Norfolk transport. While we were preparing for sea, I took a boat and a party with a siene, and went on shore on a sandy point of the island, where I had not been before, and in a short time caught a fine load of fish, mostly grey mullet, with which we returned on board, greatly to the satisfaction of all those who shared in them. Every thing being now ready, we weighed and bid adieu to America on the 4th April, shaping our course for the Havannah, where our captain intended to call for various purposes, but principally to replenish his stock, which had begun to get exceedingly low.

On our passage thither we encountered a heavy gale, which detained us longer than we had calculated for our voyage. We did not reach that place till the 19th. Here we found ourselves once more in Espana, every thing here being exactly like what you meet with in the mother country,—the same stink of oil, garlic, and dried fish. Speaking of the latter, which is called by them Bacalao, an officer of ours who kept a journal, when describing this place, says, " The natives catch a great quantity of fish on the coast, called Bacalao." Unfortunately it is not called Bacalao till after it is dried, but Piscado. This brough, ast it might be expected, lots of laughter upon his head.

I need not describe the Havannah, because any one who has a Gazetteer, may there read an account of it; and which, though perhaps not altogether a correct one, will be sufficient to give him an idea of what it is; suffice it to say, it is an exceeding strong place, and would not, I apprehend, be so easily taken, if the inhabitants are true to their country, as it was in the year 1762. The capture of it at the time above stated, made the place extremely interesting to me, for one of my earliest and best friends served as a lieutenant in the 56th grenadiers at the taking of it; and often have I heard him expatiate, with great delight and animation, on the scenes he witnessed, and the dangers he encountered, in this most arduous undertaking. He is now, poor man, no more, having died only very lately, and I sincerely trust and hope he is in peace. The Moro and the Punta, and all the other immense fortifications, attracted my particular regard, on this old gentleman's account; but so extremely jealous were the Spaniards, that they would not permit even us, their late faithful helpers and friends, to view the works. We visited the theatre, which is a fine building, but heavy and badly lighted but apparently well supplied with performers. The piece on this occasion was Anthony and Cleopatra. There were also some equestrian performers here from the United States. They had built a fine circus, at about half a mile's distance from the city, to which every one of course repaired. All the world was there ; even little Connolly, whom I had known at Cadiz as a major in the Spanish service, was here in the command of a regiment, and had attained the rank of full Colonel. He did not seem over anxious to recognise any of his former acquaintances, nor even to let it be known that he was so much of a Briton as to have acquaintance with any people of that country ; in short, he wished to be considered a complete Spaniard. I doubt not he is now a rank apostolical. We paid a visit also to old Woodville, the famous cigar-maker. He was an expatriated Englishman, from Portsmouth I believe, obliged to flee his country on account of some smuggling transaction, and, in doing this, he had changed his name. We found the old man ill in bed, but able to sit up and speak with us. He wore an immense long white beard, reaching down nearly to the bed as he sat up. Yet this old man had a young black wife, and a whole fry of young mulattoes running about the house like as many little pigs. He was very kind, but apparently not over well to do. We bought each a considerable quantity of his famed cigars, for which we paid him, I think, four dollars a thousand—more, I apprehend, than he usually gets from the Spaniards for them.'

Having laid in such sea stock as we could conveniently procure, and having stored ourselves well with the delicious preserves of this country, and withal bought a fine turtle, weighing about two cwt., on the 24th we set sail for old and happy England, glad once more to set our faces homeward.

We had a quickish run through the Gulf of Florida, or,
as it is more properly called, the Bahama Channel, and,
keeping to the northward of Bermuda, shaped our course
so that we passed a little to the south of the Great New-
foundland Bank.   From hence the wind was roughish
generally, but quite fair, so that we frequently ran at the
rate of 200 miles in the twenty-four hours, the transport
being an excellent sailer.

Nothing particular occurred till we were within a few
days' sail of Ireland, when we fell in with an American who
had just left England.   From him we learned the totally
unlooked-for information, that Bonaparte had made his
escape from Elba, and had returned to France, and that the
whole continent was once more involved in war.   Nothing
could exceed the change which this unexpected news produced among our people.   Some who were desponding at
the gloomy prospect of half-pay, revived in a moment, and
again set honour, glory, and promotion, once more before
the eyes of their imagination.   Indeed, I think no one
seemed sorry at the change ; but some probably would have
preferred a short repose, before they were called upon again
to leave that home which they had painted to themselves
so comfortable and happy.

On the   we arrived at Plymouth, where the good
folks received us with great cordiality ; but the news from
Flanders now engrossed all attention, and our unfortunate
business seemed forgotten.   It was as well perhaps that it
was so, for we had no victory to boast ; and with the world
it is but too often the case, that a want of good fortune is
almost tantamount to a want of good conduct.   We were
ordered on to Portsmouth, which we reached in two days ;
and from thence proceeded still onwards to the Downs.
Our arrival was telegraphed to London, from whence, after

some communication by post also with the Commander-in-Chief, we were ordered to disembark, which we did on the 2d June. The cause of this being ordered, and of our not-proceeding direct to Flanders, was, that we were extremely ill off for equipment, nearly one-fourth of our men being without arms or appointments, all those who had been prisoners, and many of those who had been severely wounded, having been deprived of them. In some respects the order for our landing was unfortunate, as far as regards the honours of that great and crowning victory of Waterloo, in which we consequently had no share; and, on the other hand, as far as regards my own public accounts, at least it was fortunate for me, for I was thus enabled to have them prepared, and forwarded to the War Office, and finally settled without loss of time, which I could not have done had we left England again immediately.

We were ordered from Deal to Thorncliffe, our old quarters, where we found three companies of my battalion, and five or six of the other two. All our old friends were of course glad to see us; and, under such circumstances, the meeting of those between whom friendship has long subsisted, is in a great measure a compensation for the toil and sufferings of a soldier's life. We continued at Thorncliffe for some time, but busily preparing once more to take the field; and had Bonaparte not been so precipitate in his movements, we might have shared in the glory of his final overthrow.

I was compelled to go to London while we remained here, for the purpose of settling a variety of accounts, &c., and while there was persuaded to appear before the Medical Board, for the purpose of obtaining a certificate as to the nature of my wound, on which to found a claim for a year's pay, the amount at this time given to all whom that Board recommended as fit subjects for this bounty. I had omitted doing so when in London before, because I thought no one had any claim for it, except such as had suffered most materially in health in consequence of their wounds. However, at the suggestion of my friends I did appear before the Board, who considered my wound of such severity as to entitle me to that bounty; and I accordingly soon after received the sum of L.118, 12s. 6d., the amount of one year's pay. I have reason to be thankful both to the government and to my friends for this unlooked-for augmentation of my funds, and trust I did not make an ill use of it.

But at length the news of the memorable battle of Waterloo arrived, and we had no share in it. I know not whether I shall be believed, but I think there were few of my companions in the late expedition but felt somewhat disappointed, and rather vexed, that this decisive action should have taken place so early, and almost wished that the government had despatched us even as we were on our first arrival in England; for really, as it turned out, it was most unfortunate to those of my friends, who had been undergoing probably as severe and hazardous a service as any our army had lately been engaged in, and that all that should be looked upon as almost worse than nothing, while some young fellows, who had never before seen an enemy, should be covered with the honours and distinctions which were so amply lavished on them, merely because they had the good fortune to share in that brilliant and decisive victory. But regret is vain and unprofitable, and a soldier must make up his mind to meet with bad as well as good fortune, or he will only render his life the more miserable.

On the 10th of July we embarked at Dover, and on the

13th landed at Ostend; but we were entering only on a barren service, the honours having been all acquired previous to our arrival. We moved forward by the way of Bruges, Ghent, Oudenarde, and Mons, and then through Bavay and Chatelet to Peronne; from Peronne through Roye, Pont Lant, Maxence, and Louvre, to Paris. Here we were posted to the brigade in which our other two companies were stationed, and occupied the Champs Elysées as our camp. Certainly the sights we witnessed in this far-famed capital amply repaid us for our trip to France, however devoid of military glory that might be.

It will not be expected that I should enter into a detail of all the lions which this splendid city contains, and which have attracted the curiosity of nearly half the gentry of this country. Suffice it to say, we saw the palaces of the Tuilleries, St Cloud, Luxemburg, and Versailles, with all the splendour they contain—the churches of Notre Dame and the Pantheon—the Hospital of Invalids—the Garden of Plants—the Hotel de Ville—the Palais Royal, and the far-famed Louvre. In this latter, a person might at that time spend a twelvemonth, without exhausting the curiosities and beauties it contained; but, during our stay here, we witnessed its divestment of nearly all its most valued specimens of art, to the great regret, grief, and annoyance of those who had ransacked almost all nations to decorate this splendid gallery. This was undertaken and executed by our illustrious Chief, in the name and on the behalf of this our generous nation. He dealt out with a just and impartial hand, to all who had claims upon this magnificent collection, the specimens of art which had formerly adorned their national churches and palaces, without one painting or one statue of the meanest description being reserved for himself, who had been mainly instru-

mental in this restoration, or for the nation which he represented.

We saw also the triumphal arch of Bonaparte, in the
Place de Carousel, stripped of its four matchless Venetian
horses. The stately pillar in the Place Vendome was also
deprived of the effigy of him who erected it. In short,
every thing was done by the Bourbons at this period, sanctioned by the Allies, to obliterate even the very remembrance of such a character as Bonaparte. We visited also
the splendid manufactory of china at Sevres—the National
Museum of Antiquities—the Royal Library, and the Theatre
Français, to witness Talma's performance of Hamlet, with
various other places of curiosity, too tedious to notice here;
and, finally, the catacombs, the repository of millions of
human bones.

Here it is where man is taught to remember what he is
—a worm—a shadow that departeth—even a vapour, which
appeareth for a moment, and then passeth away for ever.
Oh, how does all human greatness dwindle into nothing,
while you stand viewing these silent memorials of our
frailty! The myriads of generations that have passed away,
multitudes of whose bones are collected in this vast, dark
cavern! Now how noiseless those who perhaps once
shook the world with alarms! I love to meditate on this
sad scene, which, if duly considered, teaches the soundest
wisdom. How apt are we to be allured by the gay fan-
tastic follies of an hour, to forget that we must soon, so
very soon, take up our abode in the dark and silent tomb!
Oh! to be ready, when called upon, to descend into the
house appointed for all living! But though these meditations may be pleasing to myself, they may not be so to my
reader. I will therefore leave this dark, deep, and capacious charnel-house, and once more ascend with him to the
light of the sun.

We had· not remained long in Paris, till there was a grand review of the Emperor of Russia's Guards, and which took place in the Place of Louis XV., immediately in front of the Tuilleries. Nothing could exceed the uniformity and the steadiness of these Northern warriors. There were troops of all armies amongst them; the Cossacks, the hussars, the artillery, the grenadiers, and the regular infantry, all vied with each other in their endeavours to please their beloved Czar. Here were all the great ones of the earth assembled to witness this imposing spectacle ; exhibited, no doubt, as much as any thing, for the purpose of showing the French the power of those who now held them in subjection. But that arbitrary power which is so intolerable to the ideas of an Englishman, was here exhibited in all its native deformity. A Colonel of one of the regiments, whose movements did not please the Emperor, was, without the least ceremony, taken from the head of his regiment, and rammed into a common guard-house, where an English officer was on duty. He hesitated to receive him, until assured that such was the custom in the Russian service, and that it was the Emperor's orders.

My battalion was soon after removed from the brigade it was originally posted to, and joined another, stationed on Montmartre. Here the adjutant and myself were quartered on a proprietor of the pits out of which the famous plaster of Paris is dug. These pits are situated on the side of this hill, facing the city. From hence I often took a fishing, or a shooting, or a coursing excursion. The first was generally confined to the Canal del Ourq, in which I found pike, perch, and tench. I never was very successful, however, both from the vast numbers of fishermen which frequented this water, and from the scarcity of fish. Partridges

and hares were abundant in the neighbourhood of Paris, but
we had not a good dog among us. We obtained leave from
the Duke of Orleans to shoot in one of the royal preserves,
the Forest of Bondy. In our coursing expeditions we were
more successful, sometimes bringing in to the amount of
seven hares in a day. This would be looked upon almost as
poaching in England, but in France it was otherwise ; they
know nothing of coursing there ; and nothing could exceed
the beautiful country round Paris for that sport ; it was a
dead level generally, without a hedge, sometimes for miles
together, and a rich corn country, so that hares abounded.
Towards autumn, we had two or three reviews of the British troops ; these were splendid exhibitions of the tactics
of our great General. But though the army had the appearance of a fighting army, I do not think it equalled the Russians in point of regularity and uniformity ; with them the
whole army is nearly dressed alike, especially the infantry ;
while the variety of our facings, and other distinctions of
regiments, detracts greatly from the appearance of the army
as a whole. Here also the crowned heads of Europe assembled in this city, paid us the compliment of their presence,
the Emperor Alexander inspecting most minutely every
regiment and division as it passed him. The Austrians and
the Prussians also occasionally showed themselves in bodies,
but I do not remember to have seen a general review of
either of these armies ; indeed neither of them had a large
force in or near Paris, they being mostly at some distance
from the capital, I believe. But we were often delighted
with the Austrian Emperor's band, in which there were no
less, I believe, than seventy performers, and all these the
very first-rate musicians. We also had horse-races occasionally, that is, among the English officers ; at one of which I
witnessed poor old Blucher receive a hurt, from which he

never recovered. Near the winning-post, the course was roped in, which the brave old fellow, as he came galloping down, all life, from the city, did not perceive, and coming up against them with great force, he was thrown from his horse, and unfortunately broke his arm. He lingered some time afterwards, but never got well of it, till death released him. We had two English boxers over there also, to amuse the people; they only sparred of course, with gloves on; and I rather think they realized a good deal of money by these exhibitions. Balloons also were set up from the gardens of Tivoli, with various other sources of amusement, so that to recount them all would only tire out my reader; suffice it to say, that in Paris, with plenty of money, and with an inclination to enter into all the gaieties of the place, no city on earth, I believe, is so fruitful of the means of pleasure and dissipation; but they leave a sting behind, which far outweighs these momentary gratifications; and if I was asked which I considered the most sinful city in the world, I would without hesitation say Paris.

Towards December arrangements were made for the army leaving Paris, and going into cantonments on the north-eastern frontier; but the remainder of the troops above the number required for the army of occupation were ordered home to England. My battalion was among the latter number; and, accordingly, we left the French capital on the 3d December, and marched out to St Denis, that famous burying-place of French royalty. From thence we passed near Beaumont, through Noailles to Beauvais, thence through some small villages, where we halted for the night, and on the 11th reached Abbeville.

On the 14th we quartered in Montreuil-sur-Mer, and on the 20th reached Calais, where we embarked for Dover.

We landed at the latter place on the 22d, and the next
morning proceeded to our old quarter Thorncliffe.

All warlike proceedings having now terminated, I made
application for, and obtained, leave of absence to revisit my
wife and my family, whom I had not seen for four years. I
need not describe my feelings on once more beholding those
I loved, and the reader will best appreciate them by placing
himself in my situation. But I had not long enjoyed this
pleasure till I heard that my battalion had been ordered to
Ireland. I confess I did not much relish the information.
When my leave expired I started for that country, and endeavoured to procure a passage across to Dublin; first from
Maryport, in Cumberland, but without success. I then tried
Workington, next Whitehaven, but was equally unable to
get off from either of these. I then moved on to Liverpool, and took my place in one of the packets; but, after
waiting several days, I was obliged to start for Holyhead,
the only place from whence I was able to proceed to Ireland.
All this disappointment and fatigue, together with some
sad punches which a large woman in the coach had given
my wife with her masculine elbows, so preyed upon her
health and spirits, that three days after our arrival in Dublin she breathed her last. She had been in delicate health
for a number of years, of an affection in the chest, but she
complained mostly of this woman's elbows, which she said
had injured her much. It will easily be conceived how
afflictive such a dispensation must have been to him who
had to bear it. But God does all things well; and even in
the midst of our severest chastisements, we should view
Him as a kind and tender parent, who only chastens us for
our good, and who does not willingly afflict the children of
men. A part of the battalion had arrived in Dublin when
the melancholy event took place, almost all the officers of

which favoured me by their presence at the funeral. I had her buried in St Mary's churchyard, Mary being her own name.

We remained in Dublin for twenty-seven months—a longer period than any other regiment I believe ; and here I think I may truly say I acquired the first knowledge of the only way of salvation ; for although born and reared a Christian, and having, as the reader may recollect, been brought sensibly to the knowledge of myself as a condemned sinner, I had as yet no distinct knowledge or apprehension of the nature of the Christian faith ; and I think I may, under the blessing of God, attribute my earnest search after a sure foundation of hope to the reading of Doddridge's "Rise and Progress of Religion in the Soul," and to the truly evangelical sermons I heard from the many eminent preachers which fill the pulpits of this capital, but more particularly to the Rev. Mr Matthias, chaplain to the Bethesda Institution. My narrative will contain nothing interesting from this period to the general reader. I will, therefore, generalize as much as possible. From Dublin we marched to Birr, in the King's County ; and while here, it was determined upon by government to reduce the battalion to which I belonged, which was carried into effect in January 1819 ; but as I was then the senior quartermaster of the regiment, I was ordered to join the 1st battalion of the corps at Gosport, which I did in February. Here we remained till September, when the Radical war called us to the north.

We embarked on board the Liffy frigate and ——— corvette, in about three or four hours' notice, on the 18th of that month, and landed at Leith on the 28th, whence we marched to Glasgow, the seat of this unhappy disturbance. I need not describe the Radical war, it being well known.

Here my health began to be much impaired. The affection of my chest, occasioned by the rupturing of the bloodvessel at Cadiz, produced most distressing effects upon my general health. I consequently obtained leave, and returned home for a few months.

During my stay at home my dear father departed this life; and I had thus the melancholy satisfaction of witnessing the last sad scene, and of paying the last duties of a child to a beloved parent. He was not, as I mentioned at the beginning of my narrative, a religious man when I left home; but towards the close of his life I have every reason to believe he was a sincere penitent, and a believer in Him through whom alone our sins can be forgiven; and I have a well-grounded hope that he is now enjoying eternal felicity in heaven, whither I hope myself to come through Him that loved me, and washed me from my sins in his own blood, and to whom be praise and glory for ever. Amen.

I joined again in the spring, and remained there all that summer, during which I had many pleasant fishing excursions into the country. I visited the falls of the Clyde, and proceeded to some a considerable distance higher up, where another officer and myself caught abundance of trout. I also took a trip into the Highlands of Argyleshire, where I had excellent sport. But at the approach of winter I was again obliged to leave Glasgow, the damp atmosphere of which, together with the smoke of the numerous steam-engines employed in its manufactories, fairly drove me out. I again went home for the winter; but during this period this battalion also got an order to embark for Ireland, and I joined them in Belfast in January 1821. From hence we marched in the spring to Armagh, where I had the high privilege of becoming acquainted with a sincere and pious clergyman, one of the reading vicars of the cathedral; and I trust I benefited by this favourable opportunity. From Armagh we marched to Naas, the country to the south having become much disturbed by the Whiteboys, as they termed themselves. We did not remain long at Naas, but were pushed on to Kilkenny, where I first became acquainted with that truly Christian minister, the Rev. Peter Roe, a gentleman well known in the religious world. I am proud and happy that I ever had the privilege of knowing him. May God prosper his pious and unceasing endeavours to benefit the souls of his fellow-creatures!

We did not remain long, however, at Kilkenny, but moved on to Fermoy, and thence to Newcastle, in the county of Limerick, the cradle of the Whiteboy insurrection. Here we were for a time actually shut up as in a besieged town; and no individual belonging to the army durst attempt to move out without a sufficient number being together, to deter the misguided peasantry from attacking us. Innumerable were the murders that were committed about this neighbourhood at this time; and one's blood runs chill to think that these miscreants, when taken and brought to the gallows to atone for their crime, protested their innocence with their last breath, although hundreds around them could attest their guilt. This Rockite war gave us considerable trouble, and it was not for a long time after that it was finally put down.

We remained in Newcastle till September, when we marched to Rathkeale, in the same county. Here we continued stationary till October 1823, when we marched again for Dublin. I had thus an opportunity of again hearing my favourite preacher; but the place was always so crowded that it was seldom practicable for strangers to obtain seats.

From Dublin we marched to Belfast, in September 1824,

where we continued till July 1825, when my battalion was ordered for service in Nova Scotia. The orders of the army being now for only six companies out of the ten to go abroad, the other four remained at home, to form what is termed the depôt. Application was made for me to remain and act as paymaster to this body ; but it having been decided that quartermasters could not act as paymasters, according to the new regulations, this boon was refused me, although I had acted four times before. This is to be attributed to the ill conduct of many of my brother quartermasters who had obtained paymasterships during the war, but who generally did not conduct themselves as men of honour and integrity ought to do, and many were consequently dismissed from the service. It was perfectly correct for those in authority to consult the good of the public in all appointments of this nature, but it was hard on those who were thus made to suffer for the sins of others,—nay, this ineligibility of quartermasters extended farther than to the appointment of acting paymaster. They have since 1817 been precluded from holding the situation of full paymaster, however well recommended they might be. I was a second time recommended, in 1820, by Lieutenant-General the Hon. Sir William Stewart for the paymastership of his own battalion, that is, the one in which I was serving, but received the same answer from the Secretary-at-War, that quartermasters were ineligible to the situation. I cannot but feel keenly the degradation to which the ill conduct of certain individuals has reduced that situation, which formerly was only like a step towards the more lucrative and more respectable one of paymaster; but, as I said before, we must not murmur at the dispensations of Providence, however severely they affect our worldly prospects ; and no doubt all this was done by the direction of Him who cannot err. However, I have great reason also to be thankful to Lord Palmerston, notwithstanding my disappointments as above stated; for he—taking into consideration the injury that the present quartermasters had sustained, in consequence of the ill conduct of the individuals before noticed, and their consequent deprivation of all prospects of farther promotion, however eligible in other respects they might be, and however exemplary their conduct—brought in a bill in the session of 1826, to allow these officers to retire on *full* pay after twenty years' service in the army, provided their health was such as to render them incapable of farther service. This could not formerly take place till after thirty years' service. I have, therefore, abundant cause of gratitude to that Right Honourable Lord, for his kind remembrance of us on this occasion, as well as for his kindness in permitting me to avail myself of the benefit of this act; and I have on this, as on all other occasions, abundant cause of thankfulness to the Great Disposer of all events, not only for what He has permitted me to enjoy, but for what He has withheld from me; for He only knows what is really good for me, and I doubt not will give me always that. I may with great truth declare, that goodness and mercy have followed me all my days, notwithstanding my seeming disappointments, and which I believe were inflicted on me solely for my everlasting good. To Him, therefore, be praise and glory for ever.

But to return. Having been disappointed of obtaining the acting paymaster's place, I remained with the depôt in my capacity as quartermaster till the spring of 1826, when I received an order to be ready for embarkation to join the battalion in Nova Scotia. Accordingly I embarked, with four other officers, at Liverpool, on the 14th of June, on board the Robert Burns merchant brig, and reached Halifax

after a rather tedious passage, in which we encountered
some roughish weather on the 22d July.

I scarcely need say any thing of Halifax, which, being
one of our oldest colonies, must be well known to almost all
my readers.   Neither was I there a sufficient time to enable me to enter into a minute description of the town or
country : suffice it to say, it appears to be a town built
mostly of wood along the face of a hill, on the left-hand side
of the harbour, reaching close down to the latter, which is
so deep, capacious, and sheltered, that I question whether
there is a better in the world : a seventy-four can lie close
alongside the wharfs.   The town contains, I understand,
about 13,000 inhabitants, composed of settlers from different
countries, but chiefly English, Irish, Scotch, and Dutch.
There are a few negroes, a part of the slaves taken from
the Americans during the late war having been located
here.

The colony is not so flourishing as it was during war,
as it was then greatly supported by the immense number of ships and troops which always were stationed here.
The country round Halifax is barren in the extreme, except a very small portion, where hay is generally grown.
It seems incapable of cultivation, being little else than
rock, with forests of stunted pines, &c. growing upon it.
In some parts of Nova Scotia, however, there is excellent
land, which yields a great return for cultivation; and were it
not for the severity of the winter, which in this country is
both long and severely trying to weak constitutions, it would,
I doubt not, be an excellent country to which to emigrate.
The waters in every direction afford abundance of fish, but
not of the best quality.   There are portions of two tribes
of Indians occasionally in the neighbourhood of Halifax.   I
forget their names; but the men of one tribe are exceed-

ingly tall, being seldom below five feet ten inches, and many reaching to six feet three inches. The men of the other are in general short. Both tribes are fast diminishing in point of numbers. They are greatly addicted to the fatal vice of drunkenness, whenever they can command the means of becoming so; and in Halifax it is no difficult matter, for the abominable rum which is sold here may be had almost as cheap as ale in England.

These unfortunate wanderers have hitherto resisted all efforts to induce them to settle and cultivate the land, although many of them are *good Christians*, their progenitors having been converted by the Roman Catholic priests while the French held the country.

The woods, &c. in the neighbourhood of Halifax contain little game of any kind. There are a few what they call partridges, which, I believe, roost on trees; but they have more the appearance of grouse than the partridge of England. There are some woodcocks also in the season, but they are rather scarce. Snipes also, and several species of plover, may be met with occasionally; but you will seldom be able to fill your game-bag with any thing. There are some hares of a very small description, little larger than our rabbits; but these are rare. Bears also, with a few other wild animals, occasionally show themselves; but in winter, I am told, a deathlike silence pervades the whole face of the country, as if every living animal had totally deserted it, and I believe with all the winged tribes this is actually the case.

The women here are remarkably fair and beautiful, and, generally speaking, are, I believe, as virtuous as at home; but among the lower orders, whose virtue is so frequently assailed by the temptations which a large naval and military force always brings with it, like our Portsmouth,

6

and other places of a similar description, the scenes of vice and abomination are extremely disgusting. A great many of the unfortunate blacks before mentioned are included in the number of these unhappy prostitutes.

The places of worship in Halifax are both good and pretty numerous. There are two churches, two or three Presbyterian or Scotch churches, two Baptist, two or three Methodist, and one or two Roman Catholic places of worship.

I did not remain here long; for, finding that my broken and debilitated constitution could not possibly withstand the severity of a winter in this climate, I was ordered to be examined by a board of medical officers, who recommended my return to England without delay. Accordingly, on the 20th of September, I embarked on board the Borodino transport. We sailed on the 22d, and on the 25th encountered one of the severest gales I almost ever witnessed. It carried away every sail we had set, and swept away our jolly-boat from the quarter. I often wished I was once more snug in England, and my hope was, I should then tempt the sea no more. That same all-gracious Being who had so long watched over me, and had brought me in safety that far on my journey, He also brought me to my native land once more in peace; for on the 13th of October I landed at Portsmouth, having been only three weeks in returning from, while we had been nearly six in going to, Halifax.

I immediately set off for London, where, having reported myself to the Secretary at War, I was ordered to be examined by the Director-General of Hospitals as to the state of my health, and with a view to avail myself of the benefits of the act of Parliament before mentioned, and being prospered by Him who has always been better unto me than I could possibly deserve, I have been permitted to set myself down in peace in this my own native village for the remainder of my life, having the unspeakable privilege of being surrounded by many kind and dear relations, who vie with each other in their endeavours to render me comfortable and happy, and where I can in serenity watch the gradual approach of that enemy which my Saviour has overcome for me, and which, my hope is, He will deprive of all his terrors, as I trust he has done of his sting, and that, when I shall have continued my appointed time in this vale of tears, I, as well as the reader of this narrative, shall be taken to Himself, to dwell with Him for ever.

APPENDIX.

———

THE following are copies of fifteen testimonials addressed to the late Quartermaster Surtees.

No. 1.—FROM LIEUT.-COL. DUFFY.

Birr, 24th January, 1819.

DEAR SIR,

As you are on the point of removing to the 1st battalion, I take this opportunity of expressing my entire satisfaction at the very regular and orderly manner in which your department has been conducted during the time you have been placed under my command; and it will give me great pleasure should an occasion occur where my testimony to your gentlemanlike conduct can be of service to you.

I remain, Dear Sir,
Very faithfully yours,
J. DUFFY,
Lt.-Col. Rifle Brigade.

Quartermaster Surtees,
1st Bat. Rifle Brigade.

No. 2.—From Major Travers.

Tuam County, Galway, 19th April 1820.

Dear Surtees,

With feelings of most sincere regret I read your letter to me, which I received yesterday, and lose not a moment in complying with your request, which, should it prove to be of any use to you, I am sure will be productive of the most heartfelt gratification to every one of those concerned, whose opinions of you are, as they always have been, of the highest description.   Your conduct, both as a gentleman and soldier, has ever been such as to excite in the breast of your brother officers sentiments peculiarly favourable; and for myself, I have only to say, that few of my old acquaintances in the corps have had my esteem in a higher degree.   I send you the sentiments of such of your old brother officers, in the shape of a certificate, as I could obtain, whose standing may have some influence in the procuring the accomplishment of your wishes, and regret that the dispersed state of the regiment prevents its being more general.

Dear Surtees,
Yours faithfully,

Jas. Travers.

Wm. Surtees, Esq.
Quartermaster, Rifle Brigade.

No. 3.—From Officers of the 2d Battalion Rifle Brigade.

The following testimonial is subscribed by us, in hopes it may prove beneficial to an officer who has so long supported the character which we are desirous to portray in the terms it deserves.

We certify, that Mr William Surtees, late Quartermaster in the Rifle Brigade, has been for a considerable number of years known to us in the regiment, and that for soldierlike and gentlemanly conduct, no person bore a higher character.   He served in the situation he filled in the corps, particularly that of Acting Paymaster, for two considerable periods in the Peninsula, and with the expedition to New Orleans, with credit to himself, and satisfaction to his superiors, and, to our knowledge, obtained the general esteem and approbation of all his brother officers of the regiment who knew him.

> S. MITCHELL, Brevet Lieut.-Col. and Major,
> 2d Bat. Rifle Brigade.
> JAS. TRAVERS, Brevet-Major, Rifle Brigade.
> WM. COX, Capt. Rifle Brigade.
> BOYLE TRAVERS, Capt. Rifle Brigade.
> CHAS. GEO. GRAY, Brevet-Major, Rifle Brigade.
> WM. HALLEN, Capt. Rifle Brigade.
> T. H. RIDGWAY, M.D., Surgeon, Rifle Brigade.

Tuam, 19th April 1820.

No. 4.—FROM LIEUT.-COL. ROSS, C.B.

Paisley, 15*th July* 1820.

DEAR SIR,

I learn with extreme regret that you consider it to be expedient to make application to be removed as Quartermaster to a veteran battalion. I have stronger reason to feel this regret than I believe any other of your brother officers, as I have known you longer, it being now about twenty years since we met at the formation of the Rifle Corps; during the greater part of this time you served, I may say, under my immediate command; and I can bear the most ample and unqualified testimony to the zeal, intelligence, and gallantry with which you discharged the duties of the different situations you have filled in the corps.

I shall have great pleasure in hearing of your future welfare; and should it ever happen to be in my power to promote your views in any way, I hope you will consider that you will only have to make them known.

> Believe me, my Dear Sir,
> Ever yours most sincerely,
> JOHN ROSS, Lt.-Col.
> Major, Rifle Brigade.

Quartermaster Wm. Surtees,
    Rifle Brigade.

No. 5.—From Lieut.-Colonel Smith, C.B.

Halifax, Nova Scotia, 25*th August* 1826.

My Dear Sir,

Were it permitted a soldier to regret the loss of his comrades, then truly should I deplore yours; I have only just learned that you are about to avail yourself of Lord Palmerston's permission to retire from the service on account of ill health, after having in your present situation completed your period of twenty years. You have struggled against indisposition with manly fortitude in various climes, and have ever performed your duty zealously and conscientiously.

I, as well as the other officers of the corps, have ever lamented that your natural zeal and talent as a soldier, should not have been called forth in a more conspicuous situation; and there is not an old officer in the regiment who has not witnessed your intrepid bravery in the field.

I must again assure you, that you leave us with the most heartfelt good wishes for your welfare, and the universal regret of the corps, in which you have served so many years with the most rigid integrity and zeal; and should I have it in my power upon any future occasion to render you any service whatever, it will afford me as much satisfaction as I now feel distress, in losing one of my old companions in arms, with whom I have been so many years happily associated.

And ever believe me,
Your very sincere friend,
H. G. SMITH,
Brevet Lieut.-Col. Rifle Brigade.

Quartermaster Surtees,
Rifle Brigade.

No. 6.—From Officers of the 1st Batt. Rifle Brigade.

Halifax, Nova Scotia, 30*th August* 1826.

We the undersigned officers present with the 1st Battalion Rifle Brigade, who have had the satisfaction of an intimate acquaintance with Mr Surtees for a series of years at home and abroad, beg leave to add our testimony as to the valour, integrity, zeal, and gentleman-like conduct which we have ever witnessed in him ; and beg to express our sincere regret at the prospect of losing his society and services.

> J. LOGAN, Major.
> W. JOHNSTONE, Captain.
> A. WADE PEMBERTON, Captain.
> G. HOPE, Captain.
> JOHN COX, Captain.
> J. KINCAID, Lieutenant.
> JOSEPH BURKE, M. D. Surgeon.
> GEORGE SIMMONS, Lieutenant.

No. 7.--FROM COLONEL NORCOTT, C. B.

Halifax, Nova Scotia, 30th August 1826.

MY DEAR SIR,

I most truly and sincerely regret that your long, zealous, and inde-fatigable duties have so seriously undermined your constitution, as to oblige you to retire from the service.

Although I feel a very lively gratification in bearing testimony to your merit and gallantry in the field, as well as to your public and private character as an officer and a gentleman, in the most unqualified sense, during a period of twenty-four years which I have known you, I cannot, at the same time, but lament the circumstances which bind me, in justice to your meritorious services, to tender you this my humble tribute of regard and esteem for all you have done for the service and the corps, and for such unremitted integrity and worth. You have my ardent wishes for your health and happiness wherever you go.

> Believe me to be,
> My Dear Sir,
> Always sincerely yours,
> A. NORCOTT, Colonel.

No. 8.—From Lieut.-Colonel Fullarton, C. B.

Halifax, Nova Scotia, 25th August 1826.

Dear Sir,

Having served in the same battalion with you for eighteen years, during which time I had every opportunity, both public and private, in various situations of home and on foreign service, of witnessing your very exemplary conduct, both as an officer and a gentleman, I, with my brother officers, have to regret that your ill health has deprived the regiment of a valuable officer, and your companions of a friend, whose amiable and excellent qualities will ever be revered by them.

With regard to myself, it will afford me the greatest pleasure if at any future period I can in any way be of service to you.

Believe me, my dear Sir,

Yours most truly,

Jas. Fullarton, Lt.-Col.

Major, Rifle Brigade.

Quartermaster Surtees,
Rifle Brigade.

No. 9.—From Lieut.-Colonel Balvaird.

Naas, 2d June 1826.

My dear Sir,

It affords me much pleasure to assure you, that during the time I was in the Rifle Brigade (13 years), and more particularly when you served under my immediate command, I can bear the most ample and unqualified testimony to the zeal, intelligence, and gallantry with which you discharged your duty—and wherever you may go, you carry with you the good wishes of,

Yours most sincerely,

W. Balvaird, Lt.-Col.

late Major, Rifle Brigade.

Quartermaster Surtees,
Rifle Brigade.

No. 10.—From Major-General Sir A. F. Barnard, K.C.B.

Albany, 18*th October* 1826.

Dear Sir,

I have heard with great regret that your state of health has obliged you to avail yourself of the regulation which enables you to retire from the Rifle Brigade, in which corps I had such frequent cause to praise the gallantry and assiduity which you showed in the discharge of your duties in the field, and your regularity and assiduity in quarters.

The officers of the corps, I am confident, will all regret the loss of a person whose mild and gentlemanlike manners and disposition had so much endeared him to them.

With every wish for your future welfare,

I remain, dear Sir,

Very sincerely yours,

A. F. Barnard.

Quartermaster Surtees,
Rifle-Brigade.

No. 11.—From Major Logan.

London, 18*th October,* 1826.

My dear Surtees,

I have just learnt with much regret that you are about to retire from the Rifle Brigade, from an impaired constitution, owing to your unwearied and zealous exertions in the service.

From the period of my entering the Corps, *twenty-two years ago,* I have had the pleasure of being intimately acquainted with you, and I must do you the justice to state, that a more gallant, zealous, and indefatigable officer, I have seldom fallen in with. As a gentleman, your conduct always won and gained the esteem of your brother officers.

Believe me I shall ever feel warmly interested in your welfare.

Yours, my dear Surtees,

Most faithfully,

J. LOGAN,

Major 1st Bat. Rifle Brigade.

To Quartermaster Surtees,
1st Bat. Rifle Brigade.

No. 12.—FROM LIEUT.-COLONEL BECKWITH, C.B.

London, 20th October, 1826.

MY DEAR SURTEES,

I cannot suffer you to return to your home, without adding my mite of applause to that of our brother officers, who have, together with myself, known you so well and so long.

From the day that we were employed together at Ipswich, in obtaining volunteers from the Militia, when you were so instrumental in obtaining so large a number of men for the service, and during the whole of our services in the Peninsula, and elsewhere, when my situation as Assistant Quartermaster-General of the Light Division threw us so constantly together, until the last period of our regimental service, I have always known and respected your courage, your active discharge of your duties in times of difficulty and hardship, and your zeal and affection for the Rifle Brigade.

Your present poverty is the surest testimony of your integrity, which you have always kept in times of strong temptation, when very many others similarly placed have not resisted so well.

All my feeble services are constantly at your disposal, and wishing you content, and as much happiness as we can reasonably expect here,

I remain, my dear Surtees,

Yours, most sincerely,

CHARLES BECKWITH,

Lieut.-Colonel.

Quartermaster Surtees,
Rifle Brigade.

No. 13.—From Lieut.-General the Honourable
Sir Wm. Stewart, G.C.B.

Cumloden, Newtonstewart, Nov. 19, 1826.

If the three or four-and-twenty years, my dear sir, that I have
had the satisfaction of having had you under my command in the
Rifle Regiment or Brigade, suffice not to authorize my full approval
of your conduct, both towards that corps and towards the public
service, I know not what experience would do so. To this extent
and to still farther extent, if it be required in detail, I am gratified
by your having given me this opportunity of certifying the above.
The loss that my battalion will sustain by the deprivation of your
services will be great, and the only consolation that I shall have will
be in learning that your present object of retiring on full pay be obtained, and that your health, injured, as my own has been, by perhaps
too great a zeal in the fulfilment of our respective duties, may be
somewhat amended by your retirement in private life. I have much
to thank you for the most justly merited encomiums from your several commanders and from your elder brother officers, enclosed in
your letter of the 13th instant, and to these honourable documents
favour me by adding this one. I wish it was in my power to be of
any service to your views towards a civil appointment under government, but as your age much exceeds that to which all official nomi-
nations are now limited, application for such will be fruitless.

I have the honour to be, my dear Sir,
    With repeated assurance of regard,
        Your faithful friend and obedient servant,
            Wm. Stewart,
            Lieutenant-General.

Quartermaster Surtees,
1st Bat. Rifle Brigade.

T

No. 14.—From Major Eeles.

Dublin, Nov. 28, 1826.

My Dear Surtees,

I enclose herewith copies of two letters which I have received from the office of his Royal Highness the Commander-in-Chief.

In congratulating you on their contents, I cannot refrain from expressing, strange as it may seem, not only my gratification but also my regret ; gratification that you have succeeded in obtaining the object of your wishes, and regret the most lively, that your state of health should have obliged you to quit the corps; the more particularly, as the regiment will not only by your retirement be deprived of the benefit of your zealous and meritorious services, but I shall lose the society of one of my oldest and most valued friends.

The senior part of the regiment will ever remember with pride the glorious occasions in which you so often signalized yourself in the field, while the younger members of the corps will not fail, equally with the former, to admire the gentlemanlike conduct and urbanity of manners which have secured to you the friendship and good wishes of us all.

Believe me, my Dear Surtees,
Very sincerely yours,
WILLIAM EELES,
Major, Rifle Brigade.

To Quartermaster Surtees,
Rifle Brigade.

No. 15.—From Major-General Sir T. S. Beckwith, K.C.B.

Gilsland, June 26, 1827.

My Dear Sir,

In returning to you the packet you have favoured me with the perusal of, I cannot refrain from expressing, in common with all your old friends and brother officers of the Rifle Brigade, my regret that your health made it necessary for you to retire from a corps, where your faithful and unremitting services for nearly thirty years had been so eminently useful, and where you possessed the friendship and confidence of every individual of any standing in it.

That your concern is as sincere as theirs in parting with them, I am perfectly convinced; yet it will be matter of real consolation to you to be able to reflect that you never gave just cause of offence to any member of the corps, and never neglected an opportunity of rendering them a service when in your power.

That you have not retired a richer man is a subject of regret to us all; and we shall learn with great satisfaction of any event, that may tend to increase your means of doing good to those who look to you for protection.

Should any such opening present itself, I do not hesitate to express my conviction, that whoever may employ you, will never have reason to repent doing so; as I am well assured you will undertake no situation, without due reflection, and the nature of which you do not understand; and that, once taken in hand, you will discharge the duties of it with the same diligence and fidelity that you have performed those of your public life for so many years past.

Earnestly wishing that a little repose after such a lengthened series of toils and dangers, may restore you to health and strength,

    I remain,

      My Dear Surtees,

        Your sincere and faithful friend,

            THOS. SIDNEY BECKWITH,

            Col. 2d Bat. Rifle Brigade.

To William Surtees, Esq.
    Late Rifle Brigade.

FINIS.

EDINBURGH: PRINTED BY BALLANTYNE AND COMPANY,
PAUL'S WORK, CANONGATE.

FORTESCUE'S HISTORY OF THE BRITISH ARMY: COMPLETE SET - 14 VOLUMES + MAPS
9781474537780

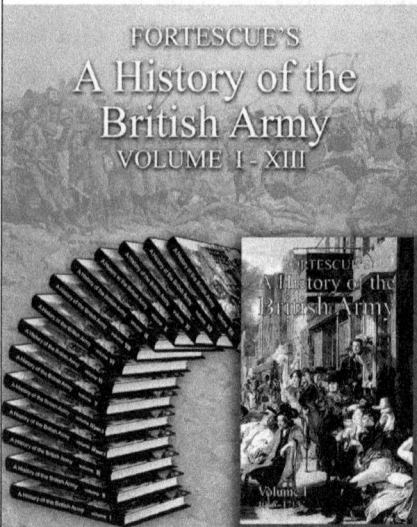

This work, which is a classic, covers the history of the British Army from the Norman Conquest down to the Cardwell reforms of 1870, when commission by purchase was finally abolished. The very last chapter of the work looks at the British Army up to 1914.

Naval and Military Press have reprinted this valuable and timeless work in its entirety, faithful to the originals in all respects. The contents of the individual volumes are as follows:

Vol. I - from the Battle of Hastings to the end of the Seven Year's War (1713). Includes such battles as Bannockburn, Crecy, Agincourt, Flodden, the battles of the English Civil War, Dunkirk Dunes, Tangiers, and the battles during Marlborough's campaigns. The volume also traces the development of European Armies, infantry, cavalry and artillery, and the specific changes in Britain during the period.

Vol. II - covers from the 1713 to 1763 and includes the Jacobite Rebellion of 1715, the scandals of the reign of King George I, the war with Spain and the dispute over the Austrian Succession, and the Battles of Fontenoy and Culloden. It also covers the situation in India and the contest for mastery with the French. The expansion into North America is described and the differences that arose between the French and the British, together with Wolfe's campaigns in North America. The volume includes much material on the development of the British Army, and the problems that arose with regard to recruitment and conditions of service at that time.

Vol. III - continues the story from 1763 to 1792. The continuing problems in North America are joined by the growing pains of Empire. The loss of the Americas is covered in detail, as is the state of the British Army, especially in the light of Cornwallis' disastrous contributions to the American failure. Developments in India follow, and again Cornwallis makes a contribution to failure.

Vol IV Part I - Deals with the French Revolution from 1789 to the Treaty of Amiens in 1798. It includes British operations in the Netherlands, the West Indies, South Africa and Ireland. The whole European area is described with the French and Allied nations included. Naval matters are also included, and the campaigns in Egypt and the Mediterranean are treated in detail. At the same time a close eye is kept on developments within the British Army.

Vol. IV Part 2 - continues the theme of the previous part, and goes up to 1801. The examination of the British Army is also expanded, and an important appendix gives exact details of British Army pay.

Vol. V - the period 1803 to 1807. Detailed treatment of the situation and operations in the East Indies and Ceylon, the West Indies, Europe and the Mediterranean. There are important chapters on conditions at home,and the air of war-weariness that was appearing. Finally, there is a description of operations in South America.

Vol. VI - 1807-1809. The Napoleonic War continued, with further details of operations in Egypt and in the Mediterranean. The Swedish situation is covered, the British expedition to Copenhagen and operations in Portugal. The Spanish theatre is also examined in fine detail.

Vol. VII - 1809-1810. This volume is concerned mainly with these two years in the Peninsula, but also covers the expedition to the Scheldt, and operations in the East Indies, Mauritius and Java.

Vol. VII - 1809-1810. Maps

Vol. VIII - 1811-1812. This volume covers two more years of the campaign in the Peninsula, together with the War with the United States. There are details of many battles, including Barosa, Badajoz, Fuentes de Onoro, Albuera, Ciudad Rodrigo, Salamanca and others of fame during the Peninsula War. the United States. There are details of many battles, including Barosa, Badajoz, Fuentes de Onoro, Albuera, Ciudad Rodrigo, Salamanca and others of fame during the Peninsula War.

Vol. IX - 1813-1814. The French invasion of Russia is

followed by descriptions of the situation in the Peninsula, and in North America. Throughout developments in Europe are covered so that the picture of the war for the reader in these years is complete, and second to none in detail.

Vol. X - 1814-1815. The whole of Europe was aflame in these two years, and Fortescue writes most effectively of the military activity and the political background. Italy, the Peninsula, the Low Countries and the American War are all interwoven from the British point of view in a tour de force of military history. He then includes a really valuable summary of events in Europe from 1803 to 1814 before setting out to describe the culminating battle at Waterloo. From the Duchess of Richmond's Ball to the exhaustion on the night after the battle, Fortescue maintains a pace and directness which is fascinating to read.

Vol. XI - 1815-1838. Fortescue looks at the British Army in 1815, and particularly the recruit in England. Every detail of his life is included, and the picture is an important one for all who are interested in this period of military and social history. The War with Nepal, the Pindari War, the War in Ceylon and the War with Burma all occupy the subsequent pages followed by the Ashanti campaign and the Kaffir War of 1834-35. This volume also includes details of Home Affairs and Foreign Policy.

Vol. XII - 1839-52. This volume is mainly concerned with India, and covers operations in Afghanistan and on the Khyber Pass, together with internal security operations in India itself. There is also a section dealing with the revolt in Australia and operations in New Zealand. Finally there is a description of the Kaffir War and the Boer revolt.

Vol. XIII - 1852-1870. This volume includes the Crimean War, the War in Persia and the Indian Mutiny and the campaign in China. It then goes on to look at the Ambela and Abyssinian campaigns, and the Wars in New Zealand. Finally Fortescue looks at affairs in Great Britain and the position of the East India Company. He then turns his attention to the new army from 1870 to 1914, and includes the territorial system, the new social engineering going on for men's wefare in the army, The series ends however with an important look at the end of the era of purchase, and what the army was going to do next.

Map Compendium - includes all six separate map volumes that came with the original work in one binding.

www.ingramcontent.com/pod-product-compliance
Lightning Source LLC
Chambersburg PA
CBHW030939150426
42812CB00064B/3051/J